CLINICAL ASPECTS

of

CHILD DEVELOPMENT

*An Introductory Synthesis of
Developmental Concepts and
Clinical Experience*

MELVIN LEWIS, MB., B.S. (London)
F.R.C.Psych., D.C.H.

*Professor of Pediatrics and Psychiatry
Yale Child Study Center*

Second Edition

LEA & FEBIGER   *Philadelphia   1982*

Lea & Febiger
600 Washington Square
Philadelphia, PA   19106
U.S.A.

Library of Congress Cataloging in Publication Data

Lewis, Melvin, 1926–
Clinical aspects of child development.

Includes bibliographies and index.
1. Child development. 2. Sick children—
Psychology. 3. Child psychiatry. I. Title.
[DNLM: 1. Child development. WS 105 L671c 1981]
RJ131.L42 1982   155.4'024616   81-11825
ISBN 0-8121-0796-9   AACR2

First Edition, 1971
        Reprinted 1973
        Reprinted 1974
        Reprinted 1976
        Reprinted 1978

PRINTED IN THE UNITED STATES OF AMERICA

Print No.   4   3   2   1

To Dorothy, Gillian, and Eric

Preface

to First Edition

This book is written primarily for medical students. Other students may also find it useful. Its goal is to provide the student with an introductory synthesis of certain basic psychological concepts and their use in understanding the wide range of behavior seen during the stage of human development we call childhood. To the extent that sound diagnosis and treatment are based upon the principles and findings in child development, this book will also serve as a basis from which principles of management may be inferred. However, no attempt will be made here to describe specific techniques of management.

Many medical students have an urge to learn "first things first," and since they want to become doctors, "first" to their minds means basic functioning, normal and abnormal. It is recognized that to teach a course of normal development without any reference to deviant or pathological patterns is often thought at best to lack correlation and at worst to be quite irrelevant. On the other hand, to teach psychopathology before the student has an idea of normal psychological development is to leave the student floundering in a sea of symptoms and signs, with no normal reference points by which he can chart his course.

The obvious resolution is to teach normality and abnormality simultaneously. An attempt, therefore, is made here to paint in broad strokes the essential framework, or skeleton, for such a resolution. At the same time, this overview should enable the student to fill in for himself the gaps in his knowledge, the gaps in the teacher's knowledge, and the gaps in any course on the subject. In working toward this goal, I of course have had to be selective in the material used.

Others will differ from me in the selection and emphasis made. I have changed the balance several times myself. Each year students come to medical school better informed. Curricula in many medical schools are themselves in a state of flux. Further, the introduction of new findings and new concepts and the challenge to old beliefs are changing the face of medicine more rapidly than ever before. Nevertheless, I have tried to present the broad range of material fairly and consistently within a more or less unified theoretical frame of reference.

This brings me to a special characteristic of this book. The original literature is now so large that it cannot be encompassed by one person. Moreover, the mere physical act of trying to retrieve original works, papers, and other material from a library is enormously time consuming, if not actually frustrating. Yet, if the medical student reads only someone else's synthesis, he is the poorer for the development of his own ideas.

In an effort to reduce this difficulty, a series of "notes" consisting of more or less extensive, but hopefully always relevant, quotations from the literature are appended to the end of each chapter. In this way I hope the student will at least get a taste of the joy of reading an original contribution, and perhaps be encouraged to make further explorations as he proceeds in his studies.

Implicit in this book is a particular pedagogical concept. This concept views medical education as a kind of spiral process, in which the student first goes once over lightly, and relatively briefly, the broad sweep of the curriculum. At subsequent periods he can then go over similar ground, this time with more familiarity and greater depth. This concept underlies some of the thinking, for example, of the new curriculum at Yale University School of Medicine. It is hoped, therefore, that this text will form the basis for such a first go-around by the student interested in human behavior. And as such it is purposefully brief. In fact, it contains the essential information and concepts presented in a 36-hour course consisting of lectures, demonstrations, interviews, clinical exercises and seminars given during the first 9 weeks of medical school. It may also serve as a "refresher" course when the student returns to the basic sciences in the "track system" now in use in the clinical years.

Many colleagues and friends have helped me in the preparation of this book, and of course the literature belongs to us all. If I have not assiduously acknowledged every thought, concept, or finding uttered or written by everyone I have listened to or read over the years, it is because I have come to regard many of them now as part of the common domain of accepted knowledge. Yet, I have tried to indicate certain landmarks in the literature that might be used as a guide for those who wish to explore the subject further.

My thanks go especially to my wife, Dorothy, for her ideas, her stimulation, and her encouragement. I also wish to thank Herbert D. Kleber, M.D., Ernesto E. Pollitt, Ph. D., Milton J.E. Senn, M.D., and Randall M. Zusman, medical student, for their helpful criticisms and suggestions. My particular thanks go to my secretary, Mrs. Arthur Eberlein, for her unflagging enthusiasm and helpful suggestions, as well as her astonishing capacity to keep things in order and correct my errors. Lastly, I thank Lea & Febiger for their unfailing courtesy and cooperation.

New Haven, Connecticut Melvin Lewis

Preface

For this second edition, the book is divided into four parts. Part One consists of brief capsule or summary reviews of certain essential human functions seen in longitudinal perspective during childhood. The functions selected include biological development, attachment behavior, cognitive development, language development, psychosexual and aggressive drive development, moral development, psychosocial development, and family development.

Part Two consists of a description of the child seen in cross-section at various stages of development, when these various functions coalesce to form the whole child. Where possible, clinical correlations are described but no attempt has been made to provide a comprehensive account of psychopathology in childhood.

Part Three describes the effects of illness, hospitalization, dying and death in the context of the development of the child.

Part Four is an introduction to clinical psychiatric diagnosis that draws on all of the preceding chapters.

Since the goal is to provide a short introductory synthesis for the clinician, oversimplification is inevitable. Some attempt has been made to correct for this oversimplification by increasing the number and range of Notes (readings from original sources).

Since the child is here looked at first in longitudinal and then in cross-sectional perspective, as well as under stress and in the context of psychiatric evaluation, repetition is also inevitable. I have tried to keep such repetition to a minimum.

What is the theoretical framework for this book? Until a new creative genius gives us the gift of a new vision of nature that will reshape our overview of life, the way Darwin, Freud, and Watson and Crick have done, we must struggle with the multiple theories we now have to account for human behavior. Explorations of the biology of the cell and the psychology of the unconscious continue to account for bits of human behavior, in some cases better than in others. We do not yet have a unified theory of human behavior although we do have some fragile and tantalizing wisps of connections that several authors have tried to elucidate (Heilbrunn, 1979; Kendel, 1979; Meyersburg and Post, 1979).

Scientists experience first and then try to account for that experience by inferring a law or constructing a model. If the law or the model is a good one, then consequences of that law or model will predict certain new events or phenomena and will "explain" certain other previously known but perhaps disparate facts. And the more scientists can use measurement and the experimental method, the more confident they can be about their theories. Unfortunately, when a theory exists for which there is no relatively satisfactory scientific test that includes measurement (there is no absolutely ultimate test for truth), there is the risk of authoritarianism—a thing is held true because someone said it was so.

In the chapters that follow, I have tried to present some of the scientific findings that support a few of our theories of human behavior, at the same time keeping open the question of the validity of those theories that are still for the most part at the level of experience, inference, and speculation. My reason for including the latter, "unproven" theories is that in clinical practice we must often decide on the basis of experience and judgment when we do not have the necessary scientific knowledge. In doing this I hope I have avoided the risk of authoritarianism.

Last, this book continues to strive toward its overall aim: to be useful to all who wish to review and utilize basic psychological concepts and findings relevant to clinical work with children.

I wish to thank Ms. Lonna Thiem for typing the manuscript with devotion, care, and attention, and Ms. Dorothy Oyler for her valuable assistance in proofreading the manuscript. I also wish to thank David Fassler, medical student, and Dr. Joseph Woolston for their many helpful criticisms and suggestions. Special thanks and love go to Dorothy Otnow Lewis for her passionate advocacy, clarity, and uncompromising regard for scientific evidence. Finally, as before, I thank Lea & Febiger for their patience and support.

New Haven, Connecticut   Melvin Lewis

REFERENCES

Heilbrunn, G. (1979), Biologic correlates of psychoanalytic concepts. *J. Am. Psychoanal. Assoc.*, 27:597–626.
Kendel, E.R. (1979), Psychotherapy and the single synapse. *New Engl. J. Med.*, 301:1028–1037.
Meyersburg, H.A., and Post, R.M. (1979), An holistic developmental view of neural and psychological processes. *Br. J. Psychiatry*, 135:139–155.

Acknowledgments

I should like to express my thanks to the following individuals and publishers for permission to use the material quoted in the Notes.

Note 1
H.A. Meyersburg; R.M. Post; British Journal of Psychiatry.

Note 2
J. Bowlby; Basic Books, Inc.

Note 3
M.D.S. Ainsworth; S.M. Bell; Child Development.

Note 4
J. Piaget; International Universities Press, Inc.

Note 5
E.H. Lenneberg; John Wiley & Sons, Inc.

Note 6
N. Geschwind; W.H. Freeman & Co.

Note 7
Sigmund Freud Copyrights; The Institute of
Psycho-Analysis; The Hogarth Press Ltd.; Basic Books, Inc.

Note 8
B. Bornstein; International Universities Press, Inc.

Note 9
S. Feshbach; John Wiley & Sons, Inc.

Note 10
A. Freud; International Universities Press, Inc.

Note 11
J. Piaget; Macmillan Publishing Co., Inc.

Note 12
L. Kohlberg; Russell Sage Foundation

Note 13
E. Erikson; W.W. Norton

Note 14
T. Lidz; John Wiley & Sons, Inc.

Note 15
T. Benedek; Little, Brown and Company

Note 16
H. Hartmann; International Universities Press, Inc.

Note 17
M.J.E. Senn; Josiah Macy, Jr., Foundation

Note 18
A. Gesell; C.S. Amatruda; Paul Hoeber Medical Division, Harper & Row

Note 19
E.H. Erikson; International Universities Press, Inc.

Note 20
J. Bowlby; Penguin Books Ltd.

Note 21
R.A. Spitz; International Universities Press, Inc.

Note 22
J. Piaget; International Universities Press, Inc.

Note 23
D.W. Winnicott; Tavistock Publications Ltd.

Note 24
A. Freud; D. Burlingham; International Universities Press, Inc.

Note 25
Sigmund Freud Copyrights; The Institute of Psycho-Analysis; The Hogarth Press Ltd.; W.W. Norton

Note 26
J. Piaget; B. Inhelder; Basic Books, Inc.

Note 27
G.H.J. Pearson; Bulletin of the Philadelphia Association for Psychoanalysis

Note 28
M. Rutter; J. Tizard; K. Whitmore; Longman Group Limited.

Note 29
L.E. Peller; The Psychoanalytic Study of the Child; International Universities Press, Inc.

Note 30
J. Piaget; Basic Books, Inc.

Note 31
E.H. Erikson; W.W. Norton & Co., Inc.

Note 32
D.G. Prugh; E.M. Staub; H.H. Sands; R.M. Kurschbaum; E.A. Lenihan; American Journal of Orthopsychiatry

Contents

Part One
Longitudinal Perspectives

Chapter 1

BIOLOGICAL DEVELOPMENT

It has long been known that the highest integrative functions are contained in the cerebral cortex (Sherrington, 1906). Our mind is a function of our brain and, in the last analysis, all psychological disturbances reflect changes in neuronal and synaptic function (Kendel, 1979). At the same time, there is a sequence of development in many biological structures and functions. This chapter therefore will focus on some of the more prominent developmental sequences and their possible relationships to behavior.

BRAIN MATURATION

During the fetal period, the development of the brain, as measured by volume percentage, proceeds (surprisingly) in a caudocranial direction (Tanner, 1970). Thus at birth, midbrain and spinal cord are more advanced than pons, medulla, and cerebrum. The cerebellum, which is least advanced at birth, grows rapidly from just before birth to about age 1. Cortical synaptic density appears to increase during infancy, reaching a maximum of about 50% *above* the adult mean at age 1 to 2, and thereafter declines until about age 16, when it remains constant until about age 75 (Huttenlocher, 1979). This phenomenon may help explain why immature brains may recover more completely from injury than fully matured brains. Thus a young child who has a severe injury to the speech areas of the brain may recover his or her speech within a few days, whereas an adult with the same injury may remain permanently aphasic. The apparent excess of synapses may also account for the plasticity in the developing child. For example, children can more easily learn to speak second languages without an accent than can adults.

Among the primary areas, the motor area is the most advanced part of the cortex during the first 2 years of life. Development subsequently spreads out from each of the primary areas (sensory, visual, and auditory). Subsequent development within the motor and sensory areas then proceeds in a cephalocaudal direction—arms first, then legs. Visual association areas develop somewhat ahead of auditory areas, suggesting that the infant understands what he sees before he understands what he hears. At 1 month of age, the primary motor area appears to be functioning, and by 3 months of age all the primary cortical areas serving such functions as vision and learning appear to be relatively mature. By 2 years of age, the primary sensory area has essentially caught up with the motor area (Tanner, 1970).

MYELINATION

Myelination in the brain continues to develop through adolescence and possibly into adulthood (Yakovlev and Lecours, 1967). Myelination tends to occur in arcs or functional units rather than in geographical areas (Anokhin, 1964). Thus the reticular formation, which is concerned with the maintenance of attention and consciousness, continues to myelinate as a system through to puberty and possibly beyond. Myelination also seems to occur in waves, starting in one system, say, and then being overtaken later by myelination in another system (Bekoff and Fox, 1972). Ultimately, all the areas concerned with emotions become active. Heilbrunn (1979) has stated that the "central stations" concerned with emotions include (1) the medial portion of the amygdalate nucleus and areas in the hypothalamus—for rage, (2) the anterior cingulate gyrus—for fear, (3) the central gray—for rage and fear, (4) the lateral amygdalate—for complacency and fearlessness, and (5) the limbic system—for appetitive, pleasurable, and sexual impulses. A ventral branch originating in the reticular formation and innervating the hypothalamus regulates motivational activities, and a dorsal pathway originating in the locus ceruleus and innervating the hippocampus regulates cognitive functions. The locus ceruleus appears to coordinate all the pleasure centers (Cooper et al., 1974). Cells of the aversive systems originating in the raphe nuclei extend through the mesencephalon (Stein and Berger, 1975). The hippocampi appear to be the site for memory formation, and the temporal cortex is involved in recall of past events.

Myelination correlates with a number of behaviors. For example, a delay in myelination may account for the fact that the smile of premature infants is delayed up to 10 weeks later than the smile of normal infants of the same postnatal age (Bronson, 1969). Other behavioral correlations have been described or speculated about by Meyersburg and Post (1979; see Note 1).

NEUROTRANSMITTER DEVELOPMENT

Neuroendocrine control undergoes a similar developmental sequence. For example, the hypothalamic-pituitary gonadotropin-gonadal axis first appears to be functioning during fetal life and early infancy. During childhood it then is suppressed to a low level of activity. Finally, at puberty, the system is reactivated. Thus the 10 years or so between late infancy and the onset of puberty can be viewed as an interval of functional gonadotropin-releasing hormone (GnRH) insufficiency, ending when GnRH secretion by neurosecretory neurons is reactivated (Grumbach, 1980). The GnRH neurons, located in the medial basal hypothalamus in the region of the arcuate nucleus, seem to be controlled by extrahypothalamic neural pathways and brain monoamines.

At the level of biogenic amine and other neurotransmitter substances too, some evidence of a developmental sequence exists (Himmich, 1971; Coyle and Axelrod, 1972), leading to speculations regarding further correlations between neurochemistry, neurophysiology, neuroanatomy, and behavior. For example, it has been reported that dopamine-beta-hydroxylase (DBH) activity is low during the first year of life and increases 10-fold from birth to the second decade (Molinoff et al., 1970) and that the levels of DBH in the newborn correlate with the scores of irritability, unsociable responses, 1-year anomaly scores, and activity levels at birth, 5, and 12 months, respectively (Rapoport et al., 1977).

Some investigators have reported that high levels of CSF homovanillic acid (HVA) are found in neuropsychiatrically disturbed children compared to adult psychiatric patients and that this phenomenon may represent a developmental change in dopamine receptor sensitivity or the maturation of other neuromodulators (Leckman et al., 1980).

Recent animal studies have also suggested that two kinds of dopamine receptors exist in the basal ganglia of mammalian species, one excitatory and the other inhibitory and that these tracts may complete their development at different stages (Rosengarten and Friedhoff, 1979), giving rise to different patterns of vulnerability at different stages of life. A ribonucleic acid (RNA) developmental life curve has also been described. The amount of cellular RNA increases from the third to the fortieth year, then maintains a plateau between ages 40 and 60, after which it decreases sharply. Concomitantly, there is a constant increase of ribonuclease which destroys RNA, accounting perhaps in part for the difficulty of remembering recent events during old age (Heilbrunn, 1979).

EEG DEVELOPMENT

EEG patterns also show a developmental progression. Interestingly, birth in itself does not seem to affect neurological maturation. The EEG of an infant born at 28 weeks is much the same 6 weeks later as that of an infant born at 34 weeks (Dreyfus-Brisac, 1966). However, the interaction with the environment is thought to bring about some developmental shift, even in this largely maturational sequence of EEG change in the premature infant. Thus the intermittent sharp-and-slow bursts (the so-called *trace-alternant)* EEG, representing unmodulated cortical activity, disappears earlier in the premature infant than it does in the full-term infant of comparable gestational age. Presumably the change in early quiet sleep EEG reflects the organization that takes place after birth.

At about 3 months of age, when the smile response generally occurs (the "first organizer," as described by Spitz [1965]), there is another associated EEG change: the onset of sleep EEG changes from a simple direct change (waking →REM state) to a stepwise change (waking →Stage 1 nonREM Stage 2 nonREM →REM sleep) (Metcalf and Jordan, 1971). There is some evidence to suggest that waking EEG changes also occur at about the ages of 2 years, 6 years, and 11 years, which happen to be the ages at which important cognitive changes occur (Gibbs and Knott, 1949). For example, sleep spindles in the EEG during Stage 2 sleep decrease between 6 and 12 months of age, at about the time that an increase in memory occurs and so-called stranger anxiety becomes manifest (Tanguay et al., 1975). An individual's characteristic pattern (usually about 8–13 c/sec) becomes established by about 15 or 16 years of age.

GENETIC FACTORS IN DEVELOPMENT

Genetic factors play an important role in development. Torgerson and Kringlen (1978) studied the development of temperamental characteristics in 53 same-sexed twins. They studied such temperamental attributes as activity level, rhythmicity, approach/withdrawal, adaptability, intensity, threshold, mood, distractibility, and attention span/persistence. Monozygotic twins were found to be temperamentally more similar than dizygotic twins, particularly in activity level, approach/withdrawal, and threshold. The evidence suggested that this phenomenon was a genetic effect. Cantwell (1976) reviewed the evidence for the role of genetic factors in the hyperkinetic syndrome (hyperactivity, impulsivity, distractibility, and excitability) and found that evidence from family studies, adoptive studies, and twin studies suggested a polygenic inheritance mechanism for the disorder. Genetic disorders, of course, account for a large number of syndromes in childhood. For example, of the half million moderately and severely mentally retarded children, nearly 50% have a genetic disorder (Crandall, 1977). Other disorders in which genetic factors play an important role include dyslexia (Hallgren, 1950), enuresis (Hallgren, 1957) , and stuttering (Carter, 1969).

ENVIRONMENT AND BIOLOGICAL DEVELOPMENT

It is important to note that the genetic factors previously mentioned do not operate in a void: the environment is an essential element in the final expression of a trait or disorder. For example, in studies of children of schizophrenics, genetic theory and empirical data suggest that children with severely affected parents and with many affected relatives will have the highest risks, whereas children with only one mildly affected parent may have risks that approach the population base rates (Hanson et al., 1977). Yet as Hanson et al. point out, some children of diagnosed schizophrenics will have *no* genetic risk for schizophrenia, and some of those who do will still enjoy a life of adequate mental health, even without intervention. In fact, the concordance rate for schizophrenia in identical twins is only about 50%. Thus environmental factors are at least as important as genetic factors in the emergence of the schizophrenia syndrome. So far, no specific environmental factor is known.

Environmental factors may affect biological development in

other ways. For example, psychosocial stimulation may have a profound effect on biogenic amine metabolism, which in turn may affect behavior and emotions (Axelrod et al., 1970). While much of this knowledge is still at the level of research, increasingly it is influencing clinical approaches to child and adolescent development.

BRAIN DAMAGE AND BRAIN DEVELOPMENT

Damage to the brain in children clearly affects behavior; brain damage is accompanied by a much increased rate of psychiatric disorder, and the rate of disorder is in proportion to the extent of damage. Thus psychiatric disorder is significantly commoner in children with bilateral brain lesions than in children whose conditions are confined to one side of the brain (Rutter et al., 1970). At the same time, the range of psychiatric disorders in brain-damaged children is heterogeneous, without specific features for the most part (Rutter, 1977).

STATE AND EARLY DEVELOPMENT

The organization of behavior in the infant also appears to be partially dependent on the state of the infant. Brazelton has noted that "an infant who manifests all states of consciousness and who can change state appropriately with or without environmental stimulation indicates a greater capacity for organization and control than an infant who cannot demonstrate this range of behavior or who is 'locked into' a state in an obligatory way" (Eagle and Brazelton, 1977, p. 43).

It is important to distinguish between the term state as used simply to connote in general regularly occurring clusters of behavior and the term state as used to mean specifically a manifestation of central nervous system arousal. In the latter use of the term, the very fluctuations, or rhythms, of state are themselves important data about CNS integration, not just confounding variables. Behavior in the infant, then, is a function of the state of the organism, the specific stimuli acting on the organism, and the environment in which these act (Escalona, 1962). In turn, state includes:

1. The infant's position at the time of stimulation
2. The response characteristics of an infant to state
3. The baseline level of behavioral activities of the infant at the time of observation
4. The maturational level of competence

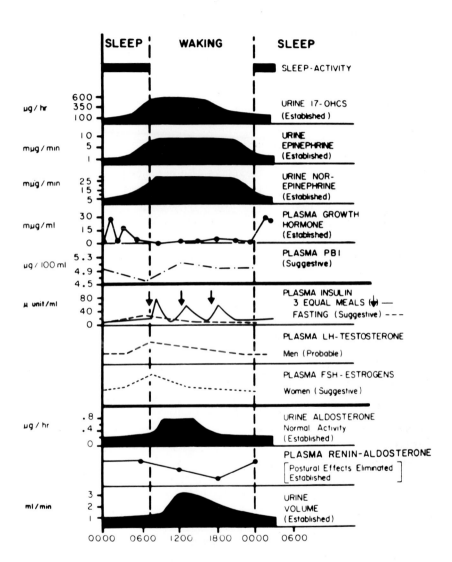

Fig. 1–1. Phase map of daily cycle of endocrine measures and urine volume in man in relation to habitual sleep and feeding schedule (Reprinted by permission of publisher from: Psychosomatics and chronobiology, by G. Curtis, *Phychosomatic Medicine,* 34:235. Copyright 1972 by Elsevier North Holland, Inc.)

> 5. Various time-elapsed variables, such as time since last feeding and time since last startle response

State is also considered to be a rhythmic process, with a temporal component. This time dimension is important in considering the phasic aspects of states of hunger or sleep, or of alertness, or of endocrine activity (Anders, 1978) (see Fig. 1–1).

THEORETICAL MODELS OF DEVELOPMENT

How does development proceed? For present purposes, we may classify theories of child development into two classes, reactive and structural. Reactive theories postulate that the child's mind begins as a *tabula rasa* and that the child then reacts to the environment. Major examples of this type of theory include stimulus-response theory, learning theories, classical conditioning theory, and operant conditioning theory. The clinical implications for treatment that flow from reactive theories are that symptoms are regarded as learned behavior; i.e., the symptom is the disorder and that through re-learning and/or environmental change the symptom is removed and therefore the disease is cured.

Structural theories postulate that there is a genetically determined capacity for the development of patterns, or systems, of behavior and that the child acts on his or her environment from the very beginning. The continuing sequence of behavior patterns that then emerge is described as stages that are qualitatively different from each other. Major examples of structural theories include the general theories of Bowlby, Freud, and Erikson and Piaget's special theory of cognitive development. The clinical aspects of some structural theories will be discussed shortly. The clinical implications for treatment that flow from structural theories are that some kind of reorganization within the child is required; e.g., resolution of intrapsychic conflict, alteration of the family homeostasis, and acquisition of new schema.

The concept of stages is important in structural theories since it enables one to analyze behavior, just as classification in biology serves as a basis for subsequent analysis and understanding. The criteria for stages include:

> 1. A stage, or structure, is characterized as a whole ("the final form of equilibrium") and not just as the juxtaposition of parts. The concept of definable stages means

behavioral characteristics that have some degree of stability and autonomy.

2. There is an invariant sequence, or constant order of succession, from one stage to another.

3. While multiple and interrelated lines of stage development are present, each line may also have its own rate of development ("level of preparation, level of completion"), giving rise to a multi-leveled organism at any given moment.

4. Each successive stage in normal development represents an advance from the previous stage.

5. Each later stage supersedes all earlier stages in that structures constructed at a given age become an integral part of structures that follow.

6. The change is qualitative, and not just quantitative.

7. Each stage proceeds in the direction of increasing complexity of organization, from a state of relative globality to a state of increasing differentiation and integration.

8. Biogenetic, environmental, experiential, and psychological factors guarantee and facilitate the developmental process, coping, and adaptation.

9. There are presumed critical, or sensitive, periods during which conditions are ideal for the normal development of important functions, such as attachment, gender identity, and language.

Is development a continuous process?

Certain phenomena, such as the enhancement of memory between 8 and 12 months of age and the shift from a perceptual mode to a symbolic-linguistic mode at about 17 months, seem to emerge more or less suddenly, perhaps more in relation to maturation of special areas in the central nervous system than to the mother-child bond (Kagan, 1979). Kagan argues that such phenomena suggest the possibility of some discontinuities in development and that the experiences of the average infant with its parents might not, after all, have any long-lasting, cumulative effects.

In the chapters that follow we will concentrate on some of the major structural theories of development. At the same time, we will remember that there is a biological aspect and social context for all human behavior and that in medicine we observe at least three dimensions: "the patient as a living organism, the patient as a member of society, and the patient as a person" (Tosteson, 1979, p. 691).

Note 1

H.A. Meyersburg and R.M. Post (1979), *Br. J. Psychiatry* 135–139.

TEMPORAL CORRESPONDENCE OF SEVERAL NEUROLOGICAL AND PSYCHOLOGICAL DEVELOPMENTAL SEQUENCES

	FIRST DECADE																				SUCCEEDING DECADES					
	MONTHS OF FIRST YEAR																									
	-9	-6	-2	0	1	2	3	4	5	6	7	8	9	10	11	12	2nd yr.	3rd yr.	4th yr.	5th yr.	6th yr.	7th yr.	8th yr.	9th yr.	10th yr.	2nd	3rd	4th	5th	6th	7th & beyond

MYELINATION CYCLE

STRIATO ACOUSTIC SYSTEM

MOTOR ROOTS

OPTIC RADIATIONS & TRACTS

SENSORY ROOTS

AND TRACTS

YAKOVLEV & LECOURS

PYRAMIDAL TRACTS & STRIATUM

CEREBELLAR PEDUNCLES

LIMBIC SYSTEM

ACOUSTIC RADIATIONS

GREAT CEREBRAL COMMISSURES

RETICULAR FORMATION

INTRACORTICAL NEUROPIL ASSOCIATION AREAS ?! — ?! — ?! — ?!

NEUROMOTOR — Tonic Neck Reflex — Head Balanced — Sits — Creeps — Stands Alone — Walks — Runs — Rides tricycle — Stands on one foot — Skips

FREUD — ORAL — ANAL — PHALLIC OEDIPAL LATENCY — ADOLES-CENCE — ADULTHOOD

Delay of the Drives Leads to Secondary Thinking

PIAGET — SENSORI-MOTOR PERIOD — PERIOD OF PRE-OPERATIONAL THOUGHT — STAGE OF CONCRETE OPERATIONS — FORMAL OPERATIONS

1st Abstraction

1st Internalized Thinking

SPITZ

INFANT MATERNAL DIALOGUE
PRIMAL CAVITY PREOBJECT
OBJECT SPECIFICITY
Smiling Response (1st Organizer of the Psyche)
Stranger Anxiety (2nd Organizer of the Psyche)
"No" Response (3rd Organizer of the Psyche)

MAHLER

SEPARATION INDIVIDUATION PROCESS
Autistic Phase Hatching Period
Omnipotence
Practising
Rapprochement (Refueling)
Object Constancy (Libidinal)
Separation
Resolution of Omnipotence

ERICKSON

ORAL-RESPIRATORY SENSORY STAGE (SUCKING)	MUSCULAR-ANAL INCORPORATIVE MODE (BITING)	LOCOMOTOR-GENITAL	LATENCY	PUBERTY & ADOLES-CENCE	YOUNG ADULT-HOOD	ADULTHOOD MATURITY POST-MATURITY
Trust vs. Mistrust	Autonomy vs. Shame & Doubt	Initiative vs. Guilt	Industry vs. Inferiority		True Genitality	

Identity vs. Role Confusion
Intimacy vs. Isolation
Generativity vs. Stagnation
Ego Integrity vs. Despair

REFERENCES

Anders, T. (1978), State and rhythmic processes. *J. Am. Acad. Child Psychiatry*, 17:401–420.

Anokhin, P.K. (1964), Systemogenesis as a general regulation of brain development. *Prog. Brain Res.*, 9:54–86.

Axelrod, J., et al. (1970), Changes in enzymes involved in the biosynthesis and metabolism of noradrenaline and adrenaline after psychosocial stimulation. *Nature*, 225:1059–1060.

Bekoff, M., and Fox, M. (1972), Postnatal neural ontogeny: Environment-dependent and/or environment-expectant. *Dev. Psychobiol.*, 5:323–341.

Bronson, G. (1969), Vision in infancy: Structure-function relationships. In: *Brain and Early Behavior Development*, ed. R.J. Robinson. New York: Academic Press.

Cantwell, D.P. (1976), Genetic factors in the hyperkinetic syndrome. *J. Am. Acad. Child Psychiatry*, 15:214–223.

Carter, C.O. (1969), Genetics of common disorders. *Br. Med. Bull.*, 25:52–57.

Cools, A.R., and Van Rossum, J.M. (1976), Excitation-mediating and inhibition-mediating dopamine receptors. *Psychopharmacologia*, 45:243–254.

Cooper, J.R., Bloom, F.E., and Roth, R.H. (1974), *The Biochemical Basis of Neuropharmacology*. New York: Oxford University Press.

Coyle, J.T., and Axelrod, J. (1972), Tyrosine hydroxylase in the rat brain: Developmental characteristics. *J. Neurochem.*, 19:1117–1123.

Crandall, B.F. (1977), Genetic disorders and mental retardation. *J. Am. Acad. Child Psychiatry*, 16:88–108.

Curtis, G. (1972), Psychosomatics and chronobiology. *Psychosom. Med.*, 34:235–256.

Dreyfus-Brisac, C. (1966), The bioelectrical development of the central nervous system during early life. In: *Human Development*, ed. F. Falkner. London: Saunders.

Eagle, D.B., and Brazelton, T.B. (1977), The infant and risk-assessment and implications for intervention. In: *Child Psychiatry: Treatment and Research*, ed. M.F. McMillan and S. Henao. New York: Brunner/Mazel.

Escalona, S. (1962), The study of individual differences and the problem of state. *J. Am. Acad. Child Psychiatry*, 2:11–37.

Gibbs, F.A., and Knott, J.R. (1949), Growth of the electrical activity of the cortex. *Electroencephalogr. Clin. Neurophysiol.*, 1:223–229.

Grumbach, M.M. (1980), The neuroendocrinology of puberty. *Hosp. Pract.*, 15:51–60.

Hallgren, B. (1950), Specific dyslexia ("congenital word-blindness"): A clinical and genetic study. *Acta Psychiatr. Neurol. Scand.*, (Suppl.) 65.

Hallgren, B. (1957), Enuresis: A clinical and genetic study. *Acta Psychiat. Neurol. Scand.*, 32(Suppl. 114):1–159.

Hanson, D.R., Gottesman, I.I., and Meehl, P.E. (1977), Genetic theories and the validation of psychiatric diagnoses: implications for the study of children of schizophrenics. *J. Abnorm. Psychol.*, 86:575–588.

Heilbrunn, G. (1979), Biologic correlates of psychoanalytic concepts. *J. Am. Psychoanal. Assoc.*, 27:597–626.

Himmich, W.A. (1971), Biochemical processes in behavioral development: Biochemical processes of nervous system development. In: *The Biopsychology of Development*, ed. E. Tobach et al. New York: Academic Press.

Huttenlocher, P. (1979), News release, July 16, 1979, quoted in *Pediatr. Currents*, 28(9):72.

Kagan, J. (1979), The form of early development. *Arch. Gen. Psychiatry*, 36:1047–1054.

Kendel, E.R. (1979), Psychotherapy and the single synapse. *New Engl. J. Med.*, 301:1028–1037.

Leckman, J.F., Cohen, D.J., Shaywitz, B.A., Caparulo, B.K., Heninger, G.R, and Bowers, M. B., Jr. (1980), CSF monoamine metabolites in child and adult psychiatric patients: A developmental perspective. *Arch. Gen. Psychiatry*, 37:677–681.

Metcalf, D.R., and Jordan, K. (1971), EEG ontogenesis in normal children. In: *Drugs, Development and Cerebral Function*, ed. W.L. Smith. Springfield, Ill.: Charles C Thomas, pp. 125–144.

Meyersburg, H.A., and Post, R.M. (1979), An holistic developmental view of neural and psychological processes. *Br. J. Psychiatry*, 135:139–155.

Molinoff, P.B., Brimijoin, W.S., Weinshilboum, R.M., et al. (1970), Neurally mediated increase in dopamine-beta-hydroxylase activity. *Proc. Natl. Acad. Sci. U.S.A.*, 66:453–458.

Rapoport, J.L., Pandoni, C., Renfield, M., et al. (1977), Newborn dopamine-beta-hydroxylase, minor physical anomalies and infant temperament. *Am. J. Psychiatry*, 34:676–679.

Rosengarten, H., and Friedhoff, A.J. (1979), Enduring changes in dopamine receptor cells of pups from drug administration to pregnant and nursing rats. *Science*, 203:1133–1135.

Rutter, M. (1977), Brain damage syndromes in childhood: Concepts and findings. *J. Child Psychol. Psychiatry*, 18:1–21.

Rutter, M., Graham, P., and Yule, W. (1970), A Neuropsychiatric Study in Childhood. *Clinics in Developmental Medicine*, Nos. 35, 36. S.I.M.H. London: Heinemann.

Sherrington, C.S. (1961), *Integrative Action of the Nervous System* (1906). New Haven, Conn.: Yale University Press.

Spitz, R. (1965), *The First Year of Life*. New York: International Universities Press.

Stein, L., and Berger, B.D. (1975), Noradrenergic reward mechanisms, recovery of function, and schizophrenia. In: *The Chemistry of Mood, Motivation and Memory*, ed. J.L. McGaugh. Advances in Behavioral Biology, Vol. 4. New York: Plenum, pp. 81–103.

Tanguay, P.E., Ornitz, E.M., and Kaplan, A. (1975), Evolution of sleep spindles in childhood. *Electroencephalog. Clin. Neurophysiol.*, 38:175–181.

Tanner, J.M. (1970), Physical growth. In: *Carmichael's Manual of Child Psychology*, ed. P.H. Mussen. New York: Wiley.

Torgerson, A.M., and Kringlen, E. (1978), Genetic aspects of temperamental differences in infants: A study of same-sexed twins. *J. Am. Acad. Child Psychiatry*, 17:433–444.

Tosteson, D.C. (1979), Learning in medicine. *New Engl. J. Med.*, 301:690–694.

Yakovlev, P.I., and Lecours, A.R. (1967), The myelogenetic cycles of regional maturation of the brain. In: *Regional Development of the Brain*, ed. A. Kinkowski. Oxford: Blackwell.

Chapter 2
ATTACHMENT BEHAVIOR

In the study of the origin of man, parenting and social relationships, monogamous pair bonding, specialized sexual-reproductive behavior, and bipedality have been proposed as vital precursors for the development of brain and human intelligence (Lovejoy, 1981). Embedded in this pivotal capacity for social relationships in general and the nuclear family in particular is the ability to form attachments. This basic function therefore deserves our first consideration.

The infant at birth is preadapted, so to speak, for survival and sociability. The infant sees, hears, sucks, and grasps in highly specific ways from the beginning (Bornstein and Kessen, 1979). The development of these functions depends upon the mutual, synchronous interactions between the infant and another person over time, with the infant often setting the pace for this interaction (Schaffer, 1977). Thus the infant appears to have innate active functions that (1) perform selectively, (2) have intrinsic rhythms and changes of state, and (3) are modifiable through interaction with another person. The mothering person is an almost equal partner in this interaction.

Klaus and Kennell (1976) have emphasized the importance of early contact between parents and neonate for the formation of attachment. They have stated that the mother and father must have close contact with the neonate during the sensitive period of the first minutes and hours of life, during which the mother and father appear to exhibit species-specific responses to the infant when they are first exposed to the infant, and the infant responds to the mother with some signal, such as a body movement or an eye movement.

Subsequent studies have confirmed the ease with which bonding occurs in the first few hours of life (Hales et al., 1977). All this is part of a new direction in the progress of the concept of attachment, in which the role of maternal attachment in the reciprocal process during the newborn period, including the care of the premature infant, is now considered equally important (Barnett et al., 1970; Klaus et al., 1972). Interference in this interaction may be a factor in certain instances of child abuse (Klaus and Kennell, 1976), divorce, and subsequent giving up of the infant (Leifer et al., 1972). Again, fathers can be and are involved in attachment as much as mothers (Parke, 1978).

In their original work, Bowlby (1958; 1969) and Ainsworth (1963; 1973), drawing on ethology, evolutionary theory, psychoanalysis, cognitive-developmental theory, and control-systems theory, described and conceptualized how this earliest bond, or attachment, between an infant and another person is formed. From the beginning, other individuals will exercise an attention-compelling influence on the infant that is unrivaled by any other single feature of the environment. By the same token, parents are attracted to the infant, leading to a situation in which an enmeshing of parent-infant interaction patterns occurs. There is then a progression in the infant from responding to rather primitive stimulus configurations which he abstracts from the total sensory input, to taking in people as a whole. Since the infant is exposed to just a few specific individuals initially, he learns their characteristics first.

The motivation is the process of learning itself: the more the infant seems interested in things, the more he wants to see; and since human beings appear to be by far the most interesting objects to him, those are the objects he wants to see more of.

What is the evidence for this?

The infant does, in fact, discriminate sounds and visual stimuli at birth; i.e., there is an innate cognitive structure in the infant. Visual fixation occurs within a few hours after birth. During the first month, the eyes are locked at a focal distance of about 8 inches; images nearer or farther are blurred. It so happens that 8 inches is about the distance of the mother's face during feeding. By 4 months the infant's accommodation is about the same as that of adults. Interestingly, there appear to be sex-linked differences in visual attention behavior at 6 months and again at 13 months: girls show more sustained attention to visual stimuli than do boys at these ages (Kagan and Lewis, 1965). Other sensory modalities are also present early, such as pressure and touch sensitivity, as well as smell, taste, and proprioception (position). In short, all the infant's sensory systems are "go" and are functioning at birth or shortly thereafter.

The infant at 1 week of age is apparently attracted to strongly patterned stimuli, e.g., horizontal stripes, concentric circles, and facelike mosaics. Also, pattern is preferred over color or brightness or size, so that some degree of form perception again appears to be innate. Infants appear to be attracted by complex patterns rather than by simple ones, and they also prefer movement. The interesting point is that the infant in a sense chooses what he will look at (if he is given the choice). It so happens that the one object that has all the characteristics just mentioned—i.e., is (1) in almost constant motion, (2) emits a great deal of highly varied stimuli, (3) appeals to a number of different sensory modalities, (4) is quite complex, (5) possesses a distinctive pattern, and (6) is also responsive to the infant's own behavior—is the human object, and the human *face* in particular—not the breast, but the *face* (Fagan, 1979; Fantz, 1975).

The infant, then, appears to be genetically programmed to respond to and learn about and become attached to that aspect of his environment that is most likely to ensure his survival—namely, another person.

The concept that there is a primary, given, inevitable, characteristic for each child, no matter what his or her environment, is an interesting one because it says something about differences as well as similarities. One has only to go into a newborn nursery to see babies behaving in a variety of ways. Fries and Woolf (1953) described some of these differences as "congenital activity types," and Chess and Thomas (1977) have elaborated the concept of "temperament" in the child. Escalona and Heider (1959) too have observed that "as one notes behavioral alterations from infancy to . . . later preschool ages, one knows that not a single behavior has remained the same yet here one is stuck with the inherent continuity of behavioral styles and of the child's pattern" (p. 9).

There is no question that there is some kind of inborn characteristic for each child. It suggests that, given an "average expectable environment," children do have individual, intrinsic personalities of their own, a fact that parents have known for centuries.

Attachment, then, is an affectional tie that one person forms to another person, binding them together in space and enduring over time. Attachment is discriminating and specific. One may be attached to more than one person, but there is usually a gradient in the strength of such multiple attachments (Schaffer and Emerson, 1964b). Attachment implies affect, predominantly affection or love.

Bonding implies a selective attachment (Cohen, 1974) which is maintained even when there is no contact with the person with whom the bond exists.

Attachment behavior is behavior that promotes proximity to or contact with the specific figure or figures to whom the person is attached. Attachment behavior includes signals (crying, smiling, vocalizing), locomotions (looking, following, approaching), and contacts (clambering up, embracing, and clinging). Sucking, clinging, following, crying, and smiling become incorporated by 8 or 9 months. Attachment behavior is strongest in toddlers; bonding is most secure in older children (Rutter, 1976).

Bowlby (1958; 1969) in particular and later Ainsworth (1963; 1973) developed the idea that the act of smiling in infancy may be one of a group of "innate release mechanisms" that release a particular protective response in the mother. Thus at about 6 to 8 weeks, the infant first recognizes the facial configuration of the smile in the mother and can be said to be imprinted on the mother as the person to whom he will turn. In turn, the mother is affected by this recognition of her by the infant in a way that increases her affectionate bond to the infant. The reciprocal behavior of the parents is the "caretaking behavior."

Bowlby also proposed that the biological function of the attachment behavior is to protect the infant from danger, especially the danger of attack by predators. The system may be activated by the hormonal state, environmental stimulus situation, and CNS excitation. The system is terminated in response to a specific terminating signal (e.g., attachment achieved) or by habituation. The attachment behavior system is in equilibrium with other important behavior systems, e.g., exploratory behavior, which is elicited by stimuli that have novelty and complexity or change (and may draw the infant away from the mother).

At least 15 kinds of attachment behavior have been described (Ainsworth, 1963):

1. Differential crying: The infant cries when held by someone other than the mother and stops crying when taken by her.

2. Differential smiling: The infant smiles more readily and more frequently in interaction with the mother than in interaction with another person.
3. Differential vocalization: The infant vocalizes more readily and more frequently in interaction with the mother than in interaction with another person.
4. Visual-motor orientation: The infant, when apart from his mother but able to see her, keeps his eyes more or less continuously oriented toward her.
5. Greeting responses: On the mother's return after an absence, the infant smiles and shows general attachment.
6. Lifting of arms in greeting
7. Hand clapping in greeting
8. Crying when the mother leaves
9. Scrambling over the mother: The infant climbs over the mother, exploring her person and clothes.
10. Following the mother: Once able to crawl, the infant attempts to follow the mother when she leaves the room.
11. Burying the face in the mother's lap
12. Clinging: The infant clings tightly to the mother when apprehensive.
13. Kissing: The infant returns the mother's kiss.
14. Exploration from the mother with the mother as a secure base: The infant makes little excursions away from the mother but returns to her from time to time.
15. Flight to the mother as to a haven of safety.

These attachment behaviors may vary in intensity, and in certain pathological states, such as infantile autism, one or more of them may be absent.

WHEN DOES ATTACHMENT OCCUR?

The proportion of the life cycle during which attachment behavior is seen is highly species specific and is sometimes sex specific. In female sheep, for example, attachment to the mother may continue into old age, so that a flock of sheep consists of young sheep who follow their mothers, who follow the grandmothers, who follow the greatgrandmothers, and so on. Male sheep, however, break away from their mothers at adolescence, and become attached to older males. In geese, on the other hand, attachment ends by the end of the second or third winter, in both males and females. Examples of the evidence for attachment behavior in primates other than humans are found in the work of Harlow (with monkeys) and Goodall (with chimpanzees). The evidence, starting with that from Lorenz's early work on imprinting (Lorenz, 1935) is very impressive.

Attachment behavior in the human is modified by an important human characteristic: the extreme biological helplessness of the human infant. Yet during the first few days of life babies are soothed by being picked up, talked to, and cuddled, and they soon enjoy watching people, independent of being fed (although *not* being hungry helps). The human infant can distinguish his mother as a person by about 4 months of age, long before he can move toward her or cling to her. But he can smile and vocalize and can follow her more readily.

Ainsworth (1963) showed that by 6 months of age, most infants in her study cried when their mothers left the room, and greeted their mothers with smiles, crows of delight, and lifting of the arms when the mothers returned—all examples of attachment behavior—and that this behavior increased in vigor between 6 and 9 months of age, so that when their mothers returned, the infants would quickly crawl toward them to reestablish proximity. Furthermore, clinging to the mother was shown to become especially evident after 9 months of age, particularly if the infant is alarmed by the presence of a stranger. This phenomenon has been confirmed in studies by Schaffer and Emerson (1964a) in Scotland.

Attachment during the first half-year is more or less indiscriminate; almost anyone can satisfy the infant's need for attention. After 6 months of age, a change occurs; people *other* than the mother *upset* the infant when they approach him or her. The infant shows so-called stranger anxiety. There is now a significant emotional relationship between the infant and the mothering adult or adults. Actually, the age range when this relationship occurs is probably from 5 to 12 months. In stranger anxiety, the infant's recognition of incongruity of perceptions means that he now can recall a representation of the familiar face when looking at the stranger's face. At this point the specific mother-child or, rather, child-mother bond becomes a very specific entity, having some constancy or permanence and capable of being recalled. "Mother" has become an internalized object, a memory, that can be recalled and used as a basis for comparison.

CONSEQUENCES OF ATTACHMENT

There are certain consequences of attachment. We will consider two: (i) *generalization* to other people and (ii) development of *schema* as a prerequisite for stranger anxiety and separation anxiety.

Generalization

Rheingold (1965) studied 16 6-month-old infants in an institution in which many volunteers cared for the children. For 8 babies Rheingold herself played the role of mother, 8 hours a day, 5 days a week, for 8 weeks (e.g., she bathed, diapered, played with, and smiled at the babies). Thus *one* person gave these babies *extra nurturance*. The other 8 babies were kept to the regular institutional routine, in which several different women cared for each child. All 16 babies were tested each week for the 8-week period and then each week for 4 weeks after the 8 weeks. The tests were of the babies' social responsiveness to three different groups of people: (1) the experimenter, (2) the examiner who gave the tests, and (3) a stranger (at the end of the 8 weeks).

The results of this study were that the 8 babies who had the special care showed more social responsiveness *not only* to the mother surrogate but *also* to the examiner than did the control group. That is to say, *generalization* had occurred.

Thus if an infant makes a set of responses to one class of objects, or people, he is likely to make them to similar objects, or people, provided that they are not too dissimilar from the original ones.

Development of Schema as a Prerequisite for Stranger Anxiety and Separation Anxiety

Stranger Anxiety. At 6 to 8 months of age, the infant has developed such a good schema of the mother's face that a stranger's face is now a discrepant one. One could, therefore, call stranger anxiety *a reaction to a discrepancy that is beyond the infant's capacity to assimilate or to make some other constructive response to*, such as asking, "Who is that?" (which he cannot do at 6 months but can do later).

Of course, by a later date the infant will also have been exposed to many strange faces, so that he will have also had opportunities to generalize and to form new schema. Later the strange face is also less discrepant and thus causes less anxiety. As a matter of fact, stranger anxiety is rare in institutionalized infants, who see a constant stream of strange faces, and it diminishes spontaneously in normal infants.

There is some evidence for a genetic factor in stranger

anxiety; this evidence is found in a twin study carried out by Freedman (1965). Identical twins were compared with fraternal twins for the intensity of the fear of strangers. Freedman found that there was a greater concordance in the timing as well as the intensity of the fear of strangers between identical twins than between fraternal twins. There is also a sex difference. Schaffer (1966) found that stranger anxiety began earlier in girls than in boys.

Separation Anxiety. Separation anxiety, which begins at about 10 months and wanes at about 18 months, has two components: (1) the discrepancy produced when the child is placed in a strange environment without his mother and (2) the child's inability to make a relevant response that will bring him to his mother. The closer the attachment of the baby to the mother, the more frequent and intense is the separation anxiety.

Let us look at these two components of separation anxiety, particularly the child's inability to make a relevant response that will bring him to his mother.

Rheingold put a group of 10-month-old infants one by one in a strange room under 4 conditions: (1) with the mother, (2) with a stranger, (3) with toys, and (4) alone. Rheingold found that when the mother was present, nothing much happened and that when the infant was put in a *strange room and was without the mother* the infant cried (toys or strangers were of no help). When an infant was placed in a room with the mother—a room that had an open door that led to the strange, empty room in which the infant had cried—the infant crawled into the empty room, *but he did not cry, even though he was alone.* Instead, the infant stayed for a short period, looked around, and then crawled back to talk to the mother. The infant could now do something effective when he became anxious by the discrepant environment.

What the evidence adds up to is that once the mother's absence is no longer a discrepant event or once the child can do something about the mother's absence, separation anxiety, like stranger anxiety, should also vanish. It is of interest that the greater the number of figures to whom a child was attached, the more intense his attachment to mother as his principal figure was likely to be. Incidentally, the intensity and consistency with which attachment behavior is shown varies from day to day, and even from hour to hour. Hour-to-hour variation is due to such organismic factors as hunger, fatigue, illness, unhappiness, and pain, all of which lead to increased crying and following. Environmental factors, such as the presence of a stranger, arouse alarm, especially after 40 weeks of age. This alarm in turn intensifies attachment behavior.

Also important is that from at least 2 months of age the infant often takes the initiative in seeking interaction. He does this by crying, calling, looking, and smiling.

The subsequent course of attachment behavior is something like this:

During the second year, the child begins to protest impending separation. Parents in turn often anticipate the protest, and try to hide from the child signs that they are about to leave.

By the end of the third year, most children are able to accept the mother's temporary absence, to engage in play with other children, and to be sufficiently comforted by a secondary attachment figure (e.g., a nursery school teacher) provided that (1) the figure is a familiar person, (2) the child knows where his mother is, and (3) the child is not upset for any other reason, such as illness. Note again that the child's attachment to other children and teachers has nothing to do with his having his physiological needs met.

Attachment behavior after the age of 3 is less urgent and less frequent but still important. Rutter (1976), after reviewing the evidence, concludes that children may have difficulty in developing stable selective attachments for the first time after the age of 3 or 4 years.

Attachment persists through to age 6 or even older, when it is expressed sometimes as a wish to hold a parent's hand when going on an outing. It probably exists all through childhood, adolescence, adulthood, and even old age; daughters remain attached to their mothers, older people attach themselves to younger people, adults attach themselves to a group. These attachment behaviors intensify at times of stress, such as sickness and death, when people are drawn close to people they trust. Bowlby is at pains to point out that this reaction is an intensification of attachment behavior and *not* regression in the psychoanalytic sense.

Attachment behavior also has a strong affective component. The attachment figure is loved by the infant, and the sight or return of the mother is greeted with joy. Threat of loss creates anxiety and anger.

Detachment may occur following prolonged separation. When young children are admitted to the hospital and thus undergo separation, they may first react with acute distress and crying ("protest"), then with misery and apathy ("despair"), and finally with apparent disinterest ("detachment")

(Bowlby, 1975). Single separation experiences rarely have long-term consequences. Long-term consequences follow acute stresses only if they are also associated with chronic stresses (Rutter, 1972). At the same time, recurrent stressful separations, such as recurrent hospital admissions, are associated with an increased risk of psychiatric disorders (Quinton and Rutter, 1976).

SUMMARY OF PHASES IN THE DEVELOPMENT OF ATTACHMENT

First Phase: Undiscriminating Social Responsiveness (0 to 3 months)

Primitive Behaviors	Orienting Behaviors	Signaling Behaviors
Sucking	Visual fixation	Smiling
Grasping	Visual tracking	Crying
	Listening	Vocalizations
	Rooting	
	Postural adjustment	

From the beginning the infant has some capacity to respond differentially to different stimuli, and thus to discriminate them. Further, the range of stimuli to which the infant is most responsive includes the range commonly emanating from human adults, including visual stimuli, auditory stimuli, and stimuli associated with feeding. Yet the infant does not initially discriminate between the persons presenting these stimuli.

When the infant does begin to discriminate between persons, he or she does so more readily through some modalities than others, e.g., tactile-kinesthetic discrimination first, then auditory discrimination, and then visual discriminations at, say, 8 weeks.

Second Phase: Discriminating Social Responsiveness (3 to 8 months)

The infant discriminates between familiar figures (mother and one or two others) and those who are relatively unfamiliar.

First Subphase: Discrimination and differential responses to figures close at hand, e.g., differential smiling, vocalization, and crying.

Second Subphase: Discrimination between figures at a distance, e.g., as evidenced by differential greeting and crying when a particular figure leaves the room.

Third Phase of Active Initiative in Seeking Proximity and Contact (7 months to 3 years)

At about 7 months, a striking increase occurs in the infant's initiative in promoting proximity and contact. Voluntary movements of the infant's hands and arms are now conspicuous in his or her attachment behavior. Following, approaching, clinging, and similar behaviors become more significant. The infant is now attached.

In psychoanalytic theory, the infant at this stage is said to have an anaclitic-type of object relation. In cognitive-developmental theory, the infant at this stage is said to be at the fourth subphase of sensorimotor development and to have acquired "object permanence."

It is interesting to note here that Spitz talked of "organizers" as a concept to account for the factors which govern the process of transition from one level of development to the next.

1. The smiling response is the visible manifestation of a certain degree of organization in the psychic apparatus.
2. The second organizer is the 8-month anxiety, which marks a new stage in development.
3. The third organizer is the achievement of the sign of negation and of the word no. In Spitz's view it is the first abstraction, or symbol, formed by the child, usually at the beginning of the second year (around 15 months), when the infant turns his or her head away to refuse food (a response that has its origins in the rooting reflex).

Fourth Phase: Goal-Directed Partnership (3 years)

The infant in the fourth phase infers something about the mother's "set goals" and attempts to alter her set goals to fit better with his or her goals in regard to contact, proximity, and interaction (provided the mother does not dissemble about what her set goals are, e.g., to leave the infant at nursery school).

NECESSARY CONDITIONS FOR THE DEVELOPMENT OF ATTACHMENT

The following conditions are prerequisites for the development of attachment:

1. "Sufficient" interaction with the mother
2. The ability of the infant to discriminate his mother or other attachment figure from other persons
3. The ability of the infant to have at least begun to conceive of a person as having a permanent and independent existence even when that person is not present to the infant's perception

An infant's goal-corrected behavior probably becomes increasingly smooth and effective in parallel with the later stages of development of the concept of the object, which, according to Piaget, is completed at about 18 months. Piaget suggested that the concept of *persons* as permanent objects evolves in homologous stages but in advance of the development of things as permanent objects, presumably because an infant finds people the most interesting of objects.

FACTORS THAT INFLUENCE THE DEVELOPMENT OF ATTACHMENT

The following factors influence the development of attachment:

1. Sensitive phases in the development of infant-mother attachment. The sensitive phase during which attachments are most readily formed spans a period of months in the middle of the first year. It probably starts in the neonatal period. Provence and Lipton (1962) showed that infants kept in an institution until they are 8 to 24 months old find it difficult to become attached to a foster mother later; and that age range seems to be the upper limit of the sensitive phase for becoming attached for the first time.
2. Infant-care practices (e.g., feeding practices)
3. Maternal care, infant behavior and mother-infant interaction. The mother's contribution to attachment is affected by such factors as her hormonal state, her parity and experience, and her personality. The infant's contribution is affected by such factors as wakefulness and activity level, crying, temperament, genetic make-up, and organic make-up.
4. Maternal deprivation

   Strong attachments occur under the following five conditions:
   (a) When the interaction has a certain degree of intensity, as when a sensitive, responsive parent gives a

great deal of attention to the child, talks with the child, and, especially, plays with the child (Stayton and Ainsworth, 1973).

(b) When the parent responds regularly and readily to the child's needs as signalled, say, by crying. The child is likely to become strongly attached to a parent who can recognize and respond to the child's signals.

(c) When the number of caretakers is limited. The fewer the caretakers, the greater the attachment.

(d) When the child's own contribution is strong; that is, when his needs and signals are strong.

(e) When the child is in the early sensitive phase (of imprinting), i.e., during his first 2 years.

Curiously, parental rejection, even to the extent of physical abuse, appears to increase the attachment behavior of the child. In 1963 Kovak and Hess did an experiment with chicks that confirms the existence of that phenomenon. First these investigators determined the critical attachment phase for imprinting in the chicks. Then they gave the chicks who were in this critical phase electrical shocks while the chicks were with their parents. (They did not give shocks to a control group.) They gave shocks to a group of chicks at a later time, well beyond the critical attachment phase. The chicks who were given shocks during the critical attachment phase actually followed their parents significantly more than did those who were not given shocks. The chicks who were given shocks after the critical attachment phase avoided their parents, presumably because they associated their parents with the shocks. Thus it appeared that the chicks who experienced pain during the phases when they depended on their parents to a tremendous degree for survival sought to get even closer to their parents.

Interestingly, infants in institutions have also been found to show more clinging and following behavior but to be less likely to show bonding and deep, lasting relationships than 4-year-olds reared in families (Tizard and Rees, 1975).

Attachment theory, detailed as it is, is still incomplete in that it does not account for a large area of functioning and behavior, even within the line of the development of the affectional tie between child and adult. However, it is a promising avenue of inquiry. Attachment theory is important because it provides a basis for proper care of the premature infant, suggests principles for adoption practices, and provides clues for understanding child abuse and delinquency.

Note 2

From *Attachment and Loss,* Volume 1, *Attachment* by John Bowlby. © 1969 by the Tavistock Institute of Human Relations, Basic Books, Inc., Publishers, New York. Reprinted by permission.

So far as can be seen at present, the development of attachment behavior in human infants, though much slower, is of a piece with that seen in sub-human mammals. Much evidence supports that conclusion and none contradict it.

Present knowledge of the development of attachment behavior in humans can be summarized briefly under the same eight heads that were used.... to describe present knowledge of imprinting in birds:

i. In human infants social responses of every kind are first elicited by a wide array of stimuli and are later elicited by a much narrower array, confined after some months to stimuli arising from one or a few particular individuals.

ii. There is evidence of a marked bias to respond socially to certain kinds of stimuli more than to others.

iii. The more experience of social interaction an infant has with a person the stronger his attachment to that person becomes.

iv. The fact that learning to discriminate certain faces commonly follows periods of attentive staring and listening suggests that exposure learning may be playing a part.

v. In most infants attachment behavior to a preferred figure develops during the first year of life. It seems probable that there is a sensitivity period in that year during which attachment behavior develops most readily.

vi. It is unlikely that any sensitive phase begins before about six weeks and it may be some weeks later.

vii. After about six months, and markedly so after eight or nine months, babies are more likely to respond to strange figures with fear responses, and more likely also to respond to them with strong fear responses, than they are when they are younger. Because of the growing frequency and strength of such fear responses, the development of attachment to a new figure becomes increasingly difficult towards the end of the first year and subsequently.

viii. Once a child has become strongly attached to a particular figure, he tends to prefer that figure to all others, and such preference tends to persist despite separation.

We may conclude, therefore, that, so far as is at present known, the way in which attachment behavior develops in the human infant and becomes focused on a discriminated figure is sufficiently like the way in which it develops in other mammals, and in birds, for it to be included, legitimately, under the heading of imprinting—so long as that term is used in its current generic sense. Indeed, to do otherwise would be to create a wholly unwarranted gap between the human case and that of other species.

Note 3

M.D.S. Ainsworth, and S.M. Bell (1970), Attachment, exploration and separation: Illustrated by the behavior of one-year-olds in a

The following propositions are suggested as essential to a comprehensive concept of attachment. They are based on an ethological-
evolutionary point of view, and have been formulated on the basis of
reports of a broad range of investigations, including naturalistic
studies of mother-infant interaction, and studies of mother-child
separation and reunion in both human and nonhuman primates, as
well as the illustrative strange-situation study reported here.

1. Attachment is not coincident with attachment behavior. Attachment behavior may be heightened or diminished by
conditions—environmental and intraorganismic—which may be
specified empirically. Despite situationally determined waxing
and waning of attachment behavior, the individual is nevertheless predisposed intermittently to seek proximity to the object of
attachment. It is this predisposition—which may be conceived as
having an inner, structural basis—that is the attachment. Its
manifestations are accessible to observation over time; a short
time-sample may, however, be misleading.

2. Attachment behavior is heightened in situations perceived as
threatening, whether it is an external danger or an actual or
impending separation from the attachment object that constitutes the threat.

3. When strongly activated, attachment behavior is incompatible
with exploratory behavior. On the other hand, the state of being
attached, together with the presence of the attachment object,
may support and facilitate exploratory behaviors. Provided that
there is no threat of separation, the infant is likely to be able to
use his mother as a secure base from which to explore, manifest-
ing no alarm in even a strange situation as long as she is present.
Under these circumstances the relative absence of attachment
behavior—of proximity-promoting behavior—can not be considered an index of a weak attachment.

4. Although attachment behavior may diminish or even disappear
in the course of a prolonged absence from the object of attachment, the attachment is not necessarily diminished; attachment
behavior is likely to reemerge in full or heightened strength upon
reunion, with or without delay.

5. Although individual differences have not been stressed in this
discussion, the incidence of ambivalent (contact-resisting) and
probably defensive (proximity-avoiding) patterns of behavior in
the reunion episodes of the strange situation is a reflection of the
fact that attachment relations are qualitatively different from
one attached pair to another. These qualitative differences,
together with the sensitivity of attachment behavior to situational determinants, make it very difficult to assess the strength
or intensity of an attachment. It is suggested that, in the present
state of our knowledge, it is wiser to explore qualitative differences, and their correlates and antecedents, than to attempt
premature quantifications of strength of attachment.

REFERENCES

Ainsworth, M.D.S. (1963), The development of infant-mother interaction among the Ganda. In: *Determinants of Infant Behavior*, Vol. 2, ed. B.M. Foss, London: Methuen, pp. 67–112.

Ainsworth, M.D.S. (1973), The development of infant-mother attachment. In: *Review of Child Development Research*, Vol. 3, ed. B.M. Caldwell and H.N. Ricciuti. Chicago: University of Chicago Press, pp. 1–94.

Ainsworth, M.D.S., and Bell, S.M. (1970), Attachment, exploration and separation: Illustrated by the behavior of one-year-olds in a strange situation. *Child Dev.*, 41:49–67.

Barnett, C., et al. (1970), Neonatal separation: Maternal side of interactional deprivation. *Pediatrics*, 46:197–205.

Bornstein, M.D., and Kessen, W. (Eds.) (1979), *Psychological Development from Infancy: Image to Intention*. Hillsdale, N.J.: Lawrence Erlbaum Associates.

Bowlby, J. (1958), The nature of the child's tie to his mother. *Int. J. Psychoanal.*, 39:350–373.

Bowlby, J. (1969), *Attachment*. Attachment and Loss, Vol 1. New York: Basic Books.

Bowlby, J. (1975), *Separation: Anxiety and Anger*. Attachment and Loss, Vol. 2, Harmondsworth: Penguin.

Chess, S., and Thomas, A. (1977), Temperamental individuality from childhood to adolescence. *J. Am. Acad. Child Psychiatry*, 16:218–226.

Cohen, L.J. (1974), The operational definition of human attachment. *Psychol. Bull.*, 81:107–217.

Escalona, S., and Heider, G. (1959), *Prediction and Outcome*. New York: Basic Books.

Fagan, J.F. (1979), The origins of facial pattern recognition. In: *Psychological Development from Infancy*, ed. M.H. Bornstein and W. Kessler. Hillsdale, N.J.: Lawrence Erlbaum Associates.

Fantz, R.L. (1975), Early visual selectivity. In: *Infant Perception: From Sensation to Cognition*, ed. L.B. Cohen and P.H. Salapatek. New York: Academic Press.

Freedman, D.G. (1965), Hereditary control of early social behavior. In: *Determinants of Infant Behavior*, Vol. 3, ed. B.M. Foss. New York: Wiley, pp. 149–159.

Fries, M.E., and Woolf, F.J. (1953), Some hypotheses on the role of the congenital activity type in personality development. *Psychoanal. Study Child*, 8:48–62.

Hales, D., Lozoff, B., Sosa, R., and Kennell, J. (1977), Defining the limits of the sensitive period. *Dev. Med. Child Neurol.*, 19:454.

Kagan, J., and Lewis, M. (1965), Studies of attention in the human infant. *Merrill-Palmer Q.*, 2:95–122.

Klaus, M.H., and Kennell, J.H. (1976), *Maternal-Infant Bonding*. St. Louis: Mosby.

Klaus, M.H., et al. (1972), Maternal attachment: Importance of the first postpartum days. *N. Engl. J. Med.*, 286:460–463.

Kovach, J.K., and Hess, E.H. (1963), Imprinting: Effects of painful stimulation upon the following response. *J. Comp. Physiol. Psychol.*, 56:461.

Leifer, A., Leiderman, P.H., Barnett, C., and Williams, J. (1972), Effects of mother-infant separation on maternal attachment. *Child Dev.*, 43:1203–1218.

Lorenz, K.Z. (1935), Der Kumpan in der Umvelt des Vogels. *J. Ornithol. Berl.*, 83. English translation in *Intinctive Behavior*, ed. C.H. Schiller. New York: International Universities Press.

Lovejoy, C.O. (1981), The origin of man. *Science*, 211:341–350.

Parke, R.D. (1978), Perspectives on father-infant interaction. In: *The Handbook of Infant Development*, ed. J.D. Osofsky. New York: Wiley.

Provence, S., and Lipton, R.C. (1962), *Infants in Institutions*. New York: International Universities Press.

Quinton, D., and Rutter, M. (1976), Early hospital admissions and later disturbances of behavior: An attempted replication of Douglas' findings. *Dev. Med. Child Neurol.*, 18:447–459.

Rheingold, H.L. (1965), The modification of social responsiveness in institutional babies. *Monogr. Soc. Res. Child Dev.*, 21:2, #63.

Rutter, M. (1972), *Maternal Deprivation Reassessed*. Harmondsworth: Penguin.

Rutter, M. (1976), Separation, loss and family relationships. In: *Child Psychiatry*, ed. M. Rutter and L. Hersov. Oxford: Blackwell.

Schaffer, H.R. (1966), The onset of fear of strangers and the incongruity hypothesis. *J. Child Psychol. Psychiat.*, 7:95–106.

Schaffer, H.R. (1977), Introduction: Early interactive development. In: *Studies in Mother-Infant Interaction*, ed. H.R. Schaffer. London: Academic Press.

Schaffer, H.R., and Emerson, P.E. (1964a), The development of social attachments in infancy. *Monogr. Soc. Res. Child Dev.*, 29:1–77.

Schaffer, H.R., and Emerson, P.E. (1964b), Patterns of response to physical contact in early human development. *J. Child Psychol. Psychiatry*, 5:1–13.

Stayton, D.J., and Ainsworth, M.D. (1973), Individual differences in infant responses to brief, everyday separations as related to other infant and maternal behaviors. *Dev. Psychol.*, 9:226–235.

Tizard, B., and Rees, J. (1975), The effect of early institutional rearing on the behavior problems and affectional relationships of four-year-old children. *J. Child Psychol. Psychiatry*, 16:61–74.

Chapter 3

COGNITIVE DEVELOPMENT

The beginning of thinking is in the body. The infant reacts to a *sensory* stimulus with a *motor* reaction: place a finger in his hand, and he grasps; place a nipple in his mouth, and he sucks; place a pattern in front of his eyes, and he looks. This sensorimotor pattern is the earliest kind of thinking, and it starts with those innate patterns of behavior that were just noted: grasping, sucking, looking, and gross body activity.

The basic element in Piaget's theory of the child's cognitive development is the *schema*, which consists of a pattern of behavior in response to a particular stimulus from the environment. However, the schema is more than just a response, because the child also acts upon the environment. For example, the infant sucks in response to a nipple. The schema of sucking then becomes increasingly complex as the child reacts to and acts upon a wider range of environmental stimuli. Thus when the child can put his thumb into his mouth, the schema of sucking evoked by a nipple is gradually broadened to include this new and similar but not identical stimulus, the thumb. The new object (the thumb) is said to be assimilated (see Note 4) into the original schema. At the same time, the infant has to modify his sucking behavior slightly because the thumb is different in shape, taste, and other characteristics from the nipple. This act of modification, which Piaget calls accommodation, results in a new equilibrium. These two processes, assimilation and accommodation, proceed in ever increasing complexities.

Four major stages of development are described in Piaget's theory:

1. A sensorimotor stage—from about birth to 18 months
2. A preoperational stage—from 18 months to 7 years
3. A stage of concrete operation—from 7 years to adolescence
4. A stage of abstract operations—adolescence

Each of these stages is subdivided. Clearly, Piaget is presenting a developmental theory, or system, with stage sequences. However, what moves a child from one stage to the next, beyond the intellectual effort required to resolve a cognitive discrepancy, is still unclear, even in Piaget's theory. And although Piaget has a great deal to say about cognition, he has relatively little to say about affects or about the influence of the environment on thinking.

SENSORIMOTOR STAGE

In the *sensorimotor stage* (0 to 18 months of age) there are six substages. They can be described as follows:

1. In the first month, the infant exercises a function, such as looking or grasping, simply because it exists.
2. During the next 3 or 4 months (from 1 to 4½ months of age) new schemas are acquired: they are usually centered on the infant's own body (e.g., his thumb) (so-called primary circular reactions).
3. Sometime between 4½ months to 8 or 9 months of age, the infant tries to produce an effect upon the object he sees or grasps, i.e., he now involves events or objects in the external environment (e.g., a rattle) (secondary circular reactions).
4. By 8 or 9 months to 11 or 11½ months of age, the infant begins to be aware of the existence of unperceived objects, hidden, say, behind a pillow or in peek-a-boo games. This is also the time of so-called stranger anxiety. The mental image of the object has now achieved some degree of permanence in the infant's mind (object permanence).
5. In the first half of the second year—11 or 12 months to 18 months of age—the child explores more thoroughly an object and its spatial relationship; e.g., by putting smaller objects into and taking them out of larger ones.
   (a) The child initiates changes which produce variations in the event itself; e.g., dropping, say, bread and then toys from different heights or different positions.
   (b) The child actively searches for novel events (tertiary circular reactions).
6. By the end of the second year—18 months to 2 years of age—the child shows some evidence of reasoning; mental

trial and error replaces trial and error in action; e.g., the child uses one toy as an instrument to get another.

The use of toys and play for a child is essentially a form of thinking. If one gives a 2-year-old some beads, a box lid, and a Teddy bear, the child will soon place the beads on the box lid and set the Teddy bear beside it. The child will then pick up the beads, one by one, and put them to the mouth of the Teddy bear. In this way, the child recalls in play his experience of eating. The box lid and the beads seem to symbolize the plate and the food, and the Teddy bear seems to represent the child. Thus these external objects are organized in such a way as to represent the child's internal symbolization of, say, eating. And in playing in this way, the child clarifies for himself or herself the mental representation of eating and is able to develop it further. Piaget calls this evocation of past activity in the present *deferred imitation*, a characteristic of symbolic thought.

By this time, words have emerged. At this stage, language is first of all an accompaniment to action that is derived from or based on deferred imitations. Gradually, a change occurs, and language, like play, becomes the verbal representation of a past action. The word then begins to function as a sign. But at this stage, the child's language is still a private one; the child does not at first use adult meanings, syntax, and so on. In fact, it is very difficult for the 2-year-old to conceptualize; he may know Tom, Dick, Harry, and Daddy, but he cannot understand man as an abstract concept; if he says the word man, he means a particular person (usually his father). It is not until the child is about 7 or 8 years old that his or her image and private language give way to the public verbal sign. At that age the *verbal sign* rather than the image, is the signifier used in thought.

Deferred imitation, symbolic play, graphic imagery, mental image, and language constitute what Piaget calls the semiotic function, by which he means the ability to represent something (the signified) by means of something else (the signifier). The semiotic function is consolidated between 2 and 4 years of age.

PREOPERATIONAL STAGE

The *preoperational stage*, occurring roughly between the ages of 2 and 7, clearly reflects progress over the preceding stage of sensorimotor intelligence. Two substages are described, the stage of symbolic activity and make-believe play and the stage of decentration.

Symbolic Activity and Make-Believe Play (2 to 4 Years)

One can see in this substage the development of symbolic thought and of representation. Language becomes increasingly important as the child learns to distinguish between actual objects and the labels used to represent them. As a result, the child gradually becomes able to reason symbolically rather than motorically, as was the case in the sensorimotor period, when he or she was limited to the pursuit of concrete goals through action. However, despite these significant advances, there are striking cognitive limitations to preoperational thinking which distinguish it from the logical thought processes which will emerge in the subsequent stages of concrete and, ultimately, formal operations.

There are a number of hallmarks of preoperational thinking. Principally, the child in the preoperational stage is unable to reason logically or deductively; rather, his judgments are dominated by his *perceptions* of events, objects, and experiences. A further limitation is that the child can attend to only one perceptual dimension or attribute at a time, to the exclusion of all others. The concept of *time* is also not available to a child at this stage. The child can recognize sequences and daily routines (e.g., mealtime, play time, sleep time, day and night, and Daddy's or Mommy's going and coming), but he has no concept of an hour, a minute, a week, or a month.

The preoperational child is also extremely egocentric. By that Piaget does not mean that the child is selfish per se. Rather, Piaget employs the term egocentric to refer to a certain cognitive limitation of the preoperational stage, namely, that the young child is conceptually unable to view events and experiences from any point of view but his own. The child is clearly the center of his own representational world. Similarly, the child is unable to differentiate clearly between himself and the world, between the subjective realm of thoughts and feelings and the objective realm of external reality.

In addition, at the preoperational stage the child's reasoning is neither inductive nor deductive but what Piaget terms transductive. That is, the young child tends to relate the particular to the particular in an alogical manner. Events may be viewed as related not because of any inherent cause-and-effect relationship but simply on the basis of spatial and/or temporal contiguity or juxtaposition. Furthermore, the child at this stage is unaware of and therefore unconcerned about possible contradictions in his logic.

Let us look at Piaget's example of transduction in a 2-year-old child who makes the statement: "Daddy's getting hot water, so he's going to shave" (Piaget, 1951). The child is attempting to make an inference although he does not have the concepts yet to carry out the reasoning process. He does have certain preconcepts; i.e., symbols which are neither general nor particular. For example, the child's symbol (preconcept) of *shaving* has in it, say, Daddy, face, hot water, razor, soap, bathroom, and the child's symbol (preconcept) of *hot water* has in it, say, washing, face, soap, bathroom; and so the child makes the inference, "hot water is shaving."

The child does *not*, however, have a true concept (general symbol) of, say, *shaving*, which would have in it a number of exemplars, such as shaving with hot water, shaving with an electric razor, and shaving with a brush. Nor does he or she have the true concept (general symbol) of, say, *hot water*, which would have in it such exemplars as hot water for shaving, hot water for making tea, and hot water for washing.

The child in Piaget's example is simply reasoning from preconcept to preconcept (i.e., if x, then y) although there is not necessarily any relationship between the two preconcepts. That is what is meant by transduction, one of several forms of thinking at this stage.

Let us look at some of the other forms of thinking Piaget describes for the preoperational stage:

1. *Juxtaposition*, which simply means that parts are collected together, or juxtaposed, but are not related to each other. For example, Piaget asked a 4-year-old child, "What makes...[an]...engine go?" The child answered, "The smoke." Piaget then asked, "What smoke?" And the child replied, "The smoke from the funnel." Here the child juxtaposed "smoke" and "engine" as cause and effect, without any knowledge of their actual relationship.

   One sees juxtaposition in the child's drawings at the preoperational stage. For example, a child's drawing of a bicycle* might consist of

---

*Reproduced from J. Piaget (1927), *The Child's Conception of Physical Causality*. Humanities Press, Inc., New Jersey 07716. By permission.

in which the chain, cogwheel, and pedals are seen as necessary for the wheels to turn, but how they are actually related, attached, and work is a mystery to the child. The child concentrates on the parts, or details, of the experience without being able to relate the parts into a whole.

2. *Syncretism* is the term used when the child relates everything to everything else. The child concentrates on the whole of the experience without relating the whole to the parts. For example, Piaget asked a 4-year-old, "How does the bicycle go?" The child answered, "With wheels." Piaget then asked, "And the wheels?" and the child answered, "They are round." Piaget then asked him, "How do they turn?" You can guess what the child said: "It's the bicycle that makes them turn."

3. *Centration* denotes the child's tendency to concentrate on one aspect of a changing relationship to the exclusion of other aspects (Piaget, 1952). For example:

A row of eggs in egg cups is arranged as follows:

A 4-year-old child is asked if there is the same number of eggs as egg cups. He usually says yes. The eggs and the egg cups then are rearranged as follows:

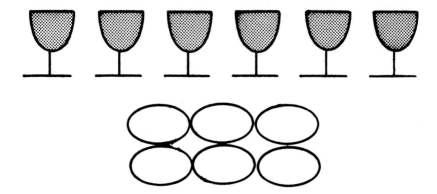

And the child is asked if they are the same now. The child usually answers no, and gives as his reason that there are more egg cups than eggs.

But if the eggs and egg cups are rearranged as follows:

the child will say that there are now more *eggs*. That is to say, the young child can concentrate on the arrangement of the eggs or on the arrangement of the egg cups—but not on both.

Also, whichever is spread apart more is an aspect of the relationship that dominates his thinking. That is, the child concentrates only on the aspect *spread apart*, which gives the appearance of an increase in number, and he or she cannot notice that the number of parts has not changed, that only their arrangement has changed.

4. Piaget calls this inability to manipulate mental representations in a rapid and flexible way *static representation*.

5. Another characteristic of the preoperational stage is *egocentrism* (Piaget, 1951), in which the child credits inanimate things with having feelings like his own and in which the child believes that his thoughts have the power to change things. The child believes things exist because someone (e.g., his mother) put them there, and he does not yet have any notion of a viewpoint other than his own. An example of potentially exasperating egocentrism occurs when a child makes up a new word and assumes that everyone knows what he is talking about. He may, for example, talk of "stocks," an ordinary word but one that he has coined to mean socks and stockings.

Here are some other examples provided by Piaget:

—A 3½-year-old said, "The stairs are horrid; they hit me." (This could also be seen as an example of animism, which will be described shortly.)

—A 3-year-old girl heard a car that was moving on a road at a right angle to the road she was on, and she became frightened. She said, "I don't want the car to come here. I want it to go there." It so happened that the car went in the direction she wished. At that, she said, "You see, it's gone over there because I didn't want it to come here."

—A 6-year-old was asked, "Why are there waves on the lake?" Her reply was, "Because they've been put there."

6. Another characteristic Piaget describes is the *animistic thinking* of the young child. The young child believes that virtually anything that moves is alive. Things such as stones or clouds are invested with feelings and motives. At the same time, mental events such as dreams are viewed as things that come in from the outside.

Let us now discuss animism in more detail to illustrate two other points besides the concept itself: (1) the *detailed complexity* that is involved in the apparently simple concept of animism and (2) *Piaget's method*.

Let us take the example of the child's concept of the sun and the moon. Here are a 6-year-old's responses to various questions Piaget asked:

Questions and answers about the sun:

—How did the sun begin?...*It was when life began.*

—Has there always been a sun?...*No.*

—How did it begin?...*Because it knew that life had begun.*

—What is it made of?...*Of fire.*

—But how?...*Because there was a fire up there.*

—Where did the fire come from?...*From the sky.*

—How was the fire made in the sky?...*It was lighted by a match.*

—Where did it come from, this match?...*God threw it away.*

Questions and answers about the moon:

—How did the moon begin?...*Because we began to be alive.*

—What did that do?...*It made the moon get bigger.*

—Is the moon alive?...*No...Yes.*

—Why?...*Because we are alive.*

The child just quoted believes that the sun and moon are *alive* (animism) and that the sun resulted from the actions of an outside agent (artificialism). The child also believes there is some connection between human activities and activities of things (participation). Such is the *first stage* of the child's understanding of the origins of the sun and the moon.

Now let us look at the responses of an 8-year-old.

—How did the sun begin?...*It was a big cloud that made it.*

—Where did the cloud come from?...*From the smoke.*

—And where did the smoke come from?...*From houses.*

—How did the clouds make the sun shine?...*It's a light which makes it shine.*

—What light?...*A big light. It is someone in Heaven who has set fire to it.*

In the last three answers there is still evidence of artificialism, but in the first answer the child invokes only natural phenomena to explain the sun's origin. That is, in this second stage of the child's understanding of the origins of the sun and the moon, the artificialism and the animism are less blatant. In the third stage, the child gives up the notions of artificialism, animism, and participation and attributes the sun's formation to natural processes, however crudely he or she understands them.

The foregoing discussion gives a glimpse of Piaget's method. It is a clinical method; it is not a fixed-questionnaire method. Neither is it a naturalistic method of simply observing the child's spontaneous utterances. It is clinical in the sense that the child's responses are followed up with nonleading questions. It has much in common with the *clinical interview*, in that it opens up things in an exploratory way. And this fact is not surprising since Piaget really first came across the clinical method when he visited Bleuler, the Swiss psychiatrist well-known for his study of schizophrenia.

Decentration (4 to 7 years)

The second substage of preoperational thinking occurs from 4 to 7 years of age, when an increased accommodation to reality, with progressive "decentering" from the child's own interests, perception, and points of view, gradually takes over. The decentering comes about partly because of the child's increased social involvement (e.g., at school). Social interaction virtually demands that the child use language, and he discovers that what he thinks is not necessarily the same as what his peers think. The child begins to see himself and the world around him from other points of view.

CONCRETE OPERATIONS

Let us take a close look now at the stage of *concrete operations*, from 7 to 11 years of age. The child at this stage is no longer bound by the configuration he perceives at a given moment. He or she can now take into account two variables at once (e.g., height and width). Piaget (1952) performed what is now a classic experiment. One form of Piaget's experiment is as follows: A child is first asked to make sure that the amount of water in two identical beakers is the same:

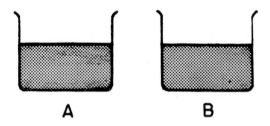

Water from one of the beakers is then transferred into a tall cylinder:

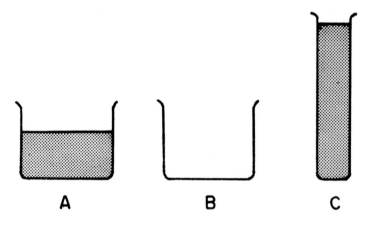

And the child is asked, "Is the amount of water the same?"

A child who is in the *preoperational* stage will say *no*, and then, if asked, will say why. He will say either that the water in the cylinder has more "because it's higher," or the water in the beaker has more "because it's wider."

A child who is at the stage of *concrete operations* will be able to say, "*Yes*, the amount of water is the same," and if asked why he thinks so, he will be able to say, "Because it's narrower [in the cylinder] and wider [in the beaker]."

The child has, in fact, mastered what Piaget calls the concept of *conservation*. The child acquires the concept of conservation not only for volume but also for number, class, length, weight, and area.

These types of conservation occur at different ages. The conservation of *objects* occurs quite early, usually by the end of the sensorimotor period. *Quantity* is conserved at 6 to 8 years of age, and *weight* at 9 to 12 years of age. Probably the variation in age at which different conservations are achieved is related to how easily the property can be dissociated from the child's own action. As Piaget (1958) puts it, "It is more difficult to...equalize....objects whose properties are less easy to dissociate from one's own action, such as weight, than to apply the same operation to properties which can be objectified more readily, such as length" (p. 249).

This example of unevenness in the ontogenetic emergence of certain logical operations Piaget calls *décalage;* conservation, for example, does not appear in "full bloom." In the stage of

Stage: Sensorimotor
　　　　period (ages
　　　　0—2). The
　　　　child is most
　　　　concerned
　　　　with acting upon
　　　　his environment.
Goal: Kinesthetic
　　　　pleasure

Fig. 3–1.　Reproduced with permission of David Fassler.

concrete operations the child cannot think about his own thinking; that would be too abstract for him or her at this stage. Hence the difficulty the child at this stage has in conceptualizing his emotions, a difficulty that Susan Harter calls *affective décalage*.

The child under the age of 6 or 7 is, in fact, tied to his immediate perceptions when he sees the same quantity of water transferred from a beaker to a taller cylinder. He is not able at first to reason that although the shape of the container is different, the amount of water is the same. Instead, he will be more influenced by his perception of which looks more to him because of the particular dimension that affects him.

After the age of 6 or 7, the child is no longer bound by his perception, and he can apply reasoning. The age of 6 or 7 marks

Stage: Pre-operational
          stage (ages 2–
          7). The child
          is busy constructing
          theories about his body
Goal: The drawing is a
          representation
          of the child's theories
          (not of reality).

Fig. 3–2.   Reproduced with permission of David Fassler.

a key turning point in the child's thinking. It is the age at which the child starts first grade. It also corresponds in psychoanalytic theory to the time when the oedipal struggle is thought to be resolved and the superego consolidated. Now the child can more readily distinguish between fantasy and reality. An interesting graphic representation of this cognitive change may be found in the child's drawings (Figs. 3–1, 3–2, 3–3).

In short, the major advance in the concrete operations stage is that the child can apply basic logical principles to the realm of concrete experiences and events without letting his or her perceptions interfere. Gradually his or her logical thought processes become organized into an increasingly complex and

Stage: Concrete operations, or logical thinking (age 7 to 11). The child now draws what he *knows* to be there.

Goal: The child is now representing what he knows to be there.

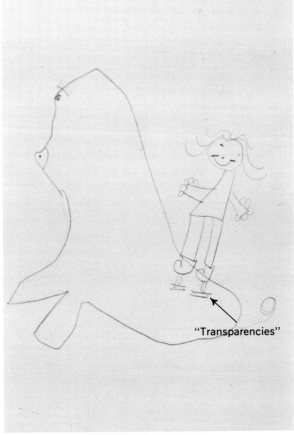

"Transparencies"

Fig. 3–3. Reproduced with permission of David Fassler.

integrated network through which he or she confronts and systematically responds to the world around him or her.

FORMAL OPERATIONS

Piaget observed that "the great novelty that characterizes adolescent thought and that starts around the age of 11 to 12, but probably does not reach its point of equilibrium until the age of 14 or 15...consists in the possibility of manipulating ideas in themselves and no longer in merely manipulating objects" (Piaget, 1969, p. 12). The young adolescent can now use hypotheses, experiment, make deductions, and reason from the particular to the general. He is no longer tied to his environment.

In fact, the difference between the formal operations stage and the concrete operations stage is that in the concrete operations stage the child can make statements about the environment based on relationships between objects or classes of objects, whereas in the formal operations stage the adolescent can produce new statements by combining previously arrived at statements. That is, he can make theoretical statements independent of specific content, and he can apply this way of thinking to all kinds of data. .

The result of this is a further release from the concrete world. To quote Piaget (1958) again: "The most distinctive property of formal thought is this reversal of direction between reality and possibility; instead of deriving a rudimentary type of theory from the empirical data, as is done in concrete inferences, formal thought begins with a theoretical synthesis implying that certain relations are necessary and this proceeds in the opposite direction" (p. 251).

Let us look in more detail at the stage of formal operations. Again, Piaget used the clinical method. The classic experiment involved a pendulum. The adolescent is given a pendulum:

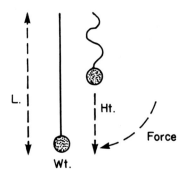

and then is asked "What determines how fast it swings?" In response, the adolescent:

1. Begins by imagining a series of purely hypothetical possibilities.
2. Then holds some factors constant while varying others.
3. Then observes the results, without bias.
4. He then draws the correct conclusion; i.e., length is a necessary and sufficient determinant of the speed of oscillation: a short pendulum swings fast, a long pendulum swings slowly. In propositional logic terms, this particular pattern (i.e., of length determining oscillation) is called reciprocal implications. As such it forms one of a set of 16 binary operations or logical relations, usually called functions. The names of the 16 binary operations are:

Negation
Conjunction
Inverse of implication
Inverse of converse implication
Conjunctive negation
Independence of variable A to variable B
Independence of variable B to variable A
Reciprocal implication
Reciprocal exclusion
Inverse of independence of variable A to variable B
Inverse of independence of variable B to variable A
Disjunction
Converse implication
Implication
Incompatibility
Tautology

The essence of a binary model is that only statements involving two values are made; e.g., the pendulum is long or short. Following this arrival at the correct conclusions through the analytic use of these functions, the adolescent can then go further: he can now manipulate the conclusions to derive further concepts. These new manipulations are entirely mental operations, *completely* free from the original observations.

These new manipulations, or mental operations, are classified by Piaget into four groups, which comprise the so-called INRC groups.

I = Identity
N = Negation
R = Reciprocity
C = Correlativity

The achievement of these formal operational cognitive structures represents the final stage in the process of human thought (but not, of course, in the *content* of human thought).

According to Ginsburg and Opper (1969), these logical models are in general:

1. Unknown, i.e., unconscious to the adolescent
2. Qualitative, not quantitative
3. Abstractions, not protocols
4. An integrated system, in which each function operates in relation to all the others
5. Ideal capabilities, not actual measures of performance
6. Explanatory and, to some extent, predictive; i.e., given the knowledge of the structure of the adolescent's mental operations, one can predict in general terms how he will perform other, similar tasks.

Finally, the discussion returns to the question of how this cognitive development comes about. Among the possible explanatory factors are (1) neurological maturation, (2) the social environment (education), (3) experience (experimentation, and (4) internal cognitive reorganization (equilibration) in response to contradiction and failure.

We may also ask, what are the practical implications of Piaget's system of cognitive development? First, at a theoretical level, besides adding to the understanding of thought processes Piaget's system sheds light on the particular difficulty the preoperational child may have in resolving emotional as well as intellectual problems. For such a child, reality and fantasy may be poorly differentiated and affects more difficult to conceptualize (conserve). Second, at a practical level, Piaget's system has implications for the way in which therapy is conducted with a child in the prelogical stage. Lastly, Piaget's system has proved to be a useful instrument in school consultation (Poulsen and Lubin, 1979) and pediatric care (Bibace and Walsh, 1980).

Note 4

J. Piaget, (1936), The origins of intelligence in children. (Margaret Cook, translator). "Assimilation: Basic Facts of Psychic Life." International Universities Press.

Three circumstances induce us to consider assimilation the fundamental fact of psychic development. The first is that assimilation constitutes a process common to organized life and mental activity and is therefore an idea common to physiology and psychology. In effect, whatever the secret mechanism of biological assimilation may be, it is an empirical fact that an organ develops while functioning (by means of a certain useful exercise and fatigue). But when the organ in question affects the external behavior of the subject, this phenomenon of functional assimilation presents a physiological aspect inseparable from the psychological aspect; its parts are physiological whereas the reaction of the whole may be called psychic. Let us take for example the eye which develops under the influence of the use of vision (perception of lights, forms, etc.). From the physiological point of view it can be stated that light is nourishment for the eye (in particular in primitive cases of cutaneous sensibility in the lower invertebrates, in whom the eye amounts to an accumulation of pigment dependent on environing sources of life). Light is absorbed and assimilated by sensitive tissues and this action brings with it a correlative development of the organs affected. Such a process undoubtedly presupposes an aggregate of mechanisms whose start may be very complex. But, if we adhere to a global description—that of behavior and consequently of psychology—the things seen constitute nourishment essential to the eye since it is they which impose the continuous use to which the organs owe their development. The eye needs light images just as the whole body needs chemical nourishment, energy, etc. Among the aggregate of external realities assimilated by the organism there are some which are incorporated into the parts of the physico-chemical mechanisms, while others simply serve as functional and general nourishment. In the first case, there is physiological assimilation, whereas the second may be called psychological assimilation. But the phenomenon is the same in both cases: the universe is embodied in the activity of the subject.

In the second place, assimilation reveals the primitive fact generally conceded to be the most elementary one of psychic life: repetition. How can we explain why the individual, on however high a level of behavior, tries to reproduce every experience he has lived? [This] is only comprehensible if the behavior which is repeated presents a functional meaning, that is to say, assumes a value for the subject himself. But whence comes this value? From functioning as such. Here again, functional assimilation is manifest as the basic fact.

In the third place, the concept of assimilation from the very first embodies in the mechanism of repetition the essential element which distinguishes activity from passive habit: the coordination of the new with the old which foretells the process of judgment. In effect, the reproduction characteristic of the act of assimilation always implies the incorporation of an actual fact into a given schema, this schema being constituted by the repetition itself. In this way assimilation is the greatest of all intellectual mechanisms and once more constitutes the relation to them, the truly basic fact....

REFERENCES

Bibace, R., and Walsh, M.E. (1980), Development of children's concept of illness. *Pediatrics*, 66:912–917.

Ginsburg, H., and Opper, S. (1969), *Piaget's Theory of Intellectual Development*. Englewood Cliffs, N.J.: Prentice-Hall, Inc.

Piaget, J. (1936), The origins of intelligence in children, trans. Margaret Cook. In: *The Essential Piaget*, ed. H.E. Gruber and J.J. Vonèche. New York: Basic Books, 1977, pp. 215–249.

Piaget, J. (1951), *Play, Dreams and Imitation in Childhood*, trans. C. Gattegno and F.M. Hodgson. New York: Norton.

Piaget, J. (with Alina Szeminska) (1952), *The Child's Conception of Number*, trans. C. Gattegno and F.M. Hodgson. London: Routledge & Kegan Paul.

Piaget, J. (1954), *The Child's Conception of Physical Causality*, trans. M. Cook. New York: Basic Books.

Piaget, J. (1958), *The Growth of Logical Thinking*. New York: Basic Books.

Piaget, J. (1969), The intellectual development of the adolescent. In: *Adolescence: Psychosocial Perspectives*, ed. G. Caplan and S. Lebovici. New York: Basic Books, pp. 22–26.

Poulsen, M.K., and Lubin, G.I. (Eds.) (1979), *Piagetian Theory and Its Implications for Helping Professionals*. Proceedings, Eighth Interdisciplinary Conference, Vol. II. Co-sponsored by University Affiliated Program, Children's Hospital of Los Angeles and the University of Southern California Schools of Education and Religion. USC Bookstore, University Park, Los Angeles, CA 90007.

Chapter 4

LANGUAGE DEVELOPMENT

According to Lenneberg (1969), language has the following six characteristics:

1. It is present in all cultures.
2. Its onset is age-correlated.
3. There is only one acquisition strategy for infants everywhere.
4. It is based intrinsically upon the same formal operating characteristics, whatever its outward form.
5. These operating characteristics have apparently remained constant throughout recorded history.
6. It is a form of behavior that may be impaired specifically by circumscribed brain lesions.

Actual language begins when the brain has matured to two-thirds of its full extent (the brain has reached about four-fifths of its adult weight by age 3 [Marshall, 1968]). Conversely, when the brain is fully matured, language acquisition becomes more difficult. Bogen (1969) has also suggested that there are two distinct minds, each related to a particular hemisphere (the left for language and verbal activity; the right for nonlanguage and nonverbal functions, such as the capacity for apposing or comparing perceptions, schemas, and engrams). For example, musical capacity has been associated with the right hemisphere (Alajouanine, 1948; Critchley, 1953; Luria, 1966; Schlesinger, 1962).

Studies prior to the 1950s provided a vast amount of detailed information on the milestones and form of children's language (McCarthy, 1954). Subsequently, attention was (and still is) directed at how the child's understanding of the basic linguistic system, or grammar, comes about. Is it a biological phenomenon (Lenneberg, 1967)? An innate given (Chomsky, 1957)? An acquired or a learned function (Staats, 1971)? Does cognitive development determine language (Piaget, 1923; Inhelder, 1971)? Or does language structure thought and culture (Vygotsky, 1962 [1934]; Luria, 1976; Whorf, 1956)? This search for an explanation of how language develops continues, and how language develops remains a mystery. In any event, children seem to learn fundamental language rules rather than specific grammatical constructions (Brown, 1973).

The capacity to discriminate between different sounds is present in the newborn (Friedlander, 1970). Indeed, from the beginning the infant is virtually programmed to move in rhythm to the human voice (Condon and Sander, 1974), and will orient with eyes, head, and body to animate sound stimuli (Mills, 1974). Subsequent language development correlates most closely with motor development although the two functions are not necessarily causally related in any specific way (see Note 5). Crying, which is present during fetal life, soon becomes differentiated during the first few months into recognized cries related to hunger, discomfort, pain, pleasure, and other stimuli (Wolff, 1969). As crying decreases, cooing increases and vowel sounds (e.g., "oo") begin to dominate. Consonants begin to appear at about 5 months of age and words at about 1 year of age, with a range of 8 to 18 months of age (Morley, 1965). At the same time, by 1 year of age the infant discriminates between and responds to differences in language, depending on who is speaking and how he is speaking (e.g., the intonation and the amount of repetition he uses). Vocabulary gradually increases to about 200 words by age 2. Nouns appear first, then verbs, adjectives, and adverbs. Pronouns appear by about age 2, and conjunctions after age 2½. By this time, too, the child's understanding of language has increased immensely. The child's play at this stage in effect represents his or her "inner language." Between ages 2 and 4 the child has acquired, or learned, most of the fundamental (as opposed to the academic) rules of grammar although how he or she does it is not known.

Although the developmental rate of the basic capacity for language remains more or less constant from culture to culture, the rate of acquisition of vocabulary and syntax is affected by the social environment. Interestingly, the earliest development of human sounds is relatively unaffected by reduced speech in the parents, as occurs in, say, families with congenitally deaf mothers (Lenneberg et al., 1965), and subsequent emergence of language and stage sequences may occur at the usual times even under such an adverse circumstance.

The child apparently has a built-in capacity to abstract various universal relationships and regularities in the particular language he or she hears, and he or she uses this capacity to construct an operation by means of which he or she can apply its principles for the formulation of an infinite number of sentences. Such an operation for language is obviously far more economical and powerful than anything the child might accrue or learn from simple imitation. Moreover, the capacity for this operational work seems not only to be related to the child's general cognitive capacities but also to be an integral part of the child's uniquely human cognition.

As the child develops and moves from stage to stage, he or she develops the capacity to react to increasingly complex stimuli, starting with intonation and moving through articulation of specific sounds to special syntactical and semantic stimuli. In this way, the child learns a linguistic code. All children appear to follow the same sequence in the development of phonology, syntax, and semantics.* Chomsky's theory of generative transformational grammar (1957) suggests that in some way, perhaps through "innate intellectual structures," the child develops a basic grammar that can generate an infinite number of sentences and an optional transformational grammar that transforms the basis of a sentence into its various forms (e.g., passive and interrogative).

Alternatively, these inner structures may derive from the sensorimotor schemas (Piaget, 1954). Indeed, the formation of such schemas during the long sensorimotor stage may be essential for the subsequent emergence of language and linguistic competence. Language in this view is one expression of what Piaget terms the semiotic function, which includes symbolic games, imagery, and imitation (Inhelder, 1971). Early schemas of experience precede symbolic language, and language comprehension precedes language production (children understand words and sentences long before they can say them) (Lovell and Dixon, 1967).

There is no satisfactory psychoanalytic theory for language acquisition (Wolff, 1967). The child begins to use language as a

---

*Phonology = the sound structure of morphemes, phonemes, and words;
Syntax = categories, such as noun, verb, sentence;
Semantics = the meaning of words and utterances and the relationships between them.

symbolic instrument, initially—and necessarily—through the help of the mothering person, whom we can call "the mother." For example, the mother uses a word (e.g., "Dada" or "Mama," then "Daddy" or "Mommy") as a symbol, and in so doing she helps in the organization of the symbolizing process that is taking place within the infant. She does not create that process within the infant; she facilitates its development. Initially, of course, considerable overextension occurs; a child may call all men Daddy (or all four-legged animals doggie) until further accommodation of the concepts, or schemas, of Daddy (or doggie) occurs.

It is very likely that the mother's spoken words initially are experienced by the infant as tones and rhythms, rather than as words with meanings, and as such are part of the unprecedented kinesthetic, tactile, visual, auditory, olfactory, and gustatory bombardment that the infant tries to assimilate and organize into schemas. Eventually, the child's percept of, say, "mother" and the word "Mother," already linked, becomes better defined. In this sense mothers are sensitive language teachers of their children (Moerk, 1974). The sensitive timing, repetition, and associated pleasurable affects with which the mother uses words for labeling, shaping, and so on, serve to stimulate the development of language. (Curiously, mothers seem to talk more to their baby girls than to their baby boys [Halverson and Waldrop, 1970]).

Reinforcement may be more important for phonetic and semantic development than for syntactic development (Brown and Hanlon, 1970). The best stimulus for syntactical development appears to be a rich conversational interchange without any attempt to modify the child's utterances (Cazden, 1966).

Children continue to learn phonology, syntax, and semantics throughout the school years. The utterances of young children appear to depend on the support of the nonlinguistic environment. For example, if one asks a young child a question "out of the blue," one often draws a blank (Bloom, 1975). Young children tend to respond more readily when they are asked to talk about events that are in a more immediately perceived context (Brown and Bellugi, 1964).

Linguistic shifts occur continuously. For example, at about age 6 or 7, children shift from making syntagmatic responses to making paradigmatic responses (Francis, 1972). (Syntagmatic associations are response items that are in a grammatical class different from that of the stimulus (i.e., the words just "go together," e.g., hot–bath, or apple–eat); whereas paradigmatic associations are response items that belong to the same grammatical class as the stimulus (e.g., hot–cold, or apple–pear). Also, prior to age 6 or 7, children link temporal succession to succession of enunciation; e.g., a young child will interpret the sentence "The girl goes upstairs when the boy has parked the car" to mean that the girl goes upstairs first and the boy parks the car afterward (Ferreiro, 1971). After age 6 or 7, the child is no longer tied to this concrete perception of sequence. Furthermore, sometime between ages 5 and 10, children become more conscious of the structure of the language they use (Nelson, 1977).

Finally, the child is able to speak and understand language independently of the context in which it occurs. At about age 12, when the child is in the stage of logical operations, language becomes a means of knowing.

Several external factors may influence this early development, particularly early symbolic language development. Infants who have been "maternally deprived," and perhaps particularly deprived of verbal stimulation (Langmeir and Matejcek, 1975), have an incomplete development of the capacity to symbolize, especially the capacity for language and abstract thinking (Provence and Lipton, 1962).

More recently, attention has been paid to the long-range effects of patterns of care in the neonatal period. For example, Ringler and his colleagues (1975) have demonstrated that the amount of mother-child contact in the neonatal period influences the amount and kind of speech patterns used by mothers interacting with their children as late as 2 years of age. Specifically, they found that mothers who had had an additional 16 hours of contact with their infants (i.e., besides the usual minimum contact in the first 3 days after birth) used significantly more questions, adjectives, and words per proposition and fewer command words and content words when talking with their children than did the mothers in the control group. Ringler and his colleagues suggested that this difference in maternal language stimulation, brought about by hospital care practices, might be an important factor in shaping linguistic behavior in the young child.

Certain other environmental and child-rearing practices also influence language development and, consequently, social development. For example, twins who are reared in close proximity and without much adult stimulation will develop idioglossia. Luria and Yudovich (1959) gave a dramatic example of gross speech retardation in their study of two 5-year-old identical twin boys: "As a rule, our twins' speech acquired meaning only in a concrete-active situation. Outside this situ-

Note 5

E.H. Lenneberg, (1967), *Biological Foundation of Language.* New York: Wiley, pp. 128–130.

DEVELOPMENTAL MILESTONES IN MOTOR AND LANGUAGE DEVELOPMENT

At the completion of:	Motor Development	Vocalization and Language
12 weeks	Supports head when in prone position; weight is on elbows; hands mostly open; no grasp reflex	Markedly less crying than at 8 weeks; when talked to and nodded at, smiles, followed by squealing, gurgling sounds usually called *cooing*, which is vowel-like in character and pitch-modulated; sustains cooing for 15–20 seconds
16 weeks	Plays with a rattle placed in his hands (by shaking it and staring at it), head self-supported; tonic neck reflex subsiding	Responds to human sounds more definitely: turns head; eyes seem to search for speaker; occasionally some chuckling sounds
20 weeks	Sits with props	The vowel-like cooing sounds begin to be interspersed with more consonantal-sounds; labial fricatives, spirants and nasals are common; acoustically, all vocalizations are very different from the sounds of the mature language of the environment

6 months	Sitting: bends forward and uses hands for support; can bear weight when put into standing position, but cannot yet stand with holding on; reaching: unilateral; grasp: no thumb apposition yet; releases cube when given another	Cooing changing into babbling resembling one-syllable utterances; neither vowels nor consonants have very fixed recurrences; most common utterances sound somewhat like ma, mu, da, or di
8 months	Stands holding on; grasps with thumb apposition; picks up pellet with thumb and finger tips	Reduplication (or more continuous repetitions) becomes frequent; intonation patterns become distinct; utterances can signal emphasis and emotions
10 months	Creeps efficiently; takes side-steps, holding on; pulls to standing position	Vocalizations are mixed with sound-play such as gurgling or bubble-blowing; appears to wish to imitate sounds, but the imitations are never quite successful; beginning to differentiate between words heard by making differential adjustment
12 months	Walks when held by one hand; walks on feet and hands—knees in air; mouthing of objects almost stopped; seats self on floor	Identical sound sequences are replicated with higher relative frequency of occurrence and words (mamma or dadda) are emerging; definite signs of understanding some words and simple commands (show me your eyes)
18 months	Grasp, prehension and release fully developed; gait stiff, propulsive and precipitated; sits on child's chair with only fair aim; creeps downstairs backward; has difficulty building tower of 3 cubes	Has a definite repertoire of words—more than three, but less than fifty; still much babbling but now of several syllables with intricate intonation pattern; no attempt at communicating information and no frustration for not being understood; words may include items such as thank you or come here, but there is little ability to join any of the lexical items into spontaneous two-item phrases; understanding is progressing rapidly

ation a word either did not possess any kind of permanent meaning, or only indicated what they were talking about without disclosing sufficiently clearly in what sense it was being used" (p. 40). When the twins were separated and placed in a special social situation in which they were compelled to speak with others in order to communicate with them, a rapid development of speech occurred.

Hearing children reared by deaf parents are able to develop adequate spoken language when oral stimuli are provided by others and the parents use gestures (Critchley, 1967). Children reared in bilingual households have no difficulty in developing speech, unless they are of low intelligence or social prejudices are present (Peal and Lambert, 1962; Soffietti, 1955).

The role of physical deprivation in the development of language is less clear. The lack of clarity has to do principally with the difficult methodological problems of researching the subject. All that can be said with certainty is that factors such as severe malnutrition, associated as they often are with multiple insults, produce a language deficiency which is not easily reversed by nutritional rehabilitation (Lefevre, 1975).

Delayed speech and language development may occur with mental retardation, deafness, cerebral palsy, developmental disorders, and infantile autism. Before age 4, injury to the left hemisphere may result in transient aphasia; however, language development will resume if the right hemisphere is intact. Persisting language impairment does not usually occur after unilateral lesions in the first few years of life (Lenneberg, 1967). Disease or injury to the left hemisphere that occurs after the early teens may result in permanent loss of language. At this age, the brain has fully matured, and further development does not occur (Geschwind, 1972; see Note 6).

Note 6

When a word is heard, the output from the primary auditory area of the cortex is received by Wernicke's area. If the word is to be spoken, the pattern is transmitted from Wernicke's area to Broca's area, where the articulatory form is aroused and passed on to the motor area that controls the movement of the muscles of speech. If the spoken word is to be spelled, the auditory pattern is passed to the angular gyrus, where it elicits the visual pattern. When a word is read, the output from the primary visual areas passes to the angular gyrus, which in turn arouses the corresponding auditory form of the word in Wernicke's area. It should be noted that in most people comprehension of a written word involves arousal of the auditory

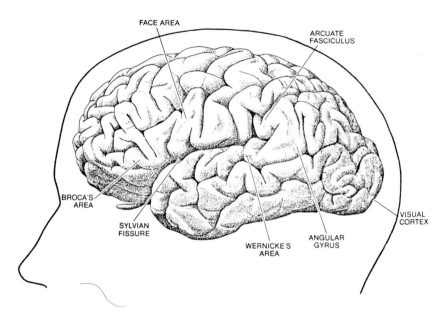

FACE AREA

ARCUATE
FASCICULUS

BROCA'S
AREA

VISUAL
CORTEX

SYLVIAN
FISSURE

ANGULAR
GYRUS

WERNICKE'S
AREA

PRIMARY LANGUAGE AREAS of the human brain are thought to be located in the left hemisphere, because only rarely does damage to the right hemisphere cause language disorders. Broca's area, which is adjacent to the region of the motor cortex that controls the movement of the muscles of the lips, the jaw, the tongue, the soft palate and the vocal cords, apparently incorporates programs for the coordination of these muscles in speech. Damage to Broca's area results in slow and labored speech, but comprehension of language remains intact. Wernicke's area lies between Heschl's gyrus, which is the primary receiver of auditory stimuli, and the angular gyrus, which acts as a way station between the auditory and the visual regions. When Wernicke's area is damaged, speech is fluent but has little content and comprehension is usually lost. Wernicke and Broca areas are joined by a nerve bundle called the arcuate fasciculus. When it is damaged, speech is fluent but abnormal, and patient can comprehend words but cannot repeat them.

form in Wernicke's area. Wernicke argued that this was the result of the way most people learn written language. He thought, however, that in people who were born deaf but had learned to read, Wernicke's area would not be in the circuit.

According to this model, if Wernicke's area is damaged, the person would have difficulty comprehending both spoken and written language. He should be unable to speak, repeat, and write correctly. The fact that in such cases speech is fluent and well articulated suggests that Broca's area is intact but receives inadequate information. If the damage were in Broca's area, the effect of the lesion would be to disrupt articulation. Speech would be slow and labored but comprehension should remain intact.

REFERENCES

Alajouanine, T. (1948), Aphasia and artistic realization. *Brain*, 71:229–241.
Bloom, L. (1975), Language development review. In: *Review of Child Development Research*, ed. F.R. Horowitz. Chicago: University of Chicago Press, 4:245–303.

Bogen, J.E. (1969), The other side of the brain. *Bull. Los Angeles Neurol. Soc.*, 34:135–162.

Brown, R. (1973), *A First Language: The Early Stages*. Cambridge, Mass.: Harvard University Press.

Brown, R., and Bellugi, N. (1964), Three processes in the child's acquisition of syntax. *Harvard Educ. Rev.*, 34:133–151.

Brown, R., and Hanlon, C. (1970), Derivational complexity and order of acquisitions of speech. In: *Cognition and the Development of Language*, ed. J.R. Hayes. New York: Wiley.

Cazden, C. (1966), Subcultural differences in child language: An interdisciplinary review. *Merrill-Palmer Q.*, 12:185–219.

Chomsky, N. (1957), *Syntactic Structures*. The Hague: Mouton.

Condon, W.S., and Sander, L.W. (1974), Neonate movement is synchronised with adult speech: Interactional participation and language acquisition. *Science*, 183:99–101.

Critchley, M. (1953), *The Parietal Lobes*. London: E. Arnold.

Critchley, E. (1967), Language development of hearing children in a deaf environment. *Dev. Med. Child Neurol.*, 9:274–280.

Ferreiro, E. (1971), *Les relations temporelles dans la langue de l'enfant*. Geneva: Droz.

Francis, H. (1972), Toward an explanation of paradigmatic-syntagmatic shift. *Child Dev.*, 43:949–959

Friedlander, B.Z. (1970), Receptive language development in infancy: Issues and problems. *Merrill-Palmer Q.*, 16:7.

Geschwind, N. (1976), Language and the brain. In: *Progress in Psychobiology*, ed. R.F. Thompson. San Francisco: Freeman, pp. 341–348.

Halverson, C.F., and Waldrop, M.F. (1970), Maternal behavior towards own and other preschool children: The problem of "ownness." *Child Dev.*, 41:839.

Inhelder, B. (1971), The sensory-motor origins of knowledge. In: *Early Childhood: The Development of Self-Regulatory Mechanisms*, ed. D.N. Walcher and D.L. Peters. New York: Academic Press, pp. 141–155.

Langmeir, J., and Matejcek, Z. (1975), *Psychological Deprivation in Children*, 3rd Ed. New York: Halsted Press.

Lefevre, A.B. (1975), Language development in malnourished children. In: *Foundations of Language Development*, ed. E.H. Lenneberg and E. Lenneberg. New York: Academic Press, 2:279–296.

Lenneberg, E.H. (1967), *Biological Foundations of Language*. New York: Wiley.

Lenneberg, E.H. (1969), On explaining language. *Science*, 164:635–643.

Lenneberg, E.H., Rebelsky, F.G., and Nichols, I.A. (1965), The vocalizations of infants born to deaf and hearing parents. *Hum. Dev.*, 8:23–37.

Luria, A.R. (1966), *Higher Cortical Functions in Man*. New York: Basic Books.

Luria, A.R. (1976), *Cognitive Development*. Cambridge, Mass.: Harvard University Press.

Luria, A.R., and Yudovich, F.I. (1959), *Speech and the Developmental Process in the Child*. London: Staples Press.

Lovell, K., and Dixon, E.M. (1967), The growth of the control of grammar in imitation, comprehension and production. *J. Child Psychol.*, 8:31.

McCarthy, D. (1954), Language development. In: *Manual of Child Psychology*, ed. L. Carmichael. New York: Wiley.

Marshall, W.A. (1968), *Development of the Brain*. Edinburgh: Oliver & Boyd.

Mills, M. (1974), Recognition of mother's voice in early infancy. *Nature*, 31.

Moerk, E. (1974), Changes in verbal child-mother interactions with increasing language skills of the child. *J. Psycholinguist. Res.*, 3:101–116.

Morley, M.E. (1965), *The Development and Disorders of Speech in Childhood*, 2nd Ed. Edinburgh: E. & S. Livingston.

Nelson, K.E. (1977), Aspects of language acquisition and use from 2 to age 20. *J. Am. Acad. Child Psychiatry*, 16:584–607.

Peal, E., and Lambert, W.E. (1962), The relationship of bilingualism to intelligence. *Psychol. Monogr.* 76 (27).

Piaget, J. (1923), *The Language and Thought of the Child.* London: Routledge & Kegan Paul.

Piaget, J. (1954), Language and thought from a genetic point of view. *Acta Psychol.*, 10:88–98.

Provence, S., and Lipton, R.C. (1962), *Infants in Institutions.* New York: International Universities Press.

Ringler, N.M., et al. (1975), Mother-to-child speech at 2 years. *J. Pediatr.*, 86:141–144.

Schlesinger, B. (1962), *Higher Cerebral Functions and Their Clinical Disorders.* New York: Grune & Stratton.

Soffietti, J.P. (1955), Bilingualism and biculturalism. *J. Educ. Psychol.*, 46:222–227.

Staats, A. (1971), Linguistic-mentalistic theory versus an explanatory S-R learning theory of language development. In: *The Ontogenesis of Grammar*, ed. D.I. Slobin. New York: Academic Press.

Vygotsky, L.S. (1962), *Thought and Language.* New York and Cambridge, Mass.: Wiley and MIT Press. (Original Russian edition, 1934.)

Whorf, B.L. (1956), Language, mind and reality. In: *Language, Thought and Reality*, ed. J.B. Carroll. Cambridge, Mass.: MIT Press, pp. 246–270.

Wolff, P. (1967), Cognitive considerations for a psychoanalytic theory of language acquisition. In: *Motives and Thought: Psychoanalytic Essays in Honor of David Rappaport*, ed. R. Holt. New York: International Universities Press, pp. 300–343.

Wolff, P. (1969), The natural history of crying and other vocalizations of early infancy. In: *Determinants of Infant Behavior*, ed. B.M. Foss. London: Methuen, p. 81.

Chapter 5

PSYCHOSEXUAL DEVELOPMENT

The link between hormonal conditions, brain functions, and sexual behavior provides the foundation for any consideration of psychosexual development (Hamburg and Lunde, 1966). At the same time, the process of socialization influences sex-typed behaviors (Mischel, 1970). The concept of the development of infantile sexuality (psychosexual drive development), briefly summarized in the following paragraphs, must eventually relate to both these sources of information.

The first systematic psychoanalytic account of the psychosexual development of children was attempted by Freud in "Three Essays on the Theory of Sexuality" (S. Freud, 1905). An instinct, or drive, in psychoanalysis was defined as "the psychical representative of an endosomatic, continuously flowing source of stimulation" or as "an elementary urge, rooted in bodily tensions, which environmental influences may deflect from its course and modify in many ways but probably cannot eradicate" (Waelder, 1960). The sexual drive was said to change in its objects and its aims as the individual proceeded in his or her development. A sequence of development in sexuality was proposed, while sexual development was seen as intimately involved in all the many other simultaneous lines of development (A. Freud, 1965). At the same time, an organic substructure was thought to be the basis of these provisional ideas, making it "probable that it is special substances and chemical processes which perform the operations of sexuality . . ." (S. Freud, 1914, p. 78) and that "deeper research will one day trace the path further and discover an organic basis for the mental event" (S. Freud, 1900, pp. 41–42).

Four major psychoanalytic sources of evidence are available for study, all of them at the level of clinical inference. Historically, the first source was in the recovery or reconstruction of what psychoanalysts believed to be early infantile feelings that occurred during the psychoanalysis of adults (e.g., S. Freud, 1909a). Second, remnants of such infantile sexuality have been inferred in normal adult behavior and in certain psychological disturbances in adults, such as the sexual perversions, eating disturbances, gastrointestinal disturbances, and certain characterological disorders (e.g., Abraham, 1921, 1925, 1934). Third, the analysis of children provided additional anecdotal data (e.g., Bornstein, 1949; S. Freud, 1909b). Fourth, and more recently, direct observation of children has added a new dimension to psychoanalytic data (e.g., Spitz, 1965). It should be remembered, however, that just as certain behavior in children may represent infantile sexuality even though it does not look "sexual," other phenomena which may involve the sex organs may not necessarily represent psychosexual behavior. For example, penile erections in infants and children may occur regularly in association with REM sleep and may represent a metabolic change rather than any particular sexual wish or fantasy (Fisher et al., 1965).

PSYCHOSEXUAL DEVELOPMENT

In psychoanalytic theory, the sexual aim of a young infant is simple: to obtain a feeling of pleasure and satisfaction and the relief from discomfort by the most immediate means possible. The young infant derives pleasure from a wide variety of visual, tactile, kinesthetic, and auditory stimuli—but by far the most sensitive and apparently the greatest source of pleasure appears to be in the region of the mouth. The object of the sexual instinct is the infant himself or herself, seen in autoerotic activities, such as mouthing and sucking at the breast, fist, or thumb. Recently, questions have been raised about some of the viewpoints subsumed under the heading of orality (Sandler and Dare, 1970). Moreover, Freud did note that "the phylogenetic foundation has so much the upper hand over personal accidental experience that it makes no difference whether a child is really sucked at the breast or has been brought up on the bottle and never enjoyed the tenderness of a mother's care. In both cases the child's development takes the same path...." (S. Freud, 1940, pp. 188 ff.). Lastly, it is important to note that certain genetic factors and biological orienting patterns are in operation prior to any psychological mechanisms. For example, the suck reflex is coordinated to the cyclic flow of breast milk (Dubignon and Campbell, 1969), and by 6 days of age the infant can selectively orient to smell, preferring his own mother's milk (MacFarlane, 1975).

As the infant develops and as speech and the capacity for symbol formation emerge, the child begins to experience feelings about his separateness and worth. He or she develops a sense of autonomy which has to be reconciled with ambivalent feelings, all at about the same time that he or she is acquiring new skills, only one of which is sphincter control. During this process, according to psychoanalytic theory, the anal mucosa is said to become erotogenized and may serve in part the aims of the ambivalent feelings just mentioned. Indeed, the young child may express his or her ambivalence in the (pleasurable) holding in and letting go of feces during bowel movements. However, this ambivalence may also be expressed in the controlling and clinging behavior seen in some 2- and 3-year-old children, and the central role of the anal mucosa at this stage has probably been exaggerated, reflecting the practices that prevailed at the time Freud made his observations more than current behavior.

When the child is between 3 and 6 years of age, behavior that is more clearly recognizable as "sexual" appears. The child at this stage is very much aware of the anatomical differences between the sexes and is curious about pregnancy, childbirth, and death. Sometimes this interest is represented in the play of the child. For example, play with toys that involve filling and emptying, opening and shutting, fitting in and throwing away, and building up and knocking down has been interpreted as representing a curiosity about the body and sexual functions. The opportunities for the sequential development of play in childhood thus become as important for the sexual development of the child as they are for other purposes (e.g., problem solving, mastery of body skills, functional pleasure in play, coping with anxiety, facilitating object relations, and communication purposes). The child at this stage is said to experience intense sexual and aggressive urges toward both parents, but the aim is less well defined. Boys and girls may become absorbed by fairy-tale or television characters that serve to represent children's own fantasies. Such fantasies also emerge in the dreams of children. Children of this age may also play at being mothers and fathers or doctors and nurses—working toward a partial fulfillment of their sexual aims, which at this time may be partially fused with their aggressive fantasies. Boys and girls may inflict pain on each other in keeping with their understanding of the sexual act as an act of violence. They may also be quite exhibitionistic and possessive, especially of the parent of the opposite sex. Hostility to the same-sex parent seems to be influenced by certain characteristic family patterns of relationships present in a particular society (Honigmann, 1954).

Between 6 and 12 years of age, during the elementary-school years, concepts of inevitability regarding birth, death, and sex differences become clarified, and the sense of time and the ability to differentiate between fantasy and reality become established. Defense mechanisms, which in general bar from consciousness certain unacceptable impulses and fantasies and at the same time provide some substitute gratification, are strengthened. The child consolidates earlier reactions, such as shame against exhibitionistic urges, disgust against messiness, and a sense of guilt that contains sexual and aggressive wishes. The child's play at this time is usually characterized by organization, whether in a board game or team game. Sex play, far from being dormant, continues actively, especially with voyeuristic tendencies and the urge to touch. The sex play often may be more discreet at this age (that is, adults may see it less often) yet it may also be quite overt, with much interest and curiosity (Reese, 1966). The object of the sexual instinct may be a peer, but the actual playmate may be of either sex.

When puberty comes, the young adolescent struggles to achieve mastery of his or her body and of sexual and aggressive urges at the same time that he or she is trying to separate from his or her family, find new and appealing sexual objects, and achieve a sense of identity. In the course of this struggle, the sexual behavior of the adolescent may range from an indiscriminate regression (toward expressions of earlier forms of the sexual drive, manifested in impulsive behavior, messiness, and alternating labile affects) to petting and mutual masturbation, which may be heterosexual or homosexual and, eventually, intercourse. Sometimes earlier aims and objects are temporarily gratified and used, as, for example, in isolated acts of fellatio or in exhibitionistic behavior. Occasionally, an adolescent sexually molests a young child, especially during babysitting. Adolescent boys who do so have been reported to be identified with a dominant mother.

Ultimately, a mature primacy of the genital zone is established, with an appropriate heterosexual object choice and an appropriate achievement of the new sexual aims of a love relationship, sexual intercourse, orgasm, discharge, and childbirth.

Rutter (1971, 1976) reviewed the scientific literature on normal psychosexual development and concluded that Freud's description of the oral and anal stages is too narrow and somewhat misleading, that the oedipal situation is not universal, that Freud's description of the latency period is wrong in most respects, and that Freud's concept of an innate sex drive that has a quantifiable energy component is only a half-truth. Rutter noted that at present there is insufficient evidence to decide between the various psychological theories of sexual development. Rutter, it appears, is not one to mince words. However, even though the level of scientific reliability and validity in psychoanalytic research is generally low, Rutter may be confusing the levels of abstraction in psychoanalytic writings (Waelder, 1962; Achenbach and Lewis, 1971). The "artificial structure of hypothesis" (S. Freud, 1920, p. 60) that psychoanalysts use in their metapsychology may indeed be "blown away" by the answers provided by biology (S. Freud, 1920, p. 60), but in the meantime the clinical data derived from the psychoanalytic situation should, so to speak, be placed in escrow pending confirmation or refutation by accepted scientific methods.

Sexual Preference

Saghir and Robins (1973) have provided considerable support for a childhood behavioral pattern associated with both male and female homosexuality. Of the males studied, 67% of the 89 homosexuals versus 3% of the heterosexuals reported that they had played mostly with girls and were considered "sissy" or effeminate during boyhood. In the prehomosexual female sample (N = 56), there was a significantly higher proportion of "tomboys," both in childhood (70% versus 16%) and adolescence (35% versus 0%), with lack of interest in doll play discriminating prehomosexual from preheterosexual "tomboys."

Green (1979), in a review of some of the retrospective and prospective research regarding sexual preference, noted that Whitham (1977), who had studied 107 exclusively homosexual males and compared them to exclusively heterosexual males, had found that 47% of the homosexuals recalled being more interested in doll play than other boys their age, 44% recalled liking to cross-dress more, and 42% recalled preferring girls' games and having a female peer group. In contrast, such behaviors were recalled by less than 1% of the heterosexuals. Of course, heterosexuals might simply repress such memories to a greater extent.

Green (1979) noted that "feminine boyhood behavior, as defined by clothing, toy, peer group, activity, and role-playing preferences, does not consistently predict later homosexual orientation. However, from preliminary data, it does appear to load in favor of such an outcome in some persons" (Green, 1979, pp. 107 ff.). Green went on to note that his "data so far indicate a moderate amount of homosexual fantasy, arousability, and overt behavior in a sample of boys who were previously 'feminine.' However, of considerable importance is the current variation in sexual orientation in these boys. One mid-adolescent is a 'drag queen' and has had an extensive series of same-sex partners. One is genuinely bisexual, with an equal distribution of erotic fantasies and overt behaviors involving males and females. One prepubertal boy reports erections in response to fantasies or pictures of nude males but not females, although he has had no interpersonal genital experience. Others report an exclusively heterosexual orientation.

"This variation in outcome is noteworthy. Clearly all boys who show behaviorial patterns considered 'feminine' are not prehomosexual. Parents of boys whose behavior does not fit the conventional stereotype of 'masculinity' should not be rendered anxious by the belief that their children are prehomosexual.... However, many parents do become grief-stricken if they believe their children are or will become homosexual" (Green, 1979, p. 108). Green therefore feels it is important to stress the markedly atypical early childhood behavior of the sample described here and the considerable variability in their later sexual behaviors. Since there is a wide range of ultimate behaviors, there is a need for caution in making any prediction about outcome.

Note 7

S. Freud (1905), *Three Essays on the Theory of Sexuality*. Standard Edition. London: The Hogarth Press, 1953, pp. 125–243.
Summary[1]
...We started out from the aberration of the sexual instinct in respect of its object and its aim and we were faced by the question of whether these arise from an innate disposition or are acquired as a result of experiences in life. We arrived at an answer to this question

---

1. All footnotes omitted.

from an understanding, derived from psychoanalytic investigation, of the workings of the sexual instinct in psychoneurotics, a numerous class of people and one not far removed from the healthy. We found that in them tendencies to every kind of perversion can be shown to exist as unconscious forces and betray their presence as factors leading to the formation of symptoms. It was thus possible to say that neurosis is, as it were, the negative of perversion. In view of what was now seen to be the wide dissemination of tendencies to perversion we were driven to the conclusion that a disposition to perversions is an original and universal disposition of the human sexual instinct and that normal sexual behavior is developed out of it as a result of organic changes and psychical inhibitions occurring in the course of maturation; we hoped to be able to show the presence of this original disposition in childhood. Among the forces restricting the direction taken by the sexual instinct we laid emphasis upon shame, disgust, pity and the structures of morality and authority erected by society. We were thus led to regard any established aberration from normal sexuality as an instance of developmental inhibition and infantilism. Though it was necessary to place in the foreground the importance of the variations in the original disposition, a cooperative and not an opposing relation was to be assumed as existing between them and the influences of actual life. It appeared, on the other hand, that since the original disposition is necessarily a complex one, the sexual instinct itself must be something put together from various factors, and that in the perversions it falls apart, as it were, into its components. The perversions were thus seen to be on the one hand inhibitions, and on the other hand dissociations, of normal development. Both these aspects were brought together in the supposition that the sexual instinct of adults arises from a combination of a number of impulses of childhood into a unity, an impulsion with a single aim . . . .

. . . We found it a regrettable thing that the existence of the sexual instinct in childhood has been denied and that the sexual manifestations not infrequently to be observed in children have been described as irregularities. It seemed to us on the contrary that children bring germs of sexual activity with them into the world, that they already enjoy sexual satisfaction when they begin to take nourishment and that they persistently seek to repeat the experience in the familiar activity of "thumb-sucking". The sexual activity of children, however, does not, it appeared, develop *pari passu* with their other functions, but, after a short period of efflorescence from the ages of two to five, enters upon the so-called period of latency. During that period the production of sexual excitation is not by any means stopped but continues and produces a store of energy which is employed to a great extent for purposes other than sexual—namely, on the one hand in contributing the sexual components to social feelings and on the other hand (through repression and reaction-forming) in building up the subsequently developed barriers against sexuality. On this view, the forces destined to retain the sexual instinct upon certain lines are built up in childhood chiefly at the cost of perverse sexual impulses and with the assistance of education. A certain portion of the infantile sexual impulses would seem to evade these uses and succeed in expressing itself as sexual activity. We next found that sexual excitation in children springs from a multiplicity of forces. Satisfaction arises first and foremost from the appropriate sensory excitation of what we have described as erotogenic zones. It seems probable that any part of the skin and any sense-organ—probably, indeed, *any* organ—can function as an erotogenic zone, though there are some particularly marked erotogenic zones whose excitation would seem to be secured from the very first by certain organic contrivances. It further appears that sexual excitation arises as a by-product, as it were, of a large number of processes that occur in the organism, as soon as they reach a certain degree of intensity, and most especially of any relatively powerful emotion, even though it is of a distressing nature. The excitations from all these sources are not yet combined; but each follows its own separate aim, which is merely the attainment of a certain sort of pleasure. In childhood, therefore, the sexual instinct is not unified and is at first without an object, that is, auto-erotic.

The erotogenic zone of the genitals begins to make itself noticeable, it seems, even during the years of childhood. This may happen in two ways, Either, like any other erotogenic zone, it yields satisfaction in response to appropriate sensory stimulation; or, in a manner which is not quite understandable, when satisfaction is derived from other sources, a sexual excitation is simultaneously produced which has a special relation to the genital zone. We were reluctantly obliged to admit that we could not satisfactorily explain the relation between sexual satisfaction and sexual excitation, or that between the activity of the genital zone and the activity of the other sources of sexuality.

We found from the study of neurotic disorders that beginnings of an organization of the sexual instinctual components can be detected in the sexual life of children from its very beginning. During a first, very early phase, oral erotism occupies most of the picture. A second of these pregenital organizations is characterized by the predominance of sadism and anal erotism. It is not until a third phase has been reached that the genital zones proper contribute their share in determining sexual life, and in children this last phase is developed only so far as to a primacy of the phallus.

We were then obliged to recognize, as one of our most surprising findings, that this early efflorescence of infantile sexual life (between the ages of two and five) already gives rise to the choice of an object, with all the wealth of mental activities which such a process involved. Thus, in spite of the lack of synthesis between the different instinctual components and the uncertainty of the sexual aim, the phase of development corresponding to that period must be regarded as an important precursor of the subsequent final sexual organization.

The fact that the onset of sexual development in human beings occurs in two phases, *i.e.* that the development is interrupted by the period of latency, seemed to call for particular notice. This appears to be one of the necessary conditions of the aptitude of men for developing a higher civilization, but also of their tendency to neurosis. So far as we know, nothing analogous is to be found in man's animal relatives. It would seem that the origin of this peculiarity of man must be looked for in the prehistory of the human species.

It was not possible to say what amount of sexual activity can occur in childhood without being described as abnormal or detrimental to further development. The nature of these sexual manifestations was found to be predominantly masturbatory. Experience further showed that the external influences of seduction are capable of provoking interruptions of the latency period or even its cessation, and that in this connection the sexual instinct of children proves in fact to be polymorphously perverse; it seems, moreover, that any such premature sexual activity diminishes a child's educability. . . .

Note 8

B. Bornstein (1949), The analysis of a phobic child. *The Psychoanalytic Study of the Child*, III/IV, New York: International Universities Press, Inc., pp. 181–226.

Frankie, a 5½-year-old boy of superior intelligence who was eager to learn, was brought into analysis because of a severe school phobia. He liked to play with the other children and was friendly and amenable with them, but shy and withdrawn in the presence of any stranger. He became panic-stricken if his mother or nurse were out of sight. Even when left with his father in his own home, he was occasionally overwhelmed by attacks of anxiety. His phobic symptom had existed for more than 2 years. . . .

When Frankie was 2, it became especially difficult to put him to bed at night. Regularly, he screamed for an hour before he fell asleep, and also whenever he awoke during the night. A third screaming period occurred at the age of 4½ years and was stopped only after the nurse threatened to punish him. . . .

The child's anxiety reached its peak when he was brought to nursery school at the age of 3 years and 9 months. At that time, his sister's nurse had just left the home, and he had to share his own nurse with the baby (aged 9 months). He went to school for only 2 days. Each time, he had to be taken home because of his wild attacks of fear and screaming, and nothing could make him return to school. . . .

The analyst suggested that treatment be postponed until after a period of preparation for analysis in which the school was to cooperate with the analyst. . . .

Frankie started his first session by building a hospital which was separated into a "lady department", a "baby department", and a "men's department." In the lobby, a lonely boy of 4 was seated all by himself, on a chair placed in an elevated position. The child's father was upstairs visiting "a lady" who, he informed us, when questioned, "is sick or maybe she's got a baby, maybe—I don't know, never mind." He made the point that newborn babies and mothers were separated in this hospital. Casting himself in the roles of a doctor and a nurse, he attended to the babies in a loving way, fed and cleaned them. However, toward the end of the play, a fire broke out. All the babies were burnt to death and the boy in the lobby was also in danger. He wanted to run home, but remembered that nobody would be there. Subsequently he joined the fire department, but it was not quite clear as to whether the firemen had started the fire or put it out. Frankie announced: "Ladies, the babies are dead; maybe we can save you!" Actually only those lady patients who had no babies were rescued by him. The one whom he several times—by a slip of the tongue—had addressed as "Mommy", however, was killed in the fire. No particular attention was given to the men's department. Most of the men had died anyway.

This game, which was repeated in the analysis for many weeks, betrayed the intensity of the boy's fury against his mother and sister. He could not forgive his mother for her unfaithfulness. He took her going to the hospital as a desertion of him and a sign of her lack of love. She must suffer the same tortures which he had suffered when she left him. He said, as it were: "I don't love you either; I hate you, I don't need you, you may die in the hospital. If you hadn't had a baby I would love you.". . .

Frankie, who so thoroughly punished his mother by the withdrawal of his love, naturally lived in continual fear of retaliation. He could not stay at home or go out without his mother because he needed the presence of just that person against whom his aggressive impulses were directed. The presence of the ambivalently loved person prevents the phobic from being overwhelmed by his forbidden impulses and assures him that his aggressive intentions have not come true. But while the unconscious hatred directed at the protecting person is usually difficult to uncover in the analysis of adults, it was still very close to the surface in this 5½-year-old boy. . . .

The danger which threatened the mother from relations with men would result in what was the gravest danger to him: the arrival of a new baby. He had to guard against a repetition of this traumatic experience.

It was this concern that was responsible for the insomnia which became acute at this point of his analysis. There had been previous occurrences of insomnia when he was 2½ and again when he was 4½. Now again it took him hours to fall asleep. He listened silently and anxiously to the noises at night. Whenever his parents spent an evening at home, he ran back and forth between the living room and his bedroom. He wanted to know, as he expressed it, what plans they were making. They might eat something special and he wanted to share it. Or someone might come and hurt his Mommy. Ideas about the problem of procreation filled the hours of his severe insomnia. . . .

One element which was already present in his wild performances became the predominant and all-important feature: a strong inclination to gain pleasure by use of his eyes. This voyeuristic element led him to a new impersonation, that of an omniscient God.

In this new role he made the analyst a frightened, sleeping child into whose ears God whispered dreams of wild colliding horses, of violent scenes in which "Daddy throws Mommy out of the window so that she has to go to the hospital for eighteen days." The "sleeping games" revealed his suspicions of something frightful happening between his father and mother during the night—something he would have liked to observe. As God, he had the right to see and watch everything. His new role of God provided him with a greater power than he had previously enjoyed as attacker, judge, or policeman—roles in which he had experienced the triumph of the conqueror, but also suffered the pain of the conquered. . . .

Later, however, when he realized that God was not only his own creation but a concept shared by others and that he could not rule "his" God to the extent necessary to be protected from anxiety, he replaced his fantasy of an omniscient God by an imaginary television apparatus which belonged exclusively to his fantasy and thus was completely at the disposal of his wishes and plans. ("God sees everything, but the television apparatus sees only if I turn it on.") The television apparatus brought the child closer to reality. When he was God, he made the analyst dream about those frightful scenes between his parents, while with the introduction of his imaginary television apparatus, he himself attempted to face those scenes. The analyst was made a co-observer of eating scenes for which Frankie provided the music (another auditory manifestation) while explaining the observed events to the analyst. He reassured the analyst many times that the observations were "make believe" and actually he never again reached the previously described state of excitement and anxiety. By means of his invention of the television apparatus, he removed himself not only from the scenes he imagines, but also from the feelings of desire and concomitant guilt which those scenes aroused. . . .

The following is one of the scenes observed through the apparatus: Father was in the restaurant and ordered the most delicious food for Mother from the restaurant owner. Then he had a secret talk with the owner. As soon as Mother had eaten, she collapsed and died; the food was poisoned. (In his thoughts, eating was linked with being impregnated, for which Frankie had not yet forgiven his mother, and for which he still punished her by death.) Father and the owner of the restaurant were unconcerned by her death; they continued their pleasant talk and play, shoving Mother under the table.* Some drawings of this time show God and God's wife feasting at a dinner table, disturbed by "little gnomes" who alternately attack God and his wife.

These games helped the investigation and understanding of a past period of his life: We had reason to assume that when he was 4½, his screaming attacks had reappeared as his reaction to audible primal scene experiences. His father once wrote us that in former times, "in his prankish days," he used to pinch his wife and throw her into the air, "all in fun and for exercise . . . I can imagine what it must have seemed like to someone who heard it but did not see what actually happened." Frankie's running back and forth between his bedroom

---

*The scene is rich in its overdetermined factors; it permits the reconstruction of Frankie's oedipus complex. The element, "Mother is shoved under the table," refers to the child's resentment against his mother, who did not pay any attention to him when he, sitting under the table, tried to disturb his parents' meal. The next element, "Father and restaurant owner confer about the food for Mother (from which she dies)" is an indication of Frankie's wish to participate in his father's sexual activities. Frankie's position as restaurant owner was evident in many daydreams: he possessed "all the restaurants in New York." This detail makes us anticipate that Frankie's hostility toward his mother contained also some envy of her role as father's wife. Owner and father-Frankie and father do together what otherwise mother and father do. We shall see later how strong the child's desire was to take the passive role with the father.

and the living room occurred in reaction to auditory stimuli and continued until his nurse quenched his active interest, and nightly curiosity by a threatening and punishing attitude.

With the process of internalization of his conflicts the actually threatening nurse was replaced by imaginary objects, mainly wolves, who stood guard under his bed and kept him from getting up and investigating what might be happening in the parental bedroom.

These imaginary wolves under the bed were able, like the God he had played, to see what he did and to surmise his intentions. As soon as he put out hand or foot to go into his parents' bedroom,* the wolves would snap at him; "but they would let me go to the bathroom." For a protection from their attacks the boy armed himself with many weapons, preferably with a long stick, in order to beat the wolves down when they raised their heads. He maintained that they observed all his movements, and he in turn countered with an equally watchful attitude. His configuration of the wolves contained as elements the punitive and protective parent figures as well as his own impulses. The wolves punish his intentions and prevent their fulfillment. Their symbolic role as superego was strikingly confirmed in a drawing which Frankie called the WOLVES' STATUE. It showed an oversized wolf (in human form) with outstretched arms, floating above Frankie in his bed, under which a number of smaller-sized wolves (also in human form) were engaged in mysterious activities, obviously of a sexual nature. In his comments on this picture, Frankie said: "It shows what the wolves hope for, what they will look like some day."

The dread of wolves which had haunted the child for weeks finally led to the analysis of his castration fear. In his stories and in his play, the mother's attackers who previously had been punished by death, now were punished by almost undisguised castration. In his pictures he endowed God with monstrously elongated arms and legs, only to cut off these limbs with scissors. Immediately after such operation he tried to undo this symbolic act of castration by drawing innumerable new arms and legs. Frankie derived reassurance from the idea that destruction is not necessarily irrevocable and consequently dared to express the thoughts of castration without any symbolic disguise. Mother's attackers were imprisoned and he, as a doctor, subjected the prisoners to operations which usually threw him into a state of exaltation. Playing the doctor, he exclaimed: "Those criminals, they have to be operated on. Off with their wee-wees. It has to come off!" In his play he guarded himself against any awareness of his fear by identifying himself with the person performing the act of castration. His fear of the anticipated retaliation found expression in his behavior toward his pediatrician. Frankie had always been a difficult patient, but during this period he absolutely refused to be examined, and assaulted the doctor by throwing blocks or potatoes which he carefully had stored under his bed for this purpose.

---

*The element of uncovering the hands and feet is overdetermined and it is obviously a presentation of its opposite, *i.e.*, a reverse of the original warning against touching his genital under the bedcover.

REFERENCES

Abraham, K. (1949), The influence of oral eroticism on character disorders (1934); Contribution to the theory of the anal character (1921); Character formation on the genital level of the libido (1925). In: *Selected Papers on Psychoanalysis*. London: The Hogarth Press.

Achenbach, T.M., and Lewis, M. (1971), A proposed model for clinical research and its application to encopresis and enuresis. *J. Am. Acad. Child Psychiatry*, 10:535–554.

Bornstein, B. (1949), The analysis of a phobic child. *Psychoanal. Study Child*, 3/4:118–226.

Dubignon, J., and Campbell, D. (1969), Sucking in the newborn during a feed. *J. Exp. Child Psychol.*, 7:282–298.

Fisher, C., et al. (1965), Cycle of penile erection synonymous with dreaming (REM) sleep. *Arch. Gen. Psychiatry*, 12:29–45.

Freud, A. (1965), *Normality and Pathology in Childhood*. New York: International Universities Press.

Freud, S. (1900), *The Interpretation of Dreams*. Standard Edition, 4, 5 (1953). London: The Hogarth Press, pp. 41–42.

Freud, S. (1905), *Three Essays on Sexuality*. Standard Edition, 7 (1953). London: The Hogarth Press.

Freud, S. (1909a), *Notes Upon a Case of Obsessional Neurosis*. Standard Edition, 10 (1955). London: The Hogarth Press.

Freud, S. (1909b), *Analysis of a Phobia in a Five-Year-Old Boy*. Standard Edition, 10 (1955). London: The Hogarth Press.

Freud, S. (1914), *On Narcissism: An Introduction*. Standard Edition, 14 (1975). London: The Hogarth Press.

Freud, S. (1920), *Beyond the Pleasure Principle*. Standard Edition, 18 (1955). London: The Hogarth Press.

Freud, S. (1940), *An Outline of Psycho-Analysis*. Standard Edition, 23 (1969). London: The Hogarth Press, pp. 188–189.

Green, R. (1979), Childhood cross-gender behavior and subsequent sexual preference. *Am. J. Psychiatry*, 136:106–108.

Hamburg, D.A., and Lunde, D.T. (1966), Sex hormones in the development of sex differences in human behavior. In: *The Development of Sex Differences*, ed. E.E. Maccoby. Stanford, Calif.: Stanford University Press, pp. 1–24.

Honigmann, J.J. (1954), *Culture as Personality*. New York: Harper.

MacFarlane, J.A. (1975), Olfaction in the development of social preference in the human neonate. In: *Parent-Infant Interaction*. CIBA Symposium No. 333. ASP.

Mischel, W. (1970), Sex-typing and socialization. In: *Carmichael's Manual of Child Psychology*, Vol. 2, ed. P.H. Mussen. New York: Wiley, pp. 3–72.

Reese, H.W. (1966), Attitudes toward the opposite sex in late childhood. *Merrill-Palmer Q.*, 12:157–163.

Rutter, M. (1971), Normal psychosexual development. *J. Child Psychol. Psychiatry*, 11:259–283.

Rutter, M. (1976), Other family influences. In: *Child Psychiatry*, ed. M. Rutter and L. Hersov. Oxford: Blackwell, pp. 74–108.

Saghir, M., and Robins, E. (1973), *Male and Female Homosexuality*. Baltimore: Williams & Wilkins.

Sandler, J., and Dare, C. (1970), The psychoanalytic concept of orality. *J. Psychosom. Res.*, 14:211–222.

Spitz, R.A. (1965), *The First Year of Life*. New York: International Universities Press.

Waelder, R. (1960), *Basic Theory of Psychoanalysis*. New York: International Universities Press.

Waelder, R. (1962), Review of psychoanalysis, scientific method, and philosophy. *J. Am. Psychoanal. Assoc.*, 10:617–632.

Whitham, F. (1977), Childhood indicators of male homosexuality. *Arch. Sex. Behav.*, 6:89–96.

Chapter 6

AGGRESSION

The definition of aggression is fraught with ambiguity, since the term has been used to refer to such varied levels as descriptive (apparent fighting); motivational (conscious or unconscious, either with intent to injure or simply as instrumental in achieving some goal); and theoretical construct (the "aggressive drive"). Injurious or destructive behavior also may or may not be associated with such affects as rage and anger. Such affects in turn may result in harmful behavior, either as their primary aim or in an effort to reduce the intensity of the affect. Sometimes the welling-up of anger is necessary to energize, so to speak, an assertive act. Even at the manifest descriptive level, there is often confusion between what is a normal assertive act and what is an aggressive act. To confuse the matter further, some psychoanalysts have made the assumption that the energy for self-assertive, nonhostile, adaptive behavior is derived almost exclusively from "aggressive drive energy" (Hartmann et al., 1949).

Normal aggressive behavior, then, may be either associated with the drive to achieve a goal, which in itself is not destructive, or may be motivated by actual hostile, destructive intentions (Sears et al., 1957). The original source of either kind of aggression may be primarily "instinctual" in the psychoanalytic sense, i.e., the "aggressive drive" (Freud, 1920), or it may be "innate" in the ethological sense (Storr, 1968). Aggression may be heightened by frustration (Dollard et al., 1939), or reinforced in social learning (Miller, 1941; Feshbach, 1964).

Clearly, several attempts have been made to define and classify aggression, without much agreement. Moyer (1967) has provided one useful classification for mammalian aggression in general (see Note 9). Wasman and Flynn (1962) also have suggested a distinction between affective and predatory aggression. Affective aggression involves defensive postures and autonomic arousal, and it is motivated by a desire to avoid. Predatory aggression involves active stalking and directed attack, and it is motivated by appetitive needs.

Neurotransmitters have a role in the regulation of aggression, and recent research is beginning to suggest possible mechanisms (Alpert et al., 1980). The centers in the brain that appear to generate aggressive behavior are located in the hypothalamus, posterior cingulate gyrus, central gray, and the dorsomedial half of the amygdala. The parts of the limbic system that are involved in rage behavior include the amygdala and the hippocampus in the temporal lobe, hypothalamus, cingulate gyri and cingulum, septum pellucidum and septal area, and related portions of the thalamus, basal ganglia, orbital region of the frontal lobe, and midbrain (Fig. 6–1).

Moyer (1971) suggested that predatory aggression is related to hypothalamic and amygdala function, that fear-induced aggression is related to the amygdala, septum and

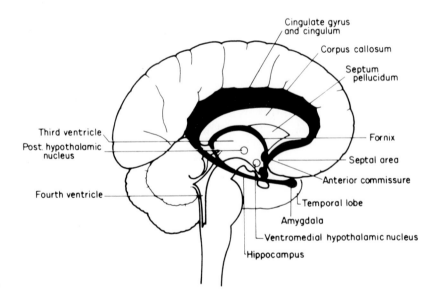

Fig. 6–1. F.A. Elliott (1978), Neurological factors in violent behavior (the dyscontrol syndrome). Reprinted by permission from the figure on page 65, Chapter 5, in *Violence and Responsibility: The Individual, the Family and Society* by Robert L. Sadoff, Ed. Copyright 1978, Spectrum Publications, Inc., New York.)

hypothalamus, and that irritable aggression occurs via the hypothalamus, amygdala and caudate nucleus. Maternal aggression (in response to a perceived threat to the mother's offspring) is related to estrogens. Territorial aggression and aggression stimulated by the appearance of a competitive male are mediated by androgens. Instrumental aggression is learned through rewards for aggressive behavior.

The level of aggression is clearly responsive to sex hormones (Money and Ehrhardt, 1968). Differences in the frequency of aggressive behavior between males and females may be related to prenatal variations in hormone levels (Reinisch, 1981). A higher level of androgen in young girls is associated with a greater interest in rough play (Ehrhardt and Baker, 1974), whereas boys whose mothers had less progesterone and more estrogen during pregnancy appear to be less aggressive (Yalom et al., 1973). Testosterone may act on the fetal brain to facilitate particularly the learning of aggressive patterns of behavior (Hamburg, 1974). In women, premenstrual tension may lower the threshold for violence. In one study of women in prison, it was found that 62% of their violent crimes had been committed during the premenstrual week (Morton et al., 1953). In a recent study by Mattsson et al. (1980), 40 male delinquent recidivists had a slightly higher mean plasma testosterone (T) level than a group of normal adolescents of the same age and pubertal stage. Furthermore, delinquents who had committed armed robbery tended to have higher mean T levels than less violent offenders.

An increased tendency toward aggressive behavior also may be associated with an additional Y chromosome (Nielson and Christensen, 1974), although the data are conflicting. XYY males are present in the prison population more frequently than in the general population (Hook, 1973), but not among those imprisoned for violent crimes.

Increased aggressiveness in boys is found in all cultures, and this sex difference is present from early life. Boys also elicit more aggressive responses from other children (Hutt, 1972). The trait of aggressiveness also tends to be more stable over a period of time in boys than in girls (Kagan and Moss, 1962). Aggressive behavior is common in preschool-age children and then declines until adolescence, when it rises again (Werry and Quay, 1971). Adolescent boys give significantly more aggressive projective test responses than do girls (Rosenzweig, 1970). Aggressivity may be a result of polygenetic influences, expressed in the individual temperament of a given child (Thomas et al., 1963).

In psychoanalytic theory, "aggressive drive" is said to serve the adaptive needs and functions of the child at the same time that it finds an avenue for discharge through these functions. Some psychoanalysts think that aggression at all times has direction in that it is primarily object seeking (Fairbairn, 1952). The concepts of amount and direction are implied when the term cathexis is used in psychoanalytic theory. Later in development, aggressive drive is said to be fused with the sexual drive (Hartmann et al., 1949). Aggression is said in psychoanalytic theory to be "neutralized" when it serves conflict-free, adaptive ends, notably in intellectual functioning and problem solving. Sublimation through, say, artistic work, is then perhaps a special case of the general process of neutralization by which unbound aggression is modified and used to serve higher purposes, including socialization. Aggression is needed to achieve whatever mastery of the external world is possible for an individual. Aggression is also pleasurable.

Aggression in the assertive sense seems to have a developmental sequence. Observations of young infants suggest that from the very moment of independent life the infant assertively exercises certain rudimentary functions that in part serve to facilitate adaptation. Such functions have been said to represent "primary autonomous apparatuses" (Hartmann, 1950). Perhaps it would be more correct to say that the adaptive aspect of these functions is rudimentary (the functions themselves may be quite complex) and the functions are rudimentary only insofar as they are manifested only during the earliest period of development. Examples of such functions are the rooting reflex, the grasp reflex, the tonic neck reflex, and certain behavioral reactions, such as anticipatory posturing and changes in activity that represent attention following an external stimulus, whether it is visual, auditory, or tactile. All these functions may operate in the service of adaptation and survival. Thus, the newborn infant alerts with human holding (Korner and Thoman, 1970) and quiets with picking up and rocking (Korner and Thoman, 1972). In short, the infant is a sucking, looking, grasping, learning individual. In some cases the survival value of these functions is readily seen; in others it is less obvious. Anticipatory posturing and changes in attention states, reflected in changes in activity, clearly serve to alert the infant to his environment. In doing so they actively (aggressively?) serve the adaptive and survival interests of the infant. For example, in one study of infants under the age of 5 months who were in an institution, those infants who were most active were least likely to show developmental retardation (Schaffer, 1966).

Each of these functions, or activities, results in and is enhanced by the infant's experiencing a measure of control (to whatever extent control is possible in the infant) over his or her environment. An early measure of control, for example, is the extent to which the infant is able to mentally assimilate the nipple, the breast, or the mother through the exercise of sensorimotor activities. Subsequent activities, such as crawling, climbing, standing, walking, and running, increased skills with hand, thumb, and forefinger, coordinated balancing skills, and so on, similarly require energy to function; and each activity in turn can act as a motor pathway for the adaptive efforts of the infant as well as for the discharge of aggression. Later, play, symbolic language, and intellectual development serve similar adaptive and aggressive purposes.

Aggression in the hostile sense similarly seems to show a developmental progression. The young infant may seem to turn his aggression inward (e.g., he may bang his head) or outward (e.g., he may have temper tantrums or show destructive behavior). When the 2- or 3-year-old child is able to manipulate his bowel and bladder functions, they too may be used to discharge aggression outwardly, albeit in such indirect forms as soiling and wetting. Later, the child may discharge his aggression in more subtle forms, and in doing so his or her behavior is no different from that seen in many adults. The child may, for example, manage not to hear the request of an adult, whether parent or teacher. The child's aggression also may be disguised by slyness or may be covered by such reaction formations as shyness and embarrassment. Occasionally, a child will remove himself from any situation that invites his or her own aggression, or he or she may deny to himself or herself as well as others that he or she has ever had an aggressive wish. At other times, the child may cunningly stick to the letter of a rule; e.g., he or she may do something which is allowed in one situation but which in the present context is clearly an aggressive act. In the young school-age child, aggression may be dealt with by the child by being turned into its opposite; e.g., the child may be too sweet or too good.

As social conflict with hostile aggression develops, such aggression is dealt with in part by defense mechanisms, including repression, displacement, projection, and various reaction formations, particularly guilt. A child, for example, may feel guilt about a hostile wish, then blame another person for his or her aggressive behavior, and subsequently identify with that person. Or the child may attempt to rationalize his or her actions. A 7- or 8-year-old child may begin to attempt to exercise his or her capacity for moral judgment to help control his or her hostility and aggression.

At the same time, aggressive behavior itself may be a defense. Thus aggressive behavior may be used to ward off depression, giving rise to a so-called masked depression (Burks and Harrison, 1962).

VARIATIONS OF AGGRESSIVE DRIVE DEVELOPMENT AND BEHAVIOR

What factors influence aggressive drive development? Observations in the newborn nursery reveal that there is an enormous range of activity among infants in a standard environment, suggesting that there are variations in aggressive drive endowment. There also seems to be a reciprocal relation between aggression and dependency. For example, the active exploratory behavior of an infant may be in conflict with the attachment behavior of the same infant, who seeks proximity and the gratification of his or her dependency needs. In some children, the more the child remains dependent, the more aggression will be latent, producing in some instances a fantasy life filled with aggression. On the other hand, perhaps this realm of fantasy life is essential, given the prolonged period of relative biological helplessness during human development. Aggressive expression is thus thought by some to be a necessary human need (Storr, 1970).

Excessive, overt stimulation may give rise to frustration and heightened aggressive tension, leading to such affects as rage and hate. Covert stimulation may take place as the result of spankings. Actual child abuse may be a forerunner of hostile aggressive behavior in children. Parents who then punish frequently or severely tend to have children who are more aggressive (Feshbach, 1970). Parental role models and permissiveness in regard to aggressive behavior between siblings at home, reinforced by peer relationships outside the home, may facilitate the development of aggression through learning and may pave the way toward producing an aggressive child. Suppressive parental attitudes may exceed the child's capacity to control himself or herself, leading to behavior which is beyond the tolerance of the parents. Weak emotional ties between parent and child may result in inadequate love to bind the aggression; the child, for example, may have little incentive or wish to please and may act on his or her aggressive impulses with little, if any, feeling of guilt. Similarly, conflict in the mother and father about their own aggressive impulses may lead them to become more or less paralyzed when it is necessary to control the child and set limits. Such parents are prone to react excessively, and often inconsistently, usually on the basis of their own needs rather than those of the child. Violence on television may contribute to aggressive behavior in young school-age children, at least in terms of immediate effects (U.S. Public Health Service Report, 1972; Friedrich and Stein, 1973).

Aggressive behavior as a disorder in children can be the manifestation of a variety of underlying causes, including genetic disorders, brain damage, borderline or psychotic states, abuse, neglect, abandonment, and inadequate parental models (Lewis et al., 1979a). Loss of the father as a result of divorce may lead to aggressive behavior, especially in boys (Tuckman and Regan, 1966). Aggressive disorders are more common in boys from lower socioeconomic backgrounds, and the disorders are often accompanied by academic difficulties and anxiety (Wolff, 1961; 1967; 1971).

Violence in children and adolescents, except in self-defense, is usually abnormal (Lewis et al., 1979a). Organic brain conditions, such as psychomotor epilepsy and episodic dyscontrol, may underlie violent behavior. The organic dyscontrol syndrome (Mark and Ervin, 1970) is thought to be more common in males, and it occurs most frequently during adolescence and early adulthood. Genetic factors may determine whether a lesion produces temporal lobe epilepsy or dyscontrol (Elliott, 1978). In some instances, perinatal trauma, head injury, infantile convulsions, or infectious illnesses may be associated with temper tantrums in infancy and childhood, and then by intense explosions of rage and by pathological intoxication in adolescence. Children with 6- and 14-per-second spikes plus other EEG abnormalities exhibit significantly more aggressive behavior than comparison groups without the 6- and 14-per-second spikes, showing extreme outbursts of rage and violent acts with minimal provocation (Walter et al., 1960). There are no identifiable significant neuropsychiatric differences between adolescents who commit severely violent sexual acts and adolescents who commit severely violent nonsexual acts (Lewis et al., 1979b).

What can be seen from the foregoing review is that the theory of "aggression" is surprisingly undeveloped. Part of the difficulty lies in the different levels of conceptualization. Clinically, the manifest "aggressive" behavior of the child should not be taken at its face value, but rather should be examined for its biological, motivational, and sociocultural roots and influences.

Note 9

Feshbach, S. (1970), Aggression. In *Carmichael's Manual of Child Psychology*, vol. 2. ed. P.H. Mussen. New York: Wiley, p. 175. (After K.E., Moyer, (1967), Kinds of aggression and their physiological basis. Report No. 67–12. Department of Psychology, Carnegie-Mellon University, Pittsburgh, Pa.)

1. Predatory aggression. Here the eliciting stimulus is the presence of a natural object of prey.

2. Intermale, spontaneous aggression. The release of this aggressive pattern is typically the presence of a male of the same species, and a male to which the attacker has not become habituated.

3. Terror-induced aggression. This type of aggression is always preceded by escape attempts and usually occurs under conditions of confinement in which the animal is cornered by some threatening agent.

4. Irritable aggression. This response is elicited by a wide range of stimuli and is characterized by an affective display. It is not preceded by attempts to escape.

5. Territorial defense. The stimulus situation eliciting this behavior entails an area which the animal has established as its "territory" and an intruder, typically but not necessarily an animal of the same species.

6. Defense of the young. This form of aggression among mammals is usually displayed by the female. The stimulus complex evoking the aggression consists of the presence of the young and the proximity of a threatening agent to the young of the animal.

7. Instrumental aggression. Any of the preceding classes of aggression may produce a stimulus change resulting in reinforcement of the behavior. Instrumental aggression is characterized by the increase in the probability of an aggressive response to a particular stimulus situation as a result of prior reinforcement.

REFERENCES

Alpert, J.E., Cohen, D.J., Shaywitz, B.A., and Piccirillo, M. (1981), Neurochemical and behavioral organization: Disorders of attention, activity and aggression. In: *Vulnerabilities to Delinquency*, ed. D.O. Lewis. New York: Spectrum.

Burks, H., and Harrison, S. (1962), Aggressive behavior as a means of avoiding depression. *Am. J. Orthopsychiatry*, 32:416.

Dollard, J., Doob, L.W., Miller, N.E., Mowrer, O.H., and Sears, R.R. (1939), *Frustration and Aggression*. New Haven: Yale University Press.

Ehrhardt, A., and Baker, S. (1974), Fetal androgens, human central nervous system differentiation and behavior sex differences. In: *Sex Differences in Behavior*, ed. R. Friedman, R. Richart, and R.L.V. Wiele. New York: Wiley.

Elliott, F.A. (1978), Neurological factors in violent behavior (the dyscontrol syndrome). In: *Violence and Responsibility*, ed. R.L. Sadoff. New York: Spectrum, pp. 59–86.

Fairbairn, W.R.D. (1952), *An Object-Relations Theory of the Personality*. New York: Basic Books.

Feshbach, S. (1964), The function of aggression and the regulation of aggressive drive. *Psychol. Rev.*, 71:257–272.

Feshbach, S. (1970), Aggression. In: *Carmichael's Manual of Child Psychology*, Vol. 2, ed. P.H. Mussen. New York: Wiley, pp. 159–259.

Freud, S. (1920), *Beyond the Pleasure Principle*. Standard Edition, 18 (1955). London: The Hogarth Press.

Friedrich, L.K., and Stein, A.H. (1973), Aggressive and prosocial television programs and the natural behavior of preschool children. *Monogr. Soc. Res. Child Dev.*, 38. No. 4.

Hamburg, D. (1974), Ethological perspectives on human aggressive behavior. In: *Ethology and Psychiatry*, ed. N. White. Toronto: University of Toronto Press, pp. 209–219.

Hartmann, H. (1950), Comments on the psychoanalytic theory of the ego. *Psychoanal. Study Child*, 5:74–96.

Hartmann, H., Kris, E., and Loewenstein, R.M. (1949), Notes on the theory of aggression: I. Introduction. *Psychoanal. Study Child*, 3/4:9–12.

Hook, E.B. (1973), Behavioral implications of the human XYY genotype. *Science*, 179:139–150.

Hutt, C. (1972), Sexual differentiation in human development. In: *Gender Differences: Their Ontogeny and Significance*, ed. C. Orensted and C.C. Taylor. London: Churchill-Livingstone.

Kagan, J., and Moss, H.A. (1962), *Birth to Maturity*. New York: Wiley.

Korner, A.F., and Thoman, E. B. (1972), The relative efficacy of contact and vestibular proprioceptive stimulation in soothing neonates. *Child Dev.*, 43:443–453.

Korner, A.F., and Thoman, E.B. (1970), Visual alertness in neonates as evoked by maternal care. *J. Exp. Child Psychol.*, 10:67–68.

Lewis, D.O., Shanok, S.S., Pincus, J.H., and Glaser, G. (1979a), Violent juvenile delinquents: Psychiatric, neurological, psychological and abuse factors. *J. Am. Acad. Child Psychiatry*, 18:307–319.

Lewis, D.O., Shanok, S.S., and Pincus, J.H. (1979b), Juvenile male sexual offenders. *Am. J. Psychiatry*, 136:1194–1196.

Lorenz, K. (1966), *On Aggression*. New York: Harcourt, Brace & World.

Mark, V.H., and Ervin, F.R. (1970), *Violence and the Brain*. New York: Harper & Row.

Mattsson, Å., Schelling, D., Olwens, D., Löw, D., and Svensson, J. (1980), Plasma testosterone, aggressive behavior, and personality dimensions in young male delinquents. *J. Am. Acad. Child Psychiatry*, 19:476–490.

Miller, N.E. (1941), The frustration-aggression hypothesis. *Psychol. Rev.*, 48:337–342.

Money, J., and Ehrhardt, A.A. (1968), Pre-natal hormone exposure: Possible effects on behavior in man. In: *Endocrinology and Human Behavior*, ed. R.P. Michael. London: Oxford University Press.

Morton, J.H., Addison, H., Addison, R.G., Hunt, L., and Sullivan, H. (1953), A clinical study of pre-menstrual tension. *Am. J. Obstet Gynecol.*, 65:1182–1191.

Moyer, K.E. (1967), Quoted in Feshbach, S. (1970), Aggression. In: *Carmichael's Manual of Child Psychology*, Vol. 2, ed. P.H. Mussen. New York: Wiley, p. 175.

Moyer, K. E. (1971), *The Physiology of Hostility*. Chicago: Markham.

Nielson, J., and Christensen, A.L. (1974), Thirty-five males with double Y chromosome. *Psychol. Med.*, 4:28–37.

Reinisch, J.M. (1981), Prenatal exposure to synthetic progestins increases potential for aggression in humans. *Science*, 221:1171–1173.

Rosenzweig, S. (1970), Sex differences in reaction to frustration among adolescents. In: *The Psychopathology of Adolescence,* eds. J. Zubin and A.M. Freedman. New York: Grune and Stratton, pp. 90–102.

Schaffer, E.G. (1966), Activity level as a constitutional determinant of infantile reaction to deprivation. *Child Dev.,* 37:595–602.

Sears, R.R., Maccoby, E.E., and Levin, H. (1957), *Patterns of Child Rearing.* Evanston, Ill.: Row, Peterson.

Storr, A. (1968), *Human Aggression.* New York: Atheneum. (Bantam Books, 1970.)

Thomas, A., Birch, H.G., Chess, S., Hertzig, M.E., and Korn, S. (1963), *Behavioral Individuality in Early Childhood.* New York: New York University Press.

Tuckman, J., and Regan, R.A. (1966), Intactness of the home and behavioral problems in children. *J. Child Psychol. Psychiatry,* 7:225–233.

U.S. Public Health Service Report to the Surgeon General (1972), *Television and Growing Up: The Impact of Televised Violence.* Washington, D.C.: U.S. Government Printing Office.

Walter, R.D., Colbert, E.G., Koegler, R.R., Palmer, J.O., and Bond, P.M. (1960), A controlled study of the 14- and 6-per-second EEG pattern. *Arch. Gen. Psychiatry,* 2:559–566.

Wasman, M., and Flynn, J.P. (1962), Directed attack elicited from hypothalamus. *Arch. Neurol.,* 6:220–227.

Werry, J.S., and Quay, H.C. (1971), The prevalence of behavior symptoms in young elementary school children. *Am. J. Orthopsychiatry,* 41:136–143.

Wolff, S. (1961), Symptomatology and outcome of preschool children with behavior disorders attending a child guidance clinic. *J. Child Psychol. Psychiatry,* 2:269–276.

Wolff, S. (1967), Behavioral characteristics of primary school children referred to a psychiatric department. *Br. J. Psychiatry,* 113:885–893.

Wolff, S. (1971), Dimensions and clusters of symptoms in disturbed children. *Br. J. Psychiatry,* 118:421–427.

Yalom, I., Green, R., and Fisk, N. (1973), Prenatal exposure to female hormones: Effect on psychosexual development. *Arch. Gen. Psychiatry,* 28:554–561.

Chapter 7

PSYCHOANALYTIC LINES OF DEVELOPMENT

A comprehensive view of inferred intrapsychic development using the idea of "development lines" has been conceptualized by Anna Freud (1965; see Note 10). Six lines of development have been described:

1. From dependency to adult object relationships
2. From suckling to rational eating
3. From wetting to soiling to bladder and bowel control
4. From irresponsibility in body management to responsibility in body management
5. From egocentricity to companionship
6. From body to toy and from play to work

Other lines of development, such as from cooing to complex sentences and from early schema to abstract thoughts, could also be described (see the earlier chapters). The following brief summary outlines the major elements in the six lines just listed.

FROM DEPENDENCY TO ADULT OBJECT RELATIONSHIPS

This line starts with the infant in a state of more or less "biological unity" with the mother. In the first month or two the infant is said to be in a normal autistic phase, virtually oblivious to the environment. During the next 6 months the infant's behavior is conceptualized as being in a normal symbiotic phase, in which the infant behaves as though he and his mother were an omnipotent system: a dual unity within one common boundary. By 9 months, separation-individuation is said to occur; that is, the infant shows some separate functioning in the presence of and with the emotional availability of the mother. However, the relationship is still regarded as a need-fulfilling, part-object, anaclitic relationship, i.e., the object (the mother) exists for the infant only inasmuch as and so long as it (she) satisfies a need. From 18 months to 36 months, "object constancy" is achieved. During this period the child's relationship with adults is highly ambivalent, with much clinging, dominating, and torturing ("the anal sadistic stage").

From 3 to 6 years, the child is said to be in an object-centered, phallic-oedipal phase, characterized by possessiveness of the parent of the opposite sex, jealousy and rivalry of the parent of the same sex, curiosity, and exhibitionism.

From 6 years to 11 years, the child is in so-called latency, with libido transfer to teachers and other adults, fantasies of disillusionment and denigration of the parents ("family romance" fantasies), and aim-inhibited interests.

During preadolescence, a return to earlier part-object, need-fulfilling, ambivalent attitudes occurs. At adolescence a struggle with infantile object ties reemerges, accompanied by strong defenses against pre-genitality as the adolescent strives toward genital supremacy with objects of the opposite sex outside the family.

FROM SUCKLING TO RATIONAL EATING

This line begins with nursing, followed by weaning at about 3 or 4 months and the change to self-feeding at about 10 months. The equation food = mother still dominates. By age 3, "disagreements" with mother occur about the amount and intake of food ("table manners") and about eating sweets. Various food fads emerge. Gradually, the equation food = mother fades, to be replaced by certain irrational attitudes toward eating; e.g., fears of being poisoned (orally impregnated), and of getting fat (pregnant), and fears related to intake and output (anal birth), as well as a variety of reaction formations against cannibalistic and sadistic fantasies which have been inferred or interpreted as being present in the course of the psychoanalytic treatment of children. Finally, these sexualized attitudes give way to a rational attitude toward food.

FROM WETTING AND SOILING TO BLADDER AND BOWEL CONTROL

This line starts with the child's freedom to wet and soil and continues until the parents decide to intervene. Subsequently, feces are endowed with interest, love, and aggression as the infant offers his feces as gifts or as he soils as an act of aggression. The infant then identifies with his parents' wishes and he internalizes controls, a phenomenon that often is accompanied by reaction formations; e.g., disgust against the desire to mess. Finally, autonomous control is fully established.

FROM IRRESPONSIBILITY IN BODY MANAGEMENT TO RESPONSIBILITY IN BODY MANAGEMENT

This line extends from the early establishment of the pain barrier and a narcissistic interest in the body through a recognition of external dangers to, finally, a voluntary endorsement of health rules.

FROM EGOCENTRICITY TO COMPANIONSHIP

Initially, other children are perceived for the most part as disturbers of the mother-child relationship. Then other children are related to as mere inanimate objects. By age 3, other children are seen as helpmates, at least for the duration of the task at hand. Finally, other children are recognized as human objects in their own right, and true sharing, admiring, fearing, and empathy develop.

FROM BODY TO TOY AND FROM PLAY TO WORK

Initially, the infant plays only with his own body and, by extension, the mother's body. Then the infant becomes attached to a particular transitional object (see Note 23), which gradually becomes any soft and cuddly toy, especially at bedtime. Gradually, the child turns to toys that in effect represent the body. A pleasure in mobile toys can be observed. Often toys are used to express ambivalent fantasies. Later, toys (e.g., dolls) serve as displacement objects for oedipal feelings. Finally, play becomes an end in itself, with pleasure in the finished product. The ability to play in this way is the forerunner of the ability to work, marked by a capacity to delay, control, inhibit, and modify impulses in the light of social reality.

The "meaning" of the concept of developmental lines is elusive until it is realized that the concept is part of a metapsychological profile. In turn, the metapsychological profile is an integration of empirical observations and psychoanalytic theory, including structural, dynamic, genetic, economic and adaptive metapsychological points of view. These five points of view all have a developmental perspective. The strength (and limitation) of the profile lies in its view of the person as a complex organism. However, the very complexity of the psychoanalytic view of the person makes the profile cumbersome to use. Moreover, some of the concepts lack clarity, and assessment and measurement in many, if not all, of the developmental lines is difficult. The reliability of statements is low, and prediction is hazardous. Nevertheless, some child psychoanalysts still find this concept useful, in, for example, assessing a child's readiness for nursery school, arriving at a diagnosis, or deciding whether psychoanalytic treatment is indicated. In clinical practice, however, most such assessments are usually made on a much simpler basis.

Note 10

A. Freud (1965), *Normality and Pathology in Childhood*. New York: International Universities Press, pp. 64–68.

Prototype of a Developmental Line: From Dependency to Emotional Self-Reliance and Adult Object Relationships

To serve as the prototype for all others, there is one basic developmental line which has received attention from analysts from the beginning. This is the sequence which leads from the newborn's utter dependence on maternal care to the young adult's emotional and material self-reliance—a sequence for which the successive stages of libido development (oral, anal, phallic) merely form the inborn, maturational base. The steps on this way are well documented from the analyses of adults and children, as well as from direct analytic infant observation. They can be listed, roughly, as follows:

1. The biological unity between the mother-infant couple, with the mother's narcissism extending to the child, and the child including the mother in his internal "narcissistic milieu" (Hoffer, 1952), the whole period being further subdivided (according to Margaret Mahler, 1952) into the autistic, symbiotic, and separation-individuation phases with significant danger points for developmental disturbances lodged in each individual phase;

2. the part object (Melanie Klein, 1957), or need-fulfilling, anaclitic relationship, which is based on the urgency of the child's body needs and drive derivatives and is intermittent and fluctuating, since object

cathexis is sent out under the impact of imperative desires and withdrawn again when satisfaction has been reached;

3. the stage of object constancy, which enables a positive inner image of the object to be maintained, irrespective of either satisfactions or dissatisfactions;

4. the ambivalent relationship of the preoedipal, anal-sadistic stage, characterized by the ego attitudes of clinging, torturing, dominating, and controlling the love objects;

5. the completely object-centered phallic-oedipal phase, characterized by possessiveness of the parent of the opposite sex (or vice versa), jealousy of and rivalry with the parent of the same sex, protectiveness, curiosity, bids for admiration, and exhibitionistic attitudes; in girls a phallic-oedipal (masculine) relationship to the mother preceding the oedipal relationship to the father;

6. the latency period, i.e., the postoedipal lessening of drive urgency and the transfer of libido from the parental figures to contemporaries, community groups, teachers, leaders, impersonal ideals, and aim-inhibited, sublimated interests, with fantasy manifestations giving evidence of disillusionment with and denigration of the parents ("family romance," twin fantasies, etc.);

7. the preadolescent prelude to the "adolescent revolt," i.e., a return to early attitudes and behavior, especially of the part-object, need-fulfilling, and ambivalent type;

8. the adolescent struggle around denying, reversing, loosening, and shedding the tie to the infantile objects, defending against pregenitality, and finally establishing genital supremacy with libidinal cathexis transferred to objects of the opposite sex, outside the family.

While the details of these positions have long been common knowledge in analytic circles, their relevance for practical problems is being explored increasingly in recent years. As regards, for example, the much-discussed consequences of a child's separation from the mother, the parents or the home, a mere glance at the unfolding of the developmental line will be sufficient to show convincingly why the common reactions to, respectively, the pathological consequences of such happenings are as varied as they are, following the varying psychic reality of the child on the different levels. Infringements of the biological mother-infant tie (phase 1), for whatever reason they are undertaken, will thus give rise to separation anxiety (Bowlby, 1960) proper; failure of the mother to play her part as a reliable need-fulfilling and comfort-giving agency (phase 2) will cause breakdowns in individuation (Mahler, 1952) or anaclitic depression (Spitz, 1946), or other manifestations of deprivation (Alpert, 1959), or precocious ego development (James, 1960), or what has been called a "false self" (Winnicott, 1955). Unsatisfactory libidinal relations to unstable or otherwise unsuitable love objects during anal sadism (phase 4) will disturb the balanced fusion between libido and aggression and give rise to uncontrollable aggressivity, destructiveness, etc. (A. Freud, 1949). It is only after object constancy (phase 3) has been reached that the external absence of the object is substituted for, at least in part, by the presence of an internal image which remains stable; on the strength of this achievement temporary separations can be lengthened, commensurate with the advances in object constancy. Thus, even if it remains impossible to name the chronological age when separations can be tolerated, according to the developmental line it can be stated when they become phase-adequate and nontraumatic, a point of practical importance for the purposes of holidays for the parents, hospitalization of the child, convalescence, entry into nursery school, etc.[1]

There are other practical lessons which have been learned from the same developmental sequence:

that the clinging attitudes of the toddler (phase 4) are the result of preoedipal ambivalence, not of maternal spoiling;

that it is unrealistic on the part of parents to expect of the preoedipal period (up to the end of phase 4) the mutuality in object relations which belongs to the next level (phase 5) only;

that no child can be fully integrated in group life before libido has been transferred from the parents to the community (phase 6). Where the passing of the oedipus complex is delayed and phase 5 is protracted as the result of an infantile neurosis, disturbances in adaptation to the group, lack of interest, school phobias (in day school), extreme homesickness (in boarding school) will be the order of the day;

that reactions to adoption are most severe in the latter part of the latency period (phase 6) when, according to the normal disillusionment with the parents, all children feel as if adopted and the feelings about the reality of adoption merge with the occurrence of the "family romance";

that sublimations, foreshadowed on the oedipal level (phase 5) and developed during latency (phase 6), may be lost during preadolescence (phase 7), not through any developmental or educational failure but owing to the phase-adequate regression to early levels (phases 2, 3, and 4);

that it is as unrealistic on the part of the parents to oppose the loosening of the tie to the family or the young person's battle against pregenital impulses in adolescence (phase 8) as it is to break the biological tie in phase 1 or to oppose pregenital autoeroticism in phases 1, 2, 3, 4, and 7.

REFERENCES TO NOTE 10

Alpert, A. (1959), Reversibility of pathological fixations associated with maternal deprivation in infancy. *Psychoanal. Study Child*, 14:169–185.

Bowlby, J. (1960), Separation anxiety. *Int. J. Psychoanal.*, 41:89–113.

Freud, A. (1949), Aggression in relation to emotional development. *Psychoanal. Study Child*, 3/4:37–42.

Hoffer, W. (1952), The mutual influences in the development of ego and id: Earliest stages. *Psychoanal. Study Child*, 7:31–41.

---

[1]If, by "mourning" we understand not the various manifestations of anxiety, distress, and malfunction which accompany object loss in the earliest phases but the painful, gradual process of detaching libido from an internal image, this, of course, cannot be expected to occur before object constancy (phase 3) has been established.

James, M. (1960), Premature ego development: Some observations upon disturbances in the first three years of life. *Int. J. Psychoanal.*, 41:288–294.

Klein, M. (1957), *Envy and Gratitude.* London: Tavistock.

Mahler, M.S. (1952), On child psychosis and schizophrenia: Autistic and symbiotic infantile psychoses. *Psychoanal. Study Child*, 7:286–305.

Spitz, R.A. (1946), Anaclitic depression. *Psychoanal. Study Child*, 2:313–342.

Winnicott, D.W. (1955), Metapsychological and clinical aspects of regression within the psycho-analytical set-up. *Int. J. Psychoanal.*, 36:16–26.

REFERENCES

Freud, A. (1965), *Normality and Pathology in Childhood.* New York: International Universities Press.

Chapter 8

MORAL DEVELOPMENT

Moral behavior derives in part from the basic cultural rules governing social action that the child internalizes, and moral development is the increase in the degree to which the internalization of these basic cultural rules has occurred. The process of internalization is usually assumed to be influenced by punishment and reward, identification with parents as models, and role-taking opportunities during play with peers. The degree to which internalization has taken place may be measured by the child's ability to resist temptation to break a rule (e.g., against cheating) when detection or punishment may *not* be a factor, the emotion of guilt, and the child's capacity to judge behavior. This capacity is complicated because it involves:

1. Intelligence
2. The capacity to anticipate future events
3. The capacity for empathy with another person
4. The ability to maintain attention and not give in to an impulse
5. Control of fantasies (especially aggressive fantasies)
6. A sense of self-esteem and confidence in oneself

Fear of punishment is prominent in young children. Next to develop is an urge to confess. By age 12 or 13, the majority of children seem to react directly to guilt and internal self-criticism when faced with the fact of their transgression although this reaction often occurs at a much earlier age.

The reaction of guilt is caused in part by the threat of loss of love and in part by the threat of punishment. What also correlates with internal guilt is the remorse that is initially induced when a parent points out through reasoning—and within the limits of the child's understanding at any given stage of development—the harm that may be caused to others by a particular act of aggression.

Cheating in one situation does not necessarily imply that cheating will occur in another situation. Further, children are not "cheaters" or "honest"; there is a bell-shaped curve with an average of moderate cheating in the middle. Cheating may also depend on the effort required and risk of detection involved; i.e., noncheaters may simply be more cautious rather than more honest. The most influential factors determining resistance to temptation to cheat or disobey in preadolescents are situational factors (Kohlberg, 1964).

In Piaget's view, the cognitive limitations of the child 3 to 8 years old lead him to confuse moral rules with physical laws, so that he views moral rules as fixed, eternal things. Perhaps this is because the child under the age of 8 cannot distinguish between subjective and objective aspects of his experience— what Piaget terms the child's realism. Another reason may be that the child under the age of 8 cannot distinguish his own perspective on events from the perspectives of others—what Piaget terms the child's egocentrism. Piaget describes the development of moral judgment in terms of six aspects, all of which are related to, and seem to reflect, cognitive development. In general, all six dimensions reveal a development from judging in terms of immediate external physical consequences toward judging in terms of subjective or internal values. The six dimensions are (Kohlberg, 1964):

INTENTIONALITY IN JUDGMENT

Young children tend to judge an act as bad mainly in terms of its actual *physical* consequences, whereas older children judge an act as bad in terms of the *intent* to do harm. Thus when children are asked who is worse, a child who breaks five cups while helping his mother set the table or a child who breaks one cup while stealing some jam?, 4-year-olds say that the child who committed the larger accidental damage is worse, and 9-year-olds say that the "thief" is worse.

RELATIVISM IN JUDGMENT

Young children view acts as either totally right or totally wrong, and they assume that an adult is always right, whereas older children are aware of possible diversity in views of right and wrong. This point is illustrated by the responses of children who are told the following story. A lazy child had been forbidden by his teacher to get any help in his homework. But a friend helped the lazy child. The children told this story are then asked such questions as, Did the helping child think he was right or wrong for helping? Did the lazy child think he was right or wrong for accepting help? What does the teacher think? Six-year-olds say that the helping child would have thought he was wrong to help, and they expect everyone to agree with this single-minded judgment. Nine-year-olds realize that there might be more than one way to view the moral issues involved.

INDEPENDENCE OF SANCTIONS

The young child says an act is bad because it will elicit punishment, whereas an older child says an act is bad because it violates a rule or does harm to others. This point is illustrated by the responses of children who are told the following story: A child was being helpful by watching his baby brother while his mother was out. When his mother returned, she spanked the child. Four- or 5-year-olds say that the child must have done something bad to get punished; 7- or 8-year-olds say that the child was good, not bad, even though he was punished. Thus it can be seen that older children can separate issues.

USE OF RECIPROCITY

Four-year-old children do not use reciprocity as a reason for consideration of others, whereas children of 7 and older frequently do. Even 7-year-olds show mainly selfish and concrete reciprocity concerns. This point is illustrated by the responses of a group of 10-year-olds who were asked, "What does the Golden Rule say to do if a boy came up and hit you?" Most of the 10-year-olds interpreted the Golden Rule in terms of concrete reciprocity and said, "Hit him back. Do unto others as they do unto you." But by age 11 to 13, most children can clearly judge in terms of ideal reciprocity, in terms of putting oneself in someone else's shoes.

USE OF PUNISHMENT TO MAKE RESTITUTION AND TO REFORM

Young children advocate severe, painful punishment for misdeeds; older children favor milder punishments that will also lead to some reform of the person involved.

NATURALISTIC VIEWS OF MISFORTUNE

Children of 6 or 7 view accidents that follow misdeeds as punishment willed by God ("immanent justice"); older children do not make this connection.

To summarize Piaget's views on the moral judgments of the child (Piaget, 1977; see Note 11), moral development can be viewed in the context of the major stages of cognitive development:

1. *Preoperational Stage.* The morality of constraints—rules of behavior are viewed as natural laws handed down to the child by his or her parents. Violation brings retribution or unquestioned punishment, and no account is taken of motives.
2. *Stage of Concrete Operations.* Rules of behavior become a matter of mutual acceptance, with complete equality of treatment, but no account is taken of special circumstances.
3. *Stage of Formal Operations.* The morality of cooperation—rules can be constructed as required by the needs of the group so long as they can be agreed upon. Motives are now taken into account, and circumstances may temper the administration of justice.

As the child advances through these stages, a progressive decentering occurs.

Building on Piaget's views, Kohlberg (1964; see Note 12) has suggested three major levels of development of moral judgment:

1. *Level I. Premorality (or Preconventional Morality)*
   a. Type 1. Punishment and obedience orientation (i.e., obedience to parents' superior force)
   b. Type 2. Naive instrumental hedonism (i.e., agreement to obey only in return for some reward)
2. *Level II: Morality of Conventional Role-Conformity*
   a. Type 3. Good-boy morality of maintaining good relations, approval of others (i.e., conformity to rules in order to please and gain approval)
   b. Type 4. Authority maintaining morality (i.e., adherence to rules for the sake of upholding social order)
3. *Level III: Morality of Self-Accepted Moral Principles*
   a. Type 5. Morality of social contract, of individual rights, and of, say, democratically accepted law (with a reliance on a legalistic "social contract")

b. Type 6. Morality of individual principles of conscience (there is voluntary compliance based on ethical principles; this level is probably not reached until early adolescence, and it may not be reached at all)

More recently, Kohlberg (1978) and Colby (1978) have identified two types of reasoning at each stage: Type A emphasizes literal interpretation of the rules and roles of society, whereas Type B is a more consolidated form and refers to the intent of normative standards.

Interestingly, Jurkovic (1980) has noted that delinquents differ in their level of moral development just as they do in their personality and behavioral style. Indeed, "not only do they vary from one another in stage of moral development, but they also fluctuate in their own reasoning level on different moral problems" (p. 724).

Note 11

Reprinted with permission of Macmillan Publishing Co., Inc. from "Egocentric thought in the child," in *The Moral Judgement of the Child*, by J. Piaget. First Free Press Paperback Edition, 1965.

The Idea of Justice

To bring our inquiry to a close, let us examine the answers given to a question which sums up all that we have been talking about. We asked the children, either at the end or at the beginning of our interrogatories, to give us themselves examples of what they regarded as unfair.[1]

The answers we obtained were of four kinds: (1) Behavior that goes against commands received from the adult—lying, stealing, breakages, in a word, everything that is forbidden. (2) Behavior that goes against the rules of a game. (3) Behavior that goes against equality (inequality in punishment as in treatment). (4) Acts of injustice connected with adult society (economic or political injustice). Now, statistically, the results show very clearly as functions of age:

	Forbidden	Games	Inequality	Social Injustice
6–8	64%	9%	27%	—
9–12	7%	9%	73%	11%

Here is an example of the identification of what is unfair with what is forbidden:

Age 6: "A little girl who has a broken plate," "to burst a balloon," "children who make a noise with their feet during prayers," "telling lies," "something not true," "it's not fair to steal," etc. . . . .

Here are examples of inequalities:

Age 6: "Giving a big cake to one and a little one to another."

---

[1]As a matter of fact, this term is not understood by all, but it can always be replaced by "not fair" (Fr. *pas juste*).

Age 10: "When you both do the same work and don't get the same reward." "Two children both do what they are told, and one gets more than the other." "To scold one child and not the other if they have both disobeyed."

Age 12: "A referee who takes sides."

And some example of social injustice:

Age 12: "A mistress preferring a pupil because he is stronger, or cleverer, or better dressed."

"A mother who won't allow her children to play with children who are less well dressed."

"Children who leave a little girl out of their games, who is not so well dressed as they are."

These obviously spontaneous remarks, taken together with the rest of our inquiry, allow us to conclude, insofar as one can talk of stages in the moral life, the existence of three great periods in the development of the sense of justice in the child. One period, lasting up to the age of 7–8, during which justice is subordinated to adult authority; a period contained approximately between 8–11, and which is that of progressive equalitarianism; and finally a period which sets in toward 11–12, and during which purely equalitarian justice is tempered by considerations of equity.

The first is characterized by the nondifferentiation of the notions of just and unjust from those of duty and disobedience: whatever conforms to the dictates of the adult authority is just. As a matter of fact even at this stage the child already looks upon some kinds of treatment as unjust, those, namely, in which the adult does not carry out the rules he has himself laid down for children (e.g., punishing for a fault that has not been committed, forbidding what has previously been allowed, etc.). But if the adult sticks to his own rules, everything he prescribes is just. In the domain of retributive justice, every punishment is accepted as perfectly legitimate, as necessary, and even as constituting the essence of morality: if lying were not punished, one would be allowed to tell lies, etc. In the stories where we have brought retributive justice into conflict with equality, the child belonging to this stage sets the necessity for punishment above equality of any sort. In the choice of punishments, expiation takes precedence over punishment by reciprocity, the very principle of the latter type of punishment not being exactly understood by the child. In the domain of immanent justice, more than three-quarters of the subjects under 8 believe in an automatic justice which emanates from physical nature and inanimate objects. If obedience and equality are brought into conflict, the child is always in favor of obedience: authority takes precedence over justice. Finally, in the domain of justice between children, the need for equality is already felt, but is yielded to only where it cannot possibly come into conflict with authority. For instance, the act of hitting back, which is regarded by the child of 10 as one of elementary justice, is considered "naughty" by children of 6 and 7, though, of course, they are always doing it in practice. (It will be remembered that the heteronomous rule, whatever may be the respect in which it is held mentally, is not necessarily observed in real life.) On the other hand, even in the relations between children, the authority of older ones will outweigh equality....

The second period does not appear on the plane of reflection and moral judgment until about the age of 7 or 8. But it is obvious that this comes slightly later than what happens with regard to practice. This period may be defined by the progressive development of autonomy and the priority of equality over authority. In the domain of retributive justice, the idea of expiatory punishment is no longer accepted with the same docility as before, and the only punishments accepted as really legitimate are those based upon reciprocity. Belief in immanent justice is perceptibly on the decrease and moral action is sought for its own sake, independently of reward or punishment. In matters of distributive justice, equality rules supreme. In conflicts between punishment and equality, equality outweighs every other consideration. The same holds good a fortiori of conflicts with authority. Finally, in the relations between children, equalitarianism obtains progressively with increasing age.

Toward 11–12 we see a new attitude emerge, which may be said to be characterized by the feeling of equity, and which is nothing but a development of equalitarianism in the direction of relativity. Instead of looking for equality in identity, the child no longer thinks of the equal rights of individuals except in relation to the particular situation of each. In the domain of retributive justice this comes to the same thing as not applying the same punishment to all, but taking into account the [extenuating] circumstances of some. In the domain of distributive justice it means no longer thinking of a law as identical for all but taking account of the personal circumstances of each (favoring the younger ones, etc.). Far from leading to privileges, such an attitude tends to make equality more effectual than it was before.

Note 12

L. Kohlberg (1964), Development of moral character. In: *Review of Child Development Research*, ed. M.L. Hoffman and L.W. Hoffman. New York: Russell Sage Foundation, Vol. I, pp. 400–404.

In an initial study of 72 boys of ages ten to sixteen, with Piaget procedures, six types of moral judgment were defined after extensive study. . . .

Each of the six general types of moral orientation could be defined in terms of its specific stance on 32 aspects of morality. In addition to areas suggested by the Piaget dimensions, the aspects ranged from "Motives for Moral Action" to "Universality of Moral Judgment," from "Concepts of Rights" to "Basis of Respect for Social Authority." As an example, the six types were defined as follows with regard to Aspect 10, "Motivation for Rule Obedience or Moral Action":

Stage 1. Obey rules to avoid punishment.

Stage 2. Conform to obtain rewards, have favors returned, and so on.

Stage 3. Conform to avoid disapproval, dislike by others.

Stage 4. Conform to avoid censure by legitimate authorities and resultant guilt.

Stage 5. Conform to maintain the respect of the impartial spectator judging in terms of community welfare.

Stage 6. Conform to avoid self-condemnation.

Aspect 10: Motivation for Moral Action
Stage 1: Punishment—Danny, Age 10:
(Should Joe tell on his older brother to his father?)
"In one way it would be right to tell on his brother or his father
might get mad at him and spank him. In another way it would be
right to keep quiet or his brother might beat him up."
Stage 2: Exchange and Reward—Jimmy, Age 13:
(Should Joe tell on his older brother to his father?)
"I think he should keep quiet. He might want to go someplace like
that, and if he squeals on Alex, Alex might squeal on him."
Stage 3: Disapproval Concern—Andy, Age 16:
(Should Joe keep quiet about what his brother did?)
"If my father finds out later, he won't trust me. My brother
wouldn't either, but I wouldn't have a *conscience* that he (my
brother) didn't."
"I try to do things for my parents; they've always done things for
me. I try to do everything my mother says; I try to please her. Like
she wants me to be a doctor, and I want to, too, and she's helping me
to get up there."
Stage 6: Self-condemnation Concern—Bill, Age 16:
(Should the husband steal the expensive black market drug needed
to save his wife's life?)
"Lawfully no, but morally speaking, I think I would have done it. It
would be awfully hard to live with myself afterward, knowing that I
could have done something which would have saved her life and yet
didn't for fear of punishment to myself."

The stages just listed would be generally taken to reflect moral
internalization rather than cognitive development. Cognitive development is more immediately apparent in the following stages of
thought about Aspect 3, "The Basis of Moral Worth of a Human Life":
Stage 1. The value of a human life is confused with the value of
physical objects and is based on the social status or physical attributes of its possessor.
Stage 2. The value of a human life is seen as instrumental to the
satisfaction of the needs of its possessor or of other persons.
Stage 3. The value of a human life is based on the empathy and
affection of family members and others toward its possessor.
Stage 4. Life is conceived as sacred in terms of its place in a
categorical moral or religious order of rights and duties.
Stage 5. Life is valued both in terms of its relation to community
welfare and in terms of life being a universal human right.
Stage 6. Belief in the sacredness of human life as representing a
universal human value of respect for the individual.

Aspect 3: Basis of Moral Worth of a Human Life
Stage 1: Life's Value Based on Physical and Status Aspects—Tommy,
     Age 10:
(Why should the druggist give the drug to the dying woman when
her husband couldn't pay for it?)
"If someone important is in a plane and is allergic to heights and
the stewardess won't give him medicine because she's only got
enough for one and she's got a sick one, a friend, in back, they'd

probably put the stewardess in a lady's jail because she didn't help the important one."

(Is it better to save the life of one important person or a lot of unimportant people?)

"All the people that aren't important because one man just has one house, maybe a lot of furniture, but a whole bunch of people have an awful lot of furniture and some of these poor people might have a lot of money and it doesn't look it."

Stage 2: Life's Value as Instrumental to Need-Satisfaction—Tommy at age 13:

(Should the doctor "mercy-kill" a fatally ill woman requesting death because of her pain?)

"Maybe it would be good to put her out of her pain, she'd be better off that way. But the husband wouldn't want it, its not like an animal. If a pet dies you can get along without it—it isn't something you really need. Well, you can get a new wife, but it's not really the same."

Stage 4: Life Sacred Because of a Social and Religious Order—John, Age 16:

(Should the doctor "mercy-kill" the woman?)

"The doctor wouldn't have the right to take a life, no human has the right. He can't create life, he shouldn't destroy it."

Stage 6: Life's Value as Expressing the Sacredness of the Individual—Steve, Age 16:

(Should the husband steal the expensive drug to save his wife?)

"By the law of society he was wrong but by the law of nature or of God the druggist was wrong and the husband was justified. Human life is above financial gain. Regardless of who was dying, if it was a total stranger, man has a duty to save him from dying."

....The age trends for the six stages, considered as including all aspects of morality, are indicated in the accompanying figure. It is evident that the first two types decrease with age, the next two increase until age thirteen and then stabilize, and the last two continue to increase from age thirteen to age sixteen. These age trends indicate that large groups of moral concepts and attitudes acquire meaning only in late childhood and adolescence and require the extensive background of cognitive growth and social experience associated with the age factor.

There are two possible interpretations of these age findings. Both common sense and most psychological theory would view such age differences as the effect of increased learning of the verbal morality characteristic of the adult American culture. Some patterns of moral verbalization are presumably easier to learn than others, are perhaps explicitly taught earlier, and hence are characteristic of younger ages.

Developmental theories suggest a second interpretation. The stages of moral thinking may not directly represent learning of patterns of verbalization in the culture. Instead, they may represent spontaneous products of the child's effort to make sense out of his experience in a complex social world, each arising sequentially from its predecessors.

As an example, Tommy, the ten-year-old exemplar of a Stage 1 conception of life's value, implies that one should decide whose life to

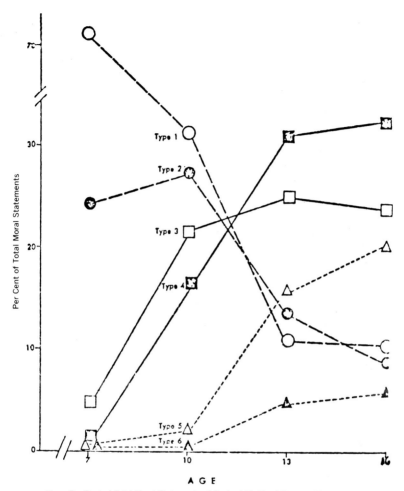

Per Cent of Total Moral Statements

Type 1
Type 2
Type 3
Type 4
Type 5
Type 6

A G E

Mean Per Cent of Total Moral Statements of Each of Six Moral Types at Four Ages

save in terms of the amount of furniture owned. While Tommy's response probably reflects his parent's high concern about acquiring or preserving furniture, his derivation of the value of life from the value of furniture is his own. The naive or primitive quality of Tommy's belief arises from a characteristic failure of younger children (usually under eight) to distinguish the value of an object to its owner and its (moral) value to others (moral "egocentrism") . . . when Tommy made this distinction three years later, he set off on quite a different path in considering the value of a life, one based on its replaceability in terms of the needs of others. Each line of thinking reflects his organization of values presented to him by his world in terms of assumptions characteristic of his current development level.

The writer has been led to accept this second, or developmental, interpretation by evidence suggesting that his stages form an invariant developmental sequence. This evidence suggests that the use of a more advanced stage of thought depends upon earlier attainment of each preceding stage and that each involves a restructuring and displacement of previous stages of thought. . . .

REFERENCES

Colby, A. (1978), Evolution of a moral-developmental theory. In: *New Directions in Child Development: Moral Development*, ed. W. Damon. San Francisco: Jossey-Bass.

Jurkovic, G.J. (1980), The juvenile delinquent as a moral philosopher. A structural-developmental perspective. *Psychol. Bull.*, 88:709–727.

Kohlberg, L. (1964), Development of moral character. In: *Review of Child Development Research*, Vol. I, ed. M.L. Hoffman and L.W. Hoffman. New York: Russell Sage Foundation, pp. 400–404.

Kohlberg, L. (1978), Revisions in the theory and practice of moral development. In: *New Directions in Child Development: Moral Development*, ed. W. Damon. San Francisco: Jossey-Bass.

Piaget, J. (1977), Egocentric thought in the child. In: *The Essential Piaget*, ed. H.E. Gruber and J.J. Vonèche. New York: Basic Books, pp. 186–188.

Chapter 9

PSYCHOSOCIAL DEVELOPMENT

A broader, psychosocial perspective of the life cycle has been described by Erikson (1959), who propounded what he called the epigenetic principle: anything that grows has a *ground plan* and out of this plan the *parts* arise, each part having its *time* of special ascendancy until all parts have arisen to form a *functioning whole.*

Each item of the healthy personality to be discussed is *systematically related to all other items:* all items depend on the *proper development in the proper sequence of each item,* and each item *exists in some form before its decisive and critical time arrives* (see Table 9–1).

Table 9–1. DIAGRAM ILLUSTRATING PROGRESSIVE
DIFFERENTIATION OF PARTS*

First Stage (about first year)	BASIC TRUST	Earlier form of AUTONOMY	Earlier form of INITIATIVE
Second Stage (about second and third years)	Later form of BASIC TRUST	AUTONOMY	Earlier form of INITIATIVE
Third Stage (about fourth and fifth years)	Later form of BASIC TRUST	Later form of AUTONOMY	INITIATIVE

*E. Erikson, (1959), *Identity and the Life Cycle.* New York, W.W. Norton, 1979. By permission.

Each stage becomes a *crisis* because of a *radical change in perspective.*

In order to do Erikson justice, the description of his theory that follows will quote extensively from his monograph "Identity and the Life Cycle" (Erikson, 1959; see Note 13).

BASIC TRUST VS. BASIC MISTRUST

This is an "incorporative oral stage" of receiving and accepting, with a mutuality between mother and child, as well as an "active incorporative stage," with biting, and so on. It includes conscious experiencing and ways of behaving and unconscious inner states. Erikson described how mothers create a sense of trust in their children by a kind of caring that combines sensitive care of the baby's individual needs along with a firm sense of personal trustworthiness.

AUTONOMY VS. SHAME AND DOUBT

In this stage Erikson believed that the maturation of the muscle system, and the ability to coordinate such conflicting action patterns as 'holding on' and 'letting go,' were important to the child, along with the child's investment in his autonomous will. The so-called anal zone was thought by Erikson to lend itself more than any other to the expression of stubborn insistence on conflicting impulses because:

a. It is the modal zone for 2 contradictory modes, i.e., retention and elimination.
b. The sphincters are part of the muscle system, which in general alternates between rigidity and relaxation, flexion and extension.

The whole stage, then, becomes a battle for autonomy. As he stands on his own two feet, the child delineates "I" and "you," "we" and "mine." The child here is apt to both hoard things and discard them, to both cling to possessions and throw them out the window. Erikson conceptualized a sense of autonomy and pride arising from a sense of self-control without loss of self esteem. Concomitantly, a sense of doubt and shame might arise from a sense of muscular and anal impotence, loss of self control, and parental overcontrol.

"To develop autonomy, a firmly developed and a convincingly continued stage of early trust is necessary.... At around 8 months the child seems to be somehow more aware, as it were, of this separateness; this prepares him for the impending sense of autonomy.

"Shame supposes that one is completely exposed and conscious of being looked at—in a word, self-conscious. One is visible and not ready to be visible.

" . . .be firm and tolerant with the child at this stage, and he will be firm and tolerant with himself. He will feel pride in being an autonomous person; he will grant autonomy to others; and now and again he will even let himself get away with something."

INITIATIVE VS. GUILT

By age 4 to 5, the child knows that he *is* a person, and he tries to discover what kind of a person he will be. Like his parents? Powerful? Beautiful? Dangerous?

The child at this stage:

1. Moves around very freely and more violently
2. Has a greater command of language and asks many questions
3. Is highly imaginative, a trait that leads at times to a sense of guilt, as though the fantasy itself were a crime.

The child seems to "grow together" psychologically and physically, and he is "self activated." Not only can he walk and run, he tries to find out what he *can* do with the ability and what he *may* do with it. The child at this stage makes comparisons (e.g., about sexual differences).

There is what Erikson calls an *intrusive mode* , characterized by (1) intrusion into other *bodies* by *attack*, (2) intrusion into other *people's ears and minds* by *aggressive talking*, (3) intrusion into *space* by vigorous *locomotion*, and (4) intrusion into the *unknown* by *consuming curiosity*.

The child at this stage feels ashamed that his fantasies or behavior will be discovered. He or she also begins to feel guilty automatically, even for thoughts and for deeds which nobody has watched. Yet at the same time the child is ready to learn quickly and avidly, and to become grown up (in regard to responsibility, discipline, and performance). The child now is willing to make things together, to collaborate with other children for the purpose of constructing and planning (instead of bossing and coercing), to profit by his or her association with teachers and ideal prototypes, and to feel equal to others in worth.

INDUSTRY VS. INFERIORITY

This stage differs from others in that it does not consist of a swing from a violent inner upheaval to a new mastery. The violent drives are said to be normally dormant at this time. It is a stage of "outer hindrances." The child sooner or later becomes dissatisfied and disgruntled; he or she may have a sense of not being useful and may feel unable to make things and to make them well, even perfectly. "It is as if he knows . . . (Erikson says). . . he must begin to be somewhat of a worker and potential provider before becoming a biological parent." The dangers at this stage are:

1. That the child will develop a sense of inferiority, a feeling that he or she will never be any good
2. That the child's sense of identity (through identification) will remain prematurely fixed on being nothing but a good little worker or a good little helper, which may not be all he could be
3. That the child may never acquire the enjoyment of work and the pride of doing at least one kind of thing well

In summary, this is a socially decisive stage. A sense of division of labor and of equality of opportunity develops at this time, and the ground is set for the child's sense of identity.

IDENTITY VS. IDENTITY DIFFUSION

The concept of ego identity is one of Erikson's major contributions, and it is necessary here to quote him directly. Ego identity is more than the sum of childhood identification; "It is the inner capital accrued from all those experiences of each successive stage . . . when successful identification led to a successful alignment of the individual's basic drives with his endowment and his opportunities. . . . The sense of ego identity, then, is the accrued confidence that one's ability to maintain inner sameness and continuity (one's ego in the psychological sense) is matched by the sameness and continuity of one's meaning for others. . . Thus, self esteem, confirmed at the end of each major crisis, grows to be a conviction that one is learning effective steps toward a tangible future, that one is developing a defined personality within a social reality which one understands. . . Accruing ego identity gains real strength only from wholehearted and consistent recognition of real accomplishment. . . The danger of this stage is identity diffusion. . . ."

To continue in Erikson's words, "To say ... that the identity crisis is *psycho* and *social* means that:

1. It is a subjective sense as well as an observable quality of personal sameness and continuity, paired with some belief in the sameness and continuity of some shared world image ...
2. It is a state of being and becoming that can have a highly conscious ... quality and yet remain, in its motivational aspects, quite unconscious and beset with dynamics of conflict ...
3. It is characteristic of a developmental period [adolescence and youth].
4. It is dependent on the *past* for the resource of strong identifications in childhood, while it relies on new models encountered in youth, and depends for its conclusion on workable roles offered in young adulthood. In fact, each subsequent stage of adulthood must contribute to its preservation and renewal ... Psychosocial identity ... also has a *psycho-historical* side. The study of psychosocial identity ... depends on ...
    (1) the personal coherence of the individual and role integration in his group;
    (2) his guiding images and the ideologies of his time;
    (3) his life history—and the historical moment ...

The unconscious complexities .. can be grouped thus:

1. Every person and even group harbors a *negative identity* as the sum of all those identifications and identity fragments which the individual had to submerge in himself as undesirable or irreconcilable or which his group has taught him to perceive as the mask of fatal "difference" in sex role or race, in class or religion ...
2. In some young people, in some classes, at some periods in history, the personal identity crisis will be noiseless and contained within the rituals of passage marking a second birth; while in other people, classes, and periods, the crisis will be clearly marked off as a critical period intensified by collective strife or epidemic tension. Thus the nature of the identity conflict often depends on the latent panic or, indeed, the intrinsic promise pervading a historical period. ... Psychosocial identity ... is ... situated in three orders in which man lives at all times:
    (1) The *somatic order,* by which an organism gets to maintain its integrity in a continuous reciprocal adaptation of the *milieu intérieur* and other organisms.

(2) The *personal order* —that is, the integration of "inner" and "outer" world in individual experience and behavior.

(3) The *social order*, jointly maintained by personal organisms sharing a geographic-historical setting . . . "

How is Erikson's contribution assessed today? Rapaport (1959) made the following observations on Erikson's theory:

1. It outlines the universal sequences of phases of psychosocial development.
2. The phases, for the first time in the history of psychoanalytic theory, span the whole life cycle.
3. Each phase is characterized by a phase-specific developmental task.
4. There is a mutual coordination between the developing individual and his social environment.
5. At the same time, each society has its own way to meet each phase of the development of its members through specific institutions, such as parental care, schools, and teachers.
6. The individual is *genetically* a social person, society merely influencing the manner in which he solves his developmental tasks.
7. The particular way society's caretaking institutions influence the functioning of various modes (e.g., retentive and intrusive) leads to a change of function, which eventually results in the characteristic behavior of the individual.
8. The theory as a theory is not always clear in terms of its level of abstraction.
9. Erikson relates his ego theory to Freud's id psychology of drive development.

Piaget (1960) noted that "the great merit of Erikson's stages . . . is precisely that he attempted, by situating the Freudian mechanisms within more general types of conduct (walking, exploring, etc.), to postulate continual integration of previous acquisitions at subsequent levels" (p. 13).

Erikson is not a scientist in the measuring, experimental sense. Rather, he is a perceptive observer. He began writing about ego identity in the late 1940s and early 1950s, and the body of his work stems from that period. Possibly his key concept is that of identity, which comprises a conscious sense of individual identity, an unconscious striving for a continuity of personal character, a criterion for the work of ego synthesis, and the maintenance of an inner solidarity with a group's ideals and identities.

Erikson has also approached his subject through biography (he has written about Shaw, Ghandi, Luther, and himself, including his analysis with Anna Freud), clinical work with children, and theory. Many people, especially such authors as Lifton and Kenniston, have moved farther in the direction of psychohistory. Others seem to equate Erikson with "ego psychology," and have subsequently concentrated their interest on "ego functions," particularly cognitive development.

Some of Erikson's theories have not held up under scientific scrutiny; for example, his theory of sex differences in children's play (among them, that boys tend to build towers and girls tend to build enclosures). Clinicians who work with children have found many of Erikson's concepts (e.g., of basic trust and identity) useful, albeit mostly at a general, somewhat global level. Still others have taken issue with some of Erikson's concepts (e.g., that of identity diffusion). For example, followers of Erikson have attempted to derive the diagnostic category of identity disorder (DSM-III, 313.82*), which is said to consist of (1) severe/subjective distress regarding uncertainty about three or more identity-related issues (e.g., long-term goals, career choice, friendship patterns, sexual orientation, religious orientation identification, systems of moral values, and group loyalties) and (2) subsequent impairment of social or occupational (including academic) functioning, both of more than 3 months' duration and not due to any other mental disorder. However, those who disagree with this categorization, such as Rutter and Shaffer (1980), have stated that there is now "a substantial body of research of many different kinds which runs counter to the views of adolescence which seem to underlie this concept" (see also Rutter, 1979). More empirical research is needed before the issue can be settled.

Note 13 (See page 110.)

E. Erikson (1959), *Identity and the Life Cycle*. New York: W.W. Norton, 1979. By permission.

---

*Here and elsewhere in this book, the numbers in parentheses refer to the DSM-III classification of the disorder being discussed.

NOTE 13.   ERIKSON'S LIFE-CYCLE CHART

	1.	2.	3.	4.	5.	6.	7.	8.
I. **INFANCY**	Trust vs. Mistrust				Unipolarity vs. Premature Self-Differentiation			
II. **EARLY CHILDHOOD**		Autonomy vs. Shame, Doubt			Bipolarity vs. Autism			
III. **PLAY AGE**			Initiative vs. Guilt		Play Identification vs. (oedipal) Fantasy Identities			
IV. **SCHOOL AGE**				Industry vs. Inferiority	Work Identification vs. Identity Foreclosure			
V. **ADOLESCENCE**	Time Perspective vs. Time Diffusion	Self-Certainty vs. Identity Consciousness	Role Experimentation vs. Negative Identity	Anticipation of Achievement vs. Work Paralysis	Identity vs. Identity Diffusion	Sexual Identity vs. Bisexual Diffusion	Leadership Polarization vs. Authority Diffusion	Ideological Polarization vs. Diffusion of Ideals
VI. **YOUNG ADULT**					Solidarity vs. Social Isolation	Intimacy vs. Isolation		
VII. **ADULTHOOD**							Generativity vs. Self-Absorption	
VIII. **MATURE AGE**								Integrity vs. Disgust, Despair

REFERENCES

DSM-III (1980) (*Diagnostic and Statistical Manual of Mental Disorders*, 3rd Ed.), Washington, D.C.: American Psychiatric Association, pp. 65–67.

Erikson, E.H. (1959), Identity and the life cycle. *Psychol. Issues*, 1: 101–172.

Piaget, J. (1960), The general problem of the psychobiological development of the child. In: *Discussions on Child Development*, Vol. 4, ed. J. Tanner and B. Inhelder. New York: International Universities Press, pp. 3–27.

Rapaport, D. (1959), Introduction: A historical survey of psychoanalytic ego psychology. *Psychol. Issues*, 1:5–17.

Rutter, M. (1979), *Changing Youth in a Changing Society: Patterns of Adolescent Development and Disorder*. London: Nuffield Provincial Hospitals Trust. (Cambridge, Mass.: Harvard University Press, 1980.)

Rutter, M., and Shaffer, D. (1980), DSM-III: A step forward or back in terms of the classification of child psychiatric disorder? *J. Am. Acad. Child Psychiatry*, 19:371–393.

Chapter 10

FAMILY DEVELOPMENT

Normally, children thrive when they develop within a healthy family. At the same time, the traditional family is not the only healthy setting in which the development of the child may proceed. In the United States nearly 50% of all children born today will spend an extended portion of their lives with only one parent before they reach age 18; the divorce rate was nearly twice as high in 1978 as in 1970 (it increased most drastically in the 30 to 44 age bracket); and from 1970 to 1978 there was an increase of 184% in the number of single black women who headed households (Bureau of the Census, 1978). In most of these family setups normal development of the child is possible.

The family is constantly changing both within itself and in relation to society. Within the family, individuals may be in various transition states, such as being the youngest, being the oldest, leaving home, getting married, beginning parenthood, dying. In the context of society, the family both contributes and reacts to such changes as industrialization, economic depression, overpopulation, migration, political climate, educational and welfare policies, cultural forces, and religious toleration. And both sets of factors interact.

According to Hareven (1977), a "typical" developmental sequence in American families today is marrying early, having children early, and having few children. The "typical" family experiences a compact period of parenthood in the middle years of life and then a longer period (about one-third of adult life) without children. Finally, there is often a period of living alone following the death of a spouse, most frequently the husband (Glick, 1955).

A family is a matrix of a special group with a special bond to live together, employing transactions, role divisions, and other communications for the purpose of nurturance, socialization, and enculturation (Tseng and McDermott, 1979) (see also Note 14). Socialization begins at birth (Schaffer, 1979). Parent and infant form a dyad, and their interactive behavior has a temporal patterning. Brazelton and his colleagues (1974) have described, for example, the cyclical nature of the interactions between young infants and their mothers. The infant is equipped at birth with the means to begin coping with other people in his or her environment, and he or she seems virtually to be preadapted for social interchange. At the same time, the parents seem to sense the infant's rhythms and cycles, and they try to synchronize their behavior with the infant's. Socialization has begun, and it continues to develop within the context of the family. Enculturation occurs through language use, ways of relating, values, unconscious beliefs, and role expectations (Lidz, 1968).

The essential elements of what a family has to offer a child remain important, no matter how varied the setting. These elements include a loving relationship, opportunities for attachment, continuity of care and affection, adequate stimulation, and a steady relationship with one person (Rutter, 1972).

A loving relationship means that the infant experiences someone who holds him or her in high esteem, who is delighted with the infant, and who gives the infant a warm feeling. Such a person readily and generously meets the infant's inner needs, protects the infant, and ensures that the infant gets the necessary stimulation.

Strong attachments occur when the interaction has a certain degree of intensity, as it has when a parent (or other adult) gives a great deal of attention to the child, feeds the child, talks with the child, plays with the child (especially), and responds regularly and readily to the child's needs—signalled by, say, crying. The parent who recognizes and responds to the different signals of a child is one to whom the child is likely to become strongly attached. Stronger attachments generally occur if (1) the number of caretakers is limited (the fewer the caretakers, the stronger the attachments) and (2) the attachments occur during the early sensitive period, especially the first 2 years. (3) The child's own contribution to the attachment process is strong, especially in regard to the strength of the child's needs and signals.

Criteria for what constitutes the optimum continuity of care have yet to be established. Questions about how much of what kinds of stimulation are essential for a child also remain unanswered.

Questions about the advantages, or disadvantages, of "multiple mothering" arise when one considers the need for a steady relationship with one person. When there is one major mother figure and one or more mother surrogates (as occurs when a mother goes out to work and the child is cared for by a mother surrogate), no harm is done, provided the mother surrogate is a suitable person. Again, when there are several almost primary mother figures (say, up to four or five, as in extended families), children do very well. However, when there are many different mother substitutes, each of whom may be inadequate and none of whom is intensely attached to the child, the child may suffer. This situation occurs in many institutions.

Children have roles to play within the family. They may satisfy various needs of the parents and may provide opportunities for the parents to rework various developmental tasks as the parents experience the children at different developmental stages. Children may also play pathological roles in a family, including those of scapegoat, baby, pet, and peacemaker (Rollins et al., 1973). Children with adverse temperamental features are most likely to be selected for scapegoating by parents at times of stress (Rutter et al., 1977). Children also take on what Anthony (1973) calls a "family likeness," displaying personality characteristics, coping styles, prejudices, and defense characteristics similar to those of other members of the family. Projective identification (Klein, 1946) and externalization (Brodey, 1959) are some of the processes by which this is hypothesized to occur. Projective identification is the term used to describe the putting of part of oneself or part of one's impulses and feelings into another person, leading to an identification with that other person based on attributing to him or her some of one's own qualities.

One particular definable developmental stage within the family is that of parenthood, which is a process having an early, a middle, and a late phase with respect to the developing child (Benedek, 1970). The early phase of parenthood extends from conception to adolescence. The middle phase of parenthood begins when the child begins to mature sexually as he or she starts to take a sexual interest in another person, and it continues through marriage and childbearing. The onset of old age marks the beginning of the late phase of parenthood, when the now "adult child" becomes a need-fulfilling person for the aged parent, thus completing the cycle.

At each stage of the cycle, parents seem to relive and to rework through those conflicts that they experienced when they were at the stage of development their child is now in. However, each parent is also at his or her stage of adult development, and thus there are a myriad of possible combinations of developmental levels. The principle of developmental phases is one way of understanding the complexity of both nuclear and extended family relationships.

Although numerous attempts have been made to classify families (Fisher, 1977), none of them has been universally accepted. What is abundantly clear from the literature on the family is that the development of the child must be considered in the context of the development of the family in which the child is reared, and that family developmental psychopathology and family therapy are important areas of clinical knowledge (McDermott, Jr., 1981).

Note 14

T. Lidz (1970), The family as the developmental setting. In: *The Child and His Family*, ed. E.J. Anthony and C. Koupernik, pp. 19–40. Copyright © 1970, John Wiley & Sons, Inc. Reprinted by permission of John Wiley & Sons, Inc.

The family is . . . a very special type of group with characteristics imposed upon it by the biological differences of its members as well as by the particular purposes it serves. Recognition of these characteristics leads to an appreciation of some requisites of its structure. . . .

1. The nuclear family is composed of two generations each with different needs, prerogatives, and obligations. The parents, having grown up in two different families, seek to merge themselves and their backgrounds into a new unit that satisfies the needs of both and completes their personalities in a relationship that seeks permanence. The new unit differs to a greater or lesser degree from their families of origin and thus requires malleability in both partners. The new relationship requires the intrapsychic reorganization of each spouse to take cognizance of the partner. Stated in very simple terms, the ego functioning of each is modified by the presence of an alterego including the id, ego, and superego requirements of the alterego. Wishes and desires of a spouse that can be set aside must be differentiated from needs that cannot be neglected.

The parents are properly dependent upon one another, and children must be dependent upon parents, but parents cannot properly be dependent upon immature children. The parents serve as guides, educators, and models for offspring. They provide nurturance and give of themselves so that the children can develop. Though individuals, as parents they function as a coalition, dividing roles and tasks in which they support one another. As basic love objects and objects for identification for their children, who the parents are, how they behave, and how they interrelate with one another and not simply what they do to their child and for their child are of utmost importance to the child's personality development.

The children, in contrast to their parents, receive their primary training in group living within the family, remaining dependent upon the parents for many years, forming intense emotional bonds to them, and developing by assimilating from their parents and introjecting their characteristics, and yet must so learn to live within the family that they are able to emerge from it to live in the broader society; or, at least, to start families of their own as members of the parental generation.

2. The family is also divided into two genders with differing but complementary functions and role allocations as well as anatomical differences. The primary female role derives from woman's biological structure and is related to the nurture of children and the maintenance of a home needed for that purpose, which leads to an emphasis upon interest in interpersonal relationships and emotional harmony—an expressive-affectional role. The male role, also originally related to man's physique, is concerned with the support and protection of a family and establishing its position in the larger society—an instrumental-adaptive role.

3. The relationships between family members are held firm by erotic and affectional ties. The parents who seek to form a permanent union are permitted and even expected to have sexual relationships. While all direct sexual relationships within the family are prohibited to the children, erogenous gratification from parental figures that accompanies nurturant care is needed and fostered; but it must be progressively frustrated as the need for such primary care diminishes lest the bonds to the family become too firm and prevent the child's investment of interest and energy in the extrafamilial world. The de-erotization of the child's relationships to other family members is a primary task of the family. . . .

4. The family forms a shelter for its members within the larger society. Theoretically, at least, members receive affection and status by ascription rather than by achievement, which provides a modicum of emotional security in the face of the demands of the outside world. However, the family must reflect and transmit the societal ways, including child-rearing techniques appropriate to each developmental phase, and the culture's meaning and value system, and so forth, to assure that the children will be able to function when they emerge from the family into the broader society.

These fundamental characteristics of the nuclear family, and correlaries derived from them, set requisites for the parents and their marital relationship if it is to provide a suitable setting for the harmonious development of their offspring and to foster their children's development into reasonably integrated adults capable of independent existence. . . .

The family must foster and direct the child's development by carrying out a number of interrelated functions. . . . (1) the parental nurturant functions that must meet the child's needs and supplement his immature capacities in a different manner at each phase of his development; (2) the dynamic organization of the family which forms the framework for the structuring of the child's personality or, perhaps stated more correctly, channels and directs the child into becoming an integrated individual ... (3) the family as the primary social system in which the child learns the basic social roles, the value of social institutions, and the basic mores of the society; and (4) the task of the parents to transmit to the child the essential instrumental techniques of the culture, including its language.

REFERENCES

Anthony, E.J. (1973), A working model for family studies. In: *The Child and His Family*, ed. E.J. Anthony and C. Koupernik. New York: Wiley, pp. 3–20.

Benedek, T. (1970), Parenthood during the life cycle. In: *Parenthood: Its Psychology and Psychopathology*, ed. E.J. Anthony and T. Benedek. Boston: Little, Brown, pp. 185–206.

Brazelton, T.B., Koslonski, B., and Main, M. (1974), The origins of reciprocity: The early mother-infant interaction. In: *The Effect of the Infant on Its Caretaker*, ed. M. Lewis and L. Rosenblum. New York: Wiley.

Brodey, W.M. (1959), Some family operations and schizophrenia. *Arch. Gen. Psychiatry*, 1:379–402.

Bureau of the Census (1978), Washington, D.C.:U.S. Government Printing Office. Publication No. 657.004/145.

Fisher, L. (1977), On the classification of families. *Arch. Gen Psychiatry*, 34:424–433.

Glick, P. (1955), The life cycle of the family. *Marr. Fam. Living*, 18:3–9.

Hareven, T.K. (1977), Family time and historical time. *Daedalus*, 107:57–70.

Klein, M. (1946), Notes on some schizoid mechanisms. *Int. J. Psychoanal.*, 27:99–110.

Lidz, T. (1968), *The Person*. New York: Basic Books.

Lidz, T. (1970), The family as the developmental setting. In: *The Child and His Family*, ed. E.J. Anthony and C. Koupernik. New York: Wiley, pp. 19–40.

McDermott, J.F., Jr., (1981), Indications for family therapy: question or non-question? *J. Am. Acad. Child Psychiatry*, 20:409–419.

Rollins, N., Lord, J.P., Walsh, E., and Weil, G.E. (1973), Some roles children play in their families. *J. Am. Acad. Child Psychiatry*, 12:511–530.

Rutter, M. (1972), *Maternal Deprivation Reassessed*. Harmondsworth: Penguin.

Rutter, M., Quinton, D., and Yule, B. (1977), *Family Pathology and Disorder in Children*. London: Wiley.

Schaffer, H.R. (1979), Acquiring the concept of dialogue. In: *Psychological Development from Infancy*, ed. M.H. Bornstein and W. Kessen. Hillsdale, N.J.: Lawrence Erlbaum Associates, pp. 279–306.

Tseng, W.-S., and McDermott, J.F. (1979), Triaxial family classification. *J. Am. Acad. Child Psychiatry*, 18:22–43.

PART TWO

Cross-Sectional Perspectives

Chapter 11

PRIOR TO BIRTH

PRENATAL DEVELOPMENT

The psychological development of the child has its antecedents during the prenatal period. It is known, for example, that the fetus can react to loud sounds by gross motor activity (Bernard and Sontag, 1957). Actual behavior conditioning of the fetus may even be possible, although this has not yet been convincingly demonstrated (Spelt, 1948). Nevertheless, certain behavior does occur in the fetus (Hooker, 1952), including a sucking reflex at about 20 weeks. The important points here are that heredity and environment are already interacting and that it is conceivable that future psychologically motivated behavior can be influenced by manipulating the genetic and environmental variables. In any case, from the beginning the new organism in its own right exerts an influence on the world. For example, the quickening movements of the fetus evoke a response in the mother, representing an early contribution of the child to the mother-child interaction. Throughout development the child will continue to influence his environment through his own activity.

PRENATAL ENVIRONMENT

The environment of the prenatal child of course is intrauterine, but even this relatively homeostatic environment is to some extent influenced by the mother's physical and emotional state. Weight gain during pregnancy is important for fetal growth. The normal mother who eats her regular diet will usually gain the minimum 25 pounds needed to allow her fetus to grow adequately and to prepare herself for the lactation period that may follow (Winick, 1981). Malnutrition, illness, radiation, drugs taken by the mother, and anxiety, on the other hand, may seriously affect the development of the fetus. Prenatal sex hormones in particular have a powerful effect on the developing brain and psychosexual differentiation (Ehrhardt and Meyer-Bahlburg, 1979; Imperato-McGinley, et al., 1979).

THE MOTHER'S PERSONALITY

Four major factors of the mother's attitude influence her relationship with her child: *First is the mother's personality prior to, during, and after pregnancy.* Perhaps the single most important factor here is the nature and extent of the mother's own experience of being mothered. Persisting aspects of the mother's relationship with her own parents, her sense of feminine identification, and her relationship with the child's father are further variables to be considered. Many of these kinds of prevailing personality factors affect the mother's relationship to her child. Sometimes direct displacement of the mother's feelings and attitudes onto the child will occur. At other times the child will be used as a weapon (or battlefield) in a continuing struggle, say, with the husband. At all times the mother's particular perceptual capacities, mothering skills, and ability to develop during the phase of motherhood affect the mother-child relationship (A. Freud, 1955).

ACCEPTANCE OF PREGNANCY

The Mother's Specific Attitudes Toward Pregnancy

Besides the fear or pleasure the mother may have experienced in regard to being pregnant, she may have had more or less hidden and complex motivations for getting pregnant. For example, she may have wanted to please the grandparents of the expected child. Or she may have conceived a child in an unrealistic wish to save her marriage. Or she may have become pregnant in an attempt to deal with her anxiety about frigidity or sterility. Or she may have yearned for a child, in an unconscious fantasy in which she herself was the nurtured infant. Sometimes hostile attitudes toward the fetus are crystallized during a painful or physically traumatic labor.

REACTION TO PREGNANCY

The Acute Impact of the Normal Psychological Reactions to Pregnancy

During the normal crisis of pregnancy the woman has been described as moving through a phase of enhanced preoccupation with herself ("cathexis of the self") until quickening brings about a new person ("object") with whom the woman forms a complex relationship (Bibring et al., 1961; see also Note 15). Moreover, this crisis in the mother is thought to continue beyond parturition, and it may influence the nature of the mother-child relationship. Sometimes unresolved psychological reactions to pregnancy spill over and cause disturbances in the delicate balance of the earliest mother-child relationship. For example, the multiple stresses of childbirth may temporarily upset the mother's physiological and psychic equilibrium, producing any kind and degree of psychiatric disorder (Normand, 1967). The specificity of the disorder in part depends upon such factors as the previous level of emotional maturity, including the sense of femininity, and the presence of certain unresolved conflicts, such as hostility toward the mother's own mother. However, hormonal changes after pregnancy can result in psychological problems regardless of the mother's maturity. Typically, the onset of clinical symptoms occurs during the puerperium. Perhaps the most common symptoms are depressive ones. Many normal women experience postpartum blues (Markham, 1961). This depression may lead to some degree of withdrawal, accompanied by partial rejection of the baby. The withdrawal and rejection, in turn, may result in early feeding difficulties in the baby, leading to further rejection and the creation of a vicious cycle. In this way a physiological and a consequent psychological reaction to the pregnancy and labor may interfere with the normal development of the mother-child interaction. Certainly, depression in the mother is likely to give rise to psychiatric symptoms in the child (Cohler et al., 1974). Attempts have been made to predict postpartum psychosis; the pregnant woman who is all "sweetness and kindness" was thought by Zilboorg (1957) to be at risk, while the woman who had an emotionally stormy pregnancy was thought to be least likely to develop a psychotic reaction. We now know that genetic and physiological predispositions to psychiatric disorders play major roles in the development of postpartum psychoses.

MOTHER'S LATENT EXPECTATIONS OF THE CHILD

A child may come to be used by the mother to express her own conscious or unconscious wishes. Occasionally, she may have the fantasy that she can remake herself in the child or at least "correct" (usually she over-corrects) the mistakes in the way she was brought up.

MODIFYING FACTORS

All of the foregoing influences become even more complex if either parent is absent because of separation or divorce, illness, or death. And the attitudes and expectations become more powerful when there are reinforcing reality factors, such as adoption, a difficult childbirth, brain damage, the fear of hereditary traits, illness, or an unwanted child. Pregnant women who want an abortion but cannot get one are more likely to experience child-rearing difficulties, and to produce a greater frequency of psychiatric problems in the young child (Forsmann and Thuwe, 1966). Furthermore, none of these factors remains static: they are in a continuous state of flux. Some of these factors will be discussed later as they impinge on the child at different phases in his development, but one point must be emphasized here: the child continues to make a contribution of his own to any continuing conflict between the parent and child.

ROLE OF THE FATHER

The mother is, of course, only part of the child's environment albeit usually the most important part in the child's early years. What has been said so far about the mother could also be said about the father (Earls, 1976). While the father may not have concerns about bodily harm during the pregnancy, he may resent the change in focus of attention and displace this resentment onto the child. Hopefully, the father will love the child as a natural outcome of his love for the child's mother. But the father may not love the mother, or, more commonly, may feel ambivalent. He may lack the motivation or maturity for marriage and fatherhood. Occasionally, the father will become anxious at the prospect of increased responsibility or because of identification with his own father (Zilboorg, 1931). Sometimes the father's ideas of what a mother's role and a father's role should be are in conflict with the mother's ideas on the subject. Then again, if the father is insecure in his work, he may be unable to meet the needs of the mother and child.

GRANDPARENTS AND SIBLINGS

Grandparents, uncles and aunts, and siblings also form part of the child's environment. It is obvious that some grandparents are helpful and others are intrusive. Yet it must also be said again that it takes two people to make a conflict, and usually a parent who is in conflict with a grandparent either has encouraged the conflict or has not been able, for various reasons, to take the necessary steps to resolve the conflict.

PERINATAL VARIABLES

Prematurity is an important factor in subsequent development. Prematurely born infants are poorly parented more frequently than are full-term infants (Klein and Stern, 1974), and they are more prone to abuse and/or neglect (Klaus and Kennell, 1970; Hunter et al., 1978). Minde and his colleagues (1980) have shown that a mother's activity with her premature infant in the neonatal nursery may be a good indicator of her initial adjustment to this infant and of her current emotional adjustment. Severe prematurity (birth weight less than 4½ pounds), severe complications of pregnancy and/or delivery, and severe familial stress have been shown to make their contribution to behavior disorders in later life, even when social class factors are held constant (Drillien, 1964). Overactivity and restlessness are the most common behavior problems that are related to severe prematurity (i.e., a birth weight of 3 pounds or less).

On the other hand, not all psychiatrically disturbed children have low birth weights, and complications of birth do not necessarily result in psychiatric disorder. In a study in which the obstetric histories of 100 primary school-age children referred to a psychiatric department with reactive psychiatric disorders were compared with the obstetric histories of 100 matched controls, no significant differences were found between the two groups in maternal age, birth weight, factors suggestive of an abnormal fetus, complications of pregnancy, complications of delivery, or the postnatal conditions of the child (Wolff, 1967).

SUMMARY

What was suggested in the preceding discussion is that the infant arrives in the world with an already complex development behind him or her, possessing an array of functions operating in ways that are peculiar to him or her and actively making a contribution of his or her own. Far from being a *tabula rasa*, the infant at birth has certain behavioral characteristics, brought about even prenatally by the interaction of genes and the environment, which are unique to the infant. Furthermore, these functions operate in such a way that a state of partial adaptedness may be said to exist at birth.

Once outside the womb, the active infant encounters the mother more directly. The mother now constitutes what Hartmann has called the average expectable environment (Hartmann, 1939; see Note 16). The continuing mutual relationship between infant and mother enables the infant to survive and thrive. The personality of the mother continues to influence this relationship. More specifically, the particular impact of the events of pregnancy, labor, and birth of a live child upon the mother in turn causes her to influence her child in characteristic ways.

Most children are born into an environment that is more or less prepared for the child, an environment that is virtually never "ideal" but fortunately is at least "good enough" and an environment to which they have themselves contributed. Furthermore, the mental activity of the infant turns a good-enough environment ("the ordinary good mother is good enough") into an optimum environment (Winnicott, 1958).

ANTICIPATORY GUIDANCE

Attempts have been made to forestall some of the possible difficulties between mother and infant by means of "anticipatory guidance," a method first conceptualized by Milton Senn (1947; see Note 17). Success in these attempts is dependent on the sensitivity and skill of the pediatrician on the one hand, and the capacity of the parent to change on the other hand. Unfortunately, many of the attitudes and fantasies just mentioned are often unconscious. Consequently, considerable resistance to any change is encountered in parents. Moreover, the indices for predicting what expectant mothers will have difficulties with their infants are not always sufficiently sensitive, except in extreme instances.

Note 15

T. Benedek (1970), The psychobiology of pregnancy. In: *Parenthood.* ed. E.J. Anthony and T. Benedek. Boston: Little, Brown, pp. 137–151. Copyright 1970, Little, Brown and Company.

Pregnancy is a "critical phase" in the life of a woman. Using the term as ethologists use it, it implies that pregnancy, like puberty, is a biologically motivated step in the maturation of the individual which requires physiologic adjustments and psychologic adaptations to lead to a new level of integration that, normally, represents development. For a long time the significance of the psychobiological processes of pregnancy was neglected by psychoanalysts. Freud, impressed by the emotional calmness of pregnant women, considered pregnancy as a period during which the woman lives in the bliss of her basic wish being gratified; therefore, he assumed that pregnant women are not in need of or accessible to psychoanalytic therapy. Since then psychoanalytic investigations have revealed the two opposing poles which account for pregnancy as a critical phase. One is rooted in the drive organization of the female procreative function, the other in the emotional disequilibrium caused by the stresses of pregnancy and the danger of parturition.

Recently, Rheingold collected into a large volume references regarding women's "fear of being a woman," with emphasis on the fear of death connected with childbearing. . . . This concept is so deeply ingrained in the human mind that even Freud failed to recognize the emotional manifestations of the instinctual tendency to bear children in the drive organization of women. Helene Deutsch, in her major work, attributes "the devoted patience which women of uncounted generations have shown in the service of the species" to the necessity of woman's socioeconomic dependence on man. . . . An ever-growing literature abounds in the discussion of this concept, drawing its arguments from folklore, religion, mythology, and from the history of civilizations. . . . Against such telling evidence it may seen foolhardy to propose the results arrived at by psychoanalytic investigations. Yet it seems safe to do so since investigations have revealed the psychobiologic process of the female reproductive function without which mankind would not exist. . . .

In the perspective of the psychobiologic processes of pregnancy, one can evaluate the clinical significance of the developmental conflicts and their constellation in the personality organization of women; these conflicts, revived during pregnancy, influence women's feelings about motherhood and their attitude toward their child and/or children. Psychoanalyses of pregnant women or women in the postpartum period thus provide clues to the interactions of three generations in the psychology of parenthood. . . .

On the basis of psychoanalytic observations Helen Deutsch generalized that a deep-rooted passivity and a specific tendency toward introversion are characteristic qualities of the female psyche. . . . Investigation of the sexual cycle has revealed that these propensities reappear in intensified form correlated with the specifically female gonadal hormone, lutein, during the postovulative phase of the cycle. Such observations justify the assumption that the emotional manifestations of the specific receptive tendency and the self-centered retentive tendency are the psychodynamic correlates of a biologic need for motherhood. Thus motherhood is not secondary, not a substitute for the missing penis, nor is it forced by men upon women "in the service of the species," but the manifestation of the all-pervading instinct for survival in the child that is the primary organizer of the woman's sexual drive, and by this also her personality. Thus the specific attributes of femininity originate in that indwelling quality of woman's psyche which is the manifestation and result of the central organization of receptive and retentive tendencies of the reproductive drive that becomes the source of motherliness. . . .

Pregnancy is a biologically normal but exceptional period in the life of women. At conception a "biologic symbiosis" begins that steers the woman between the happy fulfillment of her biologic destiny and its menacing failures. The heightened hormonal and metabolic processes which are necessary to maintain the normal growth of the fetus augment the vital energies of the mother. It is the interlocking physiologic processes between mother and fetus that make the pregnant woman's body abound in libidinous feelings. As metabolic and emotional processes replenish the libido reservoir of the pregnant woman, this supply of primary narcissism becomes a wellspring of her motherliness. Self-centered as it may appear, it increases her pleasure in bearing her child, stimulates her hopeful fantasies, diminishes her anxieties. One can, however, observe differences in women's reactions to this psychobiologic state. A woman whose personality organization makes her a natural mother enjoys the narcissistic state with vegetative calmness, while a less fortunate woman defends herself, often consciously, against that experience. As women succeed in adjusting to the hormonal influences of pregnancy, the initial fatigue, sleepiness, some of the physical reactions such as vertigo or morning sickness diminish. Thus women are able to respond to their physical and emotional well-being by expanding and enjoying their activities. While the pregnant woman feels her growing capacity to love and to care for her child, she experiences a general improvement in her emotional state. Many neurotic women who suffer from severe anxiety states are free from them during pregnancy; others, in spite of morning sickness or in spite of realistic worries caused by the pregnancy, feel stable and have their best time while they are pregnant. Healthy women demonstrate during pregnancy just as during the high hormone phases of the cycle an increased integrative capacity of the ego.

Yet the drive organization which accounts for the gratification of pregnancy harbors its inherent dangers. It tests the physiologic and psychologic reserves of women. Realistic fears, insecurities motivated by conception out of wedlock, economic worries, unhappy marriages make the test more arduous. Yet even such pregnancies usually have a normal course. We might assume that such pregnancies, in our age of relatively free use of contraceptives, are often deliberately or unconsciously chosen for their drive gratification and therefore have a curative effect. To this assumption one might object, since we all know that the hope for a change for the better in an interpersonal relationship or in an external situation may enhance the gratification of pregnancy. To this, however, I would answer that the increased libidinal state of pregnancy enhances hope and by this might favorably influence not only the pregnancy but also the realities of the environmental situation. Whether the hope will be fulfilled or disappointed, the fact is that hope arising from the libidinal state of pregnancy is often the motivation of motherhood. The point to be emphasized is: *only if the psychosexual organization of the woman is loaded with conflicts toward motherhood do actual conditions stir up deeper conflicts and disturb the psychophysiologic balance of pregnancy....*

Since the father's attitude toward the child might be influenced by the communicated experience of his wife, the emotional course of the pregnancy is largely responsible for the psychologic environment of the child; since it might confirm or undermine the meaning of the marriage, it may stabilize or disrupt the primary social unit, the family....

Note 16

H. Hartmann (1939), *Ego Psychology and the Problem of Adaptation.* (D. Rapaport, translator, 1958). New York: International Universities Press.

In his prolonged helplessness the human child is dependent on the family, that is, on a social structure which fulfills here—as elsewhere—"biological" functions also....

The processes of adaptation are influenced both by the constitution and external environment, and more directly determined by the ontogenetic phase of the organism....

No instinctual drive in man guarantees adaptation in and of itself, yet on the average the whole ensemble of instinctual drives, ego functions, ego apparatuses, and the principles of regulation, as they meet the average expectable environmental conditions, do have survival value. Of these elements, the function of the ego apparatuses ... is "objectively" the most purposive. The proposition that the external world "compels" the organism to adapt can be maintained only if one already takes man's survival tendencies and potentialities for granted....

A state of adaptedness exists before the intentional processes of adaptation begin....

Note 17

M.J.E., Senn (1947), Anticipatory guidance of the pregnant woman and her husband for their roles as parents. In: *Problems of Early Infancy* (Transactions of the First Conference). New York: Josiah Macy, Jr. Foundation, pp. 11–16.

At the New York Hospital pediatricians who are Fellows in Pediatric-Psychiatry, interviewed women at various periods of pregnancy.... In the experiment as set up, the pediatrician who interviewed the parents prenatally was the physician who examined the baby in the newborn period, planned its feeding program, and provided general medical care. This pediatrician was also responsible for the care of the baby throughout infancy and early childhood.

This experiment at the New York Hospital has shown that both men and women approaching parenthood do desire to talk about the coming event, and are exceedingly pleased to have an opportunity to meet and talk with the pediatrician who will care for their baby throughout the early years of its life. In fact, many women who heard about the experiment demanded pediatric consultation before the birth of their baby. Unfortunately, this could be done only for relatively few women, as the experiment was set up on a limited scale.

It was brought out that the pregnant woman often is actually more apprehensive about her role as a mother than her ability to deliver a viable infant. She is anxious about her own health and the life of the fetus and fearful of her ability to come through labor without too much discomfort or delivery without dying in the process. Even with such great anxiety about labor and delivery, however, it is significant and interesting to learn that she has an almost equally great apprehension that she may somehow fail in her role as a mother in the years when she is to care for and guide her child.

The father also was invited to meet with the pediatrician and in every case he came for at least one prenatal interview.

At each interview the prospective parent or parents are encouraged to talk about the pregnancy, about their feelings generally, and to ask any questions concerning the infant and its care. The pediatrician's role is a dual one—that of listener and adviser. He describes techniques of baby care, breast feeding, breast care before and after the birth of the baby, weaning, supplementary and complementary formula feeding, and the preparation of foods. Practical advice is given as to what to purchase in the way of equipment. The advantages of breast feeding are mentioned but there is no attempt made to "sell" breast feeding to the exclusion of bottle feeding, lest the parents be overcome with guilt or other adverse emotions in those instances where breast feeding is attempted and is unsuccessful. The psychological concomitants of infant feeding are stressed repeatedly. In the interviews talk about the baby and its care is purposely limited to the newborn period, that is, the first month of life, lest the parents become confused and confounded by the manifold material discussed.

As a result of the prenatal pediatric interviews, the incidence of breast feeding can be kept above 80%. Furthermore, the mother is able to prepare for the neonatal care well in advance, so that she can spend a good part of her time caring for the infant without feeling guilty about other duties which are neglected or taken over by substitutes. The mother has learned techniques of infant care and thereby is relaxed in her relationship to the new baby, her husband and others in the household. Where there are other children, both parents have been prepared for the usual sibling rivalry feelings and can protect the siblings as much as possible from the trauma incident to the birth of the new baby. The father is able to accept the role as mother-substitute and as housewife-substitute because he has been told what the reality situation would be like in the household after the birth of the new baby, and to act in a supportive way to his wife not only during the pregnancy, but also through the neonatal period when the mother and newborn return to the home. Where other persons in the family have to be considered, either physically or psychologically, the prospective parents are encouraged to make arrangements for their temporary care outside the family well in advance of the birth of the baby so that their presence does not influence adversely the convalescence of the mother or the early life of the baby.

In conclusion, the experiment of interviewing pregnant women and their husbands in terms of their function as parents has demonstrated to pediatricians that their role as physician-guide to the mother could best begin before the birth of the infant, through what may be called "anticipatory guidance," and that modern pediatrics should train physicians so that this role might be filled with optimum benefit to parent and child alike.

REFERENCES

Benedek, T. (1970), The psychobiology of pregnancy. In: *Parenthood*, ed. E.J. Anthony and T. Benedek. Boston, Little, Brown, pp. 137–151.

Bernard, J., and Sontag, L.W. (1947), Fetal reactivity and sound. *J. Genet. Psychol.*, 70:205–210.

Bibring, G.L., Dwyer, T.F., Huntington, D.S., and Valenstein, A.F. (1961), A study of the psychological processes in pregnancy and of the earliest mother-child relationship. *Psychoanal. Study Child*, 16:9–72.

Cohler, B.J., Grunebaum, H.U., Weiss, J.L., Gallant, D.H., and Abernethy, V. (1974), Social relations, stress and psychiatric hospitalization among mothers of young children. *Soc. Psychiatry*, 9:7–12.

Drillien, C.M. (1974), The effect of obstetrical hazard on the later development of the child. In: *Recent Advances in Paediatrics*, ed. D. Gairdner. London: Churchill.

Earls, F. (1976), The fathers (not the mothers): Their importance and influence with infants and young children. *Psychiatry*, 39:209–226.

Ehrhardt, A.A., and Meyer-Bahlburg, H.F.L. (1979), Prenatal sex hormones and the developing brain: Effects on psychosexual differentiation and cognitive function. *Ann. Rev. Med.*, 30:417–430.

Forsmann, H., and Thuwe, I. (1966), One hundred and twenty children born after application for therapeutic abortion refused. *Acta Psychiatr. Scand.*, 42:71–88.

Freud, A. (1954), Safeguarding the emotional health of our children: An inquiry into the concept of the rejecting mother. In: *National Conferences of Social Work: Casework Papers*, 1955. New York: Family Service Association of America, p. 5.

Hartmann, H. (1939), *Ego Psychology and the Problem of Adaptation*, trans. D. Rapaport. New York: International Universities Press.

Hooker, D. (1952), *The Prenatal Origin of Behavior*. Lawrence, Ka.: University of Kansas Press.

Hunter, R.S., Kilstrom, N., Kraybill, E.N., and Loda, F. (1978), Antecedents of child abuse and neglect in premature infants: A prospective study in a newborn intensive care unit. *Pediatrics*, 61:629–635.

Imperato-McGinley, J., Peterson, R.E., Gautier, T., and Sturla, E. (1979), Androgens and the evolution of male-gender identity among male pseudohermaphrodites with 50C-reductase deficiency. *N. Engl. J. Med.*, 300:1233–1237.

Klaus, M.H., and Kennell, J.H. (1970), Mothers separated from their newborn infants. *Pediatr. Clin. North Am.*, 17:1015–1037.

Klein, M., and Stern, L. (1974), Low birthweight and the battered child syndrome. *Am. J. Dis. Child*, 122:15–18.

Markham, S. (1961), A comparative evaluation of psychotic and non-psychotic reactions to childbirth. *Am. J. Orthopsychiatry*, 31:565.

Minde, K.K., Marton, P., Manning, D., and Hines, B. (1980), Some determinants of mother-infant interaction in the premature nursery. *J. Am. Acad. Child Psychiatry*, 19:1–21.

Normand, W.C. (1967), Post-partum disorders. In: *Comprehensive Textbook of Psychiatry*, ed. A.M. Freedman and H.I. Kaplan. Baltimore: Williams & Wilkins, pp. 1161–1163.

Senn, M.J.E. (1947), Anticipatory guidance of the pregnant woman and her husband for their roles as parents. In: *Problems of Early Infancy* (Transactions of the First Conference). New York: Josiah Macy, Jr. Foundation, pp. 11–16.

Spelt, D.K. (1948), Conditioned responses in the human fetus *in utero*. *Psychol. Bull.*, 35:712–713.

Winick, M. (1981), Food and the fetus. *Nat. Hist.*, 90:76–81.

Winnicott, D.W. (1958), Mind and its relation to the psychesoma. In: *Collected Papers Through Paediatrics to Psycho-Analysis*. London: Tavistock, p. 245.

Wolff, S. (1967), The contribution of obstetric complications to the etiology of behavior disorders in childhood. *J. Child Psychol. Psychiatry*, 8:57–66.

Zilboorg, G. (1931), Depressive reactions related to parenthood. *Am. J. Psychiatry*, 87:927.

Zilboorg, G. (1957), The clinical issues of post-partum psychopathological reactions. *Am. J. Obst. Gynecol.*, 73:305.

Chapter 12

EARLY INFANCY–THE FIRST YEAR

CONCEPT OF DEVELOPMENT

Development is a complex process (Escalona, 1969). The sequential emergence and linear growth of specific capacities is usually referred to as maturation. The totality of full blossoming and multiple, interlocking uses of these functions and skills, brought about by interaction between the individual and his environment, is called development. In this way development is the result of the mutual influences of endowment, maturation, environment, and experiential factors. Human development appears to follow what Erikson calls the epigenetic principle, which, as mentioned earlier, states that anything that grows has a *ground plan* and that out of this plan the *parts* arise, each part having its *time* of special ascendency until all parts have arisen to form a *functioning whole* (Erikson, 1959).

A number of abstract criteria for development have been postulated. There is, first of all, a constant order of succession from one stage to another. Each successive stage in normal development represents an advance from the previous stage. Moreover, each later stage supersedes all earlier stages in that an inferior stage becomes part of a superior stage. The change is qualitative as well as quantitative. Each stage in development is hypothesized as involving progressive structuralization of the psychic apparatus (see page 147). Development can be viewed as a whole or as a sector of the whole, such as "cognitive development." There is, lastly, an inevitable thrust toward development, given an environment that is nurturing and appropriately stimulating.

CRITICAL PERIOD

Implicit in the stage concept of theories of human development is the concept of the "critical periods," analogous to the critical period in embryogenesis, during which certain organs are irreversibly laid down at specific times and cannot be formed at other times. In a broad general way there seem to be critical periods in psychological development; for example, the first two years seem to be important for the development of the capacity to form relationships. However, attempts at greater specificity for the concept of critical periods have run into difficulties because of the multiple variables involved in the development of any given function, the unitary functioning of the individual as a whole, and the possibilities for at least partial reversibility. For example, it had once been postulated that if a child does not learn to read during the critical formative school years he will have difficulty in learning to read at a later date. To some extent this postulate is true. However, the important emphasis here is in the ease of learning to read. Some illiterate adults inducted into the Armed Services have been taught to read although not to read well. Moreover, the factors resulting in adult illiteracy are multiple. Lastly, the critical period, if any, for learning to read may extend over a long period of time, so that even illiteracy of long duration may give way to the capacity to read if the conditions change.

The difficulties involved in the irreversibility aspect of the concept of the critical period, as well as the multiple factors that are usually at work, have led to a modification of the concept to one in which the individual will, say, achieve or learn some things better, faster, or with less training at some times in his life cycle than at others. This modification has been called the concept of the sensitive period (Wolff and Feinbloom, 1969). Few functions exist in pure isolation, and most clinical phenomena have multiple determinants. For example, stimulus deprivation, somatic injury, malnutrition, and other factors at work during the sensitive period of the early years may produce as an end result a child who has failed to thrive and who appears to be arrested at a retarded level. Yet, it is still often difficult to assess the relative contribution of each of these antecedent factors, and usually impossible to say whether the function that appears to be affected (e.g., intellectual development) is affected critically or irreversibly.

The concept of a critical period may still be useful, however, particularly in very early development, when irreversibility may indeed be a factor. Perhaps the best example of the use of the critical period concept is in the studies of early separation of mother and child, when irreversibility is a strong possibility. For example, Spitz (1945), using the baby tests worked out by Hetzer and Wolf (1928), essentially studied 130 children, 61 in a foundling home and 69 in a nursery. The significant differences between the two institutions were as follows: the foundling home had few toys, the children were isolated and virtually screened from the world; they lay supine in the hollow of their mattresses, and they lacked all human contact for most of the day, particularly from the age of 3 months onward. The nursery, on the other hand, provided each child with a mother who gave, and continued to give, the child everything a good mother has to give.

Spitz found that the Developmental Quotient of children in the foundling home dropped from 124 to 72 by the end of the first year of life, and the children showed seriously decreased resistance to disease and an appallingly high mortality. Children in the nursery gained slightly in their Developmental Quotient (101.5 to 105 by the end of the first year of life).

The rapid decline in the development of children in the foundling home occurred at approximately the same time that they were weaned, i.e., between their third and fourth months. At this time, even the human contact they had during nursing stopped. Their perceptual world was emptied of human partners. All the other kinds of deprivation could be compensated for by adequate mother-child relations, the very stimulation the foundling home children lacked.

Spitz concluded that it was the deprivation of maternal care, maternal stimulation, and maternal love that produced the clear evidence of damage to the foundling home infants, and that even when put in a more favorable environment after age 15 months, the psychosomatic damage could not be repaired by normal measures (Spitz, 1946). That is to say, the absence of adequate mothering during this critical period of development to all intents and purposes led to irreversible damage.

It would appear that this study supports the concept of a critical period. However, Spitz himself was also careful to state that "whether it [the psychosomatic damage] can be repaired by therapeutic measures remains to be investigated." The qualifications of degree of irreversibility and extent of therapeutic intervention therefore are further considerations in the definition of the concept of critical period.

This study was important also because it was one of the first to document the role of maternal deprivation in the etiology of childhood disorders. Since that time the concept of maternal deprivation has undergone much revision and refinement. For example, Langmeir and Matejeck (1975) have listed at least four major types of deprivation:

1. Stimulus deprivation, in which there is a lack of sensory and motor stimulation, particularly in the earliest stages of life.
2. Cognitive deprivation, in which the environment fails to provide sufficient structure, organization, and reasonable predictability of events, making it difficult for the child to make sense out of his or her experiences, particularly in terms of his or her behavior and the response from the environment.
3. Attachment deprivation, in which there is a failure of the reliable presence and responsiveness of a person to whom the child can focus his perceptual, cognitive and affective activities; this failure leads to a failure to become attached.
4. Social deprivation, in which the absence of adequate socialization experiences gives rise to a series of impairments, including learning difficulties, a deformed value system, and an impaired facility for the performance of social functions and roles.

Rutter (1972), too, clarified the findings relating to maternal deprivation to the point that the global term should no longer be used. Instead, the effects of varying degrees, duration and reasons for separation and loss, must be assessed in the context of many other variables. These variables include the child's stage of development, experiences with brief, incremental, and happy separations, degree of attachment attained, experiences with frightening medical procedures, lack of toys or play opportunities, experiences with unfamiliar and/or unsympathetic staff or parents, and inadequate preparation and the child's having parents who have psychiatric disturbances. Overt parental discord involving the child over a considerable period of time, parental psychiatric disturbance, and the degree of attachment formed are perhaps the most important variables.

A further example of the concept of a critical period can be seen in the special case of gender identification arising out of the development of object relations. Gender identification is generally irreversibly established by 2½ years of age. Wrong assignment of sex in the case of infants with intersex problems cannot usually be changed after that age (see p. 176).

With these concepts in mind, development will be described here from the standpoints of biological maturation, personality development, cognitive development, and psychosocial development.

MATURATION

One of the great services Arnold Gesell did for pediatrics was to document in an orderly and detailed manner the sequence of skills that can be observed in a child as he advances in age (see Note 18). His work was avidly seized upon by pediatricians eager to reassure mothers that their children were normal. Unfortunately, the details of each step of maturation were sometimes taken as inviolable. The development of the child came to be viewed by some as an unfolding flower that only had to be watered and fed. Further, the precision with which each detail of any given stage was regarded in this viewpoint was unwarranted since it did not take into account the enormous variation from child to child at any given age, and from time to time in a given child. And, of course, it did not completely answer the question of why a child behaved as he did, and what factors influenced his behavior. That is to say, questions of motivation and stimulation in the context of the interaction between the child and his or her environment were largely sidestepped.

Nevertheless, important general sequences and milestones were described for the normal child, in a normal environment, and these are well worth noting.

Motor Sequence

Gesell and Amatruda (1941) observed that most children creep, can be pulled to their feet, and have a crude prehensory release by the time they are 10 months old. Within the next 2 months, they can walk with help, and can prehend a small pellet. By 2 years of age they are running with ease, although not with great skill.

Adaptive Sequence

Similarly, by 10 months of age a child can bring two cubes together as if to compare them and by 12 months can release a cube in a cup. By 2 years of age, a child can build a tower of six cubes and can imitate a circular motion with a crayon on paper.

Language Sequence

The sequence of emergence of actual sounds is broadly the same in all children everywhere (Lewis, 1963). Children vocalize. and respond to sounds from birth, possibly even prenatally. The child can be soothed specifically by the voice of his mother as early as the first few weeks. The early phonetic characteristics of discomfort-cries of the infant appear to be the vocal manifestations of his total reaction to discomfort, determined in part by the physiological contraction of his facial muscles. By about the sixth week, the infant begins to utter repetitive strings of sound called babbling. In doing so, he or she finds satisfaction in producing at will those sounds which at first have occurred involuntarily, acquires skill in making sounds, and imitates as best he can the sounds of others. The nearer the approximation of his sounds to those of the parents, the more marked will be his parents' approval of him, and the greater will be the infant's incentive to repeat sounds. In this way the child acquires the phonetic pattern of his mother tongue. What is important here is that in these earliest weeks the frequency and variety of sounds already may be restricted through inadequate fostering by the caring adult. A full account of how children learn to speak has been described by Lewis (1959).

At 5 months most infants can discriminate "p" from "t," "b" from "g," and "i" from "a," and by 12 months can discriminate and respond differently to differences in tone, vocabulary, and the person who is speaking.

At 10 months most children heed their name when called and usually understand certain simple commands (although these responses may have more to do with the tone with which the command is said than with the word itself). Often the child can say a word, as well as say "Ma-ma" and "Da-da." Most children say their first words by the end of the first year. More words are added, until by age 2 years a child usually has two sentences and can say "I." Two-thirds of children begin to use phrases by age 2 (Morley, 1965). By age 2, an average child can understand several hundred words (language comprehension usually precedes language production) and use about 200 (Rutter and Bax, 1972). Nouns are used before verbs.

Personal-Social Development

A 10-month-old child can feed himself a cracker (sloppily) and play "peek-a-boo," "pat-a-cake," and "so-big." By 12 months of age he is finger feeding and somewhat cooperative in dressing. By 2 years of age he is able to verbalize his toileting needs. He is also playing with elementary jigsaw puzzles, balls, and pull toys. He is picking things up, throwing them down, and imitating others.

ROLE OF ACTIVITY

It is important to keep in mind, however, that while the sequence just outlined is accurate, the timetable is immensely variable. Moreover, the child contributes to his own velocity of development. First of all, children start off with different innate capacities; some are active, some quiet, and some highly unpredictable. Fries attempted to classify children into various congenital activity types, suggesting that there was a continuity of a general activity level for given individuals (Fries and Woolf, 1953). Thomas et al. (1963) in their New York study, developed nine categories of behavioral style that were consistent for the individual infant (see p. 246). More significant is that the infant's level of activity is an important determinant of his development. Babies who are constitutionally very active and mobile appear to suffer less from a period of understimulation during a hospital stay than do less active babies (Schaffer, 1966).

Some children by temperament are irritable and slow to adapt to novel circumstances, and others adapt readily to changes in the environment (Thomas et al., 1968). These characteristics interact with parental attributes. An important aspect of parenting is the parents' ability to understand the infant's cues (Bell and Ainsworth, 1972). Some parents prefer an active, alert child, while others prefer a quiet, passive child (Rutter, 1976). The possible combinations for mutual enhancements or mutual disharmonies are multiple, and these interactions change in time and according to different circumstances. Later in development, the interaction between equipment factors, including motor activity and sensitivity to discomfort on the one hand, and environmental factors, including stimulation and the ability to soothe the infant on the other hand, subtly contribute to the infant's identification processes (Ritvo and Solnit, 1958).

INFLUENCE OF THE INFANT ON THE MOTHER

Maternal behavior seems to be under the control of the stimulus-and-reinforcing conditions provided by the young infant in such a way that at first the mother's behavior is shaped by the infant's behavior. This phenomenon then affects how the mother shapes the infant's behavior (Moss, 1967). For example, eye-to-eye contact seems to serve to foster positive feelings in the mother (Robson, 1967). These feelings in the mother have something to do with her "being recognized" in a highly personal and intimate way, and it is perhaps for this reason that mothers of blind children often feel rebuffed at first by their infants. Again, Bowlby (1958) believes that the smiling of an infant acts as a social releaser of instinctual responses in the mother, along with such other innate "releasers" as crying, following, clinging, and sucking. Lorenz (1966) has gone so far as to suggest that the human smile is also a ritualized form of aggression comparable to the "greeting" ceremonies that inhibit intraspecific fighting in many lower animals.

In effect, infant and parent constitute a dyad, in the context of which development occurs (Schaffer, 1977). Increasingly, recognition is being given to this dyad in developmental studies concerned with language development (Nelson, 1977), visual behavior (Stern, 1974), attention (Collins and Schaffer, 1975), and problem-solving (Kaye, 1976).

ROLE OF STIMULATION

At the same time, the amount and kind of stimulation a child receives greatly affects the degree of development and use of any particular skill that may appear on schedule and in its rudimentary form. The amount of stimulation provided by the adults is one of the major determinants of the infant's behavior (Schaffer and Emerson, 1964).

Stimulation and Language Development

Specific stimulation for language development mentioned earlier is a case in point. In a study of 75 family-reared children and 75 institutionalized infants, Provence and Lipton (1962) observed that the response of the parent contributes to the process of differentiation in the infant's mental functioning. The parent's repetition, labeling, and responses to the infant's reactions to his environment, to the infant's feelings, and to the infant's vocalizations are important to the infant's recognition of himself, other persons, and his world. Further, responses from others are essential to the child's development of meaningful speech. For example, one of the ways in which the mother appears to influence the development of speech is through a process of "mutual imitation." Moreover, the mother's speech is "both a carrier of the emotions and an organizing influence on the infant's mental apparatus." The mother, through her way of responding to the infant in action, and especially in speech, identifies or "labels" many things for the infant (e.g., people, toys, himself, his feelings and actions, and the feelings and actions of others). The infant comes to be able to identify many aspects of inner and outer reality because the mother provides the appropriate experiences.

On the other hand, for the institutionalized infant who is placed in a family at the end of the first year, there is a much later period when the speech is predominantly used to express a need or to repeat in a literal way some phrase or sentence learned by rote or from imitation of the parent: ". . . it takes much longer before the [institutionalized] children verbalize their fantasies, comment upon their play, ask questions that express a wish to learn about things or talk about feelings. . . . In these [institutionalized] children one can demonstrate on the tests during and after the second year a greater facility in the aspects of language that represents a concreteness of thought (e.g., ability to name objects or pictures) than in some of the speech that reflects a capacity for more abstract and flexible thought." The institutionalized child's understanding of the adult's language is also retarded.

Stimulation and Visual Activity

Another specific stimulus that enhances development is the increased visual attention that comes about after extra handling of institutionalized infants (White and Held, 1966). Korner and Grobstein (1966) have also observed that when a crying newborn is picked up and put to the shoulder, there is an increase in the frequency of eye opening, alertness, and scanning, as well as the obvious soothing effect. Calibration of the degree of attention to both visual and auditory stimulation in the newborn is achieved by using changes in the heart rate, motor responsivity, and other measurable responses (Lewis et al., 1966).

NEEDS OF THE INFANT

Clearly, the infant responds to an internal environment as well as to an external one. Initially, the infant's internal life appears to consist of felt needs. These needs seem to fall into two categories, immediate needs and long-range needs. The immediate needs are for the relief of hunger and discomfort, for sleep, and to suck. The infant appears to have little if any tolerance if these needs are unsatisfied.

The infant's long-range needs are for the warmth and security of a mothering person, adequate stimulation (an infant needs to be talked to), and graduated performance expectations. While the infant may appear to have greater tolerance if any of these long-range needs are not met, serious character defects may appear later as a result of significant early deprivation in any of these areas.

SLEEP

Sleep in the infant has certain interesting characteristics. During the first few weeks of life, the infant sleeps two-thirds of the time, for approximately 50-minute periods. This sleep of the infant may represent a third state of being inasmuch as a major proportion of his sleep appears to be so-called "rapid eye movement (REM) sleep." The phenomenon of rapid eye movement associated with the periodic low voltage phase that occurs in a regular electroencephalographic sleep cycle was first described by Aserinsky and Kleitman (1953). This phase of sleep appeared to have a periodicity in adults of 90 minutes and to last about 20 minutes. When adult subjects were awakened during this phase of REM sleep, a high incidence of dream recall was noted. Aserinsky and Kleitman postulated (1) a special inhibiting mechanism that blocked all motor movement except those of the eye and middle ear muscles and (2) occasional brief muscle twitches. When REM sleep was interrupted and the subject was deprived of REM sleep, there followed an increase in the number of times REM sleep appeared, an increase in the actual amount of REM sleep, and an increase in the size and duration of the twitches. There was also a shift toward hyperexcitability in the behavior of the subject. Anxiety seems to be a naturally occurring phenomenon that possibly suppresses REM sleep.

The curious fact is that the infant seems to spend much of his sleep in the REM state (Dreyfus-Brisac et al., 1958) at a time in his life when there is unlikely to be much content to his dreams, if indeed he dreams at all. A 10-week premature infant spends about 80% of his sleeping time in the REM state, and a full-term infant spends about 50% of his sleeping time in the REM state. Thereafter, there is a steady decline in the percentage of sleep spent in the REM state, to the extent that at the end of the first year it is down to 35%, and by 5 years of age it is only 20%. A shift toward a night pattern of sleeping occurs at about 16 weeks of age, although the infant at this state is still rarely awake for more than 3 hours at a time (Parmelee et al., 1964). A plausible hypothesis is that this REM state is regulated by as yet unknown biochemical mechanisms, and may well have important basic survival functions prior to any consequent hypothesized functions of dreaming. Whatever the function of REM sleep, an adequate amount of it appears to be an important need of the infant.

Full-term infants switch from active REM sleep to quiet REM sleep about every 50 to 60 minutes, and neonates have a sleep–wake cycle of about 3 to 4 hours. During the first year, prolongations of daytime wakeful periods and night-time sleep periods occur, culminating in a true diurnal rhythm by about 4 years of age (Anders, 1978). Interestingly, active REM sleep and quiet NREM sleep rhythms seem to be determined by constitution (Ellingson, 1975), while sleep–wake rhythms seem to be more culturally determined.

Modes of Need Satisfaction

Most of the needs mentioned earlier are met within the mutual adaptation that occurs between the infant, who is born with a certain degree of preadaptiveness (Hartmann, 1939), and the "ordinary devoted mother" (Winnicott, 1945), who creates a sense of "basic" trust in her child. This sense of trust is engendered by the mother's appropriate and reliable response to her sensitive and accurate perception of the baby's needs (Erikson, 1959; see Note 19). Furthermore, for the first year or two, the greatest exchange and intimacy occur when the child is being fed, in coincidence with the primacy of the buccal mucosa as the organ of greatest sensitivity. However, there are other equally important modes of exchange and gratification that should not be neglected during this early period. These modes include visual, auditory, tactile, and kinesthetic stimulation.

Signs of Unmet Needs

If the needs of the infant just discussed are not met soon, signs of acute tension appear. And if there is a chronic deficiency of need fulfillment, signs of a disorder of development appear. The signs of acute tension in early infancy are diffuse; they may be restlessness, fretfulness, whining, crying, clinging, physical tenseness, and various visceral dysfunctions, such as vomiting or diarrhea, or a sleep disturbance. The extent and duration of the deprivation are significant factors. For example, weaning that is attempted too early or is done too abruptly may cause acute anxiety in the child.

More prolonged deprivations of one or more of the need-satisfying experiences at this stage may influence the development of the child in the direction of a personality that remains clinging and dependent, or that craves food and drink to console himself in times of stress, or that strives aggressively to win love, or that is chronically envious. Inconsistent gratifications may influence the child in the direction of an untrusting personality. Massive chronic early deprivation is found in children who develop the syndrome of "affectionless characters" (Bowlby, 1951; see Note 20) or "failure to thrive" (Leonard et al., 1966), or, in some children, failure to grow in height. Complete loss of the mother in the second half of the first year without any replacement mothering gives rise to the syndrome of "anaclitic depression," the chief symptoms of which are a dejected expression and a reluctance for motility (Spitz, 1946).

EARLY PERSONALITY DEVELOPMENT AND THE SENSE OF SELF

What has been said so far implies that the rudiments of the personality are present in the earliest period of life and that the development of the personality arises, in part, from the body and its needs. The following paragraphs examine further the process by which the personality develops.

The infant's body is an obvious source of gratification as well as of discomfort for him. The infant actively touches his or her body frequently, at first through random movement and then through intentional action; for example, the infant puts his thumb or finger in his mouth, sometimes as early as age 3 to 6 weeks. (Reflex thumbsucking occurs in the fetus in utero.) Furthermore, he or she passively receives body comforts of a rich variety as he or she is fed, burped, diapered, cuddled, or whirled in the air. Indeed, the infant appears initially to perceive his environment only to the extent that it alters his body. Fingers and mouth are important at this stage. In his early months, the infant initially does not appear to discriminate between his own fingers and those of others, his own mouth and that of his mother. (Sometimes the infant puts food into his mother's mouth instead of his own, an action that is often mistaken as a sign of altruism or generosity.) Further, an external object exists for the infant (if it exists for him at all) only as long as it gratifies a need. To the extent that the external environment and his internal life are as one to the infant, the infant is said by psychoanalysts to be in a state of "primary identification" (S. Freud, 1923). To the extent also that the infant is oblivious of the external world, the infant is said by some to be in a normal "autistic" state (Mahler, 1968). The infant then gradually perceives, say, the mother's face although it is unlikely that his image of it is well formed initially. The image of the mother's face probably comes to be associated in the infant's mind with the need-fulfilling properties he attributes to the perceived mother. In psychoanalysis this stage is called the need-fulfilling (or part-object) stage of object relations. (The development of the infant's relationships with others will be discussed again shortly.)

ORIGINS OF REALITY TESTING

The infant sooner or later discerns that some stimuli and sources of gratification can only come from the outside, indicating that he is beginning to make a distinction between stimuli that come from within and stimuli that come from the outside. He or she is engaged in what is called reality testing. The function of reality testing is continually reinforced by the infant's widening experience that some things are present and some are not (experience the infant gains in peek-a-boo games) and that some feelings can be made to go away, others cannot. That is to say, the infant is becoming increasingly aware of the boundaries between himself and the external world and in doing so is becoming aware of himself as a separate person. By 9 months of age, the infant probably has attained a rudimentary sense of self (Lewis and Brooks, 1976).

DEVELOPMENT OF OBJECT RELATIONS

Pattern recognition in the 3- to 6-month-old infant can be demonstrated by the fact that the infant smiles when he or she is shown a face mask that consists of a forehead, eyes, and a nose in motion (the motion distinguishes the features from the background) (Spitz, 1965; see Note 21). During this earliest period, when the infant probably does not as yet have a full image of one particular face, he is said by psychoanalysts to be at the preobject, or part-object, stage of relations (Spitz, 1965). Feature perception begins virtually at birth, and it is a complicated process. Investigations of the looking patterns of newborns, for example, suggest that infants may be able at birth to analyze extensive visual information in selected, organized ways (Kessen, 1967; Kessen and Bornstein, 1978).

STRANGER ANXIETY

By the second half of the first year there are clear signs that the infant is now aware of a person as a whole object. He or she begins to imitate the other person and to show signs of anxiety when he is confronted with a person who is unfamiliar to him ("stranger anxiety"). This phenomenon was first described by Baldwin (1895), who called it organic bashfulness, and it has since then been the subject of continuous study (Rheingold, 1968; Sroufe, 1977). It is most prominent at about 8 months of age. Several inferences may be drawn from this phenomenon. First, since the infant can now differentiate between his mother's face and that of a stranger, he must by now have a better defined mental image of his mother—and one that he can also retain; i.e., he clearly can use the function of memory. Recognition of facial representations between 5 and 7 months of age has been well documented (Fagan, 1979). Furthermore, the infant has clearly endowed that mental representation with certain attributes (e.g., security giving). These attributes, while first bestowed on the external object (the mother), must by now be a part of the more or less constant internalized mental representation of the mother. Kagan (1971) more recently has offered a discrepancy hypothesis to account for stranger anxiety. In its most general terms, the hypothesis states that an event (such as the presentation of a stranger) that activates existing structures (the schema of a known person) but which cannot be assimilated to them creates arousal. If the discrepancy and the arousal are too great because of a failure of assimilation and accommodation, negative affect will occur.

EARLY OBJECT RELATIONS AND OBJECT CONSTANCY

The fact that the infant now begins to relate to people as people—and not simply as "need-fulfilling objects"—is a further step in the development of his or her capacity for object relations. Moreover, the infant increasingly experiences the external object (the person) as being quite firmly separate from himself. And, as already stated, the infant is now able to retain in his memory a constant image of this other person. At this point the infant is said to have reached, but not yet fully consolidated, what psychoanalysts call the stage of object constancy (see p. 176).

EARLY DEFENSE MECHANISMS

The infant appears now to have also exercised at least two further processes, or mechanisms: (1) projection of an internal state onto an external object and (2) introjection of that projected attribute to form an internalized mental object. These two mechanisms may form the earliest "defense mechanisms" (S. Freud, 1926) the infant uses to deal with anxiety.

All these functions—the sense of self, the capacity to form relationships, the ability to test reality, and the use of defense mechanisms—are relatively enduring and autonomous, and in psychoanalytic theory they are referred to as psychic "structures" and are subsumed under the general heading of "ego functions." These terms, however, are essentially metaphors, and much misunderstanding arises when they are used concretely. It is rarely necessary to use them in either practical infant psychiatry or early infant development research. They are theoretical abstractions, or, as Freud (1926) put it, they comprise "the whole of our artificial structure of hypotheses" (p. 231).

BEGINNING OF THOUGHT

At the same time that the functions just discussed are developing, the signs of early cognitive development can be discerned. In the first month of life, the infant seems to exercise a function simply because it is there, but he shows few signs of coordinated activity. The infant learns to recognize the nipple, but he cannot coordinate his head and his hand when his thumb falls out of his mouth. Although he seems to be a sucking, looking, listening, and grasping individual, it is impossible to know what he is aware of. In psychoanalytic theory, the infant is said to be in a state of "primary repression," in the sense that there is no evidence yet of conscious thought. However, within a few months the infant finds that a chance action leads to a pleasurable experience, and the pleasurable experience may act as one of the earliest stimuli to repeat the action—in what Piaget calls a "primary circular reaction" (Piaget, 1952). Thus there is now evidence of thinking, and it would appear that motor activity is one of the primary sources from which thinking develops. Piaget has put heavy emphasis on the necessity of action for cognitive growth.

The first 8 months or so are particularly important from the point of view of later perceptive and intellectual development, since it is during this period that the child lays the foundations of his cognitive structures. The actual process by which reality data are treated or modified so as to become incorporated into the psychic structure is just as important as any intrinsic connections in the external stimuli, since the infant becomes aware of these intrinsic connections only to the extent that he can assimilate them by means of his existing schema or structures. The basic cognitive structure in Piaget's account of cognitive development is, in fact, the "schema." A particular object in the environment arouses a behavior pattern, or schema, in the child. This schema is then applied to an increasing variety of objects. New objects that are similar to the first object become "assimilated" into the existing schema.

THUMB SUCKING

Take once more the phenomenon of thumb sucking, this time looking at it from the cognitive viewpoint. Fortuitous or reflex thumb sucking may occur in the prenatal period. However, sometimes as early as the second month a more "systematic" thumb sucking occurs. It involves the coordination of hand and mouth and so indicates an assimilation with a previously existing schema of the breast or the nipple. In other words, the infant's previous sucking experience (the schema of, say, the nipple) is now broadened to include a new but similar experience—the thumb. The thumb or, more specifically, the new motor act of bringing the thumb into the mouth and the new sensory experience of the thumb, have now been assimilated into the existing schema with which it was initially matched.

If the new aspect of the environment encountered is too

dissimilar from the existing schema, the existing schema in turn "accommodates;" that is, the existing schema is modified. For example, an infant encounters an animal which he calls "doggie." The schema subsumed under the concept doggie will, for a while, assimilate all new and similar animals, and the infant will for a while call all animals doggie. Eventually an encounter with an animal that is sufficiently different will stimulate the child to modify his schema of doggie. The new schema will have "doggie" as a more specific concept, and animals other than dogs will be subsumed under different names. This modification of the schema is what Piaget means by accommodation. Assimilation and accommodation are reciprocal mental operations.

It is important to note that Piaget's account of cognitive development is based on the interaction between the individual and his environment; it is not a theory of simple innate maturation, nor does it follow a simple stimulus-contingency model. As a matter of fact, Piaget's theory grew out of his study of the reasoning process that underlay the wrong answers children gave to test questions. (Piaget was attempting to standardize Cyril Burt's tests of children in Binet's Laboratory School in Paris, where he had gone in 1917 at the age of 21 following his study of psychiatry at the Burghölzli Hospital in Zurich.) It was then that cognitive structure was first studied as an internal organization of patterns of thought, fulfilling the abstract criteria of development previously mentioned.

Some time during age 6 to 12 months, the infant enters what Piaget calls the substage of secondary circular reactions, when the infant begins to alter his environment intentionally to satisfy a need. He will, for example, shake a crib to produce movement in a mobile suspended above him. But the infant may also believe that any other movement he observes while shaking the crib is the result of his action. Moreover, he seems to believe that the very existence of objects, and their movements, is entirely dependent on his actions and his perceptions. What the infant at this stage cannot see does not exist for him.

The qualitative cognitive change that occurs in the evolution of secondary circular reactions may also be associated with neurophysiological changes in the brain. Thus the change from primary to secondary circular reactions may be related to the way in which the slow delta activity seen in the EEG is interspersed with faster activity (Walter, 1956).

Toward the end of the infant's first year, an increasing coordination of schemas can be observed, and the child begins to be aware of the existence of unperceived objects. He may knock down a screen to get at a hidden toy, and he seems to behave as though he is aware that objects can be moved by external forces. Moreover, he now begins to explore an object more fully, and the beginnings of an experimental approach can be seen, with the appearance of so-called tertiary circular reactions (see Note 22). In his reactions the child will seek or create new situations to which he can react. He is learning about spatial relations, and he starts putting smaller objects into and taking them out of larger objects. However, the infant is not yet able to understand (for example) that he has to rotate a long toy through a right angle in order to pull it through the bars of a playpen; he will try to pull it through as it is. Curiously, it appears that perception often, if not usually, precedes action, at least after the foundations of the initial schemas have been laid. For example, a child often can discriminate sounds before he can articulate them (Berko and Brown, 1960) and can distinguish forms long before he can draw them (Ling, 1941).

Psychoanalysis is weak in regard to its theory of cognitive development. Essentially, two concepts are described: primary process thinking and secondary process thinking. Early primary process thinking is characterized by virtually no capacity to delay the urge for immediate gratification of a need, rapid shifting from activity to activity in search of gratification (e.g., crying, thumb sucking, mouthing, and tongue protruding when trying to gratify hunger) and by the use of such preverbal processes as visual and auditory impressions. Primary process thinking is still prominent in the first year of life. However, the infant begins to use language and exhibits a form of logic and then develops an increased capacity to tolerate delay and frustration. This subsequent form of thinking is referred to as secondary process.

INFANTILE FANTASY LIFE

Just exactly what goes on in the infant's mind during the first 6 months is not known. It *looks* as though the infant is engaged in an active fantasy life, and narrative evidence gathered during psychoanalyses of adults has led to *inferences* that this fantasy life has certain general characteristics. However, one has no direct access to the infant's thoughts at this stage, and any attempt at description is limited by (1) the boundaries of direct observation of infantile behavior, (2) the inferential nature of reconstruction from material derived from adult and child analyses, (3) the impossibility of recapturing a pure preverbal state, and (4) the handicap of sophisticated adult language.

Nevertheless, the urge to understand the infant has led to speculations about his early fantasy life. For example, Klein (1960) has suggested that in the first 3 or 4 months of life the infant is filled with fantasies of his omnipotence. These fantasies are fostered by the repeated gratifications that follow the infant's active demands. For example, when the infant screams with hunger, a nipple is immediately and consistently placed in his mouth. At the same time, the infant is thought to experience every discomfort as inflicted by the outside, as though the infant were being persecuted. This attack gives rise to anxiety (Klein calls it persecutory anxiety). Further consequences of the fantasy of being persecuted include the creation and the welling-up of revengeful, destructive fantasies. Since the infant values highly what he also perceives to be an attacking object (the nipple or the breast), he strives to "preserve" his source of gratification. He is said to accomplish this by splitting off his feelings of love from his feelings of hate. Some of the hate, which was first projected into the breast, is now turned inward and introjected in an effort to conserve an "ideal breast." The infant retains a feeling of gratitude, but he sometimes experiences envy and he often experiences greed. Klein calls this whole speculative complex the paranoid-schizoid position.

Klein postulates that at about 5 or 6 months of age, the infant becomes aware of and concerned about the harm his destructive impulses (some of which have been turned inward) and his enormous greed might do, and this fear gives rise to a depressive anxiety, the so-called depressive position. The infant then tries to placate his mother and to make reparations by trying to please her.

INFANTILE ANXIETY

What can be said with less speculation and more certainty are that the infant appears to manifest signs of tension or anxiety and that the most common anxiety-evoking situation during the first 18 months is the threat of losing the mother. Anxiety initially seems to develop automatically whenever the infant is overwhelmed by internal or external stimuli that he cannot master or discharge. As the infant develops, anxiety is produced in anticipation of such a danger. This anticipatory anxiety seems to act as a signal to activate whatever mechanisms are available to the infant to reduce the danger. The advantage of signal anxiety over automatic anxiety is that signal anxiety is less massive, does not incapacitate, and is far more economical and adaptive than is automatic anxiety.

CHILD-REARING PRACTICES

The findings and concepts just described have significance for normal child-rearing practices and for the understanding of certain pathological states. One of the goals of normal child rearing, for example, is the development of a strong personality. Some of the factors that contribute to this development may be derived from a knowledge of child development. Thus each of the functions mentioned earlier (p. 147) requires specific conditions for its optimum development. A few of the minimal requirements are discussed in the following paragraphs.

The development of the sense of self requires consistent and gratifying responses from the adult, appropriate labeling of feelings and body parts, opportunities for body play and exploration, stimulation from the environment, and protection from overwhelming anxiety.

The development of the capacity for relationships requires the reliable presence of a mother or mothering person who perceives and responds to the infant's needs in an appropriate manner. The term reliable presence implies at the very least the absence of prolonged separations, especially during the critical period of attachment that becomes prominent from age 6 to 12 months of life and proceeds to object constancy from about age 8 months to 3 or 4 . Prolonged separation may still be a hazard after that age, but it is less likely to cripple the development of relationships as severely as does separation during these early years. The term reliable presence also implies continuity of care, affection, and appropriate responsiveness.

The notion of the mother's perceiving and responding in an appropriate manner should not be construed as meaning that the mother must understand every need of her child precisely and meet each need exactly. This would be impossible and, in any case, would not promote development. The child learns what his needs are through the mother's approximate responses, and he learns also to tolerate minor frustrations through the mother's unavoidably inexact or incomplete responses. However, the notion does imply that the mother protects the child from intolerable unpleasantness and anxiety and responds with appropriate measures to meet most of the child's needs. Thus if the child is crying from hunger, he is fed, and if he is crying because of physical discomfort, he may require diapering.

The development of the ability to test reality requires an environment that labels events correctly for the child, that provides the child with appropriate visual, auditory, tactile, and kinesthetic stimulation, and that reasonably gratifies the child.

The development of the capacity to tolerate frustrations and, later, to mobilize defenses against anxiety depends in part on the kind and degree of frustration to which the child is exposed. Frustration experiences within the infant's current capacity for delay can be increasingly tolerated. Frustration that is real and rational, and not created artificially, is better tolerated by the infant, and also facilitates reality testing. Since the infant may interpret reality frustrations as hostile attacks upon him, explanations of the actuality of the frustration may minimize the tendency to form such frightening fantasies; may reduce the anxiety that such fantasies arouse; and may promote the use of secondary process logic in dealing with anxiety. However, the young child usually requires additional support when the frustration exceeds the child's tolerance. For example, if separation from mother is for too long a period of time, a substitute mothering person or aspects of the mother are required.

The findings and concepts described earlier are also helpful in understanding certain pathological states. For example, sometimes there is an intrinsic internal failure to make meaningful patterns out of sensory stimuli, with a consequent handicap in dealing with the demands of the environment. The condition of infantile autism is an extreme example of this kind of failure, although other forms of pervasive developmental disorders have been described.

INFANTILE AUTISM

The syndrome of infantile autism, which was first described by Kanner (1943), occurs in about 4 or 5 children per 10,000, with boys affected three or four times as often as girls (Lotter, 1966). The onset is almost always before age 30 months, and in many cases the condition can be diagnosed within the first year of life. At first the child may appear to have reached normal developmental milestones, at least grossly. However, closer observation may reveal that speech either is not developing at all or is replete with such disorders as echolalia, disordered naming, fragmentation, pronominal reversal, and portmanteauisms. The child may also show difficulty in developing such normal routines as sleeping, feeding, and eliminating. He has an inordinate desire for sameness. The child may also show no anticipatory or adaptive posturing, seem unresponsive, and avoid looking others straight in the eye. He shows failure of attachment. He often seems happiest when left alone or when whirled. Furthermore, he has a preference for inanimate things and lacks empathy. He may strum his fingers toward the periphery of his gaze, but he is not blind. He may ignore loud sounds, but he is not deaf. Sometimes he is excessively quiet; at other times he screams, rocks, and bangs his head. Autistic children often show a special kind of defective cognitive development, and those who are significantly mentally retarded develop seizures more often than do children who are of normal intelligence. The cognitive defect involves language ability, information processing, and temporal sequencing. A comprehensive definition of the syndrome of autism has been given by the National Society for Autistic Children (Ritvo and Freeman, 1978).

The likelihood is high that a basic brain abnormality is present (Wing, 1966; Rutter, 1977; Rutter and Schopler, 1978). Evidence of a genetic factor in some cases of autism is suggested by Folstein and Rutter's (1977) finding that more than one third of the monozygotic twins they studied were concordant for autism, whereas none of the dizygotic twins they studied were concordant for autism. Signs of brain damage or organic abnormalities are found with a greater frequency among autistic children than among normal children, and the characteristic perceptual, language, and speech difficulties seem to be specific to autism.

In many cases of autism, there have been complications during pregnancy. At the same time, no specific biological markers or biochemical abnormalities have been identified (Ritvo, 1977). No factors in the child's psychological environment have been shown to cause autism. Autism is not caused by a psychiatric disorder or a psychological problem in the parents. However, secondary reactions on the part of parents who have to deal day in and day out with a child who is emotionally draining and unresponsive may complicate the clinical picture.

Unfortunately, the prognosis for autism is guarded (Rutter et al., 1967). Most autistic children have poor outcomes. Fifty percent of one group of 63 autistic children studied remained in full-time residential settings, and 30 out of the same group of 63 remained mute. Only 3 of the 63 who had reached age 9 could be said to function well academically and socially (Eisenberg, 1956). Autistic children with a low IQ do least well. The prognosis is poor for children who have not developed speech by the age of 5. Twenty-eight percent of autistic children develop epileptic fits during adolescence (Rutter, 1970).

OTHER FORMS OF PERVASIVE DEVELOPMENTAL DISORDER

In some children, a state of "unusual sensitivity" has been postulated (Bergman and Escalona, 1949). These children appear to be easily hurt, easily stimulated, and unevenly precocious. The hypothesis is that these children, who are not sufficiently protected from stimuli either because of a "thin protective barrier or because of the failure of maternal protection," may have to resort for such protection to premature "ego" formation. The psychotic manifestations are thought to set in when this premature ego breaks down, possibly as a consequence of a trauma.

Mahler (1952) described a condition she called symbiotic child psychosis, in which the ego regresses to a mechanism, or level of functioning, of symbiosis. Symbiosis, in Mahler's terminology, is essentially a "hallucinatory or delusional somatopsychic *omnipotent* fusion with the representative of the mother and, in particular, the delusion of a common boundary between two physically separate individuals" (Mahler et al., 1975, p. 45). Such children have what Mahler postulates is a severe disturbance of individuation and psychotic disorganization. This condition will be discussed further in the next chapter (See Chapter 13, p. 186).

MATERNAL INSUFFICIENCY

The syndrome of infantile autism is an extreme example of a primary intrinsic failure in the infant's interaction with his environment. On the other hand, a number of other childhood syndromes primarily related to states of acute material insufficiency can also lead to disorders of early development. For example, the failure-to-thrive syndrome in infants and the syndrome of accidental poisoning in childhood are typical results of a breakdown in mothering which may have occurred for a variety of reasons. Certain cases of child abuse fall into this category, as do children who present themselves frequently with injuries, sometimes quite consciously self-inflicted. The resources of the mothers in these families are often markedly depleted, and such mothers often feel unsupported and overwhelmed. Complete absence of any mothering at all of course leads to the syndrome of anaclitic depression, seen in some institutionalized infants.

Failure to thrive in infants may have many causes, one of which is a disturbance in the mother-child relationship (Patton and Gardner, 1962). In one study of 13 infants ranging in age from 10 weeks to 27 months, who had fallen progressively below the third percentile in weight, Leonard et al. (1966) found multiple problems in each of their families. None of the mothers reported receiving dependable and appropriate nurturing during their own childhoods, and many expressed current feelings of inadequacy. The fathers in these families were often absent, uninvolved in family life, and unsupportive. The infants themselves showed a wide range of abnormal behavior, ranging from unusual watchfulness and an unsmiling expression in the youngest infants, through to absence of any stranger anxiety in the 4- to 10-month-old infants, and superficial personal-social relationships in the older infants. Leonard postulated that the selection of the particular child who failed to thrive might have been brought about by multiple factors, including the psychological impact upon the mother of the complications of pregnancy that frequently occurred, the dissonance between the infant's temperament and the mother's personality, and the added burden that the infant represented to an already depleted mother. All of these factors contain a component that represents the infant's role in shaping the very environmental factors that are so detrimental to his own development. What is of further interest in this study is the view of motherhood as an unfolding developmental plan which is activated by pregnancy and the birth of a child. The mothers in this study fell into the category of what Anna Freud has called "unwilling mothers" (A. Freud, 1955), although this alone did not answer the question of exactly which are the most significant psychological factors that interfere with the normal, mutual thriving of mother and infant.

SOCIAL DEPRIVATION

Maternal deprivation, itself a complex concept (see Rutter, 1972), must also be seen in its social context. It has long been known that mothers in the lower socioeconomic bracket have an increased incidence of complications of pregnancy and birth

(Baird, 1959; Drillien, 1959). Indeed, in some respects the disparity between the risks for the disadvantaged and the advantaged appears to be increasing over the years. For example, in the United States in 1930 twice as many nonwhite mothers died in childbirth as did white mothers; by 1960, four times as many nonwhite mothers died in childbirth as did white mothers (Baumgartner, 1965). The risks consequent upon the increased incidence of complications of pregnancy and labor (themselves due to multiple causes), and the increased incidence of postnatal pathology (such as iron deficiency anemia), expose infants who are economically and socially disadvantaged or who are in an ethnic group exposed to discrimination to massively excessive risks for maldevelopment (Birch, 1968). For example, malnutrition alone reduces the child's responsiveness to stimulation, and this reduced responsiveness itself can induce apathy in the adult who is caring for the child. In this sense, the child adds to his own disadvantaged environment. This underlying, mutual apathy may later result in an impairment of the capacity for satisfying relationships and, later still, learning (Cravioto et al., 1966).

Children reared in the lower socioeconomic environments also seem to have a greater exposure to external dangers. For example, there appears to be a greater incidence of burns and other accidents in children from the lower socioeconomic backgrounds (Spence et al., 1954). Moreover, many mothers in the lower socioeconomic classes are young and inexperienced and offer a different kind of mothering to an infant. Marked class differences have also been found in child-rearing methods, although the research findings are conflicting. For example, Sears found that middle class mothers are more permissive than those of the lower class (Sears et al., 1957), while Davis concluded that middle class mothers are more restrictive (Davis and Havighurst, 1947). Whiting and Child (1953) went so far as to claim that children of the American middle class are among the most restricted anywhere in the world. In socially and culturally deprived homes there is usually little space and few toys or books. Parents are often preoccupied with their own problems and may have little energy to invest in their children's achievements (Wolff, 1969).

In summary, physical, socioeconomic, cultural and educational factors in our society clearly have a significant impact upon the development of the child, and no study of the development of an individual is complete without an understanding of these factors (Eisenberg, 1968; National Institute of Child Health and Human Development, 1969).

Note 18

A. Gesell, and C.S. Amatruda (1964). *Developmental Diagnosis*, 2nd
   Ed., New York: Paul Hoeber Medical Division, Harper & Row, pp.
   8–14.
   Stages and Sequences of Development.
   Before describing diagnostic procedures it will be profitable to take
a bird's-eye view of the territory which is to be explored by the
developmental examination. Development is a continuous process.
Beginning with conception it proceeds stage by stage in orderly
sequence, each stage representing a degree or level of maturity.
There are so many such levels that we must select a few which will
serve best as a frame of reference for purposes of diagnosis. We have
determined upon the following Key Ages: 4, 16, 28, 40 weeks; 12, 18, 24,
36 months.
   To appreciate the developmental significance of these key ages it is
well to examine their position in the early cycle of human growth.
This cycle is depicted in the five charts which follow. The first chart
gives a comprehensive view of the entire scope of development; it
includes the fetal period, to indicate the continuity of the growth
cycle.
   The organization of behavior begins long before birth; and the
general direction of this organization is from head to foot, from
proximal to distal segments. Lips and tongue lead, eye muscles follow,
then neck, shoulder, arms, hands, fingers, trunk, legs, feet. The chart
reflects this law of developmental direction; it also suggests that the
four distinguishable fields of behavior develop conjointly in close
co-ordination.
   In terse terms the trends of behavior development are as follows.
   In the first quarter of the first year the infant gains control of his
twelve oculomotor muscles.
   In the second quarter (16–28 weeks) he comes into command of the
muscles which support his head and move his arms. He reaches out
for things.
   In the third quarter (28–40 weeks) he gains command of his trunk
and hands. He sits. He grasps, transfers and manipulates objects.
   In the fourth quarter (40–52 weeks) he extends command to his legs
and feet; to his forefingers and thumb. He pokes and plucks.
   In the second year he walks and runs; articulates words and
phrases; acquires bowel and bladder control; attains a rudimentary
sense of personal identity and of personal possession.
   In the third year he speaks in sentences, using words as tools of
thought; he shows a positive propensity to understand his environment and to comply with cultural demands. He is no longer a mere
infant.
   In the fourth year he asks innumerable questions, perceives
analogies, displays an active tendency to conceptualize and generalize. He is nearly self-dependent in routines of home life.
   At five he is well matured in motor control. He hops and skips. He
talks without infantile articulation. He can narrate a long tale. He
prefers associative play; he feels socialized pride in clothes and
accomplishment. He is a self-assured, conforming citizen in his small
world.

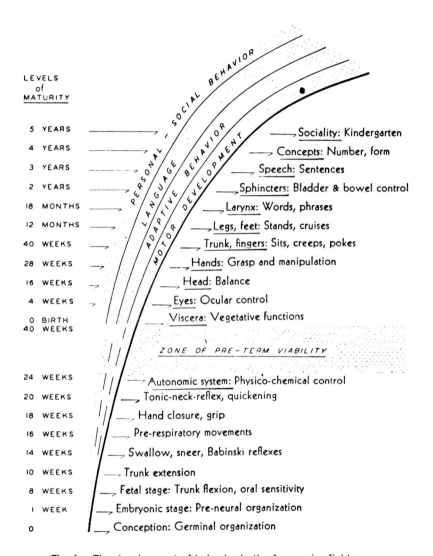

Fig. 1. The development of behavior in the four major fields.

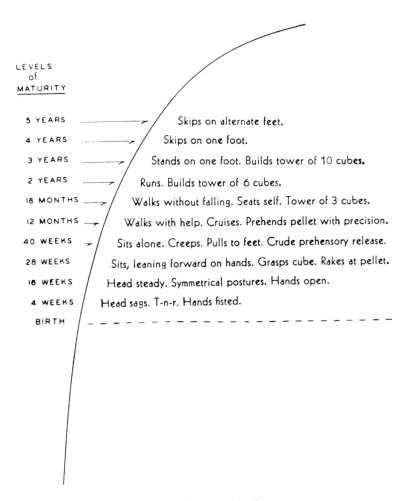

LEVELS
of
MATURITY

5 YEARS	Skips on alternate feet.
4 YEARS	Skips on one foot.
3 YEARS	Stands on one foot. Builds tower of 10 cubes.
2 YEARS	Runs. Builds tower of 6 cubes.
18 MONTHS	Walks without falling. Seats self. Tower of 3 cubes.
12 MONTHS	Walks with help. Cruises. Prehends pellet with precision.
40 WEEKS	Sits alone. Creeps. Pulls to feet. Crude prehensory release.
28 WEEKS	Sits, leaning forward on hands. Grasps cube. Rakes at pellet.
16 WEEKS	Head steady. Symmetrical postures. Hands open.
4 WEEKS	Head sags. T-n-r. Hands fisted.
BIRTH	

Fig. 2. Developmental sequences of motor behavior.

The items on this chart include both gross motor and fine motor behavior patterns. To ascertain the maturity of postural control we institute formal postural tests which reveal the repertoire of the infant's behavior: supine, prone, sitting, and standing.

Fine motor control is evaluated in a similar manner. Small objects such as cubes, pellet and string elicit patterns of fine manual control.

Such tests illustrate the principles which also underlie the developmental diagnosis of behavior in the adaptive, language, and personal-social fields.

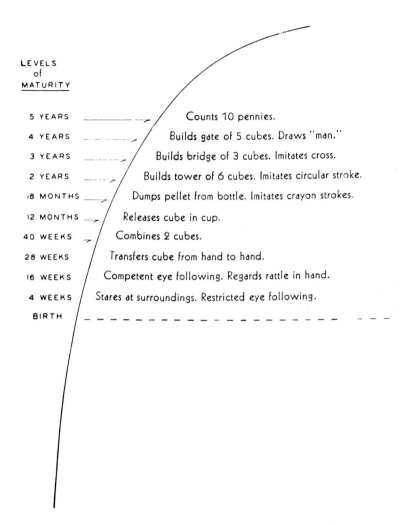

LEVELS
of
MATURITY

5 YEARS	Counts 10 pennies.
4 YEARS	Builds gate of 5 cubes. Draws "man."
3 YEARS	Builds bridge of 3 cubes. Imitates cross.
2 YEARS	Builds tower of 6 cubes. Imitates circular stroke.
18 MONTHS	Dumps pellet from bottle. Imitates crayon strokes.
12 MONTHS	Releases cube in cup.
40 WEEKS	Combines 2 cubes.
28 WEEKS	Transfers cube from hand to hand.
16 WEEKS	Competent eye following. Regards rattle in hand.
4 WEEKS	Stares at surroundings. Restricted eye following.
BIRTH	

Fig. 3. Developmental sequences of adaptive behavior.

To determine how the infant uses his motor equipment to exploit the environment we present him with a variety of simple objects. The small red cubes serve not only to test motor co-ordination, they reveal the child's capacity to put his motor equipment to constructive and adaptive ends. The cube tests create an objective opportunity for the examiner to observe adaptivity in action—motor co-ordination combined with judgment.

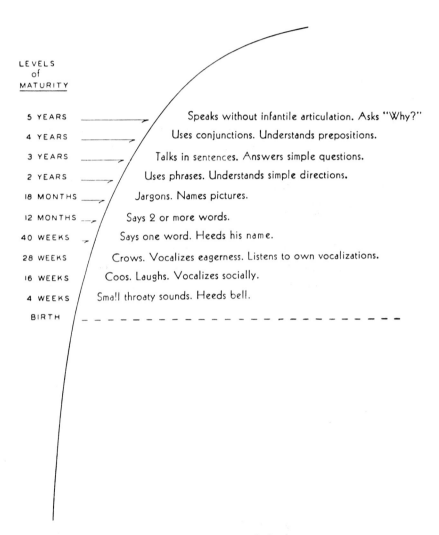

LEVELS
of
MATURITY

5 YEARS ——————→ Speaks without infantile articulation. Asks "Why?"

4 YEARS —————→ Uses conjunctions. Understands prepositions.

3 YEARS ————→ Talks in sentences. Answers simple questions.

2 YEARS ———→ Uses phrases. Understands simple directions.

18 MONTHS ——→ Jargons. Names pictures.

12 MONTHS ——→ Says 2 or more words.

40 WEEKS —→ Says one word. Heeds his name.

28 WEEKS Crows. Vocalizes eagerness. Listens to own vocalizations.

16 WEEKS Coos. Laughs. Vocalizes socially.

4 WEEKS Small throaty sounds. Heeds bell.

BIRTH

Fig. 4. Developmental sequences of language behavior.
Language maturity is estimated in terms of articulation, vocabulary, adaptive use and comprehension. During the course of a developmental examination spontaneous and responsive language behavior is observed. Valuable supplementary information may also be secured by questioning the adult familiar with the child's everyday behavior at home.

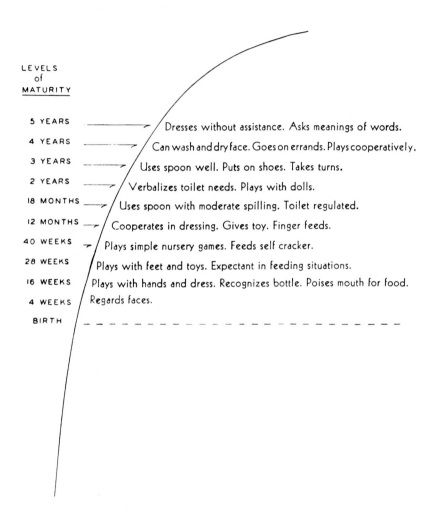

LEVELS
of
MATURITY

5 YEARS ——————→ Dresses without assistance. Asks meanings of words.

4 YEARS ———————→ Can wash and dry face. Goes on errands. Plays cooperatively.

3 YEARS ——————→ Uses spoon well. Puts on shoes. Takes turns.

2 YEARS ————→ Verbalizes toilet needs. Plays with dolls.

18 MONTHS ———→ Uses spoon with moderate spilling. Toilet regulated.

12 MONTHS ——→ Cooperates in dressing. Gives toy. Finger feeds.

40 WEEKS —→ Plays simple nursery games. Feeds self cracker.

28 WEEKS   Plays with feet and toys. Expectant in feeding situations.

16 WEEKS   Plays with hands and dress. Recognizes bottle. Poises mouth for food.

4 WEEKS   Regards faces.

BIRTH —

Fig. 5. Developmental sequences of personal-social behavior.

Personal-social behavior is greatly affected by the temperament of the child and by the kind of home in which he is reared. The range of individual variation is wide. Nevertheless maturity factors play a primary role in the socialization of the child. His social conduct is ascertained by incidental observation and by inquiry. The chart illustrates types of behavior which may be considered in evaluating the interaction of environmental influences and developmental readiness.

The remaining four charts diagram the sequences of development in Motor, Adaptive, Language, and Personal-Social fields of behavior. These four fields develop interdependently; and an adequate estimate of behavior maturity demands an appraisal of each major field. Each chart shows selected behavior patterns which illustrate the progressions of normal development. These patterns give a preliminary suggestion of the practical application of behavior norms.

Note 19

E.H. Erikson (1959). Identity and the life cycle. *Psychol. Issues*, 1 (1):55–61.

Basic Trust versus Basic Mistrust

I

For the first component of a healthy personality I nominate a sense of *basic trust*, which I think is an attitude toward oneself and the world derived from the experiences of the first year of life. By "trust" I mean what is commonly implied in reasonable trustfulness as far as others are concerned and a simple sense of trustworthiness as far as oneself is concerned. When I say "basic," I mean that neither this component nor any of those that follow are, either in childhood or in adulthood, especially conscious. In fact, all of these criteria, when developed in childhood and when integrated in adulthood, blend into the total personality. Their crises in childhood, however, and their impairment in adulthood are clearly circumscribed.

In describing this growth and its crises as a development of a series of alternative basic methods, we take recourse to the term "a sense of." Like a "sense of health" or a "sense of not being well," such "senses" pervade surface and depth, consciousness and the unconscious. They are ways of conscious *experience*, accessible to introspection (where it develops); ways of *behaving*, observable by others; and unconscious *inner* states determinable by test and analysis. It is important to keep these three dimensions in mind, as we proceed.

In *adults* the impairment of basic trust is expressed in a *basic mistrust*. It characterizes individuals who withdraw into themselves in particular ways when at odds with themselves and with others. These ways, which often are not obvious, are more strikingly represented by individuals who regress into psychotic states in which they sometimes close up, refusing food and comfort, and becoming oblivious to companionship. In so far as we like to assist them with psychotherapy, we must try to reach them again in specific ways in order to convince them that they can trust the world and that they can trust themselves. . . .

As the newborn infant is separated from his symbiosis with the mother's body, his inborn and more or less coordinated ability to take in by mouth meets the mother's more or less coordinated ability and intention to feed him and to welcome him. At this point he lives through, and loves with, his mouth; and the mother lives through, and loves with, her breasts.

For the mother this is a late and complicated accomplishment, highly dependent on her development as a woman; on her unconscious attitude toward the child; on the way she has lived through pregnancy and delivery; on her and her community's attitude toward the act of nursing—and on the response of the newborn. To him the mouth is the focus of a general first approach to life—the incorporative approach. In psychoanalysis this stage is usually referred to as the "oral" stage. . . .

During the "second oral" stage the ability and the pleasure in a more active and more directed incorporative approach ripen. The teeth develop and with them the pleasure in biting on hard things, in biting *through* things, and in biting *off* things. This active-incorporative mode characterizes a variety of other activities (as did the first incorporative mode). The eyes, first part of a passive system of accepting impressions as they come along, have now learned to focus, to isolate, to "grasp" objects from the vaguer background and to follow them. The organs of hearing similarly have learned to discern significant sounds, to localize them, and to guide an appropriate change in position (lifting and turning the head, lifting and turning the upper body). The arms have learned to reach out determinedly and the hands to grasp firmly. We are more interested here in the overall *configuration and final integration* of developing approaches to the world than *in the first appearances of specific abilities* which are so well described in the child development literature. . . .

The *crisis* of the oral stage (during the second part of the first year) is difficult to assess and more difficult to verify. It seems to consist of the co-incidence in time of three developments: (1) a physiological one: the general tension associated with a more violent drive to incorporate, appropriate, and observe more actively (a tension to which is added the discomfort of "teething" and other changes in the oral machinery); (2) a psychological one: the infant's increasing awareness of himself as a distinct person; and (3) an environmental one: the mother's apparent turning away from the baby toward pursuits which she had given up during late pregnancy and postnatal care. . . .

What the child acquires at a given stage is a certain ratio between the positive and the negative which, if the balance is toward the positive, will help him to meet later crises with a better chance for unimpaired total development. The idea that at any stage a *goodness* is achieved which is impervious to new conflicts within and changes without is a projection on child development of that success ideology which so dangerously pervades our private and public daydreams and can make us inept in the face of a heightened struggle for a meaningful existence in our time. . . .

Note 20

J. Bowlby (1951), Maternal care and mental health. World Health Organization, Monograph #2. Quoted in *Child Care and the Growth of Love*, ed. M. Fry. London: Penguin Books Ltd., 1953.

Prolonged breaks (in the mother-child relationship) during the first three years of life leave a characteristic impression on the child's personality. Such children appear emotionally withdrawn and isolated. They fail to develop loving ties with other children or with adults and consequently have no friendships worth the name. It is true that they are sometimes sociable in a superficial sense, but if this is scrutinised we find that there are no feelings, no roots in these relationships. This, I think, more than anything else, is the cause of their hard-boiledness. Parents and school teachers complain that nothing you say or do has any effect on the child. If you thrash him he cries for a bit, but there is no emotional response to being out of favour, such as is normal to the ordinary child. It appears to be of no essential consequence to these lost souls whether they are in favour or not. Since they are unable to make genuine emotional relations, the condition of relationship at a given moment lacks all significance for them. . . . During the last few years I have seen some sixteen cases of this affectionless type of persistent pilferer and in only two was a prolonged break absent. In all the others gross breaches of the mother-child relation had occurred during the first three years, and the child had become a persistent pilferer.

Note 21

R.A. Spitz (1965), *The First Year of Life*. New York: International Universities Press, pp. 89–90.
    An extremely simple experiment can be performed to show that what triggers the smile is a sign Gestalt which consists of a circumscribed part of the face. In this experiment contact is made with a three-month-old by smiling at him and nodding one's head; the infant will react by smiling, by becoming active and by wriggling.
    One now turns one's head into profile, continuing to smile and to nod; the infant will stop smiling, his expression becomes bewildered. Developmentally advanced infants frequently seem to search with their glance somewhere in the region of the experimenter's ear, as if searching for the eye which disappeared; sensitive children appear to respond with a kind of shock, and it takes time to reestablish contact. This experiment shows that the three-month-old is still unable to recognize the human face in profile; in other words, the infant has not recognized the human partner at all; he has only perceived the sign Gestalt of forehead, eyes, and nose. When this Gestalt is modified through turning into profile, the percept is no longer recognized; it has lost its tenuous objectal quality.

Note 22

J. Piaget (1952), *The Origins of Intelligence in Children*. New York: International Universities Press, pp. 266–269.
    Tertiary circular reaction is quite different: if it also arises by way of differentiation, from the secondary circular schemata, this differentiation is no longer imposed by the environment but is, so to speak, accepted and even desired in itself. In effect, not succeeding in assimilating certain objects or situations to the schemata hitherto examined, the child manifests an unexpected behavior pattern: he tries, through a sort of experimentation, to find out in which respect the object or the event is new. In other words, he will not only submit to but even provoke new results instead of being satisfied merely to reproduce them once they have been revealed fortuitously. The child discovers in this way that which has been called in scientific language the "experiment in order to see." But, of course, the new result, though sought after for its own sake, demands to be reproduced and

the initial experiment is immediately accompanied by circular reaction. But, there too, a difference contrasts these "tertiary" reactions to the "secondary" reactions. When the child repeats the movements which led him to the interesting result, he no longer repeats them just as they are but gradates and varies them, in such a way as to discover fluctuations in the result. The "experiment in order to see," consequently, from the very beginning, has the tendency to extend to the conquest of the external environment ...

Observation 141.—This first example will make us understand the transition between secondary and "tertiary" reactions: that of the well-known behavior pattern by means of which the child explores distant space and constructs his representation of movement, the behavior pattern of letting go or throwing objects in order subsequently to pick them up.

One recalls ... how, at 0;10 (2) Laurent discovered in "exploring" a case of soap, the possibility of throwing this object and letting it fall. Now, what interested him at first was not the objective phenomenon of the fall—that is to say, the object's trajectory—but the very act of letting go. He therefore limited himself, at the beginning, merely to reproducing the result observed fortuitously, which still constitutes a "secondary" reaction, "derived" it is true, but of typical structure.

On the other hand, at 0;10 (10) the reaction changes and becomes "tertiary." That day Laurent manipulates a small piece of bread (without any alimentary interest: he has never eaten any and has no thought of tasting it) and lets it go continually. He even breaks off fragments which he lets drop. Now, in contradistinction to what has happened on the preceding days, he pays no attention to the act of letting go whereas he watches with great interest the body in motion; in particular, he looks at it for a long time when it has fallen, and picks it up when he can.

At 0;10 (11) Laurent is lying on his back but nevertheless resumes his experiments of the day before. He grasps in succession a celluloid swan, a box, etc., stretches out his arm and lets them fall. He distinctly varies the positions of the fall. Sometimes he stretches out his arm vertically, sometimes he holds it obliquely, in front of or behind his eyes, etc. When the object falls in a new position (for example on his pillow), he lets it fall two or three times more on the same place, as though to study the spatial relations; then he modifies the situation. At a certain moment the swan falls near his mouth: now, he does not suck it (even though this object habitually serves this purpose), but drops it three times more while merely making the gesture of opening his mouth. ...

Observation 146.—At 1;2 (8) Jacqueline holds in her hands an object which is new to her; a round, flat box which she turns all over, shakes, rubs against the bassinet, etc. She lets it go and tries to pick it up. But she only succeeds in touching it with her index finger, without grasping it. She nevertheless makes an attempt and presses on the edge. The box then tilts up and falls again. Jacqueline, very much interested in this fortuitous result, immediately applies herself to studying it. ... Hitherto it is only a question of an attempt at assimilation ... and of the fortuitous discovery of a new result, but this discovery, instead of giving rise to a simple circular reaction, is at once extended to "experiments in order to see."

In effect, Jacqueline immediately rests the box on the ground and pushes it as far as possible (it is noteworthy that care is taken to push the box far away in order to reproduce the same conditions as in the first attempt, as though this were a necessary condition for obtaining the result). Afterward Jacqueline puts her finger on the box and presses it. But as she places her finger on the center of the box she simply displaces it and makes it slide instead of tilting it up. She amuses herself with this game and keeps it up (resumes it after intervals, etc.) for several minutes. Then, changing the point of contact, she finally again places her finger on the edge of the box, which tilts it up. She repeats this many times, varying the conditions, but keeping track of her discovery: now she only presses on the edge!

REFERENCES

Anders, T. (1978), Home-recorded sleep in 2- and 9-month-old infants. *J. Am. Acad. Child Psychiatry*, 17:421–432.

Aserinsky, E., and Klietman, N. (1953), Regularly occurring periods of eye motility, and concomitant phenomena, during sleep. *Science*, 118:273–274.

Baird, D. (1959), The contribution of obstetric factors to serious physical and mental handicap in children. *J. Obstet. Gynecol.*, 66:743.

Baldwin, J.M. (1895), *Mental Development in the Child and the Race*. New York: Macmillan.

Baumgartner, L. (1965), Health and ethnic minorities in the sixties. *Am. J. Public Health*, 55:495.

Bell, S.M., and Ainsworth, M.D.S. (1972), Infant crying and maternal responsiveness. *Child Dev.*, 43:1171–1190.

Bender, L. (1953), Childhood schizophrenia. *Psychiatr. Q.*, 27:663.

Bergman, P., and Escalona, S. (1949), Unusual sensitivities in very young children. *Psychoanal. Study Child*, 3/4:333–352.

Berko, J., and Brown, R. (1960), Psycholinguistic research methods. In: *Handbook of Research Methods in Child Development*, ed. P. Mussen. New York: Wiley.

Birch, H.G. (1968), Health and the education of socially disadvantaged children. *Dev. Med. Child Neurol.*, 10:580–599.

Bowlby, J. (1951), Maternal care and mental health. Geneva: World Health Organization.

Bowlby, J. (1958), The nature of a child's tie to his mother. *Int. J. Psychoanal.*, 39:350–373.

Collins, G.M., and Schaffer, H.R. (1975), Synchronization of visual attention in mother-infant pairs. *J. Child Psychol. Psychiatry*, 16:315–320.

Cravioto, J., DeLicardi, E.R., and Birch, H.G. (1966), Nutrition, growth and neuro-integrative development: An experimental and ecologic study. *Pediatrics*, 38:319.

Davis, A., and Havighurst, R.J. (1947), *Father of the Man*. Boston: Houghton Mifflin.

Despert, J.L. (1947), The early recognition of childhood schizophrenia. *Med. Clin. North Am.*, May, 680.

Dreyfus-Brisac, C., Samson, D., Blanc, C., and Monod, N. (1958), L'électroencephalogramme de l'enfant normal demoins de 3 ans. *Etudes Neonatales*, 7:143.

Drillien, C.M. (1959), Physical and mental handicaps in the prematurely born. *J. Obstet. Gynaecol. Br. Empire*, 66:721–728.

Eisenberg, L. (1956), The autistic child in adolescence. *Am. J. Psychiatry*, 112:607.

Eisenberg, L. (1968), Racism, the family and society: A crisis in values. *Ment. Hygiene*, 52:512–520.

Ellingson, R. (1975), Ontogenesis of sleep in the human. In: *Experimental Study of Human Sleep*, ed. G. Lairy and P. Salzarulo. Amsterdam: Elsevier, pp. 129–146.

Erikson, E.H. (1959), Identity and the life cycle. *Psychol. Issues*, 1:55–61.

Escalona, S.K. (1969), *The Roots of Individuality: Normal Patterns of Development in Infancy*. Chicago: Aldine, p. 547.

Fagan, J.F. (1979), The origins of facial pattern recognition. In: *Psychological Development from Infancy: Image to Intention*, ed. M.H. Bornstein and W. Kessen. New York: Wiley, pp. 83–114.

Folstein, S., and Rutter, M. (1977), Infantile autism: A genetic study of 21 pairs. *Child Psychol. Psychiatry*, 18:297.

Freud, A. (1955), Safeguarding the emotional health of our children: An inquiry into the concept of the rejecting mother. *National Conferences of Social Work: Casework Papers, 1956*. New York: Family Service Association of America, p. 9.

Freud, S. (1905), *Three Essays on Sexuality*. Standard Edition, 7 (1953). London: The Hogarth Press, p. 168.

Freud, S. (1923), *The Ego and the Id*. Standard Edition, 19 (1961). London: The Hogarth Press, pp. 12–59.

Freud, S. (1926), *Inhibitions, Symptoms and Anxiety*. Standard Edition, 20 (1959). London: The Hogarth Press, pp. 87–172.

Fries, M.E., and Woolf, F.J. (1953), Some hypotheses on the role of the congenital activity type in personality development. *Psychoanal. Study Child*, 8:48–62.

Gesell, A.O., and Amatruda, C.S. (1941), *Developmental Diagnosis*, 11th Ed., 1964. New York: Paul Hoeber Medical Division, Harper & Row, pp. 8–14.

Hartmann, H. (1939), *Ego Psychology and the Problem of Adaptation*. New York: International Universities Press.

Hetzer, H., and Wolf, K. (1928), Baby tests. *Zeitschrift für Psychologie*, p. 107.

Kagan, J. (1971), *Change and Continuity in Infancy*. New York: Wiley.

Kanner, L. (1943), Autistic disturbances of affective contact. *Nerv. Child*, 2:217.

Kaye, K. (1976), Infants' effects upon their mothers' teaching strategies. In: *The Social Context of Learning and Development*, ed. J.C. Glifewell. New York: Gardner.

Kessen, W. (1967), Sucking and looking: Two organized congenital patterns of behavior in the human newborn. In: *Early Behavior: Comparative and Developmental Approaches*, ed. H.W. Stevenson et al. New York: Wiley.

Kessen, W., and Bornstein, M.H. (1978), Discriminability of brightness change for infants. *J. Exp. Child Psychol.*, 25:526–530.

Klein, M. (1960), Our adult world and its roots in infancy. London: Tavistock, Pamphlet No. 2, p. 15.

Korner, A.F., and Grobstein, R. (1966), Visual alertness as related to soothing in neonates: Implications for maternal stimulation and early deprivation. *Child Dev.*, 37:867–876.

Langmeir, J., and Matejeck, Z. (1975), *Psychological Deprivation in Childhood*, 3rd Ed., trans. P. Auger. New York: Halsted Press.

Leonard, M.F., Rhymes, J.P., and Solnit, A.J. (1966), Failure to thrive in infants. *Am. J. Dis. Child.*, 3:600–612.

Lewis, M.M. (1959), *How Children Learn to Speak*. New York: Basic Books.

Lewis, M.M. (1963), *Language, Thought and Personality in Infancy and Childhood*. New York: Basic Books, pp. 15–24.

Lewis, M., and Brooks, J. (1976), Infants' social perception: A constructivist view. In: *Infant Perception: From Sensation to Cognition*, eds. L. Cohen and P. Salapatek. New York: Academic Press.

Lewis, M., Kagan, J., Campbell, H., and Kalafat, J. (1966), The cardiac response as a correlate of attention in infants. Child Dev., 37:63–72.

Ling, B.C. (1941), Form discrimination as a learning cue in infants. *Comp. Psychol. Monogr.*, 17:2.

Lorenz, K. (1966), *On Aggression*, trans. M. Wilson. New York: Harcourt, Brace & World.

Lotter, V. (1966), Epidemiology of autistic conditions in young children. I. Prevalence. *Soc. Psychiatry*, 1:124–137.

Mahler, M.S. (1952), On child psychosis and schizophrenia: Autistic and symbiotic infantile psychosis. *Psychoanal. Study Child*, 7:286–305.

Mahler, M.S., Pine, F., and Bergman, A. (1975), *The Psychological Birth of the Human Infant*. New York: Basic Books.

Morley, M.E. (1965), *The Development and Disorders of Speech in Childhood*, 2nd Ed. Edinburgh: E. & S. Livingstone.

Moss, H.A. (1967), Sex, age and state as determinants of mother-infant interaction. *Merrill-Palmer Q.*, 13:19–36.

National Institute of Child Health and Human Development (1969), *Perspectives on Human Deprivation: Biological, Psychological and Sociological*. Washington, D.C.: U.S. Government Printing Office.

Nelson, K. (1977), First steps in language acquisition. *J. Am. Acad. Child Psychiatry*, 16:563–607.

Ornitz, E.M., and Ritvo, E.R. (1976), The syndrome of autism: A critical review. *Am. J. Psychiatry*, 133:609–621.

Parmelee, A.H., Wenner, W.H., and Schulz, H.R. (1964), Infant sleep patterns: From birth to 16 weeks of age. *J. Pediatr.*, 65:576.

Patton, R.G., and Gardner, L.I. (1962), Influence of family environment on growth: The syndrome of maternal deprivation. *Pediatrics*, 30:957–962.

Piaget, J. (1953), *The Origins of Intelligence in Children*. New York: International Universities Press.

Provence, S., and Lipton, R. (1962), *Infants in Institutions*. New York: International Universities Press.

Putnam, M.D. (1955), Some observations on psychosis in early childhood. In: *Emotional Problems of Early Childhood*, ed. G. Caplan. New York: Basic Books, pp. 519–526.

Rank, B. (1955), Intensive study and treatment of preschool children who show marked personality deviations or "atypical development" and their parents. In: *Emotional Problems of Early Childhood*, ed. G. Caplan. New York: Basic Books, p. 491.

Rheingold, H.L. (1968), The effect of a strange environment on the behavior of infants. In: *Determinations of Infant Behavior*, Vol. 4, ed. B.M. Foss. London: Methuen.

Ritvo, E.R. (1977), Biochemical studies of children with the syndromes of autism, childhood schizophrenia and related developmental disabilities: A review. *J. Child Psychol. Psychiatry*, 18:373–379.

Ritvo, E.R., and Freeman, B.J. (1978), Current research on the syndrome of autism. Introduction: The National Society for Autistic Children's definition of the syndrome of autism. *J. Am. Acad. Child Psychiatry*, 17:565–575.

Ritvo, S., and Solnit, A.J. (1958), Influences of early mother-child interaction on identification processes. *Psychoanal. Study Child*, 12:64.

Robson, K.S. (1967), The role of eye-to-eye contact in maternal-infant behavior. *J. Child Psychol. Psychiatry*, 8:13–25.

Rutter, M. (1970), Autistic children: Infancy to adulthood. *Semin. Psychiatry*, 2:435–450.

Rutter, M. (1972), *Maternal Deprivation Reassessed*. Harmondsworth: Penguin.

Rutter, M. (1976), Individual differences. In: *Child Psychiatry*, ed. M. Rutter and L. Hersov. Oxford: Blackwell, pp. 3–21.

Rutter, M. (1976), Infantile autism and other child psychoses. In: *Child Psychiatry*, ed. M. Rutter and L. Hersov. Oxford, Blackwell, pp. 717–747.

Rutter, M, and Bax, M. (1972), Normal development of speech and language. In: *The Child with Delayed Speech*, ed. M. Rutter and J.A. Martin. *Clin. Dev. Med.*, No. 43. London: SIMP/Heinemann.

Rutter, M., Greenfield, D., and Lockyer, L. (1967), A five- to fifteen-year follow-up study of infantile psychosis. *Br. J. Psychiatry*, 113:1183–1199.

Rutter, M., and Schopler, E. (Eds.) (1978), *Autism: A Reappraisal of Concepts and Treatment.* New York: Plenum.

Schaffer, H.R. (1966), Activity level as a constitutional determinant of infantile reaction to deprivation. *Child Dev.*, 37:595.

Schaffer, H.R. (Ed.) (1977), *Studies in Mother-Infant Interaction.* London: Academic Press.

Schaffer, H.R., and Emerson, P.E. (1964), The development of social attachments in infancy. *Monogr. Soc. Res. Child Dev.*, 29 (3).

Sears, R.R., Maccoby, E.E., and Levin, H. (1957), *Patterns of Child Rearing.* New York: Row, Peterson.

Spence, J., Walton, W.S., Miller, F.J.W., and Courts, D.M. (1954), *A Thousand Families in Newcastle Upon Tyne.* London: Oxford University Press.

Spitz, R.A. (1945), Hospitalism: An inquiry into the genesis of psychiatric conditions in early childhood. *Psychoanal. Study Child*, 1:53–74.

Spitz, R.A. (1946), Hospitalism: A follow-up report. *Psychoanal. Study Child*, 2:113–117.

Spitz, R.A. (1946), Anaclitic depression: An inquiry into the genesis of psychiatric conditions in early childhood. *Psychoanal. Study Child*, 2:313–342.

Spitz, R.A. (1965), *The First Year of Life.* New York: International Universities Press.

Sroufe, L.A. (1977), Wariness of strangers and the study of infant development. *Child Dev.*, 48:731–746.

Stern, D.N. (1974), Mother and infant at play: The dyadic interaction involving facial, vocal and gaze behavior. In: *The Effect of the Infant on Its Caregiver*, ed. M. Lewis and L.A. Rosenblum. New York: Wiley.

Thomas, A., Birch, H.G., Chess, S., et al. (1963), *Behavioral Individuality in Early Childhood.* New York: New York University Press.

Thomas, A., Chess, S., and Birch, H.G. (1968), *Temperament and Behavior Disorders in Children.* New York: New York University Press.

Walter, G. (1956), Electro-encephalographic development of children. In: *Discussions on Child Development*, ed. J.M. Tanner and B. Inhelder. London: Tavistock, p. 146.

White, B.L., and Held, R.M. (1966), Plasticity of sensori-motor development in the human infant. In: *The Causes of Behavior: Readings in Child Development and Educational Psychology*, 2nd Ed., ed. J.R. Rosenblith and W. Allinsmith. Boston: Allyn & Bacon, pp. 783–866.

Whiting, J.W.M., and Child, I.L. (1953), *Child Training and Personality: A Cross-Cultural Study.* New Haven: Yale University Press.

Wing, J.K. (1966), *Early Childhood Autism.* London: Pergamon Press.

Winnicott, D.W. (1945), Primitive emotional development. *Collected Papers.* New York: Basic Books.

Wolff, P.H., and Feinbloom, R.I. (1969), Critical periods and cognitive development in the first 2 years. *Pediatrics*, 44:999–1006.

Wolff, S. (1969), *Children Under Stress.* London: Allen Lane, The Penguin Press.

Chapter 13

INFANCY–AGES 1 TO 3

MOTOR SEQUENCE

A steady increase in motor skills can be observed in most children, so that by age 3 a child can stand on one foot, dance, and jump. He or she is also more dextrous than previously and can build a tower of 10 cubes. Ambidexterity gives way to lateralization some time during the third year although handedness may not be firmly established for several years. Leg, eye, and ear dominance may also not become firmly established until the seventh, eighth, or ninth year, or even later.

ADAPTIVE SEQUENCE

At 18 months the child can usually imitate a crayon stroke. By age 2 he or she can imitate a circular stroke, and by age 3 years he or she can imitate a cross. At age 3 he or she is also capable of building a bridge with three cubes.

LANGUAGE SEQUENCE

Most children talk fairly well by age 3. They can talk in sentences although they do not always use the correct verb tenses and they often omit conjunctions. Nevertheless, within the limits of his vocabulary and experience, a 3-year-old is usually quite capable of telling a simple story. He can also communicate clearly using verbal language. If at age 2 most questions are "what" questions, by age 3 they are "where" and "who" questions, and by age 4 the child begins to ask "why" (Watts, 1947).

Until about age 2½, normal children may repeat what is said to them. However, after that age such repetition is considered abnormal and is called echolalia. Echolalia is found most often in autism and mental retardation; it probably reflects the child's lack of understanding of language (Fay and Butler, 1971).

PERSONAL AND SOCIAL BEHAVIOR

By the age of 3, most children can take themselves to the toilet, feed themselves, and begin to dress themselves.

FANTASY LIFE AND PLAY

Once again, the maturation sequence described by Gesell (1941) can be considered only the skeleton of the child's psychological development during these years. Fantasy life, for example, is more complex by the time the child is 2 years old. The child's fantasies can be glimpsed indirectly as they are expressed in play. The child's play style is initially repetitious, with few variations. There is little risk, no climax, and no real plot. The play materials are usually stuffed animals, balls, push toys, and elementary puzzles. By the end of the first year, the child has usually acquired a transitional object (Winnicott, 1951; see Note 23), which often is a piece of rag, a pillow, or a blanket to which he has become very attached and to which he resorts to comfort himself. Such times may be at bedtime or following any stress, such as separation. The transitional object seems to represent a halfway step between attachment to himself (say, his thumb) and attachment to the outside world (the mother). Often when he holds his transitional object close to his nose, or cheek, or mouth, he also manages to insert a finger into his nostril or mouth. In terms of psychological health versus illness, no significant differences are found between children who are attached to a treasured object and those who are not, nor between those who continue to use a soft object after age 9 compared to those who never had a treasured object (Sherman et al., 1981).

The play sometimes has as its underlying motif a working through of anxiety evoked by a fantasy or fear that he will lose his mother's love. From about age 18 months to 2½ or 3, this represents the most important and commonest danger situation for the infant. As the child develops, other basic danger situations are perceived by the child, and each will be mentioned in sequence later.

MANIFEST OBJECT RELATIONS

By the end of the second year, the manifestations of ambivalent behavior can be clearly seen in the child. For example, he may attempt to control his mother through clinging, sometimes demanding, behavior that can be desperately trying to the parent. A child who feels secure about his parents' presence and love now also feels quite free to turn his aggression onto the external world. As the child feels more autonomous, his negativistic behavior increases. At the same time, although he can more or less feed himself, he still feels free to wet and soil unless his mother interferes.

PEER RELATIONS

When he perceives others at all, the young infant perceives them as disturbers of his relationship with his mother or father. Later, the child relates to other children more or less as to lifeless objects to be used, and he only gradually becomes aware that they are alive and have feelings of their own. At first he uses other children simply as playmates, limiting the partnership to the period of time needed to perform a particular task. By the time he is 2½ to 3 years of age, however, he is beginning to share with others, a task he will be helped to master in nursery school. (The role of nursery school in education is discussed on page 241.)

Even by the end of his third year the child still plays mostly within the confines of his own fantasies. Although he may want others to play with him, the play is rarely truly or continuously shared at this time. When a group of children of this age are observed playing, the activities of each child seem still to be more or less isolated. However, a tendency toward progressive social involvement can be observed. Thus a shift from solitary, independent play to parallel activity in which children play alongside but not with each other occurs during this period. Later, play occurs in which there is common activity, with sharing and taking turns, culminating in cooperative play in which there is a common goal, with each child playing a specified role (Parten, 1933).

PARENT DEVELOPMENT

The child's ambivalent behavior at this stage requires a shift in the mother's attitude to her child. She must now set limits for the child, at the same time as she must deal with the strong feelings that are now evoked in her. The two-way-street aspect of the dyadic relationship between mother and child is now much more obvious and much more demanding. Parents too are in a state of continuous development. Past unresolved feelings are evoked again at each stage of development of the child, while the parents are themselves currently developing and experiencing life differently as they grow older. Sometimes a mother fails to thrive, and the consequent failure of her infant to thrive may add to her feelings of inadequacy or guilt. This may lead to inadequate or inconsistent limits setting. Problems of poor impulse control in children often have their origins in this period, when internalization of controls firmly set from without should be occurring.

BODY IMAGE

During the second and third years, the child's concept of his body begins to take recognizable shape. The child at this stage often has a passionate interest in Band-Aids. He may become quite upset at a small graze and want to cover up the wound with a Band-Aid—as if to hide the wound and prevent the loss of body fluid. It seems as though his idea of his body is that it is a kind of sac filled with fluid that sometimes oozes out. The child may have some vague ideas about his internal organs; for example, he may think that his heart looks like the hearts he has seen on valentine cards.

Further evidence of the child's developing sense of his body and his feelings can be seen in other play typical of this stage. For example, play with toys that can be filled and emptied, opened and shut, fitted in, messed and cleaned, held on to (hoarded) and let go (thrown out) seem to reflect the child's interest in his body parts and their functions. Movable toys seem to help him use with pleasure his increased ability to move around. Toys that can be built up and then knocked down seem to serve nicely as instruments for the expression of ambivalent feelings.

GENDER IDENTIFICATION

Early gender identification also occurs during this period. In a study of 76 hermaphroditic patients, Money and his colleagues (1955) showed that one cannot attribute psychological maleness or femaleness to the chromosomal sex, gonadal sex, hormonal sex, internal accessory reproductive organs, or external genital morphology. Sex assignment and rearing are the crucial variables in the determination of gender role and orientation. Gender imprinting has begun by the first birthday, and the "critical period" is reached by about 18 months. By the age of 2½, gender role is already established in normal children. However, abnormal attitudes in the parents and certain specific external stresses may contribute to deviant sexual identity problems, such as transvestism (Stoller, 1967). The meaning of maleness and femaleness does not reach full maturity until after adolescence.

SENSE OF SELF

Literally standing on his own two feet, the child delineates "I" and "you" and increasingly expresses his sense of individuality and autonomy. The process by which the child achieves a sense of individuality and autonomy is not well understood. Mahler (1967) has attempted to delineate a series of phases during the first 3 years of life, starting with a "normal autistic phase" during the first 2 months of life. In the second month, a normal, undifferentiated, "symbiotic phase" begins. It is a phase "in which the infant behaves as though he and his mother were an omnipotent system—a dual unit within one common boundary." This phase is said to reach its height at around ages 4 to 5 months. At about age 9 months and onward, what Mahler calls the separation-individuation process takes place. This process consists essentially of the child's achievement of separate functioning in the presence and emotional availability of the mother. At about age 18 months, the child appears to be at the peak of his belief in his own magic omnipotence. During the second 18 months of life, individuation proceeds, culminating in the attainment of stable object constancy and a sense of autonomy.

OBJECT CONSTANCY

The term object constancy as used here is a psychoanalytic concept formulated by Hartmann (1952). It denotes the infant's ability to maintain constant relations with a person ("object") regardless of the state of need in the infant. In this sense, object constancy is different from what Piaget calls object permanence, which connotes the infant's ability to respond to items in his environment as if they possessed some permanence, a development that occurs perhaps around age 5 or 6 months. A prerequisite for the development of object constancy is a lessening in the strength of the infant's needs or a greater control of those needs, which will enable the infant to retain a relationship with a person instead of shifting immediately to another person in search of immediate gratification (A. Freud, 1957). Anna Freud has noted that the very young infant is so dominated by his needs (the domination of the pleasure principle) that he cannot maintain his attachment to a nonsatisfying object for more than a given period. (The period may vary from several hours to several days.) Separation of the infant from the love object causes extreme distress to the infant from about 5 months to 2 years old. As the child matures, however, and as the pleasure principle gives way to the reality principle, the child gradually develops the ability to retain attachments to and investments in the absent love object during separations of increasing length.

SENSE OF AUTONOMY

At this stage the child also increasingly experiences a sense of individuality and self-control that leads to a feeling of achievement and pride and, in contrast, to a sense of shame and self-doubt when he has an "accident" and loses control (Erikson, 1959). Erikson has said also that it is necessary to "be firm and tolerant" with the child at this stage in order for him to be firm and tolerant with himself. "He will [then] feel pride in being an autonomous person; he will grant autonomy to others; and now and again he will even let himself get away with something."

COGNITIVE DEVELOPMENT

As long as the child feels that his thoughts are omnipotent, he will also believe that others are omnipotent. Fraiberg (1959) described a 2-year-old girl who, on seeing the sun disappear in a spectacular sunset, turned to her father and said, "Do it again, Daddy!" However, by the end of the second year some symbolic representation also emerges. The child can now use "mental" trial and error instead of "action" trial and error. He looks now for external causes of movements he sees, and he of course quite clearly distinguishes between himself and an object. Piaget has called this whole first period of cognitive functioning, which lasts until about 2 years of age, the sensorimotor stage, and he describes the infant's state during these first 2 years as egocentric. Egocentrism is used here not in the common sense but as to mean that initially the boundaries between objects and self are not differentiated; the child has little or no self-perception; and he does not at first see his place in relation to the universe, which at that time does not exist for him (Piaget, 1954). Piaget uses the term egocentric then in a purely epistemological sense, without any affective or moral connotation. The child is egocentric to the extent that he considers his own point of view as the only possible one. Indeed, the child who is egocentric is unaware that the other person has a point of view at all, and for this reason he is incapable of putting himself in someone else's place. A young child, for example, may make up a word and assume that everyone knows exactly what he means by that word. He cannot conceive that the other person does not understand what he means by that word. (Egocentrism will be discussed again in reference to adolescence.)

Gradually the infant moves into a symbolic, preconceptual stage, so that by age 3 he shows evidence of attempts at verbal reasoning, as well as symbolic activity in make-believe play. However, the child still tends to endow inanimate objects (e.g., thunderstorms, clouds, and the moon) with feeling (animism) (Piaget, 1929), and he cannot yet understand the meaning of "I promise."

Toward the end of the sensorimotor stage, and as the child moves into the symbolic, preconceptual stage, he can solve problems by inventiveness. For example, he can now rotate a stick through a 90-degree angle to bring it through the bars of his crib, and he can use one toy as an instrument to get another.

DEVELOPMENTAL TASKS

Some time between 1½ and 3 years of age it becomes clear that a child is tackling several developmental tasks. He is, first of all, achieving greater physical independence. The maturation of his neuromuscular system is central to his feeling of self-worth; he has made a shift from a passive position to an active position. Furthermore, the child can now think better, using a language with symbols and concepts. Whereas the child earlier used the few words he had for the direct discharge of his feelings (primary process), he now uses language more independently, for what Hartmann (1939) has called the conflict-free ego sphere of functions and activities (secondary process). Along with this development, definite attitudes toward people are formed, especially toward those who set limits. It is toward such persons that the child behaves in a negativistic manner. Thus he or she often says, "I don't want to" and "No!" when a parent makes a request or sets a limit. It is as though the child is once more defining his autonomy through his oppositional behavior. However, in some instances the behavior may be a manifestation of anxiety as the child struggles against a regressive pull. In other instances the behavior may be a direct discharge of aggression against the parent, especially if the mother-child relationship is an ambivalent one.

TOILET TRAINING

When the adaptive tasks and developmental achievements of the child between 1 and 3 years of age are considered, it becomes clear that while the child is adapting to his environment the environment is changing its attitudes and expectations of the child. Questions of discipline arise, particularly in regard to the child's aggressive behavior. Conflicts between parents and child are now more apparent. Toilet training may become one of the many possible sources of conflicts at this time. There are three requirements for toilet training. First, a child must be physiologically capable of controlling his anal sphincter. The age at which this control is achieved is different from child to child. It may be reached, say, from ages 15 months to 2½ years. It often coincides with the maturation of the child's skill in walking. Second, the child must be psychologically capable of postponing the urge to let go of his stool as soon as he feels the impulse. That is to say, he must have some capacity to delay as well as a wish to please his parents. Third, since initially the child usually needs help using the toilet, he might be told to give a warning signal to an adult who is prepared to assist. Later, of course, he will be able to go to the bathroom on his own.

There are several possible outcomes of the toilet-training process. Children who have a satisfactory relationship with their parents usually have a strong wish to please their parents, to conform to their expectations, and to respond to the pleasure the parents show over the child's progress in toilet training. Sometimes the child will identify with the parents in their own reaction formations, such as disgust of feces. Occasionally, a child will conform out of fear. In such cases there is often an underlying rage and resentment that may be expressed as negativism, refusal to eat, or crying. Last, the child may object to the toilet training for a variety of reasons, and he may develop encopresis.

DIFFICULTIES IN THE PARENTS

Some of the problems in toilet training arise from the parent. A mother may experience anxiety or a strong feeling of disgust when she sees the child freely soil or mess. She may rush the child, punish him, or simply frustrate him. Sometimes a mother wishes to show off how clean, or precocious, her child is, and will try to master her child's fumbling early attempts. Or she may express hostility toward the child through early forceful training. Occasionally, a mother may simply be ignorant of the requirements for toilet training or may be following a cultural or family pattern.

DIFFICULTIES IN THE CHILD

The child for his part may not understand what his parents want, particularly if they themselves do not know what they want. Even when the parents are clear in their minds, the child may be confused by their behavior—first they praise him for his beautiful BM, then they promptly flush it down the toilet. In some cases the child may use bowel training as the issue over which he expresses his earlier hostility toward his parents. Hostility is sometimes induced specifically in relation to toilet training. The birth of a sibling may occur around the time the child is being toilet trained. The child may then feel a loss of love or an impending loss of love, and express this feeling in a reluctance to be toilet trained. Occasionally, actual separation and real loss may cause a relapse. An important factor is the child's ability to give up a pleasure for the sake of a greater social gain. That is to say, the child may not yet be able to give up the narcissistic gratification the creation of a BM brings him. Sometimes, too, a child is unwilling or unready to take this next step in development.

ENCOPRESIS

By age 4, almost all children have achieved bowel control (Quay and Werry, 1972) although in one study of 10- to 12-year-olds, 1.3% of boys and 0.3% of girls still soiled once a month (Rutter et al., 1970). By age 16, the number of children with encopresis is virtually zero (Bellman, 1966). When soiling occurs after the age at which control is usually acquired, the child may not have acquired control for a variety of reasons, including poor training, a neurological disorder, or mental retardation. The child who has achieved bowel control may temporarily relapse because of anxiety or rage from such causes as the birth of a sibling, parental discord, punitive child-rearing practices, illness, or hospitalization. When soiling occurs in association with a gastrointestinal disorder, the stools are often abnormal. Anthony (1957) has described three types of soiling: (1) continuous soiling, in which the child has never experienced control, (2) discontinuous soiling, in which there was a period of control prior to the episode of soiling, and (3) retentive soiling, in which the child stubbornly retains the stool and occasionally soils after a period of constipation. Other etiological factors are a family history of soiling (which suggests a genetic factor) and a painful predisposing condition, such as an anal fissure. Thus the symptom of fecal soiling may have many causes, and it requires a careful diagnostic evaluation.

The following case example of fecal soiling may now be considered as a paradigm in the context of the developmental stage we are discussing. It should be remembered that the case is a single one, with its own peculiar characteristics, and that like all clinical cases, it is not a case purely of encopresis.

Mrs. D., a high-school graduate who had been married for 14 years, was a depressed, ineffective, and somewhat confused woman. Her depression had worsened considerably at the time of her mother's illness and subsequent death, which occurred when Harvey, her middle child, was in his first year of life. Mrs. D. had never been able to cope well. A visiting nurse once described Mrs. D's home as sparsely furnished and poorly kept. Mrs. D was unable to discipline her children, and the nurse noted at the time of her visit that both Harvey (by that time aged 5) and his younger sister, Esther, were noticeably understimulated. Mrs. D. rarely interacted in a loving way with her children, and she seemed at times to be uninvolved. None of her children seemed at all eager to obey or please her; indeed, at times it looked as though her son Harvey wished to tease and provoke her.

Mr. and Mrs. D. communicated very little with each other. Mr. D. held two jobs, and he did not offer Mrs. D. much help in the rearing of the children.

When Harvey was 2 years of age, it was noted that he was constipated. He was often given suppositories. At the age of 2 years and 5 months, Harvey was hospitalized for a tonsillectomy and adenoidectomy. At this time, Harvey was still constipated; he strained at stool, holding himself rigid and soiling and screaming. He would not sit on the toilet; instead he stood up, stiffened and grew red in the face in an effort to hold back the feces. When he was 2½, his sister was born. Mrs. D. was depressed at the time and could not prepare him for the birth; Harvey reacted to it with intense jealousy and rage. At the age 4, Harvey was still constipated and his parents were now concerned that he might be retarded because his behavior was uncontrolled and babyish, and his speech was infantile and unclear. He also clung a great deal to his mother in a demanding, almost torturing, way.

When given psychological tests, Harvey was shy and did not participate actively. He was shown to have an IQ of 83, with very poor performance on verbal items. There was no sign of organicity.

This case illustrates, among other things, the impact on the child of a depression in the mother. Mrs. D. was unable to provide the protective and facilitating function needed for the optimum development of her child. Thus Harvey was exposed to his mother's withdrawal, repeated enemas, a tonsillectomy, the birth of a sibling (for which he was poorly prepared), and repeated medical work-ups, including barium enemas, all before he was 5 years of age. Furthermore, each of these stresses (the repeated enemas, the tonsillectomy, the birth of a sibling, and so on) has a potential for trauma in its own right. Finally, it should be said that this case, like every other case, was not pure and simple. Harvey's father ran a diaper service, and he used the ready availability of clean diapers as an excuse to avoid confronting his son or his wife about Harvey's encopresis.

SEPARATION

Several types of external stress may influence the course of development at this stage. Among these stresses is separation, to which reference was made in regard to toilet training. Other effects of separation are examined in the present discussion. Separation from parents during early childhood is not a simple phenomenon (Yarrow, 1964; Rutter, 1976). However, some general observations that have clinical significance can be made. During the first 6 months of life, if substitute mothering is provided, the child may experience little more upset over separation than would be expected from the change in routine separation brings. However, from ages 6 months to about 4, after the child has formed a significant attachment to the individual who is his mother, more serious reactions to separation occur. Indeed, the stronger the love tie, the greater the anxiety that separation produces. Other factors that influence the reaction to separation are the degree and duration of the separation, the way in which the separation is handled, the child's previous experiences of separation, the presence of other stresses (e.g., illness, pain, or the birth of a sibling), the child's innate individual tolerance, and subsequent experiences that may reinforce or mitigate the initial trauma.

Separation during these early years is usually accompanied by a short but significant period of grief (Freud and Burlingham, 1943; see Note 24). The child seems to experience the mother's absence as a confirmation of his negative wishes, or as a punishment for them, or even as a consequence of them. He may feel guilty, and he sometimes tries briefly to be extra good. He also tries to deal with his feelings and fantasies through his play, and at times his behavior regresses and symptoms appear. If the separation is prolonged and is more or less complete and if a substitute mother is not provided, the child may, after a "stage of protest" (Bowlby, 1961), sink into a state of despair and eventually become and remain depressed.

SEPARATION AND REACTION TO HOSPITALIZATION

Separations are, of course, sometimes inevitable, as when a child has to go into the hospital. The reaction to separation during hospitalization is difficult to assess (Vernon et al., 1965; Rutter, 1972). The stress of physical illness is itself a major factor (it will be discussed in more detail in Chapter 17). Even in the well child, however, the hospital setting, with its unfamiliarity and the threat to bodily integrity medical and surgical procedures pose, produces a reaction, particularly in relation to certain phase-specific anxieties (e.g., castration anxiety). The intensity of this reaction may be magnified when there is also a separation, particularly in the young child. Children between 7 and 12 months of age who have been hospitalized for less than 2 weeks show marked anxiety toward strangers, desperate clinging to their mothers, and loud crying when their mothers leave (Schaffer and Callender, 1959). Children 2 to 3 years of age show fear and anger at the time of their parents' departure, are acutely anxious with strangers, and manifest (1) depressive behavior (e.g., crying and withdrawal from people), (2) restlessness, hyperactivity, and rhythmic rocking, (3) regressive behavior (e.g., soiling and a refusal to chew solid food), and (4) physical disturbances (e.g., diarrhea and vomiting) (Prugh et al., 1953; see Note 29). Follow-up studies of children who had been hospitalized have shown that long-term effects are frequently seen, particularly the recurrent fear that their parents will leave them. Quinton and Rutter (1976) found, on the other hand, that single separation experiences at any age during childhood rarely have long-term consequences. Repeated hospitalization is associated with later psychiatric disorder, but the association is most marked in children who come from disadvantaged homes.

Separation may promote development. Lewis (1954) noted that children exposed to hostile mothers gained if they were placed in the care of sensitive substitute mothers (ordinarily the hostile mother would first be helped to resolve her destructive tendencies). Langford (1948) observed that many sick children in the hospital develop "constructive compensations" and come out more mature than they were before they were sick. This constructive growth experience was more likely to occur if the parent-child relationship was healthy and if the illness was handled well by parents, nurses, and physicians. A particular way in which a parent can help a child experience hospitalization as a constructive experience has been beautifully described by Robertson (1956). Further recent studies have confirmed the possibility that in older children hospitalization can have some positive effects (Solnit, 1960).

Many of the adverse reactions just described may be mitigated by specific measures (Wolff, 1973; Rutter, 1975). Having a parent live in, particularly for children under the age of 4, avoids, of course, any separation at all. Adequate preparation that offers the child explanations and opportunities for expressive play is helpful (Plank et al., 1959). Preadmission hospital visits by the child to become acquainted with the ward and the nurse and the elimination of unnecessary admission routines are also useful. The child is also comforted if he can bring with him something familiar from home, and if the daily routines (e.g., for bathing, feeding, elimination, and sleeping) approximate as far as possible those to which he is accustomed. If the mother cannot live in, frequent visits during which she actively participates in her child's care often allay the child's anxiety. And the assignment to one nurse of the responsibility for the major care and attention to the child often reassures and comforts the child.

SEPARATION AND MATERNAL DEPRESSION

Psychological separation may occur without the actual physical separation that occurs when a child enters the hospital. For example, a sense of separation and loss may be brought about in the child when the mother withdraws during, say, a state of mourning and grief following a loss she has experienced, such as the loss of her husband through separation, divorce, illness, or death. Normally the mother recovers from her grief, finds a new love object, and then reinvests her child with her maternal care. Less commonly, she attempts to substitute a child for her lost husband, with disastrous results for the child.

However, if the mother's grief continues as a state of depression, the child may be forced to deal with this state. Many children at this stage in their development cannot deal well with the loss that they feel. Instead, a child may initially deny the feelings and then deal with them on a "piecemeal" basis as he or she is faced with future developmental tasks that require the active presence of a mother. The adequacy with which a child deals with psychological loss at this stage depends on such factors as (1) his or her developmental state, (2) the relationship that he or she had had with the "lost" mother, (3) the degree of loss (the death of the mother is the most severe degree), and (4) the support available from the environment.

If the mother's depression is chronic, a characteristic phenomenon may occur. The child may attempt to deal with his loss through identification with his concept of the depressed mother. The child, so to speak, internalizes his impressions of what he considers to be certain aspects and attributes of his mother. The identification may form the basis of a true depression, in which the child feels a sense of blame and emptiness and at the same time experiences feelings of guilt and anxiety. The guilt and anxiety are thought to arise as reactions against rage and aggression, which are believed to have been turned inward against the hypothesized "introjected" mother. The child may attempt to ward off such feelings by increased motor activity and self-punishing behavior. Occasionally, the child exhibits a pseudo-depression as he identifies with the outer characteristics of the depressed mother but does not internalize the aggression.

In any event, the young child appears not to mourn adequately, in part because his need for a full, loving relationship is vital at this stage and the interruption of continuity of affection and care, even though partial, may be too great an obstacle to overcome. Anna Freud (1965) has noted that "in the young child the capacity for outgoing love is still bound up inextricably with the reliable presence of the person who has been instrumental in calling forth this emotion and in interchange with whom it has developed." If the continuity of care and affection is broken, damage is "done to the personality by the loss of function and destruction of capacities which follow invariably on the emotional upheavals brought about by separation from, death or disappearance of the child's first love-objects."

Tolerance of the break in continuity and the consequent deprivation is low at this age, and a substitute mother is not usually available for, say, a mother who is mourning. This kind of experience of loss may permanently color the child's future love relationships.

CRUCIAL DEVELOPMENTAL TASKS

Perhaps the crux of this period of development is the child's move toward greater separation, independence, and autonomy at a time when he is capable of being demanding, intrusive, and negativistic. The extent to which the child successfully emerges from this stage depends on many factors, not the least of which are, on the one hand, the child's state of preparedness for the specific tasks just mentioned and, on the other hand, the degree to which the parents facilitate or hinder the child's progress.

PERVASIVE DEVELOPMENTAL DISORDER

A special case of how inadequate preparedness affects the task of separation and the emergence of autonomy can be seen in the so-called symbiotic psychosis syndrome mentioned earlier (see Chapter 12, p. 155).

Clinically, the child with symbiotic psychosis (Mahler, 1952) exhibits panic-stricken behavior some time between ages 2 and 5, with perhaps a peak in the fourth year. The child has severe temper tantrums, and he may feverishly attempt to restore within himself the infantile feeling of omnipotence. In an attempt to deal with his massive anxiety, the child retreats into an autistic state, accompanied at times by secondary symptoms, such as a preoccupation with and pleasure in being whirled around. Later, certain so-called tertiary symptoms appear as other mechanisms of defense (e.g., repression, isolation, and reaction formations) are brought into play. Auto-aggressive and active aggressive behavior may occur. In the older group of children, a more benign form of symbiotic psychosis seems to occur, with more neurotic symptoms in evidence. These neurotic symptoms may be phobias, compulsions, conversion symptoms, and hypochondriasis.

A careful analysis of the behavior and history of the children Mahler studied led her to postulate that the onset of acute and massive anxiety occurs at a time when the children encounter a separation from the mother for which they are poorly prepared in terms of their intrapsychic development. In some cases, maturational growth itself may inadvertently enable them to separate physically prematurely; thus these children are able to move away from their mothers physically even though they are even less well prepared emotionally to do so than is usual at this age. In other cases, an external environmental event, such as illness, prematurely puts a separation stress on the child.

Thus in Mahler's view it seems as though children who suffer a symbiotic psychosis are emotionally still at the level of the need-satisfying, part-object stage of development and either remain fixated at or regress to the symbiotic phase that normally gives way to the separation-individuation phase toward the end of the first year (Mahler, 1967). The symptoms do not appear until the second, third, or fourth year because the symbiosis has not been threatened until then. This syndrome probably is a variant of what is classified in DSM-III as childhood onset pervasive developmental disorder (299.8).

NARCISSISTIC CHARACTER DISORDER

Some psychoanalysts believe that adults who suffer from a narcissistic character disorder had difficulty with this stage of separation-individuation.

According to one view (Kohut, 1971, 1980), the patient has a disorder involving his or her sense of self, which arises during the separation-individuation phase (especially the so-called rapprochement phase) of development, when he or she received inadequate responses from the parents. This disorder is perpetuated either (1) as a draining, persistent, regressive need to seek a kind of accepting, affirming mirror of the child's sense of omnipotence or grandiosity, or (2) as a tendency to overidealize and merge with another person and thereby to overcome feelings of worthlessness or helplessness.

In either event, such a patient can tolerate neither his or her own defects nor the less-than-ideal nature of others. The patient requires perfection in others and is easily overwhelmed and often chronically enraged—a rage that may be projected in the course of a projective identification. He or she may turn to drugs or other types of self-stimulating activities. Recurrent bouts of depression, low self-esteem, and preoccupation with bodily functions are common, and separations are difficult.

In another view (Kernberg, 1975), the patient has a grandiose image of self, again arising during the separation-individuation phase, but as a defense against early splitting of rage and envy directed toward internalized object representations. This may persist as a constant tendency toward splitting, seen often as rapid shifts between overidealization and devaluation of the object.

These hypotheses remain to be validated.

ACCIDENTAL POISONING IN CHILDREN

A prototypical syndrome resulting from a failure of synchronization and mutual development between mother and child is so-called accidental poisoning in children. The poisoning act in early childhood can be viewed as the result of an interaction between certain developmental characteristics of the child and certain qualities of the mothering person. For example, in one study (Lewis et al., 1966), it was clear that in children under 18 months of age, their increased maturational ability for motor exploratory behavior was uncurtailed and uncontrolled, giving the impression of a heightened level of motor activity. At the same time, a state of depletion existed in the mothers, who were unable to cope without the support they had expected from their husbands or their mothers.

In that same study, in children between approximately 18 and 30 months of age, the developmental characteristic of negativism in the child was an important factor. The negativism seemed heightened in the child, perhaps because of frustration and the relative deprivation he endured while he was in the care of his depleted mother. The child's now heightened negativism seemed to combine with the apparent increase in motor activity that followed from poor internalization of controls to produce a situation in which the child could now deliberately do what he knew he was not supposed to do, namely, swallow a forbidden substance. It was as though the child's wish and capacity to defy his mother were now greater than his wish to please her. Furthermore, there was in these children little incentive to delay the impulsive urge to imbibe the forbidden substance. Another interesting characteristic of this group of children was the developmental characteristic of imitation, which often expressed itself in the imitation of an older sibling. In some of these children, the increased motor activity also seemed to serve an adaptive purpose in that through such motor activity the child was attempting to ward off a depression that resulted from the maternal deprivation.

Children over about 30 months of age seemed to ingest poison more specifically as a reaction to loss. The poisoning act may have had the symbolic meaning of replenishment in response to the feeling of loss.

A 43-month-old girl ingested an antibacterial powder that was used for washing the diapers of her 9-month-old sister. This powder was unattractive visually, texturally, and to taste. In order to get her sister's special powder, the girl had to climb, open a cupboard door, and unscrew a cap. The home was well organized, and the family was apparently functioning well. The parents seemed to be clear and consistent about teaching the child what was safe and what was dangerous, what was acceptable and unacceptable, and what the boundaries were in regard to safety in motility and behavior. Investigation revealed that a crucial factor in the poisoning act was the mother's reaction to her own mother's moving out of the home in order to take a job and to establish a life of her own. This loss, in addition to the birth of a second child, had depleted the mother's ability to give loving attention to the older child. The father, incidentally, was not used to helping; he had regularly retired to his hobby room after supper, leaving his mother-in-law to help his wife. The child reacted with increased negativism and what appeared to be a fierce determination to get what her infant sister had received.

In many of these children, a sense of loss appeared to be felt when there was a diminution in their mother's capacity to love and attend to them, perhaps because of illness, separation, or the birth of another child. The mother's state of depletion also interfered with her capacity to provide a safe environment for the child.

Another possible consequence of a weakened love tie is that the child has less incentive to control his body as well as his impulses. Clinically, this consequence may express itself through such symptoms as bedwetting and fecal soiling, as an impairment in the child's capacity to play with other children, or as a tendency toward destructive behavior.

PERENNIAL DEVELOPMENTAL TASKS, ENVIRONMENTAL STRESSES, AND INDIVIDUAL CHARACTERISTICS

It could probably be said that throughout development the individual is reworking certain major perennial tasks. Outstanding among these tasks are learning to control his body and his impulses, achieving a sense of self, and evolving and resolving his or her feelings toward his family and others. Furthermore, the vicissitudes of life are such that there is no shortage of events which serve to sharpen and shape the conflicts involved in each of these and many other developmental tasks. Separation and loss, particularly separation and loss during ages 1 to 3, are perhaps the most poignant events (they have already been discussed). However, it sometimes happens that a particular characteristic of the child places him or her in the position of experiencing a seemingly normal environment as one that is adverse, and his or her development and resolution of any of the perennial tasks just mentioned suffer as a consequence of the vicissitudes that follow. To illustrate this phenomenon, the child who is mentally retarded will be discussed in the following paragraphs. (Mental retardation has been chosen for discussion at this developmental stage to underscore the clinical need for early diagnosis.)

THE MENTALLY RETARDED CHILD

In general, mental retardation may be defined as "significantly sub-average intellectual functioning, manifested during the developmental period, and associated with distinct impairment in adaptive behavior" (Dybwad, 1968). Although the child's level of intellectual function can be "measured" (e.g., the retarded child's IQ is usually below 70), his social performance is less easy to measure. However, even the IQ is a doubtful criterion of intelligence, since it is not a measure of personality, and in any case the IQ can change when social conditions change. In a study carried out by Skeels (quoted by Luce, 1968), 13 retarded orphans were placed as "houseguests" in a state institution at a very early age. Three of them were categorized as imbeciles. Eleven of the children so profited from the extra play and care they received that they became "normally" intelligent, were put up for adoption, and grew up to become self-supporting middle-class adults. A control group of children the same age, who initially were of normal intelligence, were left in an orphanage in which the infants received little individual attention. One child, who at first had a rating of good average intelligence, became an imbecile by age 19, having spent her life in the orphanage. After a number of years, both groups were tested. The supposedly retarded children who had been placed as houseguests had gained IQ points. The normal children who remained in the orphanage had lost IQ points. Thus the impact of environment on intelligence was dramatically demonstrated.

Many conditions are associated with mental retardation (Masland et al., 1958; Bavin, 1968). Yannet (1956), for example, reported that mental retardation was an important symptom in more than one hundred syndromes. Among the many causes is a genetic endowment that places the individual at the lower part of the normal distribution curve for intelligence (Penrose, 1963). Such a child is said to have "familial retardation." This group of children under the age of 18 years living in the United States comprises about 2,000,000 persons, of whom 65% are males, 35% females. The sex difference may be partly explained by the more difficult social role assigned to males, and by the lower tolerance for deviance that exists for males. It may also involve a genetic factor. The majority (75%) of mentally retarded people are normal in appearance, and the majority (75%) can do almost anything that does not require abstract thinking. The vast majority (80%) have no identifiable disorder, and they fall within the school-age range. The causes of the retardation in this group of psychosocial retardates (75%) include parent-child interaction problems, physical trauma, and genetic factors.

What particularly sets many mentally retarded children apart is not some postulated inherent defect or even their limited intellect, but rather the unfortunate socialization process they undergo in the course of their development. Even their low score on an intelligence test is a result of many factors, and perhaps the most important of these factors is, again, the child's social adjustment (Heber, 1962).

What is emphasized in this discussion is that both intellective and nonintellective factors play a role in the wide range of final socialization patterns achieved by retarded children. Among the nonintellective factors, personality, motivational, and environmental factors seem to be the most significant ones (Zigler and Harter, 1969). For example, the retarded child may continuously experience failure, which may lead to his performing more poorly than he would if he had had a number of successful experiences. He performs poorly partly because he comes to distrust his own solutions to problems and relies instead on others. He may also have experienced considerable deprivation in or out of an institution, leading to an exaggerated dependency. Curiously, retarded children in institutions take longer to solve concept-formation problems in a social setting with a warm, supportive experimenter than they do in a setting in which they cannot see the experimenter (Harter, 1967). It seems that the opportunity of meeting a need for warmth and support competes with the child's attention to a task and so leads to a poorer performance.

The child is, of course, especially prey to his parents' attitudes and feelings. Parents of a child who is retarded for no obvious organic cause only slowly, and painfully, become aware of their child's limitations. Every childbirth entails a risk, and the risk of having a child whose potential for what is called intelligence falls at the lower end of the normal distribution curve is a real one. Three types of parental reactions to retardation have been observed (Kanner, 1953). In one type, the parents exhibit a mature reaction, in which feelings of loss, defeat, resentment, and guilt are experienced and worked through (Solnit and Stark, 1961). In a second type, the parents recognize but do not accept the defect. Parents in this group often engage in a pursuit of the "culprit." In a third type, the parents completely deny that their child is defective.

Although no amount of improving the social adaptation of the retarded child will transform him or her into an individual with superior or even average intelligence, the difference in intelligence should have nothing to do with the rights of the child as a human being in all dimensions (Zigler and Harter, 1969). Certainly the compounding of a retarded child's difficulties by the failure of society to make a partial adaptation to the child is neither necessary nor morally defensible.

Note 23

D.W. Winnicott (1951), Transitional objects and transitional phenomena.[1] In: *Collected Papers*. London: Tavistock Publications Ltd., 1958, pp. 229–242.

... I have introduced the terms "transitional object" and "transitional phenomena" for designation of the intermediate area of experience, between the thumb and the teddy bear, between the oral erotism and true object relationship, between primary creative activity and projection of what has already been introjected, between primary unawareness of indebtedness and the acknowledgement of indebtedness. ...

By this definition an infant's babbling or the way an older child goes over a repertoire of songs and tunes while preparing for sleep comes within the intermediate area as transitional phenomena, along with the use made of objects that are not part of the infant's body yet are not fully recognized as belonging to external reality. ...

... there is the third part of the life of a human being, a part that we cannot ignore, an intermediate area of experiencing, to which inner reality and external life both contribute. It is an area which is not challenged, because no claim is made on its behalf except that it shall

---

1. Based on a paper read before the British Psycho-Analytical Society on 30th May, 1951. *Int. J. Psycho-Anal.*, Vol. XXXIV, 1953.
2. A recent example is the blanket-doll of the child in the film A Two-Year-Old Goes to Hospital by James Robertson (Tavistock Clinic. cf. also Robertson et al. (1952).

exist as a resting-place for the individual engaged in the perpetual human task of keeping inner and outer reality separate yet interrelated. . . .

In the case of some infants the thumb is placed in the mouth while fingers are made to caress the face by pronation and supination movements of the forearm. The mouth is then active in relation to the thumb, but not in relation to the fingers. The fingers caressing the upper lip, or some other part, may be or may become more important than the thumb engaging the mouth. Moreover this caressing activity may be found alone, without the more direct thumb-mouth union. (Freud, 1905, Hoffer, 1949.)

In common experience one of the following occurs, complicating an autoerotic experience such as thumb-sucking:

1. with the other hand the baby takes an external object, say a part of a sheet or blanket, into the mouth along with the fingers; or
2. somehow or other the bit of cloth[2] is held and sucked, or not actually sucked. The objects used naturally include napkins and (later) handkerchiefs, and this depends on what is readily and reliably available; or
3. the baby starts from early months to pluck wool and to collect it and to use it for the caressing part of the activity.[3] Less commonly, the wool is swallowed, even causing trouble; or
4. mouthing, accompanied by sounds of "mum-mum", babbling, anal noises, the first musical notes and so on. . . .

All these things I am calling *transitional phenomena*. Also, out of all this (if we study any one infant) there may emerge some thing or some phenomenon—perhaps a bundle of wool or the corner of a blanket or eiderdown, or a word or tune, or a mannerism, which becomes vitally important to the infant for use at the time of going to sleep, and is a defence against anxiety, especially anxiety of depressive types. (Illingworth, 1951). Perhaps some soft object or cot cover has been found and used by the infant, and this then becomes what I am calling a *transitional object*. This object goes on being important. The parents get to know its value and carry it round when travelling. The mother lets it get dirty and even smelly, knowing that by washing it she introduces a break in continuity in the infant's experience, a break that may destroy the meaning and value of the object to the infant.

I suggest that the pattern of transitional phenomena begins to show at about 4-6-8-12 months. Purposely I leave room for wide variations.

Patterns set in infancy may persist into childhood, so that the original soft object continues to be absolutely necessary at bed-time or at time of loneliness or when a depressed mood threatens. In health, however, there is a gradual extension of range of interest, and eventually the extended range is maintained, even when depressive anxiety is near. A need for a specific object or a behavior pattern that started at a very early date may reappear at a later age when deprivation threatens.

---

3. Here there could possibly be an explanation for the use of the term "wool-gathering", which means: inhabiting the transitional or intermediate area.

This first possession is used in conjunction with special techniques derived from very early infancy, which can include or exist apart from the more direct autoerotic activities. Gradually in the life of an infant teddies and dolls and hard toys are acquired. Boys to some extent tend to go over to use hard objects, whereas girls tend to proceed right ahead to the acquisition of a family. It is important to note, however, that *there is no noticeable difference between boy and girl in their use of the original Not-Me possession*, which I am calling the transitional object.

As the infant starts to use organized sounds (mum, ta, da) there may appear a "word" for the transitional object. The name given by the infant to these earliest objects is often significant, and it usually has a word used by the adults partly incorporated in it. For instance, "baa" may be the name, and the "b" may have come from the adult's use of the word "baby" or "bear". . . .

It is true that the piece of blanket (or whatever it is) is symbolical of some part-object, such as the breast. Nevertheless the point of it is not its symbolic value so much as its actuality. Its not being the breast (or the mother) is as important as the fact that it stands for the breast (or mother).

When symbolism is employed the infant is already clearly distinguishing between fantasy and fact, between inner objects and external objects, between primary creativity and perception. But the term transitional object, according to my suggestion, gives room for the process of becoming able to accept difference and similarity. I think there is use for a term for the root of symbolism in time, a term that describes the infant's journey from the purely subjective to objectivity; and it seems to me that the transitional object (piece of blanket, etc.) is what we see of this journey of progress towards experiencing. . . .

There are certain comments that can be made on the basis of accepted psychoanalytic theory.

1. The transitional object stands for the breast, or the object of the first relationship.
2. The transitional object antedates established reality-testing.
3. In relation to the transitional object the infant passes from (magical) omnipotent control to control by manipulation (involving muscle erotism and coordination pleasure).
4. The transitional object may eventually develop into a fetish object and so persist as a characteristic of the adult sexual life. (See Wulff's development of the theme.)
5. The transitional object may, because of anal-erotic organization, stand for faeces (but it is not for this reason that it may become smelly and remain unwashed. . .)

The mother, at the beginning, by an almost 100 per cent adaptation affords the infant the opportunity for the *illusion* that her breast is part of the infant. It is, as it were, under magical control. The same can be said in terms of infant care in general, in the quiet times between excitements. Omnipotence is nearly a fact of experience. The mother's eventual task is gradually to disillusion the infant, but she has no hope of success unless at first she has been able to give sufficient opportunity for illusion. . . .

. . . The transitional phenomena represent the early stages of the use of illusion, without which there is no meaning for the human being in the idea of a relationship with an object that is perceived by others as external to that being.

The idea illustrated in Fig. 19 is this: that at some theoretical point early in the development of every human individual an infant in a certain setting provided by the mother is capable of conceiving of the idea of something which would meet the growing need which arises out of instinctual tension. The infant cannot be said to know at first what is to be created. At this point in time the mother presents herself. In the ordinary way she gives her breast and her potential feeding urge. The mother's adaptation to the infant's needs, when good enough, gives the infant the *illusion* that there is an external reality that corresponds to the infant's own capacity to create. In other words, there is an overlap between what the mother supplies and what the child might conceive of. To the observer the child perceives what the mother actually presents, but this is not the whole truth. The infant perceives the breast only in so far as a breast could be created just there and then. There is no interchange between the mother and the infant. Psychologically the infant takes from a breast that is part of the infant, and the mother gives milk to an infant that is part of herself. In psychology, the idea of interchange is based on an illusion.

In Fig. 20 a shape is given to the area of illusion, to illustrate what I consider to be the main function of the transitional object and of transitional phenomena. The transitional object and the transitional phenomena start each human being off with what will always be important for them, *i.e.*, a neutral area of experience which will not be challenged.

FIG. 19   FIG. 20

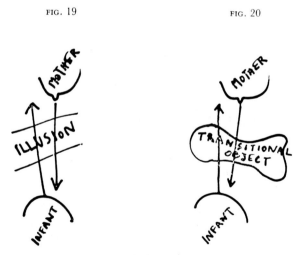

...It is assumed here that the task of reality-acceptance is never completed, that no human being is free from the strain of relating inner and outer reality, and that relief from this strain is provided by an intermediate area of experience which is not challenged (arts, religion, etc.). (cf. Riviere, 1936). This immediate area is in direct continuity with the play area of the small child who is "lost" in play.

In infancy this intermediate area is necessary for the initiation of a relationship between the child and the world, and is made possible by good enough mothering at the early critical phase. Essential to all this is continuity (in time) of the external emotional environment and of particular elements in the physical environment such as the transitional object or objects.

The transitional phenomena are allowable to the infant because of the parents' intuitive recognition of the strain inherent in objective perception, and we do not challenge the infant in regard to subjectivity or objectivity just here where there is the transitional object....

...I do consider that transitional phenomena are healthy and universal.

1. Freud, Sigmund (1905). 'Three Essays on the Theory of Sexuality.' Complete Psychological Works of Sigmund Freud. Vol. VII. London: Hogarth Press.
2. Hoffer, W. (1949). 'Mouth, Hand, and Ego-Integration.' *Psychoanal. Study Child*, Vol. III-IV. London: Imago.
3. Illingworth, R.S. (1951). 'Sleep Disturbances in Young Children.' *Brit. Med. J.*
4. Riviere, J. (1936). 'On the Genesis of Physical Conflict in Earliest Infancy.' *Int. J. Psycho-Anal.*, Vol. XVII.
5. Robertson, J., Bowlby, J. and Rosenblith, Dina (1952). 'A Two-Year-Old Goes to Hospital.' *Psychoanal. Study Child*, Vol. VII. London: Imago.
6. Wulff, M. (1946). 'Fetishism and Object Choice in Early Childhood.' *Psychoanal. Quart.*, Vol. XV.

Note 24

A. Freud, and D. Burlingham (1942), *War and Children*. New York: International Universities Press, 1943.

Reactions to parting...(during the phase from about 6 months to 2 years of age) ... are particularly violent. The child feels suddenly deserted by all the known persons in its world to whom it has learned to attach importance. Its new ability to love finds itself deprived of the accustomed objects, and its greed for affection remains unsatisfied. Its longing for its mother becomes intolerable and throws it into states of despair which are very similar to the despair and distress shown by babies who are hungry and whose food does not appear at the accustomed time. For several hours, the "hunger" for its mother, may over-ride all bodily sensations.

There are some children of this age who will refuse to eat or sleep. Very many of them will refuse to be handled or comforted by strangers. The children cling to some object or to some form of expression which means to them, at that moment, memory of the material presence of the mother. Some will cling to a toy which the mother has put into their hands at the moment of parting; others to some item of bedding or clothing which they have brought from home.

Some will monotonously repeat the word by which they are used to call their mothers, as for instance, Christine, seventeen months old, who said: "mum, mum, mum, mum, mum,"....

She repeated it continually in a deep voice for at least three days.

Observers seldom appreciate the depth and seriousness of this grief in a small child. Their judgment of it is misled for one main reason. This childish grief is short-lived. Mourning of equal intensity in an adult person would have to run its course throughout a year; the same process in the child between one and two years will normally be over in thirty-six to forty-eight hours. The difference in duration is due to certain psychological differences between the state of childhood and adultness. . . .

. . . A love object who does not give it immediate satisfaction is no good to it. Its memories of the past are spoilt by the disappointment which it feels at the present moment. It has no outlook into the future and it would be of no help to it if it had. Its needs are so urgent that they need immediate gratification; promises of pleasure are no help.

The little child will therefore, after a short while, turn away from the mother image in its mind and, though at first unwillingly, will accept the comfort which is offered. In some cases acceptance may come in slow stages. Christine, for instance, would at first only let herself be fondled or held by an unseen person. She would sit on somebody's lap, turn her head away, enjoy the familiar sensation of being held, and probably add to it in her own mind the imaginary picture of her own mother. Whenever she looked at the face of the person who held her she began to cry.

There are other children who are spared these violent reactions. They seem placid, dazed, and more or less indifferent. It takes a few days or even a week before this placidity is disturbed by a realisation of the fact that they are among strangers: all sorts of slighter depressive reactions and problems of behavior will then result. All children of this age, those with violent reactions as well as those where reaction is delayed, will show a tendency to fall ill under the new conditions; they will develop colds, sore throats, or slight intestinal troubles.

That the shock of parting at this stage is really serious is further proven by the observation that a number of these children fail to recognise their mothers when they are visited after they have "settled down" in their new surroundings. The mothers themselves realise that this lack of recognition is not due to any limitations of the faculty of memory as such. The same child who looks at its mother's face with stony indifference as if she were a complete stranger, will have no difficulty in recognising lifeless objects which have belonged to its past. When taken home again it will recognise the rooms, the position of the beds and will remember the contents of cupboards, etc.

. . . The mother has disappointed the child and left its longing for her unsatisfied; so it turns against her with resentment and rejects the memory of her person from its consciousness.

REFERENCES

Anthony, E.J. (1957), An experimental approach to the psychopathology of childhood: Encopresis. *Br. J. Med. Psychol.*, 30:146–175.

Bavin, J.T.R. (1968), The genetics of mental deficiency. In: *Foundations of Child Psychiatry*, ed. E. Miller. Oxford: Pergamon Press, pp. 457–488.

Bellman, M. (1966), Studies on encopresis. *Acta Paediatr. Scand.*, (Suppl.) 170.

198   CROSS-SECTIONAL PERSPECTIVES

Bergman, R. (1968), A case of stuttering. *J. Am. Acad. Child Psychiatry*, 7:13–30.
Bowlby, J. (1961), Separation anxiety: A critical review of the literature. *J. Child Psychol. Psychiatry*, 1:251–269.
Dybwad, G. (1968), Who are the mentally retarded? *Children*, 15:43–48.
Erikson, E.H. (1959), Identity and the Life Cycle. *Psychol. Issues*, 1 (1):65–74.
Fairbairn, W.R.D. (1952), *An Object-Relations Theory of the Personality*. New York: Basic Books, p. 176.
Fay, W.H., and Butler, B.V. (1971), Echo-reaction as an approach to semantic resolution. *J. Speech Hearing Dis.*, 14:645–651.
Fraiberg, S.H. (1959), *The Magic Years*. New York: Scribner's, p. 305.
Freud, A. (1957), The mutual influences in the development of ego and id. *Psychoanal. Study Child*, 7:42–50.
Freud, A. (1965), Continuity in theory from practice. In: *The Family and the Law*, ed. J. Goldstein and J. Katz. New York: Free Press, p. 1053.
Freud, A., and Burlingham, D. (1943), *War and Children*. New York: International Universities Press.
Freud, S. (1911), *Formulations on the Two Principles of Mental Functioning*. Standard Edition, 12 (1958). London: The Hogarth Press, pp. 213–226.
Gesell, A., and Amatruda, C.S. (1941), *Developmental Diagnosis*. New York: Paul Hoeber Medical Division, Harper & Row. (2nd Ed. 1964.)
Harter, S. (1967), Mental age, I.Q., and motivational factors in the discrimination learning set performances of normal and retarded children. *J. Exp. Child Psychol.*, 5:123–141.
Hartmann, H. (1939), *Ego Psychology and the Problem of Adaptation*, trans. D. Rapaport, New York: International Universities Press, 1958, p. 8.
Hartmann, H. (1952), The mutual influences in the development of ego and id. *Psychoanal. Study Child*, 7:7–70.
Hartmann, H. (1956), Notes on the reality principle. In: *Essays on Ego Psychology* (1964). New York: International Universities Press, pp. 241–264.
Hartmann, H., Kris, E., and Lowenstein, R.M. (1949), Notes on the theory of aggression. *Psychoanal. Study Child*, 3/4:9–36.
Heber, R.F. (1962), Mental retardation: Concept and classification. In: *Readings on the Exceptional Child*, ed. P.E. Trapp and P. Himelstein. New York: Appleton-Century-Crofts, pp. 69–81.
Kanner, L. (1953), Parents' feelings about retarded children. *Am. J. Ment. Defic.*, 57:375–383.
Kernberg, O. (1975), *Borderline Conditions and Pathological Narcissism*. New York: Jason Aronson.
Kohut, H. (1980), Self Psychology: Reflections on the present and future. November 2, 1980, Boston Psychoanalytic Association Symposium on Reflections on Self Psychology.
Kohut, H. (1971), *The Analysis of the Self*. New York: International Universities Press.
Langford, W.S. (1948), Physical illness and convalescence: Their meaning to the child. *J. Pediatr.*, 33:242–250.
Lewis, H. (1954), *Deprived Children*. London: Oxford University Press.
Lewis, M., Solnit, A.J., Stark, M.H., Gabrielson, I.W., and Klatskin, E.H. (1966), An exploratory study of accidental ingestion of poison in young children. *J. Am. Acad. Child Psychiatry*, 5:255–271.
Luce, G. (1968), The physiological imprint of learning. In: *Mental Health Programs*, Report No. 2. Washington, D.C., Department of Health, Education, and Welfare, P.H.S. Publication No. 1743, pp. 91–92.
Mahler, M.S. (1952), On child psychosis and schizophrenia: Autistic and symbiotic infantile psychoses. *Psychoanal. Study Child*, 7:286–305.
Mahler, M.S. (1967), On human symbiosis and the vicissitudes of individuation. *Am. Psychoanal. Assoc.*, 15:710–762.
Masland, R.I., Sarason, S.B., and Gladwin, T. (1958), *Mental Subnormality: Biological, Psychological and Cultural Factors*. New York: Basic Books.

Money, J., Hampson, J.G., and Hampson, J.L. (1955), An examination of some basic sexual concepts: The evidence of human hermaphroditism. *Johns Hopkins Hosp. Bull.*, 97:301–319.

Parten, M.B. (1933), Social play among preschool children. *J. Abnorm. Soc. Psychol.*, 28:136–147.

Penrose, S.L. (1963), *The Biology of Mental Defect.* London: Sidgwick and Jackson.

Piaget, J. (1929), *The Child's Conception of the World.* New York: Harcourt, Brace & World.

Piaget, J. (1954), *The Construction of Reality in the Child.* New York: Basic Books, p. xii.

Plank, E.N., Caughey, P., and Lipson, M.J. (1959), A general hospital childcare program to counteract hospitalism. *Am. J. Orthopsychiatry*, 29:94–101.

Prugh, D.G., Staub, E., Sands, H., Kirshbaum, R., and Lenihan, E. (1953), A study of the emotional reaction of children and families to hospitalization and illness. *Am. J. Orthopsychiatry*, 23:70–106.

Quay, H.C., and Werry, J.S. (1972), *Psychopathological Disorder in Childhood.* New York: Wiley.

Quinton, D., and Rutter, M. (1976), Early hospital admissions and later disturbances of behavior: An attempted replication of Douglas' findings. *Dev. Med. Child Neurol.*, 18:447–459.

Robertson, J. (1956), A mother's observations on the tonsillectomy of her four-year-old daughter, with comments by Anna Freud. *Psychoanal. Study Child*, 11:410–433.

Rutter, M. (1972), *Maternal Deprivation Revisited.* Harmondsworth: Penguin.

Rutter, M. (1975), *Helping Troubled Children.* Harmondsworth: Penguin.

Rutter, M. (1976), Separation, loss and family relationships. In: *Child Psychiatry*, ed. M. Rutter and L. Hersov. Oxford: Blackwell, pp. 47–73.

Rutter, M., Tizard, J., and Whitmore, K. (eds.) (1970), *Education, Health and Behaviour.* London: Longmans.

Schaffer, H.R., and Callender, W.M. (1959), Psychologic effects of hospitalization in infancy. *Pediatrics*, 24:528–539.

Shaw, G.B. (1903), *Man and Superman*, Act III. New York: Penguin, 1946.

Sherman, M., Hertzig, M., Austrian, R., and Shapiro, T. (1981), Treasured objects in school-aged children. *Pediatrics*, 68:379–386.

Solnit, A.J. (1960), Hospitalization: An aid to physical and psychological health in childhood. *Am. J. Dis. Child.* 9:153–163.

Solnit, A.J., and Stark, M.H. (1961), Mourning and the birth of a defective child. *Psychoanal. Study Child*, 16:523–537.

Stoller, R.J. (1967), Transvestites' women. *Am. J. Psychiatry*, 124:333–339.

Vernon, D.T.A., Foley, S.M., Sipowicz, R.R., and Schulman, J.L. (1965), *The Psychological Responses of Children to Hospitalization and Illness.* Springfield, Ill.: Charles C Thomas.

Watts, A.F. (1947), *Language and Mental Development of Children.* London: Harrap.

Winnicott, D.W. (1951), Transitional objects and transitional phenomena. In: *Collected Papers.* London: Tavistock, 1958, pp. 229–242.

Wolff, S. (1973), *Children Under Stress.* Harmondsworth: Penguin.

Yannet, H. (1956), Classification and etiological factors in mental retardation. In: *Mental Retardation: Readings and Resources*, ed. J.H. Rothstein. New York: Holt, Rinehart & Winston, 1961.

Yarrow, L.J. (1964), Separation from parents during early childhood. In: *Review of Child Development Research*, Vol. I. M.L. Hoffman and L.W. Hoffman (Eds.) New York: Russell Sage Foundation.

Zigler, E.F., and Harter, S. (1969), The socialization of the mentally retarded. In: *Handbook of Socialization Theory and Research*, ed. D.A. Goslin. Chicago: Rand McNally.

Chapter 14

EARLY CHILDHOOD—AGES 3 TO 6

MATURATION

Children become increasingly agile as they grow and develop during the period of early childhood—learning, for example, to skip on alternate feet. Their perceptual-motor skills also improve at this time: a child at age 2 can copy a circle, and a child at age 3 can copy a cross; by age 5 a child can copy a square and by age 7 years a diamond. Memory improves with age: by age 6 the child can count five digits forward and three digits backward. The use of language is, of course, extensive in early childhood and during this period the child learns to dress himself without assistance and to wash himself.

CHILDHOOD SEXUAL THEORIES

At the same time, fantasy is now much more elaborate, and is influenced by such factors as (1) the child's growing awareness of sexual differences, pregnancy, childbirth and death, (2) his life experiences, and (3) the persisting magical quality of his thinking. He begins to form theories about sex (S. Freud, 1908). For example, the child at this stage often attempts to solve the problem of how conception occurs by postulating that something is swallowed. The child also seems to view sexual intercourse between the mother and father as an act of violence. Most children initially think that the baby is delivered through the anus, and later they think that the baby comes out through the navel.

MANIFESTATION OF SEXUAL THEORIES IN FOOD ATTITUDES

Some of the theories just mentioned may manifest themselves in certain irrational postures and feelings toward food. Avoidance of all food, or the fear of being poisoned, is sometimes related to a fear of pregnancy in the later years of this stage, when pregnancy is associated with oral intake. Occasionally, avoidance of food is based on the association of fatness with pregnancy, especially if the child has been told that a baby grows in the mother's stomach. More specific food aversions, such as to sausages or the yolk of an egg, often have more specific fantasies attached to them. That is to say, like all neurotic symptoms they may represent the forbidden wish as well as the defense against the wish, and may therefore be part of a reaction formation, such as disgust. They may represent an attempt to avoid direct expression of sadistic or cannibalistic fantasies, such as the fantasy of swallowing a penis or engulfing a newborn baby.

FAMILY ROMANCE

Every child also appears to develop some form of a family romance fantasy (S. Freud, 1909a). As the child becomes increasingly aware of the discrepancy between his idealized image of his parents and the actuality of his parents, he becomes increasingly disillusioned with his parents. Part of the process of dealing with the disillusionment is the elaboration of a fantasy that his present parents are not really his parents and that he "really" comes from, say, a royal family. This fantasized family, of course, can and does possess all the idealized characteristics he had previously attributed to his parents. At the same time, this splitting may also serve to lessen the guilt he feels about his incestuous fantasies toward his parents at this time.

OEDIPAL FANTASIES

Fantasies also now appear to be more sex differentiated. The initial systematic description of these fantasies by Freud (1900) was later expanded in numerous case studies (e.g., Freud, 1905, 1909b, 1909c, 1918; Brunswick, 1940; Bornstein, 1949 [see Note 8], 1953). From these case studies it would appear that characteristic groups of drives, unconscious and conscious fantasies, and personal relationships occur in both boys and girls (see Note 25).

Before describing the psychoanalytic account of psychosexual development, it is important to note that many scientists think that the concept of psychosexual stages is oversimplified to the point of being misleading (Rutter, 1971; White, 1960). Hypotheses involving unconscious feelings are difficult to test, as is the concept of the oedipus complex. Therefore the discussion that follows must, from a strictly scientific viewpoint, be regarded as speculative (see Note 26).

PROTOTYPICAL FANTASIES OF BOYS

Boys at this stage tend to feel romantically attracted to their mothers, perhaps in the same way they imagine their fathers are. In such cases, the boy feels that his father is not only his rival but also an enemy who may hurt him. The form of the harm that a boy imagines might befall him is determined in part by his current preoccupation with the anatomical differences between boys and girls and in part by any actual threats the boy may have received. Boys, for example, observing that girls do not have penises, may believe that girls once had penises and that the penises were removed; boys may then fear that the same fate may befall them (and some adults do try to stop boys from masturbating by telling them that their penises will be cut off).

In order to avoid being hurt, the boy normally gives up his active love for his mother and identifies with his father, thus resolving his oedipal conflict. However, occasionally he retains his active love for his mother and even goes so far as to accept a "castrated" position with respect to his father. In such cases the boy virtually offers himself to the father as a love object. This position has been called the passive oedipus conflict (Brunswick, 1940).

A 19-year-old student recalled during treatment that when he was 6 years old he used to take a bath with his sister. He remembered that he used to think that she had once had a penis and that it had been cut off. At the same time, he also demonstrated unwittingly how his current behavior was largely directed at giving others the impression that he was powerless, helpless, and a threat to no one. The two "events" thus seemed to be linked together in his mind, as though he were saying, "Leave me alone, you can pass me by; I've been done already." Interestingly, he simultaneously yearned for physical contact with men.

Mothers, of course, by and large do not treat their sons as they do their husbands. The son often is resentful of this and feels some degree of inadequacy—a feeling that is reinforced by his actual physical inferiority. In order to reassure himself and at the same time attract his mother's attention, the son may, even under normal circumstances, become self-conscious about his penis—or he may have a strong wish to exhibit his penis. Sometimes this wish takes a pathological form, particularly if the parents heighten the conflict by their own behavior.

A 4-year-old boy was brought to the emergency room at 4 A.M. in an acute agitated state. For the previous four hours he had said there were spiders under his pajamas and there were shadows inside him. While in the waiting room he screamed as his aunt attempted to keep a coat over his completely nude body. He refused to wear any clothes at all, and he remained unashamedly naked.

On further study it was found that the boy and his mother slept in the same bed. There was a serious marital difficulty, which included a severe sexual problem and violent behavior between the parents, who slept apart.

Later it was learned that the boy's mother often allowed him to sit on her lap. He would feel her pelvis and ask her why she did not have the same feeling his father had. He would also be allowed to fondle his mother's breasts, and his mother noticed that he got an erection at the slightest touch—her touch. It became clear that this boy's fears about wearing his clothes were his way of reassuring himself and allaying his anxiety by keeping his genitals always in sight. For example, in a progressive play sequence the boy first exhibited his fear of spiders' crawling on his skin, then he touched his thigh and then his penis, and finally he wanted to look inside his trousers in search of his penis.

PROTOTYPICAL FANTASIES OF GIRLS

Girls during this period may tend to turn their love away from their mothers, at least to some extent, and to direct their attention increasingly to their fathers. Why this shift occurs is not entirely clear. One possible explanation is that the girl, unlike the boy, eventually does have to make a complete shift in the sex of her love object. In some cases this shift may be difficult to make, in part perhaps because of the nature or strength of the girl's tie to the mother. Probably the girl's active strivings toward the mother are never really given up but instead find their expression later, when the girl is able to complete her identification with her active mother at the time she herself is able to become a mother, to have a child of her own. In the meantime, however, the girl's wish to have a baby cannot be realized, and the girl seems to vacillate between loving her mother and loving her father and between wanting to be a girl and wanting to be a boy. She may envy the penis as a token of power, and act on her envy by becoming a tomboy.

Sometimes this tomboy behavior represents an attempt to deny her femininity. Occasionally, a girl will try to demean a boy by ridiculing him, to make him feel that he is stupid or repulsive. In some girls the disappointment about having female genitals may lead to a partial repudiation of the mother and a tendency instead to identify with the father. In other girls, the penis may be regarded as an abnormal growth on the body. There are several circumstances that may lead to this fantasy: (1) a girl may feel so secure about her femininity that it is the boy who looks odd to her, (2) the view of the penis as a growth may be a special case of the girl's wish to downgrade the boy's possession of a penis, and (3) in some families women may dominate and this circumstance may encourage the girls in the family to view males as defective.

The girl's vacillation is reinforced by the disappointment she feels at not having a baby by her father on the one hand and at not getting a penis from her mother on the other hand. Yet throughout this stage, the young girl is, of course, still dependent on her mother for the satisfaction of her daily needs, and so any jealousy of the mother because of the mother's place beside father is usually accompanied by anxiety. Thus any disapproval of the girl by the mother at this stage is acutely felt by the young girl, the more so because her thinking still lacks logic and she still tends to magically imbue the mother with omnipotent and dangerous power. Furthermore, in a sense any "punishment" is "immanently" justified, since the unconscious crime of a hostile wish against the mother has indeed been committed, and the line between a wish and an act performed is not always clear in the girl's mind at this stage. This vacillation of feelings leads to a characteristic ambivalence, found especially in women who have not adequately resolved their feelings toward their parents.

Both boys and girls feel guilty about their destructive wishes, and they are afraid of retaliation; boys at this stage more often fear physical injury, girls mostly seem to fear abandonment. According to Jones (1929), the fear of abandonment in girls may be related to an earlier fear of a loss of the personality itself and of the total annihilation of the capacity to be gratified—a condition for which the term aphánisis has been coined. Both boys and girls often seek, therefore, to reassure themselves. One common behavior pattern that serves this purpose is that of entering the parents' bedroom while the parents are together there. In so doing, the child not only is near the person he loves, but he can also be reassured that the rival is still alive. Further, since his presence prevents intercourse the child may be attempting to prevent the birth of a sibling although more probably he is acting out his own fantasies of union with a parent and defending himself against the fantasy, prevalent at this age, that parents hurt each other during intercourse.

SEDUCTION: REALITY AND FANTASY

Freud was initially convinced that his patients had been sexually molested by a parent. Later, he hypothesized that his patients' reports of such attacks during childhood resulted from the child's "phantasies" of being seduced and were not reports of actual events. However, some scholars now believe that Freud was right the first time; his patients probably had been abused sexually by a parent, often the father (Klein and Tribich, 1980; Masson, 1981). The evidence in Freud's own case reports, including the Dora case (Freud, 1905), for example, reveals abundant information about destructive behavior by the parents toward the child, and a mass of data since the 1960s shows that large numbers of children are in fact abused by their parents.

RESOLUTION OF OEDIPAL FEELINGS

The resolution of these oedipal feelings appears to require some degree of identification with the parent of the same sex and some degree of internalization of the good and bad, loving and beloved, praising and forbidding, rewarding and punishing aspects of both parents, a process that takes place over a period of time and that consolidates the formation of what Freud conceptualized as the superego (S. Freud, 1924). In addition, it is hypothesized that a repression of direct sexual and aggressive fantasies in relation to either parent occurs— to the extent that there is an amnesia for these first few years of life. Thus in spite of evidence that the child's memory functions excellently during these early years, in later life few people can remember much about their first three or four years. However, whether this apparent amnesia reflects unconscious repression or immaturity of the central nervous system is unclear.

Sometimes a displacement of sexual and aggressive impulses occurs. A child may discharge his feelings onto another family member. Usually some sublimation occurs, as seen, for example, in boys who engage in competitive but less dangerous activities with their peers. This type of sublimation will be discussed further in the next chapter (see Note 29).

FACTORS INFLUENCING OEDIPAL FANTASIES AND FEELINGS

The oedipal situation and its resolution just outlined represent the prototypical course (S. Freud, 1905; see Note 7). In actual life there are hundreds of variations, and they are brought about by a host of factors. Parts of four major clusters of factors affect almost every child. First, of course, is the state of the preoedipal organization of the child. If the child has failed to achieve, say, a sense of self or a feeling of trust, he is obviously much less well prepared than he could be to resolve the problems and tasks of this period of his life.

Sibling relationships affect the child's feelings. Sibling rivalry is almost always caused by the way parents relate to their children, but once it exists it is a force in its own right (Levy, 1937; Hawkins, 1946).

Parents themselves are an obvious reality factor. The kinds of responses a parent makes to a child are determined in part by (1) the state of the marital relationship, (2) the specific relationship between a parent and a particular child, (3) the development and changing roles demanded of parents as the child develops and as they themselves grow older, and (4) the sometimes unwelcome resurgence of previously dormant conflicts, now activated by the child at a particular stage in his development.

Last, there is a wide range of chance encounters that may befall a child, including illness, separations, births, deaths, seduction, and divorce, each of which has its characteristic impact.

SUPEREGO

The modern concept of superego began with Freud's use of the term superego in his paper "The Ego and the Id" (Freud, 1923). The paper and the date are important because they mark a significant development in Freud's theory of the functioning of the mind. This development has come to be known as the structural theory, in which certain characteristics and modes of functioning are differentiated and clustered into three systems: id, ego, and superego. Several functions and elements of these systems were, in fact, described or foreshadowed in some of Freud's earlier works (Freud, 1910, 1914).

SUPEREGO DEVELOPMENT AND FUNCTION

The term superego denotes an abstract metaphor by which certain observable phenomena, such as the sense of guilt, can be understood and to a certain extent predicted. It does not denote an anatomical or a neurophysiological entity.

From a developmental point of view, Freud argued that the superego prototypically arose from an identification with the father taken as a model, with desexualization and, perhaps, sublimation being part of that identification. When desexualization occurred, the usual power of positive, loving feelings (libidinal cathexis) to bind aggressive and destructive inclinations (aggressive cathexis) was thought to be correspondingly weakened. This was said to result in a defusion or separation of sexual and aggressive drives, leaving the aggressive drive more mobile and available. This unbound aggressive drive was then hypothesized to be converted into the general harsh and cruel prohibitions of the now internalized object representations, expressed as various forms of moral sanctions, such as, "Thou shalt" (Freud, 1923). If the original object representation (parental figure) was perceived as harsh, then that quality would be internalized: "if the father was hard, violent and cruel, the superego takes over these attributes from him . . . the superego has become sadistic" (Freud, 1928). At the same time, the original severity of the superego did not—or not so much—represent the severity which had been experienced or anticipated from the object, but expressed "the child's own aggressiveness toward the latter" (Freud, 1930). That is to say, identification with the real and attributed ethical and moral aspects of the parental figures was thought to have occurred. The identification had two aspects: one was an identification with the oedipal rival as a threatening, aggressive figure as a means of defense; the other was identification as a means of gratification—for example, a boy's merging with the father and thus sharing with him certain of his perceived attributes, such as his omnipotence. Thus an important motivation was the fear of loss of love, although avoidance of castration anxiety was thought to be the more common motivation that influenced superego organization (Freud, 1923).

The psychic energy that fueled superego functioning was

conceptualized as deriving in the first place from the reservoir of energy conceptualized as id. However, the manner in which a major portion of superego formation occurred led, it was believed, to an over-representation of aggressive drive energy. Superego demands on ego functioning were thought to be as insistent and irrational as the original instinctual demands.

Following this classic view of the development of superego functioning, progressive phases were later hypothesized (Bornstein, 1951). For example, the superego was viewed as strict initially (say, at 6 to 8 years of age), with signs of a heightened ambivalence and a marked conflict over masturbation. Gradually, this struggle might abate so that in the second half of the latency period (say, at 8 to 10 years of age), the superego might be less strict and the sublimation more successful, and the child might begin to experience pleasure again from sexual gratification. Further development was also hypothesized to occur in which conscious or unconscious guilt was replaced by reasoned judgment. At the same time, regression in superego functioning theoretically could occur. It might manifest itself clinically as a resurgence of guilt having the quality of an instinctual urge, a strong need for punishment, or a tendency to externalize and project one's own guilt onto others. That tendency was thought to be represented in dreams, for example, as spoken words attributed to parental figures.

Again, the classic psychoanalytic view conceptualized superego functioning as an internalization of ideals and prohibitions previously attributed to the representation of the parental figures in external reality. The development of superego was thought to begin in the communications, conscious and unconscious, between parents and child during infancy. The influence of the society and culture could be transmitted, in the early years, largely through the way in which parents responded to and guided the child through the expectable developmental phases. The more or less completed process would then provide a resolution of the oedipus complex, summarized in Freud's aphorism that the superego was the "heir of the oedipus complex." The major superego functions became self-observation, conscience, ego ideals, and repression. These superego functions might be reinforced by social sanctions (e.g., laws and moral codes), but would eventually assume a relative autonomy. Although more or less independent, superego functions would almost always relate to the demands of id, reality, and ego. For example, ego defenses might repress guilt feelings and rationalize superego demands as well as meet the ideals presented.

DIVERGENT VIEWPOINTS

There are other psychoanalytic views of the development of superego, the most notable of which are those of Melanie Klein. Introjection as a process in superego formation was considered in the Kleinian view to constitute the first roots of superego, particularly during the paranoid-schizoid position, when ideal and persecutory objects were said to be introjected. The persecutory object was thought to be experienced as primitive and cruel, while the ideal object with which the ego was said to long to identify became the ego ideal, although it, too, was described as harsh because of the high demands for perfection (Segal, 1964).

Klein (1960) postulated that feelings of guilt existed as early as the fifth or sixth month of life, when the baby was believed to become aware of and concerned about the harm his destructive impulses and greed might do, or might already have done, to his parental love objects. The baby was said to then experience an urge to make reparations. These feelings of guilt and the tendency to make reparations were thought to be experienced as predominantly depressive in nature, leading Klein to call this period of normal development the depressive position. Thus this self-critical and controlling function was what Klein believed to be superego and as such to operate early in life.

The superego during the depressive position was said to be experienced as an internal, ambivalently loved object, with injury to this object giving rise to feelings of guilt. However, the object was also thought to be loved and presumably felt by the child as helpful in his struggle against his destructive impulses. Thus Klein (1955) believed that "the superego is something which is felt by the child to operate internally in a concrete way; that it consists of a variety of figures built up from his experiences and phantasies and that it is derived from the stages in which he had internalized (introjected) his parents" (p. 15). In this view, "the superego of the depressive position, among other features, accuses, complains, suffers and makes demands for reparation but, while still persecuting, is less harsh than the superego of the paranoid position" (Rosenfeld, 1955, p. 188).

Klein viewed internalization, and therefore superego formation, as beginning very early, with the first internalized object.

Klein (1926) stated, "The analysis of very young children shows that, as soon as the oedipus complex arises, they begin to work it through and thereby to develop the superego" (p. 145). In Klein's view (1958), "the superego precedes by some months the beginning of the Oedipus complex, a beginning which I date, together with that of the depressive position, in the second quarter of the first year" (p. 239).

SEXUAL DIFFERENCES IN SUPEREGO FORMATION

Since superego formation was seen as a function of oedipus complex resolution, and since the oedipal conflict and its resolution were thought to be different in boys and girls, differences in superego formation in the two sexes were postulated. Perhaps the most striking difference was Freud's (1925) conclusion that women were less moral than men. "For woman the level of what is ethically normal is different from what it is in men. Their superego is never so inexorable, so impersonal, so independent of its emotional origin as we require it to be in men . . . that they show less sense of justice than men, that they are less ready to submit to the great exigencies of life, that they are more often influenced in their judgments by feelings of affection or hostility—all these would be amply accounted for in the modification of the formation of their superego" (pp. 257 ff.). Obviously, there are serious questions about the validity of Freud's views on the development and psychological characteristics of girls and women. Freud, of course, was significantly influenced by the traditional patriarchal and evolutionary values of his time (Schafer, 1974).

DEVIATIONS IN SUPEREGO FUNCTIONS

Superego deviations are said to be more likely to occur when preoedipal and oedipal development is deviant. Two particularly striking kinds of deviant development have been conceptualized—one in which the superego of the introjected parents is itself flawed, the other when a massive external event, such as the loss of a parent during the oedipal period, significantly alters the consolidation of the superego. In the case of parents who themselves have faulty values, the child is said to internalize these faulty values, leading to significant gaps in the child's superego—so-called superego lacunae (Johnson, 1949). In the case of the one-parent child, such deviations as a harsh, sadistic superego or a deficient superego are said to occur (Neubauer, 1960) (see p. 214). In almost every case reported by Neubauer, the absent parent was either "immensely idealized or endowed with terribly sadistic attributes."

SPECIAL SITUATIONS

There are other specific situations which have fairly well-defined impacts on the oedipal conflict and its resolution. Two outstanding situations that have been carefully studied are the oedipal conflict in the adopted child and the oedipal conflict in the one-parent child. Although the impacts of these situations have certain characteristics, the outcome is still dependent on the balance of all the other variables just mentioned.

ADOPTION

Adoption can act as a powerful reality that reinforces the phase-specific fantasies just described. The adopted child finds it difficult then to deal with the heightened fantasy, and tends toward an action-oriented, repetitive behavior pattern that in effect plays out the child's fantasies. Unfortunately, the result is often one of multiple psychological difficulties for the child.

Extrafamilial adoptees in the United States below the age of 18 constitute about 2% of the population (Brieland, 1965). However, a higher proportion of these children are referred for psychiatric help than would ordinarily be expected (Toussieng, 1966). The range of diagnostic categories of these children is broad, with perhaps a preponderance of children who tend to act out aggressively and sexually. The most powerful fantasies in the children are often woven around a search for the biological parents, leading at times to actual explorations. The adopted child may continue to split the two sets of parents into "good" parents and "bad" parents, in either direction.

Many other factors, however, contribute to the psychological problems of the adopted child. For example, the parents of the adopted child have to deal continuously with their own reactions to their infertility and their own fantasies about the adopted child, who is often an illegitimate child. The continuous presence and behavior of the adopted child stimulate these fantasies in the parents, and these fantasies further interfere with the rearing skills of the parents (Schechter et al., 1964). For example, the idea of "the bad seed" is a prevalent shared fantasy, and it often leads to prophecy-fulfilling behavior in the child. The way in which a child is told about his adoption can be both an indicator of existing psychological problems and part of the cause of any future psychological difficulties.

Some of the difficulties in telling a child about his adoption stem from emotional conflicts in the parents. But there are unresolved conceptual problems with even the best approach. Kirk (1964), for example, holds the views that the adoptive parents must face their own feelings and attitudes, especially those concerning their inability to produce children, and that the adoptive parents should discuss this subject openly with the child, along with the subject of the child's illegitimate birth. Peller (1961, 1963) feels that adoption should be a private matter within the family, and that "adoption day" should not be a matter of public pronouncement. Again, many workers feel that the child should be told about his adopted status very early so that the child grows up with this knowledge and so that the child and his parents can deal better with the many different aspects of the problem as the child's development proceeds. In this view, telling a child about his adoption is a continuous process that has different meanings at different stages of development. Wittenborn (1957) found that children who were told of their adoption early tended to have higher IQs, to speak better, and to appear less clumsy than children who were not told early. However, as Lewis (1965) noted, the parents who felt comfortable telling their child early that he was adopted were also parents who had many good qualities, a factor that may have been more significant than the mere fact of early telling. Other workers favor postponing telling the child about his adoption until he has accomplished some of the major tasks of development and has reached a period of relative emotional stability (say, between 6 and 10 years of age).

Neither method is simple, and many variables, such as the age and status of the siblings and the sociocultural environment, need to be considered. Moreover, much depends on how comfortable the parents feel about the position they have taken in the matter of talking with the child they have adopted and on their understanding of the kinds of problems that can arise.

Since the passage of the Children's Act of 1975 in Great Britain, British adopted persons over the age of 18 have had access to their birth records. Surprisingly, by 1980 only 1 to 2% of adopted adults had taken advantage of this legislation. The dire results that were prophesied did not materialize. However, there were some interesting sequelae. First, the number of babies available for adoption dropped from 21,299 in 1975 to

12,121 in 1978. This decline has been attributed to the inhibitory effect of the Children's Act on mothers who do not want to be traced at a later date. Second, some biological mothers who had previously given their children for adoption began to come forward in an attempt to be found. In general, the act has allowed the truth to be found and feelings to be discussed openly. A study of 70 adolescents who took advantage of the law that enabled them to obtain information about their biological parents revealed that most felt that they had a right to this information and that it was their parents' duty to give them the information, and that they were resentful of parents who were reluctant to give it. Many of these adolescents had felt confused and deprived when they were earlier denied the knowledge they later discovered for themselves (Triseliotis, 1973).

By and large, healthy, normal adoptees appeared to be more or less satisfied simply with the information they obtained (although they may have wished for more details). Less-well-adapted adoptees (those who had a poor self-image, who had an unsatisfactory home life, who had not been placed for adoption until after the age of 1, and who had an inadequate knowledge of their adoption) more often wanted to meet their biological parents and were more often disappointed (Triseliotis, 1973).

In the United States, the Child Welfare League of America in 1976 reviewed 163 adoption agencies and found that more than 3000 adult adoptees returned to these agencies in 1975. Two fifths (1200) of these wished to learn the identity of or locate their natural families. Three fifths (1800) wanted only identifying information.

The Committee on Adoption and Dependent Care (1981) of the American Academy of Pediatrics recommends that mature adoptees should have access to their birth records, but that an adult adoptee who wants this information should first have counseling with an adoption counselor to find out specifically what the adoptee wants to know and how his or her needs can best be satisfied.

THE ONE-PARENT CHILD

Having only one parent is another complication in reality that hampers the child's resolution of the oedipal conflict. In a detailed literature review of 10 reported cases and one current case presentation of a parent's being absent during the child's oedipal period, a pathogenic impact on the child's sexual identification and superego formation was inferred (Neubauer,

1960). For example, homosexuality occurred in some of the reported cases, with either a harsh, sadistic superego or a deficient superego which allowed incestuous acting out. However, it was not possible to distinguish between the effect of the parent's absence and the pathological conditions of the remaining parent, who often appeared to be seductive. Furthermore, the timing of the loss and the sex of the missing parent and the child were significant variables that could not be adequately controlled in the reported studies, although the absent parent was said to be either "immensely idealized or endowed with terribly sadistic attributes." Idealization is a process by which the child denies what is disappointing about an object without withdrawing from the object (in this case the absent parent), in contrast to pure fantasy, in which the child simply turns disappointing parents into satisfactory ones (Hoffer, 1949). Children with one parent may have difficulty in achieving a satisfactory organization in the oedipal and post-oedipal periods.

Herzog and Sudia (1968) recently emphasized that the effect of fatherlessness *in itself* is difficult to evaluate. Besides the attitudes and role of the mother in the fatherless home, the extent to which other male models influence the child is another important variable. Also, it simply cannot be said that a boy who, say, is born out of wedlock, has no father for the first 5 years of his life, and is exposed to his mother's seductions will become a homosexual. He may (Leonardo da Vinci did), but who would say that to become a genius you must be born out of wedlock, have no father, and be open to your mother's seductions? (The origins of homosexuality are discussed on page 250.)

PLAY CHARACTERISTICS

Some of the fantasies of this period and the psychological mechanisms invoked to cope with them are represented in the child's normal play. The play is quite spontaneous; the child uses a wide range of feelings and fantasy themes. Role playing is highly characteristic, with a rich use of dolls, props, costumes and so on. Time sequences and duration, however, are largely disregarded. Some sharing of fantasies occurs, at least implicitly in the common activities of the children involved. Much of the play at this stage is clearly an attempt to copy adults, sometimes with envy, sometimes out of anger or fear. Occasionally, the play seems to be an attempt at self-reassurance as the child performs big and powerful roles (as a mother or father, a doctor or nurse), or clearly expresses a family romance. In any event, the play leads to a widening experience of the world, and as such dilutes the child's sense of sexual urgency in his relationship with his parents. At the same time, play is the child's first attempt to practice the skills he will need as an adult.

FUNCTIONS OF PLAY

Play is an essential occupation of children (Waelder, 1933). The pleasure in functioning and achieving in itself motivates the child toward further exploration as well as provides him with a sense of well-being. The term function pleasure was first used by Buhlers (1930) to describe the pleasure infants show when they master simple motoric tasks. The child can now also actively repeat for himself a gratifying experience. The representational aspect of play has already been mentioned. Erikson has described three spheres of activity in the child: the macrosphere, the autosphere, and the microsphere (Erikson, 1940). The macrosphere is the world at large in the child's experience (e.g., a visit to the dentist). The autosphere is the internal fantasy life of the child (e.g., "I am being attacked and will be hurt and mutilated"). The microsphere is the play world that the child creates for himself, a world that is small, compact, manageable, and encompassable. An example is the child who plays at being a dentist. He turns a passive situation into one of active mastery, he can discharge some of his own revengeful aggressive fantasies, he can make the situation come out differently—and he can repeat the situation at his bidding. The play performs a defense function (turning passivity into activity) and a discharge function (discharging aggressive drive). The play also gives a hint of a movement toward sublimation.

There is another important aspect of play as a developmental step. Play can be viewed as an intermediary step in the development of thought. If thought is conceptualized as a trial of action through controlled reason, it can be seen how the play of the child might facilitate that process. After all, play for the child is a process in which different solutions are tried out in controlled action in the world of play before being executed in modified form in the world at large. Gradually, this kind of "play" becomes internalized, and the process is entirely carried out at the mental level.

These conceptualizations of play are not the only ones (see also Brunner et al., 1976; Piaget, 1951; Vygotsky, 1967). In a recent comprehensive review of the literature on children's play, Schwartzman (1979) listed approximately 800 references. Clearly there are many questions still to be answered on the subject of children's play.

COGNITIVE DEVELOPMENT

A more detailed account of the structure of thought at this stage is given in the studies of Piaget (1926; see also Flavell, 1963). Piaget attempted to study how the child progressively understands such concepts as (1) space, time, object, and causality, (2) spatial and numerical relations, and (3) conservation of length, area, and volume and the necessary processes that enable the child to understand how to classify. At this stage (2 to 7 years of age), which Piaget calls the preoperational stage, the child is aware of himself as a separate person. He is also aware that persons and things have a separate existence and are moved by forces other than himself. He is quite capable of permanent intrapsychic representation of objects that are not perceptually present. In the symbolic and preconceptual period of the preoperational stage (approximately 2 to 4 years of age), the child can engage in symbolic activity in make-believe play and can also make attempts at verbal reasoning. Yet he may still tend to endow inanimate objects with feeling (the animism mentioned earlier).

Some time during the second half of the preoperational stage Piaget describes an intuitive stage (approximately 4 to 7 years of age). In the intuitive stage there is an increased accommodation to reality (although the child is still bound to some extent to spatial relationships), a categorizing capacity that makes use of one characteristic of an object, and an inclination on the part of the child to follow his own line of thought when he talks to another child, with very little actual exchange of information. The child can say $6 + 4 = 10$, but he is not capable of the reversible thinking, that later will enable him to say $10 - 4 = 6$. Piaget has noted several other characteristics of the child's thinking at this stage. For example, the child increasingly tries to verify his statements by trials of action, accommodating to what he then observes. The process of assimilation becomes in this way increasingly "decentered" from the child's interests although the child still tends to see things from his point of view only. To the extent that the child does this and finds it hard to take the view of another person, he is still egocentric.

At this stage, too, the child appears to think along the lines of immanent justice. That is, the child believes that punishment for wrong deeds is inevitable and inherent in the universe—a sort of early Hollywood type of thinking. An interesting clinical aspect of this kind of thinking is its persistent quality (hence the popularity of certain early Hollywood films?) and its impact on the child who is striving to deal with not only conscious but also unconscious real or imagined misdeeds. Any punishment or, rather, any event that is seen by the child as a punishment is almost expected, is sometimes welcomed, and is often guilt relieving. The child may observe this sense of relief and so develop a behavior pattern that actively seeks punishment because it is guilt relieving. The child gets off the hook easily since he no longer has to suffer his guilt.

SIGNS OF ANXIETY

Neither boys nor girls may be entirely successful in the resolution of their conflicts and may show signs of anxiety through a conduct disorder or by suffering from excessive guilt (see p. 219), especially about masturbation (see p. 222). Perhaps the most common conduct disturbance is a heightened aggressivity in play, in which a child may threaten others or hurt himself. Occasionally, severe reaction formations against the wish to exhibit occur, with excessive shyness and withdrawal. Early learning difficulties may present themselves as the child imposes upon himself an inhibition against discovering forbidden knowledge. Nail biting, tics and other "nervous symptoms," such as nose picking, sniffing, and coughing, may also appear. Fears of the dark, animals, injury, and doctors and death may also occur, representing in part an underlying fear of being overwhelmed by the surge of unacceptable wishes and impulses.

DISORDERS OF AROUSAL

Disorders of arousal, associated with a shift from Stage 3 or 4 NREM sleep in the direction of arousal, include night terrors, somnambulism and somniloquy, and bed wetting. These disorders of arousal usually occur in the first 3 hours of sleep and are usually followed by retrograde amnesia for the episode. The actions often appear automatic and are not usually responsive to the immediate environment (Anders and Weinstein, 1972).

In night terrors (sleep terror disorder, 307.46), the child does not awaken completely, looks horrified, perspires, cries out, and often .cannot be aroused from this state for 10 to 15 minutes. The child frequently has no memory of the event when he is fully awakened. Kales and his colleagues (1968) report an incidence of at least one episode of night terrors in 1 to 3% of all children between 5 and 12 years of age. Night terrors occur during arousal from Stage 4 sleep.

Sleepwalking (sleepwalking disorder, 307.46) is also an arousal disorder. The child often has some awareness during the walking episode but usually has no memory of the event once awake. Sleepwalking is more common in boys than in girls, and it is commonly associated with night terrors. The walking usually lasts for a few minutes and occurs in Stage 3 or Stage 4 sleep. The delayed or impaired arousal out of this Stage 3 or Stage 4 sleep is thought to be the result of a delay in maturation (Broughton, 1968). Spontaneous remission usually occurs, but of those who remain sleepwalkers during young adulthood, about one-third have been reported to be schizophrenic (Sours et al., 1963). Bed wetting is discussed later (p. 226).

ANXIETY DREAMS

Bad dreams (anxiety dreams) occur during REM sleep. They are normal, recurring psychic events that occur from infancy onward, and they appear to represent controlled anxiety. The bad dreams of children at this stage often involve a monster who, say, is coming in the window and is about to attack the child. At that point, the child suddenly wakes up, often with a pounding heart. A common underlying dream process (part of the "dream work") in such dreams is the projection and displacement of the child's own unacceptable aggressive fantasies onto the monster, who then turns around and threatens to attack the child.

The concept of dream work is a crucial one in psychoanalytic theory. Indeed, Freud regarded his "The Interpretation of Dreams" as his most important work, stating that "insight such as this falls to one's lot but once in a lifetime" (S. Freud, 1900). Essentially the concept proposes a series of psychological processes and mechanisms by which the individual deals with psychological conflicts about forbidden wishes that arise during the sleeping state. The theory is too complex to be dealt with adequately in this book, and it should be studied separately. Freud (1900) did note, however, that "even when investigation shows that the primary eliciting cause of a phenomenon is psychical, deeper research will one day trace the path further and discover an organic basis for the event" (pp. 41 ff.).

Interestingly, Hobson and McCarley (1977) have in fact suggested a biologic basis for dreaming. They postulate that the giant neurons of the pontine reticular function, the so-called FTG neurons, fire off during the desynchronized sleep state (D sleep) and bombard the forebrain, which then has to make sense of the messages received, resulting in the "dreamy" quality of dreams. FTG cell activity increases just before a REM period and peaks during REM sleep. FTG cells also activate cells in other parts of the brain, including the visual centers and the vestibular system.

CHILD'S CONCEPT OF DREAMS

During the early part of this period, dreams themselves tend to be conceptualized by the child as external events, a process that Piaget calls realism (Piaget, 1951). However, the child soon begins to understand that dreams are not real external events. By their fifth birthday, most American middle-class children recognize that their dreams are not real events, and shortly afterward understand that dreams cannot be seen by others. By age 6, children are aware that dreams take place inside them, and by age 7 they are clearly aware that dreams are thoughts caused by themselves (Kohlberg, 1968).

GUILT

Guilt was mentioned earlier (p. 217) as another consequence of unresolved oedipal conflicts. In fact, guilt is a powerful affect at this stage, even with normal resolution of conflicts. If castration danger was the prototypical danger situation in the third and fourth years of life, guilt seems to be the overriding danger from about the fourth or fifth year onward, in greater or lesser degree. Erikson, for example, has described the developmental crisis at this stage as initiative versus guilt (Erikson, 1959). The child's imagination is exuberant to the point where he can frighten himself because he believes that a particular fantasy of his was virtually a committed crime. He then feels guilty. He feels guilty even about mere thoughts, not to mention deeds that nobody may have seen. Rapaport (1967) tells the story of the little boy who goes toward a candy jar. Before the boy can lay a hand on the jar, he hears a great clap of thunder. He is momentarily taken aback, looks up, and says: "Good God, isn't one even permitted to think of it?" Yet, at the same time, the child is learning quickly, is desirous of sharing in obligations and being disciplined, and seems altogether more integrated.

ORIGIN OF GUILT

The origin of guilt is still to be explained. Children in their first year of life obey the commands of adults only for the duration of the command; there is very little carry-over to the next time the same situation arises (e.g., parents must repeatedly say to a child, "Stay away from the plug," as well as place covers over all electric outlets and physically intervene when necessary). Gradually the child internalizes these commands; 2-year-old children can be observed to repeat to themselves the commands they have heard repeatedly from their parents. Occasionally children seek reinforcement of these commands from their parents by acting provocatively, by asking questions, and by inviting their parents to see how good they have been.

PURPOSE OF GUILT

Guilt, like anxiety, is an affect, and like all affects it appears to serve a purpose. The purpose, it would seem, is to provide a signal that a punishment will occur if certain behavior is persisted in, or committed at all. The stimulus for the child's response is the internalized real and imagined prohibitions of the parents (the superego described on pp. 205 ff.). Thus guilt arises essentially when there is a conflict between the child's wishes and his conscience. Like many affects, guilt may become acutely uncomfortable, causing the child to mobilize further defenses to ward off the guilt. Thus defenses may act against affects as well as against drives. Sometimes rage may be mobilized to deal with guilt. A multiple layering of such affects may thus occur.

The child's conscience requires reinforcement from the environment. The environment usually provides this reinforcing nutriment in the form of such social sanctions as marriage, parenthood, and normal social expectations in regard to ethics and morals, and so on. If this nutriment is lacking or faulty, the superego may become corrupted. If the parents themselves have faulty values, not only will the child internalize these values complete with their faults (see the discussion of superego lacunae, p. 210), but also the child's values will become further corrupted by the lack of adequate nutriments in the form of appropriate parental sanctions. On the other hand, certain strong moral attributes can be transmitted, particularly through specific family myths (Musto, 1969).

It would appear that these early prohibitions are in part internalizations of the child's perception of the parents' prohibitions, especially those that have been spoken aloud and heard by the child. However, in part they are also reinternalizations of the attributes and strictness that the child has previously externalized and projected onto the parents. Along with the spoken prohibitions of the parents is the implied threat of loss of the parents' love if the child disobeys. This threat is often conveyed by such things as a glance, a change in receptivity, or gruffness. The child feels, or should feel, a consistency and firmness in the parents' command, and a sense of guilt about disobedience. If there is inconsistency, the child will sense the double message and disobey. The parents will then be nonplussed at the child's "naughtiness" and, not recognizing their own inconsistency, may begin to punish the child, often by spanking him.

Guilt is often expressed in a form of behavior that consistently provokes punishment. It is as though the punishment will be a just retribution for the forbidden unconscious crime. Through this punishment the child is temporarily relieved of the onerous feeling of guilt. Physical punishment administered at this time usually fits in with the child's fantasies and needs.

GUILT AND SOCIALIZATION

The internal problem of guilt is perhaps central to the external socialization of the child. In order to avoid the feeling of excessive guilt, the child may, for example, try to behave in accordance with accepted social rules of conduct. However, even this solution is tempered by intrapsychic, environmental, and developmental factors. Internally, the child's ability to postpone the urge for immediate gratification, his self-esteem, his ability to empathize with the feelings of others, as well as his intelligence and his capacity for judgment—all these may modify the child's tolerance for guilt.

External modifying factors include (1) the varying impact of parental, peer, and societal sanctions; (2) the child's experiences of gratification or deprivation; and (3) the child's assessments (insofar as he can make such assessments) of the risk of detection, the effort and ingenuity required, and the possible consequences versus the possible gains when, say, he experiences the urge to cheat, lie, steal, or perform some other forbidden act.

From a cognitive-developmental point of view, the child's increasing ability to make a moral judgment parallels in part his level of cognitive development. For example, no matter what environmental influences are at work, a gradual shift takes place from making a judgment in terms of immediate external physical consequences to making a judgment in terms of subjective or internal purposes, norms, or values (Kohlberg, 1964). Most children have an understanding of the basic moral rules of society by the time they start first grade (Hartshorne and May, 1930). However, the way in which they make a moral judgment depends on the degree to which they have internalized specific moral values.

MASTURBATION

An almost universal source of guilt in the child is the urge to masturbate and the fantasies connected with masturbation. Although the term masturbation in its ordinary sense is understood to mean self-stimulation of the genitals, in its technical sense it means the gratification of the sexual drive by the self or an extension of the self. Since the sexual drive seems to have a sequence of development (S. Freud, 1905; see Note 7)—much as thinking, motility, and speech have a sequence of development—the self-gratification of the earliest manifestations of the sexual drive can also be considered as early forms of masturbation even though they are not genital. Thus, psychoanalysts consider the mouthing behavior of the infant as a rudimentary form of masturbation in that it is believed to be in part a manifestation of autoerotic activity in which the primitive so-called oral-stage sexual drive is being gratified by the self. The pleasures involved later in having a bowel movement may similarly also have a masturbatory component.

Penile erections occur in infancy, both spontaneously and in response to manipulation. Spontaneous early penile erections appear to be associated with REM sleep (Fischer et al., 1965). It is therefore plausible that such erections may represent a physiological change as well as a psychic event.

Direct manipulation of the genitals reaches its first peak somewhere between 3 and 4 years of age although accidental touching of the genitals may occur in very young infants. An interesting observation is that foundling-home infants deprived of object relations do not play with their genitals, even in their fourth year, whereas family-raised infants with good object relations play with their genitals toward the end of the first year (Spitz, 1962). More disguised masturbation takes place in the course of "horse play," as when the child contrives to rub his genital area against, say, the knee of an adult.

Another interesting detail is the fact that girls appear to masturbate mostly through pressure of the thighs rather than direct fingering of the genitals. A possible hypothesis for this phenomenon is that the girl wishes to avoid exact tactile localization that might arouse anxiety about the absence of a penis (Brunswick, 1940). On the other hand, many girls masturbate by inserting foreign objects into the vagina. Later, during adolescence, it appears that girls derive sexual gratification by stimulation in the region of the clitoris rather than the vagina, and this remains true of adult women, who achieve orgasm most regularly from stimulation in the region of the clitoris. In fact, it appears that in adults there is no such thing as a vaginal orgasm that is distinct from a clitoral orgasm (Sherfey, 1966). That is to say, clitoral and vaginal orgasms are not separate biologic entities, and regardless of where the female body is stimulated, there is absolutely no difference in the responses of the pelvic viscera provided the stimulation is sufficient to bring about orgasm (Masters and Johnson, 1966).

ORIGINS OF MASTURBATION

Several hypotheses have been offered about the origins of masturbatory activities and fantasies in the child. Brunswick (1940), for example, asserted that the early physical care of the child by the mother, a care that inevitably involves touching the genitals and that seems to be experienced by the child as a pleasurable seduction, constitutes a significant component of the basis for early childhood masturbation. Another stimulus to masturbate lies in the intense and jealous interest of the child in the sexual activity of the parents, which the child may have seen or about which he may have elaborated fantasies.

MASTURBATION FANTASIES

During the act of masturbation the child may envisage what he fantasies takes place between the parents. He may, for example, in keeping with his sexual theories, envisage either parent being suckled by the other, or his suckling either parent, or his being suckled. Such fantasies may be displaced, especially in girls, onto the image of suckling a doll. Occasionally, the child may fantasy a mutual touching of the genitals, much along the lines of his own experience of pleasure in touching his genitals or having his genitals touched, especially by the mother. Sometimes, in keeping with the child's interpretation of sexual intercourse as a sadomasochistic interaction, he may have accompanying fantasies of violence, often disguised as, say, rockets blasting off, cars crashing into each other, or wars between armies.

MASTURBATION AND FANTASIES OF BEING BEATEN

Sometimes a specific fantasy of being beaten occurs during masturbation (Freud, 1919). According to Freud, that fantasy first occurs before the fifth or sixth year, and it is accompanied by feelings of pleasure that have a masturbatory quality. Freud thought that the fantasies arose from the oedipal fantasies of the child and underwent a complicated series of changes. In boys, for example, the beating fantasy was thought to be passive from the very beginning and to be derived from a feminine attitude to the father. The sequence of changes in the fantasy that Freud reconstructed were: "I am loved by my father," leading to the unconscious fantasy, "I am being beaten by my father," which resulted finally in the conscious masochistic fantasy, "I am being beaten by my mother." In girls, the first conscious form of the fantasy appeared to be sadistic (e.g., "A teacher is beating a number of boys"), but the satisfaction was still thought to be essentially masochistic. In both boys and girls, the fantasies appeared in part to be attempts to deal with their wish to be loved by their father.

MASTURBATION AND SOCIAL RULES

Masturbation is a normal, even necessary, phenomenon, and so children of all ages need the opportunity to masturbate in private. But, like eating habits and bowel training, the practice of masturbation is also usually subject to social rules in the interests of social relationships. It has even been suggested (although without supporting evidence) that cultures that permit the unrestricted gratification of the sexual urge during the elementary-school years and early puberty have a large proportion of people whose level of personality development and intellectual functioning is lowered (Spitz, 1962). Compulsive masturbation is usually regarded as a sign of tension or disorder whose sources must be discovered and dealt with before the masturbation can be contained. Occasionally, a child becomes addicted to masturbation. Extreme anxiety and guilt are often engendered when the child is threatened with punishment or spanked for masturbating.

SPANKING

Spanking, however, does not usually eradicate this or any other behavior. Spanking may appear to have an effect at the time, but the parent usually finds that he has to spank the child for the same misdeed again and again. When spanking does seem to have a more lasting effect, that effect is often the result of fear and a strong repression of the rage in the child. Occasionally, the child who has learned to control his or her impulses only through the mobilization of fear of a strong external punishment, may repeatedly seek such punishment in order to dissipate any rising anxiety brought about by a threatened breakthrough of an impulse believed to be dangerous. Spanking may also reinforce the wish and the opportunities for the child to put his feelings into actions. This acting out comes about partially through the child's identification with parents who also hit when they are desperate.

Sometimes spanking is sexually exciting. Parents who spank report that they try to hold themselves back, feel more and more provoked, and then suddenly let go. They say that after the discharge of their anger through physical activity (spanking), their relationship with the child is calm and loving. But the calm is usually short lived, and the cycle starts again. And the parent, although he sees how ineffective spanking is, persists in spanking. The cycle of rising excitement, climax, discharge, and period of calm is suspiciously like a sexual gratification, which in some families seems to be the true, if unconscious, aim of the spanking.

Even the foregoing discussion does not touch on all the reasons that spanking is often the opposite of useful to the child in the long run. (Spanking often seems to be administered more because it is "useful" for the parents than because it is useful for the child.) For example, instead of the child's feeling guilty and learning for himself internal ways to delay and divert the direct discharge of his impulses, a child may simply be let off the hook by a spanking: the child is immediately relieved of his feelings of guilt and so is free to continue his activity, if he feels the external price he has to pay is not too high. For example, a child may reason that stealing an apple is worth the risk of a spanking and so feel free to steal. No internalization has occurred; wrong learning has taken place.

BED WETTING

Enuresis may be defined in this discussion as involuntary wetting of the bed past the age at which most children remain dry (Green and Richmond, 1954). Most normal children establish daytime control by 2½ years, and night-time control by 3½ to 4 years of age, with perhaps a range of 3 to 7 years of age (Harper, 1962). Some observers have stated that normal maturation in some children may not occur until puberty (Campbell, 1951).

Control usually comes about as a result of the interaction between this neuromuscular maturation and the psychological capacity to postpone the urge to void. The psychological capacity to delay an impulse is, in turn, part of the total psychological development of the child and is derived from many sources. Some of these sources are all those factors that contribute toward such functions as relationships, motivation, and the capacity to deal with conflict.

Furthermore, since the total psychological development of the child is integrally related to his environment, such factors in the environment as the attitudes of the child's parents and the hazards of illness, separation, and seduction also play a vital role in developing the capacity for impulse control.

Given this complex interaction of factors, it is not surprising that enuresis is a common symptom of early childhood, perhaps affecting at least 4% of children over age 4 (Lemkau, 1955).

Bed wetting can, of course, be a symptom of many different kinds of organic disorders. Several clinical findings suggest that the cause is organic: (1) the wetting is diurnal as well as nocturnal, (2) there has never been a significantly long "dry" period, and (3) there are symptoms of an infection. Bed wetting may occur also in children who have unusually small bladders (so-called primary enuresis) or as a result of a sleep disturbance. Thus, the enuretic episode occurs during arousal from nonREM sleep (usually Stage 4 sleep) (Kales and Kales, 1974). Enuretic boys ages 5 to 9 seem to skip the first REM cycles of sleep and to wet in Stage 4 sleep, the deepest stage of sleep (Pierce et al., 1961). Wetting occurs generally just before a dream, and it occurs least often in REM sleep (Gastaut and Broughton, 1964; Hawkins et al., 1965). Parents report that bed wetting seems to occur in children who are sleeping heavily and are hard to awaken. However, Graham (1973) notes that parents have less cause to awaken children who are not bed wetters, so that a valid comparison cannot usually be made. Although bed wetting, sleep walking, and nightmares occur during sudden intense arousal from slow-wave (Stage 4) sleep, other "nervous" signs, such as teeth grinding, occur during REM sleep (Reding et al., 1964).

Nevertheless, many children with enuresis (functional enuresis, 307.60) do not have an organic basis for their symptom. Among these children it is possible to group the factors as follows (Kolvin et al., 1972):

I.   Developmental delay
   1. Slow maturation
   2. Inadequate training
   3. Insufficient stimulation
II. Psychological conflict
   1. Temporary regressive phenomena
   2. Relatively stable neurotic symptom formation

The primary Group II causes of the enuresis tend to be intrapsychic and internalized in nature. Enuresis as a regressive phenomenon, for example, commonly occurs when a stress (such as illness, birth of a sibling, or separation and loss) is experienced before bladder control has been fully established. According to Katan (1946), enuresis as the expression of an internalized intrapsychic conflict tends to occur when fantasies common during this period of development (i.e., phase-specific fantasies) have been heightened by the interaction between internal and external events and produce anxiety of a degree that requires neurotic symptom formation.

For example, a common fantasy of the child during this period of development is that he will be harmed by persons of the opposite sex. This fear may arise as a fantasied consequence of destructive wishes toward the rival parent, or it may arise from an overwhelming sexual experience, which in many instances consists of a hostile seduction by the parent who (for example) handles the child's penis to direct the stream of his urine into the toilet. In the case of a boy, his fear of the mother may lead to a passive compliance in which urination is not within his control. In the case of a girl, her fear of the father as an aggressor may lead to a passive relinquishing of control (Gerard, 1939). In both instances, the bed wetting also has a passive-aggressive revenge component. Furthermore, in many children who wet the bed the symptom is brought about by the same mechanisms that produce a conversion symptom, so that the child's wishes and his defense against his wishes are represented symbolically in the outpouring of urine.

What can be seen here is the interaction between a phase-specific fantasy and an external reality that is consonant with that fantasy, resulting in a conflict which expresses itself through a symptom in which all the factors are represented.

MAJOR DEVELOPMENTAL THRUSTS

Several major developmental thrusts seem to be occurring during this stage of the child's life. The child's relationships are now much more centered on identified people and bear witness to the exciting and anxiety-arousing fantasy life just described. Thus, in the child's manifest behavior, possessiveness of the parent of the opposite sex and jealousy and rivalry with the parent of the same sex can be observed. The child is also at times protective, curious, exhibitionistic, and compliment seeking and, in the case of girls, is changing toward a somewhat masculine relationship with the mother. Children now begin to see other children as fellow children who have feelings, wishes, and rights of their own.

The child's increasing ability to take directions is matched by his better-developed internal controls system. His play and his other interactions with other children shift from parallel play to cooperative play. Language and concept development reach a new level as he observes and imitates others and acquires a sense of time. Curiosity about anatomical differences, pregnancy, and childbirth and death abounds, and masturbation is at its peak. During this stage the child strives to resolve his individual, complex oedipal feelings with the early formation of a superego, and he learns to accept his gender and his sex role.

PHOBIC ORGANIZATION

At the same time, there appears to be a general tendency toward a phobic organization that is manifested in the numerous fears that occur at this stage (e.g., fear of the dark). The phobic nature of the defense organization at this time seems to be determined in part by a number of factors. One factor is the level of cognitive development, which may not yet permit more sophisticated mechanisms, such as intellectualization. Another factor is the general maturation and development of the psychic apparatus, which may not yet have provided the individual with a very wide range of autonomous functions. A third factor thought to influence the development of phobias is the degree to which the child experiences a heightening of anxiety common at this developmental stage brought on by an event that is close to the prevailing fantasy. For example, tonsillectomy in a child who is concerned about mutilation of his body may heighten castration anxiety and stimulate specific defense mechanisms (Lipson, 1962).

DEFENSE HIERARCHY

Lewis (1971) postulated a sequential and hierarchical development of psychic defense structures that reflects in part maturation, development, and external events. A simplified schematic representation is shown in Table 14-1. In this diagram the vertical columns indicate the interacting forces of maturation, intrapsychic development, and external environment at each stage of development. This interaction would seem to determine, in part, the kind and degree of defense activity, shown in the bottom line of each vertical column. Thus, during infancy, projection, introjection, and projective identification seem to be prominent defense mechanisms reflecting the immature state of psychic organization. Later, between ages 3 to 6 ("early childhood"), the increased awareness and curiosity, the fears associated with body injury and castration, and the presence of specific real events, such as a tonsillectomy, may characteristically foster the use of phobic mechanisms. In the school-age child (say, ages 7 to 11) a more obsessional organization may be seen. Finally, during adolescence, the availability of formal operations may lend itself to intellectualization as a common defense mechanism.

Note 25

S. Freud (1940). *An Outline of Psychoanalysis.* Reprinted from *The Standard Edition of the Complete Psychological Works of Sigmund Freud.* Translated and edited by James Strachey. By permission of Sigmund Freud Copyrights, The Institute of Psycho-Analysis, and The Hogarth Press Ltd., 1964, pp. 154–155.
... With the phallic phase and in the course of it the sexuality of early childhood reaches its height and approaches its dissolution. Thereafter boys and girls have different histories. Both have begun to put their intellectual activity at the service of sexual researches; both start off from the premiss of the universal presence of the penis. But now the paths of the sexes diverge. The boy enters the Oedipus phase; he begins to manipulate his penis and simultaneously has

Table 14–1. DEVELOPMENT OF DEFENSE HIERARCHY

Correlations	DEVELOPMENTAL STAGES			
	Infancy	*Early Childhood*	*School-Age Period*	*Adolescence*
Maturational skills	Biological helplessness Limited awareness Limited motor control	Increased perceptual capacities Early motor control	Broad range of controlled perceptual, motor, and psychic activity	Extensive quantitative and qualitative changes in physical and psychological changes associated with puberty
Psychological development	Assimilation and accommodation Symbiotic state, need-satisfying object Loss of love anxiety	Preoperational thinking Object constancy Recognition of whole object Sexual development Castration anxiety	Concrete operations Autonomous ego development in latency Guilt	Formal operations Intrapsychic reorganization in the face of such adolescent tasks as identity crisis, body image changes, separation and object choice, impulse control, etc.
Reinforcing parallel external events	Loss of the object	Fear of mutilation aggravated by an actual event, e.g., tonsillectomy	School learning patterns	Career choice, move to college or military service
Simplified defense hierarchical sequence	Projection Injection Projective identification	Phobic organization	Obsessional organization	Intellectualization

phantasies of carrying out some sort of activity with it in relation to his mother, till, owing to the combined effect of a threat of castration and the sight of the absence of a penis in females, he experiences the greatest trauma of his life and this introduces the period of latency with all its consequences. The girl, after vainly attempting to do the same as the boy, comes to recognize her lack of a penis or rather the inferiority of her clitoris, with permanent effects on the development of her character; as a result of this first disappointment in rivalry, she often begins by turning away altogether from sexual life. . . .

Note 26

From: THE PSYCHOLOGY OF THE CHILD, by Jean Piaget and Barbel Inhelder, translated from the French by Helen Weaver. © 1969 by Basic Books, Inc. © by Presses Universitaires de France. By permission of Basic Books, Inc., Publishers, New York.

   . . . Yet . . . psychoanalysis . . . often sees nothing in affectivity but a series of repetitions or analogies with the past (new versions of the Oedipus complex, narcissism, etc.). It is true that Anna Freud[7] and E. Erikson[8] stressed "successive identifications" with elders who serve as models, thus liberating children from infantile choices (with the concomitant danger of identity diffusion according to Erikson), but they have neglected the role of the "concrete autonomy" acquired during later childhood and above all the role of cognitive constructions that pave the way for an anticipation of the future and a receptiveness to new values. . . .

REFERENCES

Anders, T., and Weinstein, P. (1972), Sleep and its disorders in infants and children: A review. *J. Pediatr.*, 50:311–324.

Bornstein, B. (1949), The analysis of a phobic child: Some problems of theory and technique in child analysis. *Psychoanal. Study Child*, 3/4:181–226.

Bornstein, B. (1951), On latency. *Psychoanal. Study Child*, 6:279–285.

Bornstein, B. (1953), Fragment of an analysis of an obsessional child: The first six months of analysis. *Psychoanal. Study Child*, 8:313–332.

Brieland, D. (1965), Adoption research: An overview. In: *Perspectives on Adoption Research*. New York: Child Welfare League of America, p. 58.

Broughton, R.J. (1968), Sleep disorders: Disorders of arousal. *Science*, 159:1070–1078.

Brunner, J., Jolly, A., and Sylva, R. (Eds.) (1976), *Play: Its Role in Development and Evolution*. New York: Basic Books.

Brunswick, R.M. (1940), The preoedipal phase of the libido development. *Psychoanal. Q.*, 19:293.

Buhler, C. (1930), *The First Year of Life*. New York: John Day.

Buhler, K. (1930), *The Mental Development of the Child*. New York: Harcourt, Brace & World.

Campbell, M. (1951), *Clinical Pediatric Urology*. Philadelphia: Saunders, p. 801.

[7]Anna Freud, *The Ego and the Mechanisms of Defense* (rev. ed., New York: International Universities Press, 1967).

[8]E. Erikson, *Childhood and Society* (2nd ed.; New York: W.W. Norton, 1963).

Child Welfare League of America, Inc. (1976), *The Sealed Adoption Record Controversy: Report of a Survey of Agency Policy, Practice and Opinion.* New York: Child Welfare League of America, Inc. Research Center.

Committee on Adoption and Dependent Care (1981), The role of the pediatrician in adoption with reference to "the right to know:" An update. *Pediatrics*, 67:305–306.

Erikson, E.H. (1940), Studies in the interpretation of play: I. Clinical observation of play disruption in young children. *Genetic Psychology Monographs*, 1940, p. 22. (Reprinted in *Contemporary Psychopathology*, ed. S.S. Tompkins. Cambridge, Mass., Harvard University Press, 1943, pp. 91–122.)

Erikson, E.H. (1959), Initiative versus guilt. *Identity and the Life Cycle. Psychol. Issues*, 1:74–82.

Fisher, C., Gross, J., and Zuch, J. (1965), Cycle of penile erection synonymous with dreaming (REM) sleep. *Arch. Gen. Psychiatry*, 12:29–45.

Flavell, J.H. (1963), *The Developmental Psychology of Jean Piaget*. New York: Van Nostrand, pp. 150–163.

Freud, S. (1900), *The Interpretation of Dreams*. Standard Edition, 4 (1953). London: The Hogarth Press, pp. 261–263.

Freud, S. (1905), *Fragment of an Analysis of a Case of Hysteria*. Standard Edition, 7, (1953). London: The Hogarth Press.

Freud, S. (1905), *Three Essays on the Theory of Sexuality*. Standard Edition, 7 (1953). London: The Hogarth Press, pp. 125–243.

Freud, S. (1908), *On the Sexual Theories of Children*. Standard Edition, 9 (1959). London: The Hogarth Press, pp. 205–226.

Freud, S. (1909a), *Family Romances*. Standard Edition, 9 (1959). London: The Hogarth Press, pp. 235–241.

Freud, S. (1909b), *Analysis of a Phobia in a Five-Year-Old Boy*. Standard Edition, 10 (1955). London: The Hogarth Press, pp. 5–152.

Freud, S. (1909c), *Notes Upon a Case of Obsessional Neurosis*. Standard Edition, 10 (1955). London: The Hogarth Press, pp. 155–318.

Freud, S. (1914), *On Narcissism: An Introduction*. Standard Edition, 14 (1957). London: The Hogarth Press, pp. 73–104.

Freud, S. (1918), *From the History of an Infantile Neurosis*. Standard Edition, 17 (1955). London: The Hogarth Press, pp. 7–122.

Freud, S. (1919), *"A Child is Being Beaten": A Contribution to the Study of the Origin of Sexual Perversions*. Standard Edition, 17 (1955).

Freud, S. (1923), *The Ego and the Id*. Standard Edition, 19 (1961). London: The Hogarth Press, pp. 12–68.

Freud, S. (1924), *The Dissolution of the Oedipus Complex*. Standard Edition, 19 (1961). London: The Hogarth Press, pp. 171–179.

Freud, S. (1925), *Some Psychical Consequences of the Anatomical Distinction Between the Sexes*. Standard Edition, 19 (1961). London: The Hogarth Press, pp. 243–258.

Freud, S. (1928), *Dostoevsky and Parricide*. Standard Edition, 21 (1961). London: The Hogarth Press, p. 185.

Freud, S. (1930), *Civilization and Its Discontents*. Standard Edition, 21 (1961). London: The Hogarth Press, pp. 64–148.

Gastaut, H., and Broughton, R.J. (1964), Conclusions concerning the mechanisms of enuresis nocturna. *E.E.G. Clin. Neurophysiol.*, 16:625.

Gerard, M. (1939), Enuresis: A study in etiology. *Am. J. Orthopsychiatry*, 9:48.

Graham, P.J. (1973), Depth of sleep and enuresis: A critical review. In: *Bladder Control and Enuresis*, Clinics in Dev. Med., Nos. 48/49. Eds. I. Kolvin, R. MacKeith, and S.R. Meadow. London: SIMP/Heinemann.

Green, M., and Richmond, J.B. (1954), *Pediatric Diagnosis*. Philadelphia: Saunders, p. 228.

Harper, P.A. (1962), *Preventive Pediatrics*. New York: Appleton-Century-Crofts, p. 32.

Hartshorne, H., and May, M.A. (1928–1930), *Studies in the Nature of Character*. Vol. 1, *Studies in Deceit;* Vol. 2, *Studies in Self-Control;* Vol. 3, *Studies in the Organization of Character*. New York: Macmillan.

Hawkins, D.R., Scott, J., and Thrasher, G. (1965), Sleep patterns in enuretic children. *A.P.S.S.*

Hawkins, M.O. (1946), Jealousy and rivalry between brothers and sisters. *Child Study*, 2–5.

Herzog, E., and Sudia, C.E. (1968), Fatherless homes: A review of research. *Children*, Sept.–Oct.: 177–182.

Hoffer, W. (1949), Deceiving the deceiver. In: *Searchlights on Delinquency*, ed. K.R. Eissler. New York: International Universities Press.

Hobson, J.A., and McCarley, R.W. (1977), The brain as a dream state generator: An activation-synthesis hypothesis of the dream process. *Am. J. Psychiatry*, 134:1335–1348.

Johnson, A.M. (1949), Sanctions for superego lacunae of adolescents. In: *Searchlights on Delinquency*, ed. K.R. Eissler. New York: International Universities Press, pp. 225–245.

Jones, E. (1929), Fear, guilt, and hate. *Int. J. Psychoanal.*, 10:383–397.

Kales, A., and Kales, J.D. (1974), Sleep disorders. *New Engl. J. Med.*, 290:487–499.

Kales, J., Jacobson, A., and Kales, A. (1968), Sleep disorders in children. In: *Progress in Clinical Psychology*, Vol. 8, ed. L. Abt and B.F. Riess. New York: Grune & Stratton, pp. 63–75.

Katan, A. (1946), Experiences with enuretics. *Psychoanal. Study Child*, 2:241.

Kirk, H.D. (1964), *Shared Fate*. Toronto: Collier-Macmillan, The Free Press of Glencoe.

Klein, M. (1955), The psycho-analytic play techniques: Its history and significance. In: *New Directions in Psychoanalysis*, ed. M. Klein, P. Heimann, and R. Money-Kyrle. London: Tavistock, pp. 3–22.

Klein, M. (1958), On the development of mental functioning. In: *Melanie Klein: Envy and Gratitude and Other Works, 1946–1963*. London: The Hogarth Press, 1975.

Klein, M. (1960), *Our Adult World and Its Roots in Infancy*. London: Tavistock, p. 9.

Klein, M., and Tribich, D. (1980), On Freud's blindness. *Colloquium*, 3:52–59.

Kohlberg, L. (1964), Development of moral character and moral ideology. In: *Review of Child Development Research*, Vol. 1, ed. M.L. Hoffman and L.W. Hoffman. New York: Russell Sage Foundation, pp. 383–431.

Kohlberg, L. (1968), Early education: A cognitive developmental view. *Child Dev.*, 39:1013–1062.

Kolvin, I., Taunch, J., Currah, J., Garside, R.F., Nolan, J., and Shaw, W.B. (1972), Enuresis: A descriptive analysis and a controlled trial. *Dev. Med. Child Psychol.*, 14:715–726.

Lemkau, P.W. (1955), *Mental Hygiene in Public Health*, 2nd Ed. New York: McGraw-Hill.

Levy, D.M. (1937), Studies in sibling rivalry. *Research Monograph No. 2*. New York: American Orthopsychiatric Association.

Lewis, H. (1965), The psychiatric aspects of adoption. In: *Modern Perspectives in Child Psychiatry*, ed. J.G. Howells. Springfield, Ill.: Charles C Thomas, pp. 428–451.

Lewis, M. (1971), *Clinical Aspects of Child Development*. Philadelphia: Lea & Febiger.

Lipton, S.D. (1962), On the psychology of childhood tonsillectomy. *Psychoanal. Study Child*, 17:363–417.

Masson, J.M. (1981), The seduction hypothesis in the light of new documents. Paper presented at the Western New England Psychoanalytic Society, New Haven, Connecticut, June, 1981.

Masters, W.H., and Johnson, V. (1966), *Human Sexual Response*. Boston: Little, Brown, pp. 66–67.

Musto, D. (1969), The youth of John Quincy Adams. *Proc. Am. Phil. Soc.*, 113:269–282.

Neubauer, P.B. (1960), The one-parent child and his oedipal development. *Psychoanal. Study Child*, 15:286–309.

Peller, L. (1961), Comments on adoption and child development. *Bull. Phila. Assoc. Psychoanal.*, 11:1961.

Peller, L. (1963), Comments on adoption and child development. *Bull. Phila. Assoc. Psychoanal.*, 13:1963.

Piaget, J. (1926), *The Language and Thought of the Child*. New York: Harcourt, Brace & World.

Piaget, J. (1951), *Play, Dreams and Imitation in Childhood*, trans. C. Gattegno and F.M. Hodgson. New York: Norton.

Pierce, C.M., Whitman, R.R., Maas, J.W., and Gay, M.I. (1961), Enuresis and dreaming. *Arch. Gen. Psychiatry*, 4:166–170.

Rapaport, D. (1967), *The Collected Papers of David Rapaport*, ed. M.M. Gill. New York: Basic Books, p. 589.

Reding, G.R., Rubright, W.C., Rechtshaffen, A., and Daniels, R.S. (1964), Sleep pattern of tooth grinding: Its relationship to dreaming. *Science*, 145:725–726.

Rosenfeld, H. (1955), Psychoanalysis of the superego in an acute schizophrenic. In: *New Directions in Psychoanalysis*, ed. M. Klein, P. Heimann, and R. Money-Kyrle. London: Tavistock, pp. 180–219.

Rutter, M. (1971), Normal psychosexual development. *J. Child Psychol. Psychiatry*, 11:259–283.

Schafer, R. (1974), Problems in Freud's psychology of women. *J. Am. Psychoanal. Assoc.*, 22:459–485.

Schechter, M., Carlson, P.B., Simmons, J.Q., and Work, H.H. (1964), Emotional problems in the adoptee. *Arch. Gen. Psychiatry*, 10:37.

Schwartzman, H.B. (1979), *Transformations: The Anthropology of Children's Play*. New York: Plenum.

Segal, H. (1964), *Introduction to the Work of Melanie Klein*. London: Heinemann, p. 61.

Sherfey, M.J. (1966), The evolution and nature of female sexuality in relation to psychoanalytic theory. *J. Am. Psychoanal. Assoc.*, 14:28–128.

Sours, J.A., Frumken, P., and Inderwell, R.R. (1963), Somnambulism. *Arch. Gen. Psychiatry*, 9:400–413.

Spitz, R.A. (1962), *The First Year of Life*. New York: International Universities Press.

Toussieng, P.B. (1966), Thoughts regarding the etiology of psychological difficulties in adopted children. *Child Welfare*, February 9.

Triseliotis, J. (1973), *In Search of Origins: The Experiences of Adopted People*. London: Routledge & Kegan Paul.

Vygotsky, L. (1967), Play and its role in the mental development of the child. *Soviet Psychol.*, 5:6–18.

Waelder, R. (1933), The psychoanalytic theory of play. *Psychoanal. Q.*, 2:208–224.

White, R.W. (1960), Competence and the psychosexual stage of development. In: *Nebraska Symposium on Motivation*, Vol. 8, ed. M.R. Jones. Lincoln, Neb.: University of Nebraska Press.

Wittenborn, J.R. (1957), *The Placement of Adoptive Children*. Springfield, Ill.: Charles C Thomas, p. 189.

Chapter 15

THE ELEMENTARY-SCHOOL-AGE CHILD

MATURATION

Something clearly happens in the development of the child between 6 and 11 years of age that gives rise to the impression that something qualitative as well as quantitative has locked into place. The pieces of earlier development seem almost suddenly to fit together and function in a smoother, more integrated fashion. The child not only learns new motor skills, such as balancing on a bicycle, but at some point, perhaps around age 9, does so with ease—the skill has "clicked" and become an automatic, established, unself-conscious act requiring no effort of concentration. Language skills similarly become better developed and the child becomes more capable of abstract thought. And, as noted in Chapter 1, important physiological maturities are reached at this time.

LATERALITY

Laterality is a measurable, specialized, central function of a paired faculty such as eyes, ears, hands, and feet. *Preference* is the subjective, self-reported experience of an individual and need not be the same as objectively measured laterality. Indeed, the preference of an individual may be related more to the acuity of the peripheral organ (e.g., the ear) than to anything else. *Dominance* is the term used for the concept of cerebral hemisphere specialization, e.g., information processing, language and speech lateralization.

More recently, the term *predominance* has been proposed to take into account the varying degrees of cerebral asymmetry for specific functions (Buffery, 1978). For example, right-handed subjects may have a predominance in the left hemisphere for language functions and a predominance in the right hemisphere for visual-spatial functions.

Hemispheric lateralization appears to proceed sequentially from gross and fine motor skills to sensori-motor skills to speech and language (Leong, 1976). Handedness is commonly consolidated by about age 5, footedness by about age 7, eye preference by about age 7 or 8, and ear preference by about age 9 (Touwen, 1980).

PERSONALITY DEVELOPMENT

Essentially this is a period of consolidation of all earlier developments. All the relatively autonomous, enduring functions that are conceptualized within the structural view of the personality show clear maturation as they become more firmly established. For example, the maturation of certain functions, such as defense mechanisms and reality testing, is more clearly manifested at this stage. Besides the shift from a general phobic organization to a normal obsessional organization characteristic of an elementary-school-age child, there is a much greater capacity for thinking, memory, speech, and conceptualizing. It is at this stage that certain concepts of inevitability (e.g., of death, birth, and sex differences) become established. (The child's reaction to death is discussed in Chapter 17.) Logical secondary-process thinking is clearly dominant, and the child has a far greater capacity to delay and divert the expression of a given impulse. He is able to take care of his body quite well, and he now usually thinks of food as food rather than as a symbol. His psychological defenses are greatly strengthened, with the amnesia of earlier infantile urges reinforced by such reaction formations as shame, disgust, and guilt against exhibitionistic, messing, and aggressive urges.

Concomitant with the successful management of impulses, more acceptable forms of gratification become sufficiently satisfying for the child. There is a diminution of *observable* sexuality (see p. 249), the conflicts of the oedipal period are now experienced in a less intense way, and the child is altogether more responsive to his or her environment. There may be occasional, temporary, regressive phenomena, but on the whole the child is more robust at this stage. To the extent that he or she no longer has to consume energy in dealing with his or her impulses, the child is free to pursue activities that are not ordinarily conflict laden, which allows him or her a greater degree of autonomy (Hartmann, 1955). Thus, energy becomes available for learning and exploring and for widening and deepening relationships with others.

LATENCY

This total complex of phenomena is subsumed under the term latency in psychoanalysis. However, many of the behavioral manifestations that occur during this period of psychosexual and psychosocial change are modified by cultural factors. For example, in some societies overt sexual activity occurs throughout this period of development, particularly when there are no sanctions against such activity. This was seen quite clearly in the Trobriand Islanders studied by Malinowski (1927). Moreover, in present Western society, there is an atmosphere of greater freedom which permits, for example, a more open expression of sexual interests. Recent empirical studies (Reese, 1966; Broderick, 1966; Janus and Bess, 1976; Rutter, 1980) have actually shown an *increase* in sexual activities during this period. Lastly, many other complex changes occur at about age 7 (Shapiro and Perry, 1976). All of this suggests that the original meaning of this 75-year-old term, although of historical interest, is no longer sufficient. The term latency, when used at all, should perhaps be confined to the intrapsychic changes that are taking place, particularly with respect to those functions that provide for an increase in internal controls (e.g., mechanisms of defense, increasing capacities for socialization, formation of a sense of moral values, and changes in relationships).

SUPEREGO DEVELOPMENT

While initially (say, at ages 6 to 8) the superego is said to be strict, with signs of a heightened ambivalence and a marked conflict over masturbation, gradually this struggle abates so that in the second half of this period (say, ages 8 to 10) the superego is thought to be less strict, sublimation to be more successful, and the child to begin to experience pleasure again from sexual gratification (Bornstein, 1951; Fries, 1957).

RELATIONSHIP WITH PARENTS AND PEERS

The child in his relationships with others at this stage begins to feel somewhat disillusioned with his parents, and may even feel they are not as great as the parents of his friends (Pearson, 1966; see Note 27). Family romance ideas are especially prominent. The child may turn his interests to other adults, such as teachers, scout leaders, ministers, and others, whom he may overvalue. These fantasies and behavioral tendencies are part of the process of increasing separation and autonomy. Most of all, the child needs peers with whom he can identify and play (Campbell, 1964).

IMAGINARY COMPANION

One curious form of "peer" relationship seen in childhood is that of the imaginary companion. In one questionnaire study of 700 adults asked to recall their childhood, approximately one-third of the women and one-quarter of the men recalled having an imaginary companion during their childhood (Hurlock and Burnstein, 1932). McKellar (1965) described a colleague who recalled having as a companion an imaginary blue fairy called Tinkerbell, who was a friendly figure. At age 5 the girl still had Tinkerbell as a companion even though she knew that Tinkerbell did not really exist. Tinkerbell persisted as a kind of half-belief until the girl was about 9 or 10 years old.

Sometimes the imaginary companion takes the form of a conscious fantasy of having a twin. This fantasy builds up during latency "as the result of disappointment by the parents in the oedipus situation, in the child's search for a partner who will give him all the attention, love and companionship he desires and who will provide an escape from loneliness and solitude" (Burlingham, 1945). In this sense the imaginary companion is a variant of the family romance fantasies and animal fantasies that are prevalent during this period (A. Freud, 1937).

Imaginary companions appear to serve different functions at different levels of development (Nagera, 1969): (1) they may serve as an auxiliary conscience whom the child consults, (2) they may serve as a scapegoat when the child acts upon a forbidden impulse, or (3) they may become the vehicle for some vicarious pleasure. In addition, the imaginary companion may be invoked to ward off regression and to master anxiety, thus serving healthy, adaptive aims.

SOCIAL PREPARATION

While all this development and consolidation is taking place, the child becomes noticeably more pleasant for adults. There is now a pull away from earlier childhood urges, or a strong force to push them down, which is syntonic with the adult position. This is in contrast to the regressive pull of earlier childhood to which young children frequently succumb and which adults often find distinctly annoying. The child has now become in general a more social being.

In terms of his social development, the child is also aware at this time that there is a time for play and a time for what is increasingly being called work. He seems to be aware that he must start to prepare himself more earnestly for adult roles. Erikson calls this the stage of industry versus inferiority, and notes that the child must achieve at this stage the ability to enjoy work, a sense of growing possibilities, and a feeling of capability (Erikson, 1959).

What is of further interest is that the child now begins to experience more directly the impact of the environment outside the family, especially the school and the community. Acculturation still continues to occur mostly through the family, but the family itself is also subject to the influence of society. Hence the role of society must be considered, at least in its broadest terms, at this point.

Acculturation and adaptation through this kind of cultural transmission process is, of course, much more rapid than adaptation by means of the survival of adaptive traits in the ordinary selective process of evolution. Lorenz put it well when he said, "Within one or two generations a process of ecological adaptation can be achieved which, in normal phylogeny and without the interference of conceptual thought, would have taken a time of an altogether different, much greater, order of magnitude" (Lorenz, 1966). Yet, a certain period of time, perhaps a generation, or more, is still necessary to bring about these adaptive changes that will help one make a good adjustment to a slowly evolving and changing society. But what if society evolves and changes more rapidly than usual? How is the adaptive process affected, and can it keep up?

Today the scene is one of rapidly changing social and moral values. Further, the increasing rate of automation has sometimes led to a skill's (or a career's) becoming obsolescent before it was fully developed by the individual. Moreover, new skills and careers appear much more rapidly than even the most thoughtful planning for the future can anticipate. Instantaneous telecommunications and the rapidly increasing rate of technological development add to the individual's fear of being overwhelmed and out of control. At the same time, the mobility of the American population has at times been associated with family isolation and isolation of the generations. This isolation has been aggravated in large impersonal cities and large impersonal campuses. Moreover, the temporary absolute and relative increase in the adolescent and youth population with respect to the adult population contributed to some of the polarization of viewpoints that occurred in recent years.

The effect of some of these trends is partly reflected in some of the unrest seen most vividly in adolescents. (Some of the alienation syndromes that have been described will be mentioned later.) But the effect of these trends is also beginning to affect preadolescents, partly through the uncertainty and insecurity transmitted to them by parents, teachers, and other adults who are unsettled by the rapid change.

PLAY DEVELOPMENT

Some of the personality characteristics and developments mentioned earlier permeate the play of the child at this stage also (Peller, 1954; see Note 29). The play is typically cooperative play, with team games and board games prominent. The child enjoys special clubs and, especially, making the rules. For example, in deciding to play baseball, boys at this stage may choose the teams, mark out the field, decide on the rules, and have a great time—without ever having thrown the ball! At the same time, some of the intensity with which these games are played, with aggressive attacks and sexual excitement, seem to represent the fears, wishes, and anxieties of the child in relation to his parents, brothers, and sisters. Furthermore, the fact of having a number of teammates, with the sharing of defense as well as offense, often reassures the individual child. It helps him ward off the anxiety of being alone against adults and gives him a feeling of kinship with others who have the same limitations and frustrations. The play is so gratifying at times that it absorbs some of the longings of the child.

COGNITIVE DEVELOPMENT

The increased capacity at this time for more complex thought has been studied in detail by Piaget, who has called this the stage of concrete operations (from, say, ages 7 to 11) (Inhelder and Piaget, 1958). Two outstanding characteristics of this stage have been noted by Piaget. One is the now permanent possibility of returning to the starting point of a mental operation; e.g., the child can say not only $6 + 4 = 10$ but also $10 - 6 = 4$. This "reversible operation" is an internal action resulting from the integration of other such actions. The other characteristic is that the child is no longer dominated by a configuration he perceives at any given moment but can now take into account two or more variables. A well-documented example is the child who can differentiate height and width as variables when an identical quantity of water is poured into a cylinder and a beaker; the child realizes that the amount of water in both beakers is the same (Piaget, 1928). Hitherto the child may have been bound by either the height or the width, and he or she might have said that either the cylinder or the beaker had more water because of either single dimension. Although it is known that conservation of amount of substance appears to precede observation of weight and various other measures, the precise mechanism by which conservation is attained by the child is unclear (Wallach, 1969). Nevertheless, this step in cognitive development is an important factor in the child's capacity for learning at this stage as he enters first grade at the age of 6 years. (Conservation is discussed in greater detail in Chapter 3.)

PREREQUISITES TO SCHOOL LEARNING

However, the process of learning has been developing long before the child enters elementary school or even nursery school. It is necessary, therefore, to review briefly at this point some of the child's earliest learning experiences. Learning is, in fact, to some extent dependent upon the earliest foundations for the process of learning itself. The earliest experiences form the basis for much of the later information-processing patterns, and it is possible that so-called autonomous central processes are laid down and become relatively fixed at an early age (Hebb, 1949). Many workers have demonstrated that the preschool years are of great importance for intellectual as well as social and emotional development (Stevenson et al., 1967; Scott, 1968). However, as Elkind (1970) has pointed out, this is not to say that formal instruction is indicated in the nursery school; rather, preparation for such instruction is what seems to be appropriate. Such nursery-school preparation usually includes (1) fine and gross motor play, to learn about balance, height, and gravity and to acquire the basic perceptual-motor coordination that will be needed later for reading, (2) role playing, to learn about later social roles and adult behavior, and (3) freedom to experiment, through which the child learns the pleasures of discovery and accomplishment. Through these and other kinds of experiences the child in nursery school accumulates the necessary concepts, relationships, attitudes and motivations needed for the learning that is required in elementary school (Elkind, 1970). When the child reaches elementary-school age the learning process is more complex; it involves many factors, and each factor is affected by a specific cluster of variables, some of which will be described shortly.

LEARNING

In learning, one adapts present behavior to the results of one's previous interaction with the environment. Adequate perception, memory, attention and motivation are all necessary for learning. General processes for learning include imitation, identification, habituation, sensitization, classical and instrumental conditioning, reinforcement, and generalization. Many specific processes for specific functions are also required, e.g., coding and decoding for reading skills. All of these processes involve many areas of the brain and numerous complex neurochemical exchanges. Theoretically, learning may be impaired or interrupted by interference at any point in this complex continuum. The interfering factors may be genetic, prenatal (smoking, drinking, radiation during pregnancy), congenital (birth anoxia), traumatic (head injury), infective (viral encephalitis), immunologic (food additives), nutritional, toxic (lead, etc.), maturational, neoplastic, or psychological. The learning impairment may be pure or may be part of a broader syndrome (e.g., attention deficit disorder). Unfortunately, our clinical and laboratory skills at present are not refined sufficiently to pinpoint the locus of interference, much less recommend a specific remedy.

READING DIFFICULTIES

Perhaps the single most common difficulty found in school-age children who come to child guidance clinics is some form of school learning difficulty (Rutter, 1974), usually a reading difficulty.

Reading is essentially a linguistic skill that requires a comprehension of visual symbols used for communication.

Interference with the acquisition of this skill may occur when the child has a visual or auditory handicap, a maturational lag, a specific reading or linguistic disability, an attention disorder, mental retardation, a psychological disturbance, an adverse family environment, or poor teaching.

SPECIFIC READING DISABILITY

Clinically, there is considerable evidence to suggest that certain children have a developmental lag in their capacity to understand the written symbols of language that gives rise to the syndrome called developmental dyslexia (Critchley, 1964). The problem usually becomes apparent during first grade, when the child finds reading inordinately difficult. There may be associated speech and language problems, motor awkwardness, some spatial disorientation, and mixed or delayed laterality. Comprehension is poor. The child reads only with much effort, and he often makes many omissions and guesses. The child's handwriting is poor, with many rotations, confusions, and transpositions. There is often a family history of slowness in reading development. Parents will sometimes recall that something seemed to click for them at a certain age, perhaps as late as age 12, when, more or less suddenly, reading became easy. Unfortunately, the delay in reading, especially when misunderstood, sometimes results in frustration, anger, and a feeling of defeat, causing secondary psychological difficulties that further impair the capacity to learn and read.

Children with speech retardation and articulation defects are also often delayed in reading (Ingram, 1970). Visual-spatial skills appear to be less important for reading (Robinson and Schwartz, 1973) but may be more important for arithmetic difficulties (Slade and Russell, 1971). Sequencing difficulties in the perception of temporal or spatial ordering may also be associated with reading difficulties.

Sometimes the rare syndrome of hyperlexia is encountered. It occurs most commonly in boys; the child is often described as clumsy and as having a marked apraxia (an inability to copy simple figures). The hyperlexic child also has some difficulty in comprehension, with an impaired ability to relate speech sounds to meaning, poor relationships, and such language disorders as echolalia, idioglossia, and pronoun reversal. Since these symptoms are also found in autistic children, a common neuropathology (possibly in the parietal lobe) has been postulated for both conditions (Huttenlocher and Huttenlocher, 1973).

READING AND LATERALIZATION

Lateralization itself appears to follow a logical sequence, with each higher level dependent on the level preceding it. The sequence flows from motor laterality through sensory laterality to lateralization of language (Semmes, 1968). Verbal skills represent the highest level of language differentiation and lateralization (Penfield and Roberts, 1959). Working specifically with children diagnosed as having developmental dyslexia, Sparrow (1969) found that retarded readers could be differentiated from normal readers on all the higher level perceptual-cognitive measures of lateralization in use at that time, although no differences could be found between dyslexic children and normal children on less complex measures, such as manual dexterity. Sparrow hypothesized that a developmental lag in the process of lateralization, defined as the representation or control of functions by one cerebral hemisphere, frequently resulted in deficits that interfered with learning to read, and in the case of reading-related behaviors it was almost always the left hemisphere. On the other hand, Rutter and his colleagues (1970) found no association between reading difficulties and lateralization other than an association between reading difficulties and *confusion* between right and left. Finally, Buffery (1976) concluded that "the relationship of various patterns of lateral congruity to learning disorders in general remains enigmatic."

LANGUAGE COMPLEXITY AND READING DIFFICULTIES

The specificity of a particular language is a factor that may contribute to certain reading disabilities. The prevalence of reading disability, for example, varies with the language used, being highest in English-speaking countries, lower in German-speaking countries, lower still in Latin-speaking countries (e.g., Italy and Spain), and only 0.98% among Japanese children (Makita, 1968). Makita postulates that this rarity is based upon the fact that in Japanese KANA script there is "almost a key to keyhole" situation in the script-phonetic relationship and that the reading disability of many children in English-speaking countries might be "more of a philological than a neuropsychiatric problem."

READING AND CENTRAL NERVOUS SYSTEM INTEGRATION

Intactness of both general and specific organic functions is an obvious factor in learning. Thus early brain damage impedes the acquisition of reading skills. Impulsive children also have difficulty in learning to read in part because of their inadequate strategies for learning of any kind (Egeland, 1974). Visual and auditory intactness is a necessary condition for learning in the ordinary school setting. Impairments of any of these special functions require a special adaptation of the environment to enable learning to proceed along an approximately normal course. For example, special intervention is necessary in the case of blind children if learning of the most basic kind is to occur at all (Fraiberg and Freedman, 1964; Fraiberg et al., 1966).

LEARNING PROBLEMS AND ATTENTION DEFICIT DISORDERS

Children with an attention deficit disorder comprise a heterogeneous group who may have (1) a more or less pure disturbance of activity or attention, (2) hyperactivity with developmental delay, (3) hyperkinetic conduct disorder, or (4) "other disorders" (Rutter et al., 1975). The hyperkinetic syndrome, characterized by hyperactivity, impulsivity, distractibility, and excitability, may be associated with learning problems, as well as with aggressive and antisocial behavior and emotional lability (Cantwell, 1975). The syndrome occurred at the rate of about 2 per 2199 children in Rutter's Isle of Wight study (Rutter et al., 1970). The etiology is varied and in some cases includes brain damage (Werry, 1972), central nervous system arousal disorder (Sutterfield et al., 1974), and genetic factors (Cantwell, 1976). Low academic achievement is common. The learning impairment may result from an interference with attention due to the hyperactivity, a tendency to make impulsive decisions rather than thoughtful ones, or some neurological deficit.

LEARNING AND INTELLIGENCE

General intelligence is another factor in learning. However, it is important to keep in mind that normal intellectual development is often uneven; children frequently go up or down 10 to 20 points in IQ during their school years (Rutter and Madge, 1976). Similarly, the difficulty of the subject matter waxes and wanes. Consequently, the rate of academic achievement normally may show ups and downs over the years.

Over and above native endowment, functional intelligence is in part determined by the degree of motivation, emotional stability, stimulation, model adequacy, and opportunity. For example, Zigler and Butterfield (1968) have noted that deprived nursery school children suffer from an emotional and motivational deficit which decreases their intellectual performance to a lower level than would be expected from their intellectual potential as measured in an optimizing test situation. The importance of this kind of observation of children in nursery school and kindergarten lies in the possibilities for prediction, since most studies of children who appear to develop learning difficulties in elementary school reveal a much earlier onset of problems (Cohen, 1963).

EMOTIONAL FREEDOM TO LEARN

The preceding factor leads to a further general factor, namely, that the environment may either facilitate or hamper learning. A climate of emotional freedom to learn includes the concept that the child must have such areas of functioning as attention, memory, and speech, sufficiently conflict free that he can devote himself to learning. Clearly a large number of factors that cause anxiety may reduce the level of functioning in these areas because of the anxiety aroused. Some of these factors will be described shortly.

TEMPERAMENT AND LEARNING DISABILITIES

Chess (1968) has drawn attention to the temperament of the child in learning, and has suggested that even in cases in which the cognitive or motivational element is the primary issue in a learning difficulty, the implementation of an appropriate remedial or therapeutic plan may depend on what she terms the child's temperamental individuality. Chess identified and described nine categories that constitute the temperament: (1) activity level, (2) rhythmicity of such functions as hunger, elimination, and the sleep-wake cycle, (3) approach or withdrawal in response to, say, a person, (4) adaptability to an altered environment, (5) intensity of any given reaction, (6) threshold of responsiveness, (7) quantity and quality of moods, (8) degree of distractibility , (9) attention span, and (10) persistence in the face of obstacles. The therapeutic plan was devised appropriate to the temperament as defined by these nine characteristics.

ANXIETY AND SCHOOL UNDERACHIEVEMENT

With this general background it is now profitable to describe some of the more specific psychological conflicts said to be involved in school learning difficulties. Underachievement in school is found far more often in boys than in girls, and it tends to manifest itself earlier in boys than in girls. For example, in one study boys tended to become chronic underachievers even during the first few grades of elementary school, while girls tended to show signs of underachievement in the grades just prior to and at junior high school (Shaw and McCuen, 1960). Among all the different causes of learning difficulties, anxiety from a number of sources is claimed to be the most common interfering factor (Pearson, 1952). Anxiety may be derived from tension between the parents, sexual conflicts, illness, or problems with siblings. The anxiety may interfere with the capacity to assimilate or utilize new information. Sometimes these conflicts give rise to negativism, delinquency, truancy, or school phobia, with subsequent secondary impairments of learning. At the same time, there is no clearcut relationship between anxiety and underachievement (Rutter, 1974). Most reports of a relationship between reading difficulty and neurotic conflict are based on uncontrolled and highly speculative psychoanalytic studies.

ANXIETY AND AGGRESSION

One speculation about the cause of anxiety is that anxiety arises from a difficulty in controlling aggressive impulses, giving rise to a learning block (Blanchard, 1946). The child may shut himself off from all possibility of having his aggressive fantasies stimulated, or he may experience the act of learning itself as an aggressive act, making nonlearning a counter-aggressive move. Learning difficulties are, of course, usually multidetermined; however, one component may be the hostility the child feels toward parents and his unconscious refusal to please them. In failing to perform, the child simultaneously punishes himself, thus warding off guilt.

ANXIETY AND DEPRESSION

Sometimes the anxiety may be part of a more pervasive depressive disorder (Schulterbrandt and Raskin, 1977). Depression in children may be manifested as school failure or by somatic complaints accompanied by feelings of inadequacy, worthlessness, low self-esteem, helplessness, and hopelessness. Temper tantrums, disobedience, running away, truancy, and, in adolescents, delinquency, may also be signs of depression in childhood (Glaser, 1967). The depression often consists of a persistent sense of helplessness and/or passive resignation, and the child feels unable to acquire something that he or she feels is essential to his or her well-being (Sandler and Joffe, 1965). (For a further discussion of depression in children and adolescents, see Chapter 16 and Epilog.)

ANXIETY AND THE APPEARANCE OF STUPIDITY

A child may also present himself as "stupid" when he is trying to maintain a secret, when he is reacting to his frustrated sense of curiosity, when he wishes to avoid competition, or when he is caught in a conflict between obeying and rebelling and elects to do neither and both at the same time. Secretiveness and lying on the mother's part, especially when there is a close bond between mother and child, often force the child to appear ignorant and not curious, not only about the forbidden topic but in a more generalized way too (Hellman, 1954). According to Hellman, frequently the mother's secret is that she is having an extramarital love affair.

ANXIETY AND SYMBOLIC ASSOCIATION

Very, very rarely an unconscious and symbolic association between conflicts and particular words, or even letters, that leads to a reading inhibition is discovered during intensive psychotherapy or psychoanalysis of a child (O'Sullivan and Pryles, 1962).

ANXIETY AND TRUANCY

Truancy may be a further manifestation of anxiety. The act of truancy may represent a wish to get away from an intolerable home situation. Sometimes the truancy represents a flight from reality and a retreat into fantasy. The family ties may be so weak that truancy is facilitated. At other times the truant child may be seeking a lost love object or may be attempting to create a sense of guilt in the parents. Very often, the truant child wishes to avoid school because of a primary learning difficulty or a fear of criticism, punishment, or humiliation from his classmates or teachers.

ANXIETY AND SCHOOL AVOIDANCE

Separation anxiety may become exacerbated or may make its first appearance during the elementary-school-age stage;

separation anxiety may give rise to the symptom of school avoidance (Hersov, 1980). There is often a history of a poorly resolved dependency relationship between mother and child (Waldfogel et al., 1957). Often some acute anxiety is precipitated just prior to the onset of the symptoms. This anxiety may be produced by an illness, an operation, such as a tonsillectomy, or an external event so similar to an internal fantasy the child has that the fantasy is intensified to the point that the child fears the fantasy will be realized. Sometimes hysterical or compulsive reactions may be mobilized to deal with the anxiety. In the face of this anxiety, the child may regress and experience an increase in his dependency wishes. At the same time, the mother herself may be experiencing anxiety, most often arising from some threat to her security. Such threats might arise from marital unhappiness, economic deprivation, or simply overwhelming demands that the mother resents. She then exploits the child's wish for dependence as a means of gratifying her own frustration, loss, and anxiety. Mother and child then become locked together in a mutual act of regression and dependency, usually combining hostile fantasies which each must hold in check by each keeping close to the other. Often the mother encourages her child to stay home because she has fears for his safety (which are based on her own angry wishes toward him). The child, in turn, is afraid to leave the mother for fear something will happen to her in his absence. The absence from school and the anxiety aroused may interfere considerably with the child's learning.

SEXUAL DIFFICULTIES

The expressions of normal sexuality may take a variety of forms during childhood (S. Freud, 1905). Signs of sexual problems may also emerge during this period of adjustment. However, deviant-appearing behavior does not necessarily have the same significance as similar behavior exhibited during adult years, when the individual should have reached sexual maturity. For example, manifest homosexual and heterosexual preferences have different cycles and different meanings during early development. An infant may show affection for an adult, regardless of sex, provided the adult meets the caring and protecting needs of the infant. A preschool-age child begins to show strong feelings, both positive and negative, toward both parents, based in part on the sexual attributes and roles of those parents. In this sense, a preschool-age child may show homosexual and heterosexual preferences. During the elementary school years, a boy may "love" a particular adult who has shown him empathy and understanding. If the adult is a man, the relationship appears to be homosexual; if the adult is a woman, it appears to be heterosexual. But in neither case is it necessarily based on the sex of the person; again it is based rather on the function performed by that person. At the same time, the child's relationship with his peers may appear singularly homosexual in terms of preferred sex of the playmate yet not represent homosexuality at all. For example, some school-age boys may show a disdain for girls, wishing only to play with other boys. Such boys are not at all destined to become homosexuals; as a matter of fact, boys who at this age prefer to play with girls are thought to be more likely to be vulnerable to later homosexual influences. The key to understanding this paradox lies in the realization that the choice of playmates at this stage is often made largely on the basis of identification and not of actual sexual love for the selected playmate.

HOMOSEXUALITY

Nevertheless, there are certain influences that may turn a child in the direction of homosexuality. Besides any innate bisexual or homosexual tendency that cannot as yet be documented, some children persist in forming narcissistic relationships in which they identify with persons of the same sex. Further, continuing attachments to adults on the basis of persistent attempts to gratify early needs may also lead to persisting homosexual relationships. Sometimes disguised sexual assaults on children—in the form of activities that have erotic components (e.g., the giving of enemas, rectal and vaginal douches and temperature taking)—may lead to a persisting passive homosexual longing. Also, if the oedipal feelings are not adequately resolved, the child may remain fixated at the level of an intense homosexual tie. Last, if the child is unable to mobilize effective defense reactions against homosexuality or if he has no satisfactory parent models with whom to identify, there is further likelihood that his homosexual tendencies will outweigh his heterosexual strivings (A. Freud, 1965).

Even so, the balance of factors to be weighed makes prediction of the ultimate sexual outcome difficult. For example, besides the qualities in the parents and their conflicts, there are numerous conflicts and anxieties that may arise in the child and that may be aggravated by such external factors as illness, divorce, seduction, incest, and rape (Lewis and Sarrel, 1969), not to mention the myriad opportunities and lost opportunities for satisfactions or frustrations. (Homosexuality will be discussed further on page 293.)

TRANSVESTITE BEHAVIOR

A specific variety of homosexuality seen in children is manifested by transvestite behavior. Boys who dress as girls are regarded with greater concern in our society than are girls who dress as boys. And in fact, boys who dress as girls do seem to cope less well with their intrapsychic difficulties. These boys may be trying to win their mother's love, especially if they sense that their mother does not really like them. They may also be attempting to deal with a loss through the normal process of identification. That is, if they somewhat suddenly lose the mother they love (either in reality or in psychic reality), they may attempt to make up for this loss by identifying with and holding onto the internalized image of the mother. In still other cases, the boy may be acting out hostile, aggressive impulses against the mother by caricaturing how women behave or dress.

The mothers of such children often have a disturbance in their own sexual identity and their object relations (Stoller, 1967). They may dislike men for a variety of reasons and so start their boys off on cross-dressing as soon as they show any signs of developing a masculine identity. They nip the masculine identity in the bud, so to speak. Other mothers may regard their sons as extensions of themselves and then find themselves unable to tolerate any separation from their sons. Such mothers will then so indulge their sons that the boys' gratitude becomes profound enough to lead to a strong identification with the mothers.

Unfortunately, the fathers of such children are usually poor models of masculinity and, furthermore, they fail to protect their sons from the influence of the mothers.

An important clinical point is the degree to which the child becomes sexually excited during the act of dressing in the clothes of the opposite sex. Children who get sexually excited usually find it hard to give up the gratification, and they almost become addicted to cross-dressing. They may resent any interference and may even fly into a rage.

COMPULSIVE SEXUAL BEHAVIOR IN GIRLS

Homosexuality is not the only risk of such adverse parental influences. Compulsive heterosexual activity may also be an outcome. In some instances, a girl may repeatedly and compulsively act seductively, engage in intercourse, and become pregnant. Some of this compulsion to repeat seductive acts may represent an attempt to work through an earlier traumatic incestuous relationship, as illustrated in the following very brief case summary.

When Cathy was a young girl, she lived in a home in which her father was given to violence. When she was about 6 or 7 years of age, her father committed incest with her. When Cathy became an adolescent, she found herself involved again and again with boys who were many years older than herself and who were given to violence. Her particular boyfriend at the time had a criminal record involving robbery with illegal possession of a gun. Eventually, at age 15, Cathy became pregnant by her 24-year-old boyfriend. (This case will be discussed again on page 272.)

Excessively repetitive compulsive behavior may also be part of a larger problem of poor impulse control, resulting from such factors as inadequate models for controls in the parents, overstimulation, or unresolved highly ambivalent child-parent relationships. In some cases the girl may be acting out an unconscious wish of her mother to have an affair or care for a baby again.

STEALING

The significance of stealing depends on whether it is a developmental phenomenon or a neurotic symptom. The infant simply lacks the distinction between self and object, between "what's mine" and "what's not mine." The preschool-age child has a tendency to hoard, and he may "acquire" the objects that belong to another child to add to his collection. In the nursery school-age period, object relations usually advance to the point of the child's learning what belongs to others, so that taking something that belongs to someone else begins to be called stealing. If the child is delayed in his development and continues to be relatively more immature and have poor impulse control, the impulse to take things that belong to others will continue, especially if there is added stress from any kind of deprivation.

Once the child has gone beyond this stage of development, the act of taking something that belongs to someone else is more properly called stealing. Many motivations may now lie behind the act of stealing. Sometimes it is an expression of a wish to obtain love or to bribe a person into friendship. At other times it is an expression of hostility toward the parents, who are chagrined at the act. Yet, some parents are not chagrined and some may even seem to condone the act, as in the following example. A boy confessed to stealing some table tennis balls from a large department store. His father responded by saying he was not concerned because "the store could stand the loss." The distortion of reality values and the implied condoning of the act were clear. In this case the boy had no more sense of guilt about what he had done than had the father. Such a child may have quite adequate superego injunctions in other areas, but because his parents are themselves delinquent and provide no taboos against stealing, the child takes in whole this aspect, too, of the parent and as a result has a superego or conscience that has noticeable deficits.

Occasionally the act of stealing is a poor sublimation for an intense desire to damage, mutilate, or castrate another person. Instead of hurting a part of the other person's body, the stealer takes away his "treasured possession." Sometimes such an unacceptable impulse gives rise to a feeling of guilt, which is then vitiated by the punishment which is incurred when another "crime" is committed. The act of stealing serves this function when it is performed in such a blatant way that it demonstrates a clear wish to be caught. (Sometimes the item stolen provides a clue to the initial unacceptable impulse.)

Stealing may also be a part of a more general behavior trait. For example, a child may have a tendency to behave in a counterphobic way; that is, he deals with a fear by repeatedly and increasingly risking the danger he most fears. Stealing may be just such a "daring act"; the child defies authority and experiences the thrill of near misses. Sometimes it is an act performed in the service of identification with a group or with a particular leader or as in reluctant obedience to the commands of such a person.

LYING

What has been said about stealing can also be said about lying. In infancy, fantasy and reality are not well distinguished. There is throughout childhood a tendency, especially under stress, to revert to the pleasure of fantasy and primary process thinking, so that the verbal distortion of reality (the untruth) more likely represents the lack of distinction between fantasy and reality or a regression to fantasy than a conscious effort to distort reality. Later, when the distortion of the truth can be more properly called lying, motivations similar to those found in stealing may give rise to lying.

ANTISOCIAL BEHAVIOR

Serious antisocial behavior in the 6-to-11 age group is a "particularly ominous childhood pattern" (Robins, 1966). Robins compared 524 children seen in a child guidance clinic with 100 matched normal children in a local school. Her study found that children referred to the clinic for such complaints as temper tantrums, learning problems, sleeping and eating problems, and speech problems did not differ much from the control group when they were seen as adults 30 years later; that is, shyness, seclusiveness, nervousness, tantrums, insomnia, fears, tics, speech problems, and similar complaints were *not* related to later psychiatric disorder. However, children referred to the clinic for antisocial behavior *did* differ from the control group seen 30 years later, and the more severe the early antisocial behavior was during childhood, the more disturbed was the later adjustment. Among the children referred to the clinic for antisocial behavior, (1) most of them had been held back in first grade, (2) their problems had become obvious at the age of 7, and (3) the common referral symptoms had been theft (82%), incorrigible behavior (76%), truancy (75%), running away (71%), having bad friends (52%), school discipline problems, and sexual activity, including promiscuity. (Truancy and poor school performance had been almost universally present in children who later demonstrated antisocial behaviors, and a high percentage of the antisocial children were later diagnosed as being schizophrenic.) Interestingly, in the families of these children referred for antisocial behavior, the father was "sociopathic" or alcoholic, and the homes were impoverished or broken. In short, the best single predictor of adult "sociopathy" (whatever that is) was the degree of childhood antisocial behavior, especially in the 6-to-11 age group.

Also interesting was the fact that such factors as poverty, a slum environment, maternal deprivation, foster home or orphanage placement, or even a "sociopathic" mother did not predict adult sociopathy. However, if a child had a sociopathic or alcoholic father and was also sent to a correctional institution, the prognosis for the child was poor. Lee Robins was essentially taking issue with the so-called culture-of-poverty hypothesis of sociopathy. She believed that it was the other way around; that is, that children with antisocial behavior and sociopathic fathers simply fail to rise socioeconomically. Robins concluded that antisocial behavior predicts class status more than class status predicts antisocial behavior.

In a more recent study of violent juvenile delinquents, Dorothy Otnow Lewis and her colleagues found a greater prevalence of psychotic symptoms, neurological abnormalities, and child abuse in extremely violent delinquents than in their less violent peers (Lewis et al., 1979). Lewis stated that "the combination of trauma to the central nervous system, parental psychopathology ... and social deprivation ... creates the kinds of serious, often violent, delinquent acts so prevalent in our society today" (p. 422). Further, Lewis suggested that "the combination of familial vulnerability (e.g., as indexed by the presence of a schizophrenic parent), trauma to the central nervous system (e.g., perinatal trauma, head injury), physical and psychological abuse from a parent, and social deprivation (e.g., failure of a physician to diagnose and treat correctly, or failure of society to provide adequate support systems in the form of community programs or residential treatment) is sufficient to create the violent young offender, and this combination of factors occurs frequently" (p. 423).

Finally, it is important to keep in perspective the prevalence of psychiatric disorders in children in this age group. Rutter et al. (1970) found a prevalence of only 6.8% in a total population studied of 2199 10- and 11-year-old children (see Note 28).

Note 27

G.H.J. Pearson (1966), The importance of peer relationship in the latency period. *Bull. Phila. Assoc. Psychoanal.*, 16:109–121.

As we observe children we note that around the age of five and six, the child begins to remove himself from his family and seeks friends of his own age outside the home.... Real playing together becomes more definitive from five or six on. By the time he is about six or seven, he gradually spends more and more time with his friends than with his family. He begins to share his interests and ideas more with his friends and less with his parents, and he definitely begins to keep his secrets for his friends and no longer tells them to his parents.

By the time he is eight or nine, this behavior has become quite marked and of course continues into and through adolescence. At the same time he begins to question, both by himself and with his friends, his former concept of his parents as deities who can do no wrong. He begins gradually to recognize that they, like all other adult human beings, are mortal and comes to believe that adults, as a general rule, are not to be trusted. As he finds himself being aware of his parents' and other adults' shortcomings, he relies more and more on the support and cooperation of his peer companions. Somewhere between eight and ten these form a group, tend to gang together against the adults and the adults' authority, and find pleasure in thwarting the adult as much as possible. This turning away from the former worshipful admiration of the parents and other adults and the consequent deprecating of their importance is regarded by the parents, and other adults, with distinct displeasure. . . .

Withdrawal from parents and adults and relating more closely to peers reinforces repression of the oedipal conflict and thus becomes an important factor in personality development. Relationship with peers in itself develops skill in socialization. . . . this is as necessary an individual step in the total development of the human being as is the relationship with the mother. When there is interference with it or if it does not occur, the later life adjustment of the human being is crippled. . . . This developmental process can be interfered with in two ways: as the result of environmental and adult restrictions; and as the result of inner restrictions which have been produced by frustrations during the pre-oedipal and early oedipal years.

Parents who dislike the incessant activity and use of small and large muscles in the five-, six-, or seven-year-old may insist on less active behavior. As a consequence the child is forced back into the intrapsychic life of daydreaming and fantasy and is prevented from repressing and redirecting the oedipal fantasies. . . . Similarly parents who for whatever reason restrict unreasonably their child's contact with other children or resent bitterly the child's loyalty to his peer group, and the concomitant "disloyalty" to themselves, may interfere with the child's socialization and prevent the (necessary) repression. . . .

External circumstances . . . may restrict the possibility of a child making adequate contact with his peers. . . . Sometimes an only child will be sent to a private school from the time he enters school. This school usually is a long distance from his home and no other child from his neighborhood may attend it. His peers may look with contempt on this particular child because he attends a different school. He finds that they don't accept him readily, so he comes more and more to stay by himself on his own property and often within his home. This again forces a difficulty in the solution of his oedipal problems, or at best a delay in their solution. Of course, the opportunity he has for free play with his peers during school hours will help him to some extent.

Very frequent moves from one neighborhood to another during this period also may interrupt old relationships and create difficulties in adjusting to new groups of peers so that the child eventually gives up making further attempts. Long continued illnesses during this period or marked chronic physical disabilities which actively prevent peer contact are a cause in some cases but these are special instances.

Occasionally one sees a child who restricts himself from peer contact because of former painful experiences. . . .

There are a number of cases in which the child during the late prelatent and latency periods restricts himself from peer contact for unconscious reasons, usually the result of traumatic experiences during his pre-oedipal and early oedipal periods. . . .

. . . a child who himself avoids contact with his peers during the late prelatent and latent periods or who is much, much too loyal to his parents in his thinking, must show disturbances in his development.

... In short, it is important to remember that the child utilizes a number of methods such as: motor activity, curiosity and interest in the external world, alliance with his peers against adults, increased loyalty to his peers with its accompanying increase in a more realistic appraisal of his parents and other adults, as mechanisms to aid his repressions, to promote separation from parents and to facilitate his own maturing.

Note 28

M. Rutter, J. Tizard, and K. Whitmore (1970), *Education, Health and Behaviour*. London: Longman Group Limited, pp. 200–201.

Of the total population of 2199 ten- and eleven-year-old children screened, 118 (5.4 per cent) were found to have a clinically significant psychiatric disorder. When this rate was corrected for the number likely to have been missed by the group screening procedures, a prevalence of 6.8 per cent was found. This figure does not include uncomplicated intellectual retardation, monosymptomatic disorders or uncomplicated educational retardation.

The psychiatric disorders were classified into seven main groups: neurotic disorders, antisocial or conduct disorders, mixed neurotic and antisocial disorders, developmental disorders (which were excluded from the prevalence figure given above), hyperkinetic syndrome, child psychosis, and personality disorder. Neurotic disorders and conduct disorders were much the commonest conditions and the two diagnoses were made with about the same frequency. However, whereas neurotic disorders were somewhat commoner in girls, conduct disorders were very much commoner in boys. In addition there was a large group of children who had a mixed conduct and neurotic disorder. This group resembled the antisocial group in many characteristics including sex ratio, family size and associated reading retardation. If it is pooled with the conduct disorder group, the total prevalence of antisocial or conduct disorders is found to be 3.2, or 4.0 per cent when the correction factor is applied. The observed prevalence of neurotic disorders was 2.0 per cent giving a true prevalence of 2.5 per cent.

Only two children showed the hyperkinetic syndrome (although a much larger number showed restlessness or overactivity as part of a conduct or a neurotic disorder); two were psychotic and one girl had a markedly deviant personality.

The largest subgroup of neurotic conditions was 'anxiety disorders' (30 cases) in which anxiety and worrying were the most permanent symptoms. Many of the children in this group were generally fearful and a third had handicapping specific phobias. Altogether of the 118 children with psychiatric disorder, sixteen had clinically significant phobias (although the phobia was rarely the main and never the only symptom). Specific situational phobias were the most common variety; they were about equally frequent in boys and girls. There was no case of persisting school refusal. Specific animal phobias were only half as common and occurred only in girls. In marked contrast to the type of phobias found in adults, there were no cases of agoraphobia or of handicapping social anxiety.

A smaller number of children (7) had disorders with prominent obsessive features but there were no examples of a fully developed obsessional disorder of an adult type. An overt depressive disorder was found in only three girls and no boys, although a larger number of children in other diagnostic subgroups were to some degree unhappy or miserable. In three further children the most striking feature was the presence of tics. Of the seventeen neurotic boys four were rated as severely impaired, and of the twenty-six neurotic girls thirteen were severely handicapped.

Antisocial disorders were classified according to place, severity and type. Twenty children were antisocial but not delinquent, eight showed a trivial delinquency, in five cases the delinquency was confined to the home, twenty children exhibited 'socialised' delinquency and seventeen 'non-socialised' delinquency. The distinction between 'socialised' and 'non-socialised' delinquency proved to be more difficult than would be judged from the reports of the proponents of this distinction, since the characteristics which were supposed to group together did so only to a very weak extent. In the present study most weight was placed on good peer relationships and an absence of neurotic features in the antisocial acts, in making the diagnosis of 'socialised delinquency'. The only difference which could be found between children categorised as 'socialised' and 'non-socialised' was that the latter tended to be eldest children while the former showed no particular ordinal position.

Most of the children with neurotic disorder and most of those with conduct disorder had conditions of at least three years duration.

Note 29

L.E. Peller (1954), Libidinal phases, ego development, and play. *Psychoanal. Study Child*, 9:178–198.

SURVEY OF PLAY ACTIVITIES

	CENTRAL THEME OF PLAY: OBJECT-RELATIONS:	DEFICIENCIES ANXIETY (denied):	COMPENSATING FANTASY:	FORMAL ELEMENTS, STYLE:	SOCIAL ASPECT:	PLAY MATERIAL:	SECONDARY PLAY GAINS:
Group I	Relation to *Body* Anxieties concerning body	My body is no good I am often helpless	My body (its extensions, replicas, variations) is a perfect instrument for my wishes. Imagery of grandeur, of perfect ease	Hallucinations (pos. & neg.) rather than fantasies. Imagery increases pleasure, persistence	Solitary	Extensions & Variations of Body functions & Body parts.	Increased body skills & mastery. Initiation into active search for gratification.
Group II	Relation to *Preoedipal Mother* Fear to lose love object	My Mother can— desert me; do as she pleases;	I can do to *others* what she did to *me.* I can go on (or quit)	Short fantasies. Endless, monotonous repetitions. Few variations. No risk, no climax, no real plot. Tit-for-tat	Solitary or with mother. Other children rank with pets, or things—not as co-players. Sporadic mirroring play	Maternal play with dolls, stuffed animals, with other children, and mother herself. Peek-a-boo. Earliest tools.	Rage, anxiety mitigated. Ability to bear delay, frustration. Initiation into lasting object relation.
Group III starts about 3 years	*Oedipal* Relations & Defenses against them. Fear to lose love of love object	I cannot enjoy what grownups enjoy.	I am big; I can do as big people are doing. Family Romance	Spontaneity. Infinite variety of emotions, roles, plots, settings. Time is telescoped In later times; Drama, risk	Early co-play Attempts to share fantasy. Fantasy always social Activity may be solitary or social	Dollplay; wide variety of events, of father, mother images; (pilot, nurse, magician etc.) Creative play, Imaginative play. Use of emblems, props, insignia	Preparation for adult roles, adult skills. Co-play prepares co-work. Initiation into adventure, accomplishment.
Group IV starts about 6 years	*Sibling* Relations Fear of superego and superego figures	I am all alone against threatening authority I cannot start all over again	Many of us are united. We observed rules conscientiously. I can live many lives.	Codified plot & roles. Importance of rules, program, rituals, *formal* elements. Reciprocity (Piaget)	Organized co-play Fantasy tacitly shared.	Team games Board games Organized games Games with token armies	Dissolving oedipal ties. Co-operation with brothers, with followers & leaders experienced as gratifying.

REFERENCES

Blanchard, P. (1946), Psychoanalytic contributions to the problems of reading disabilities. *Psychoanal. Study Child*, 2:163–187.

Bornstein, B. (1951), On latency. *Psychoanal. Study Child*, 6:279–285.

Broderick, C.B. (1966), Sexual behavior among preadolescents. *J. Soc. Issues*, 22:6–21.

Buffery, A.W.H. (1976), Sex differences in the neuropsychological development of verbal and spatial skills. In: *The Neuropsychology of Learning Disorders*, eds. R.S. Knights and D.J. Bakker. Baltimore, University Park Press, pp. 187–205.

Buffery, A.W.H. (1978), Neuropsychological aspects of language development: An essay on cerebral dominance. In: *The Development of Communication*, eds. N. Waterson and C. Snow. New York: Wiley, pp. 25–46.

Burlingham, D. (1945), The fantasy of having a twin. *Psychoanal. Study Child*, 1:205–210.

Campbell, J.D. (1964), Peer relations in childhood. In: *Review of Child Development Research*, Vol. 1, ed. M.L. Hoffman and L.W. Hoffman. New York: Russell Sage Foundation.

Cantwell, D.F. (Ed.) (1975), *The Hyperactive Child*. New York: Spectrum.

Cantwell, D.F. (1976), Genetic factors in the hyperkinetic syndrome. *J. Am. Acad. Child Psychiatry*, 15:214–223.

Chess, S. (1968), Temperament and learning disability of school children. *Am. J. Public Health*, 58:2231–2239.

Cohen, T. (1963), Prediction of underachievement in kindergarten children. *Arch. Gen. Psychiatry*, 9:444–450.

Critchley, MacD. (1964), *Developmental Dyslexia*. London: Heinemann, p. 104.

Egeland, B. (1974), Training impulsive children in the use of more efficient scanning techniques. *Child Dev.*, 45:165–171.

Eisenberg, L. (1957), Psychiatric complications of brain damage in children. *Psychiatr. Q.*, 31:72–92.

Elkind, D. (1970), The case for the academic preschool: Fact or fiction? *Young Child.*, 25:132–140.

Erikson, E.H. (1959), Industry vs. inferiority. *Psychol. Issues*, 1:65–74.

Fraiberg, S., and Freedman, D.A. (1964), Studies in the ego development of the congenitally blind child. *Psychoanal. Study Child*, 19:113–169.

Fraiberg, S., Siegel, B.L., and Gibson, R. (1966), The role of sound in the search behavior of a blind infant. *Psychoanal. Study Child*, 21:327–357.

Freud, A. (1937), *The Ego and the Mechanisms of Defense*. London: The Hogarth Press, pp. 73–78.

Freud, A. (1965), *Normality and Pathology in Childhood*. New York: International Universities Press.

Freud, S. (1905), *Three Essays on the Theory of Sexuality*. Standard Edition, 7 (1953). London: The Hogarth Press.

Freud, S. (1923), *The Ego and the Id*. Standard Edition, 19 (1961). London: The Hogarth Press.

Fries, M.E. (1957), Review of the literature on the latency period. *J. Am. Psychoanal. Assoc.* 5:525.

Glaser, K. (1967), Masked depression in children and adolescents. *Am. J. Psychother.*, 21:565–574.

Hartmann, H. (1955), Notes on the theory of sublimation. *Psychoanal. Study Child*, 10:9–29.

Hebb, D.O. (1949), *The Organization of Behavior: A Neuropsychological Theory*. New York: Wiley.

Hellman, I. (1954), Some observations on mothers of children with intellectual inhibitions. *Psychoanal. Study Child*, 9:259–273.

Hersov, L., and Berg, I. (Eds.) (1980), *Out of School*. Chichester: Wiley.

Hurlock, R., and Burnstein, A. (1932), The imaginary playmate: A questionnaire study. *J. Genet. Psychol.*, 41:380–391.

Huttenlocher, P.R., and Huttenlocher, J. (1973), A study of children with hyperlexia. *Neurology*, 23:1107–1116.

Ingram, T.T.S. (1970), The nature of dyslexia. In: *Early Experience and Visual Information Processing in Perceptual and Reading Disorders*, ed. F.A. Young and D.B. Lindsley. Washington, D.C.: National Academy of Sciences.

Inhelder, B., and Piaget, J. (1958), *The Growth of Logical Thinking from Childhood to Adolescence*. New York: Basic Books.

Janus, S.S., and Bess, B.E. (1976), Latency: Fact or fiction? *Am. J. Psychoanal.*, 36:339–346.

Leong, Che. K. (1976), Lateralization in severely disabled readers in relation to functional cerebral development and synthesis of information. In: *The Neuropsychology of Learning Disorders*, eds. R.M. Knights and D.J. Bakker. Baltimore, University Park Press, pp. 221–231.

Lewis, D.O., et al. (1979), Violent juvenile delinquents: psychiatric, neurological, psychological and abuse factors. *J. Am. Acad. Child Psychiatry*, 18:307–319.

Lewis, M., and Sarrel, P. (1969), Some psychological aspects of seduction, incest, and rape in childhood. *J. Am. Acad. Child Psychiatry*, 8:609–619.

Lorenz, K. (1966), *On Aggression*, trans. M.K. Wilson. New York: Harcourt, Brace & World, p. 239.

McKellar, P. (1965), Thinking, remembering and imagining. In: *Modern Perspectives in Child Psychiatry*, ed. J.G. Howells. Springfield, Ill.: Charles C Thomas, pp. 170–191.

Makita, K. (1968), The rarity of reading disability in Japanese children. *Am. J. Orthopsychiatry*, 38:599–614.

Malinowski, B. (1927), Prenuptial intercourse between the sexes in the Trobriand Islands, N.W. Melanesia. *Psychoanal. Rev.*, 14:26–36.

Nagera, H. (1969), The imaginary companion. *Psychoanal. Study Child*, 24:165–196.

O'Sullivan, M.A., and Pryles, C.V. (1962), Reading disability in children. *J. Pediatr.*, 60:369.

Pearson, G.H.J. (1952), A survey of learning difficulties in children. *Psychoanal. Study Child*, 7:322–386.

Pearson, G.H.J. (1966), The importance of peer relationship in the latency period. *Bull. Phila. Assoc. Psychoanal.*, 16:109–121.

Peller, L.E. (1954), Libidinal phases, ego development, and play. *Psychoanal. Study Child*, 9:178–198.

Penfield, W., and Roberts, L. (1959), *Speech and Brain Mechanisms*. Princeton, N.J.: Princeton University Press.

Piaget, J. (1928), *Judgement and Reasoning in the Child*. New York: Harcourt, Brace & World, pp. 181–182.

Reese, H.W. (1966), Attitudes toward the opposite sex in late childhood. *Merrill-Palmer Q.*, 12:157–163.

Robins, L. (1966), *Deviant Children Grown Up*. Baltimore: Williams & Wilkins.

Robinson, M.W., and Schwartz, L.B. (1973), Visuo-motor skills and reading ability: A longitudinal study. *Dev. Med. Child Neurol.*, 15:281–286.

Rutter, M. (1974), Emotional disorder and educational underachievement. *Arch. Dis. Child.*, 49:249–256.

Rutter, M. (1980), Psychosexual development. In: *Scientific Foundation of Developmental Psychiatry*, ed. M. Rutter. London: Heinemann, pp. 322–339.

Rutter, M., and Madge, N. (1976), *Cycle of Disadvantage: A Review of Research*. London: Heinemann.

Rutter, M., Schaffer, D., and Shepherd, M. (1975), *A Multiaxial Classification of Child Psychiatric Disorders*. Geneva: World Health Organization.

Rutter, M., Tizard, J., and Whitmore, K. (Eds.) (1970), *Education, Health and Behaviour*. London: Longman.

Rutter, M., Tizard, J., and Whitmore, K. (Eds.) (1970), *Education, Health and Behavior: Psychological and Medical Study of Childhood Development.* New York: Wiley.
Sandler, J., and Joffe, W.S. (1965), Notes on childhood depression. *Int. J. Psychoanal.,* 46:88–96.
Schulterbrandt, J.G., and Raskin, A. (Eds.) (1977), *Depression in Childhood: Diagnosis, Treatment and Conceptual Models.* New York: Raven.
Scott, J.P. (1968), *Early Experience and the Organization of Behavior.* Belmont, Calif.: Wadsworth.
Semmes, J. (1968), Hemispheric specialization: A possible clue to mechanism. *Neuropsychologia,* 6:11–26.
Shapiro, T., and Perry, T. (1976), Latency revisited: The age of seven plus or minus one. *Psychoanal. Study Child,* 31:79–105.
Shaw, M.C., and McCuen, J. (1960), The onset of academic underachievement in bright children. *J. Educ. Psychol.,* 51:103–108.
Slade, P.D., and Russell, G.F.M. (1971), Developmental dyscalculia: A brief report on four cases. *Psychol. Med.,* 1:292–298.
Sparrow, S.S. (1969), Dyslexia and laterality: Evidence for a developmental theory. *Semin. Psychiatry,* 1:270–277.
Stevenson, H.W., Hess, E.H., and Rheingold, H.L. (1967), *Early Behavior.* New York: Wiley.
Stoller, R.J. (1967), Transvestites' women. *Am. J. Psychiatry,* 124:333–339.
Sutterfield, J., Cantwell, D., and Sutterfield, B. (1974), Pathophysiology of the hyperactive child syndrome. *Arch. Gen Psychiatry,* 31:839–844.
Touwen, B.C.L. (1980), Laterality. In: *Scientific Foundations of Developmental Psychiatry,* ed. M. Rutter. London: Heinemann, pp. 154–164.
Waldfogel, S., Coolidge, J.C., and Hahn, P.B. (1957), The development, meaning and management of school phobia. *Am. J. Orthopsychiatry,* 27:754–780.
Wallach, L. (1969), On the bases of conservation. In: *Studies in Cognitive Development: Essays in Honor of Jean Piaget,* ed. D. Elkind and J.H. Flavell. New York: Oxford University Press, pp. 191–219.
Werry, J. (1972), Organic factors in childhood psychopathology. In: *Psychopathological Disorders of Childhood,* ed. H.L. Quay and J.S. Werry. New York: Wiley.
Zigler, E., and Butterfield, E.C. (1968), Motivational aspects of changes in IQ test performance of culturally deprived nursery school children. *Child Dev.,* 38:1–14.

Chapter 16

ADOLESCENCE

PUBERTY

Puberty is the term used to designate the marked physical maturation that occurs in almost every system of the body in both boys and girls at about 10 years of age, although the actual age of onset varies greatly (Tanner, 1962, 1971; Young, 1971). Menarche occurs sometime between 10 and 16 years of age, and testicular growth between 13 and 17 years. Girls, it appears, develop about two years earlier than boys, and some boys have completed their whole physical development of puberty before other boys of the same chronological age have even begun theirs (Tanner, 1971) (see Fig. 16–1 and Table 16–1). Thus the mere statement of the adolescent's age is far too vague a guide to his or her developmental stage.

Certain of these changes have profound implications for the psychological development of the individual, who at this time is at some stage of adolescence. For example, beard growth and ejaculation in the boy and breast development and the onset of menstruation (Kestenberg, 1961) in the girl may serve as organizers for consolidation of the adolescent's sexual identity.

Adolescence is usually defined as the general growing-up period between childhood and adulthood, and it has a similar but not identical age of onset of about 10 years in girls and 12 years in boys. Again, the age varies immensely from person to person.

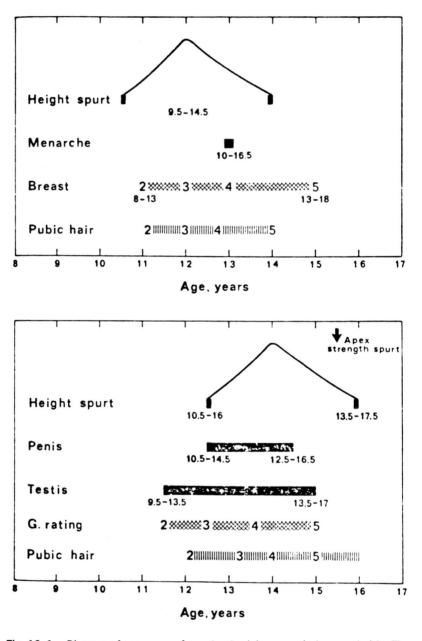

Fig. 16–1. Diagram of sequence of events at adolescence in boys and girls. The average boy and girl are represented. The range of ages within which each event charted may begin and end is given by the figures placed directly below its start and finish. (From W.A. Marshall and J.M. Tanner, "Variations in the Pattern of Pubertal Changes in Boys," *Archives of the Diseases of Childhood,* 45 [1970], 13.)

Table 16-1.   GENITAL MATURITY STAGES IN BOYS AND
SEXUAL MATURITY STAGES IN GIRLS.

Classification of genitalia maturity stages in boys

Stage	Pubic hair	Penis	Testes
1	None	Preadolescent	
2	Slight, long, slightly pigmented	Slight enlargement	Enlarged scrotum, pink, texture altered
3	Darker, starts to curl, small amount	Penis longer	Larger
4	Resembles adult type, but less in quantity, coarse, curly	Larger, glans and breadth increase in size	Larger, scrotum dark
5	Adult distribution spread to medial surface of thighs	Adult	Adult

Classification of sexual maturity stages in girls

Stage	Pubic hair	Breasts
1	Preadolescent	Preadolescent
2	Sparse, lightly pigmented, straight, medial border of labia	Breast and papilla elevated as small mound; areolar diameter increased
3	Darker, beginning to curl, increased amount	Breast and areola enlarged, no contour separation
4	Coarse, curly, abundant but amount less than in adult	Areola and papilla form secondary mound
5	Adult feminine triangle, spread to medial surface of thighs	Mature; nipple projects, areola part of general breast contour

From W.A. Daniel, Jr. (1977), *Adolescents in Health and Disease*. St. Louis,
The C.V. Mosby Co., 1977, adapted from Tanner, J.M. (1962), *Growth at
Adolescence*, ed. 2, Oxford, England, 1962, Blackwell Scientific Publications.

The concept of adolescence as a stage in development came
into prominence with the industrialization of society, and it
has undergone prolongation and repeated subdivisions as
society has become more complex and more adolescents have
been studied. Thus several phases of adolescence have been
described, including preadolescence, early adolescence,
adolescence proper, late adolescence, and postadolescence
(Blos, 1962). The onset of adolescence, which more or less
coincides with the onset of puberty, is initially mostly a
response to puberty—either its appearance or lack of appearance. In one study based on fantasy themes, late-maturing
boys were found to be more likely than normally maturing

boys to have feelings of personal inadequacy, feelings of rejection and domination by others, prolonged dependency needs, and rebellious attitudes toward their parents (Mussen and Jones, 1957). Early-maturing boys, on the other hand, were more likely to feel self-confident and independent, and they seemed to be more capable of playing a mature role in their social relationships. They also seemed to produce more student body presidents and more athletes (Jones, 1957). Early maturers also seem to have, on the average, a slightly higher level of intelligence than late maturers (Douglas et al., 1968). The young adolescent is still very much a child at this stage—dependent on family, concerned about body changes, and subject to anxiety. The young adolescent brings with him or her whatever sense of trust and certainty he or she acquired during earlier stages of childhood.

During middle adolescence (from 15 to 17 years), the adolescent turns intensely toward peers and seems to look for external certainties, presumably to counter feelings of internal insecurity. Such behavior as taking drugs, drinking alcohol, engaging in testing behavior, and becoming infatuated with parent surrogates may appear during this stage. The adolescent may criticize his or her parents, perhaps as a way of reducing their attributed power. But the parents are very much needed as an anchor: the adolescent almost needs the parents to be there to be wrong, so that the adolescent can have at least the illusion of being right, separate, and independent. The adolescent at this stage avoids thinking about his or her past, or the distant future.

In late adolescence the person becomes more adult-like in his or her commitments to work and to other people and in his or her more solid sense of self and internal integration. Sometimes adults try to prolong this stage of adolescence because they fear the adolescent's success. Different "maturities" occur at different ages. (Legislators may be responding in part to these differences when they enact various laws governing licenses for driving and marriage, for voting, and for buying liquor, all at different ages.) In any case, chronological age is a poor indicator of maturity, and maturation is asynchronous; that is, biological, social, emotional, or intellectual maturations occur at different rates and in irregular spurts.

Some of the dynamic changes that occur also seem to meet the criteria for a new developmental stage. Keniston (1970a, 1970b) has therefore conceptualized a developmental phase between late adolescence and early adulthood that at present has no fixed name although the term youth is often loosely applied to this stage.

Not surprisingly, there are wide variations among different cultures as well as different families and individuals. Mixtecan Indians of Mexico begin assuming some parental functions at age 6 or 7 and learn to perform adult tasks quite easily, with full parental approval (Phillips et al., 1973), whereas the Mundugumor adolescents in the South Seas have a far more unpleasant time, with much hostility from parents of the same sex (Paulson and Lin, 1972). The Chewa of Africa and the Lepcha of India co-habit and copulate early (by age 11 or 12), whereas the Aina of Panama remain ignorant of adult sexual information until the last stages of the marriage ceremony (Hauser, 1976). Thus, much of what follows may be true only for specific populations and cultures and may not have universal validity.

COGNITIVE DEVELOPMENT

Cognitive development during adolescence is characterized by a widening scope of intellectual activity, increased awareness, and a capacity for insight. Piaget has called adolescence a stage of formal operations (Inhelder and Piaget, 1958; Piaget, 1969; see Note 30). The essential cognitive change is that the child begins to be able to grasp abstract concepts, such as infinity, and to reason from hypotheses. He will now use such propositional phrases as, "if so and so, then such and such" and "either/or."

Egocentrism, a term which essentially refers to a lack of differentiation in some area of human interaction (Piaget, 1962), takes a unique form in adolescence. The extent to which an adolescent believes, say, that other people are as obsessed as he is with his behavior and appearance is one measure of the egocentrism of the adolescent (Elkind, 1967). Based on the (false) premise that others are as admiring or as critical of him as he is of himself, the adolescent constructs what Elkind calls an imaginary audience, whose reaction the adolescent can of course anticipate. The adolescent constantly feels under scrutiny and often feels shame, self-critical and self admiring. But in his egocentrism he fails, of course, to differentiate between what he believes to be attractive and what others actually admire.

Yet at the same time the adolescent also regards his or her own feelings as unique, and he or she develops what Elkind calls personal fables. These fables are stories about himself or herself that the adolescent believes, such as stories that reflect a belief that he is immortal, or, in the case of a girl, that she will not become pregnant and therefore has no need to take precautions when she has sexual intercourse, or that only the adolescent can feel with extraordinary intensity.

Gradually, by age 15 or 16, the imaginary audience gives way to a perception of the real audience through a process of repeated testing against reality. The personal fable also diminishes as the adolescent discovers in the intimacy of a relationship of mutuality that others have feelings similar to his or her own.

Some of these cognitive characteristics have been described from a psychoanalytic viewpoint. For example, Fountain (1961) described five qualities that distinguished the adolescent from the adult.

1. The adolescent tends to show a special intensity and volatility of feeling, with a rapid fluctuation of object choice. He seeks emotional experiences, and he seems compelled to go out of his way to find emotion.

2. The adolescent has a need for frequent and immediate gratification. He cannot tolerate much anxiety and has a need to be kept constantly interested.

3. The adolescent is likely to be unaware of the probable consequences of his actions and to misunderstand the feelings and behavior of others.

4. The adolescent has a failure of self-criticism—that is, a failure to perceive contradiction, incongruity, and absurdity in himself.

5. The adolescent's awareness of the world about him is different from that of the adult. According to Fountain, the adolescent is less capable than the adult of concerning himself with people and events that do not impinge upon him personally.

In summary, Fountain observed that "as the adolescent matures, the world about him begins to exist in its own right; he sees people as having needs of their own, independently, and he no longer perceives them only as they relate to him. He becomes to some degree 'responsible' for his fellow men."

The adolescent's cognitive and emotional development in relation to society will be discussed again when the syndrome of alienation is considered (see p. 273).

PERSONALITY DEVELOPMENT: UNIVERSAL TASKS

Associated with the cognitive changes just mentioned, there are clear manifestations of personality development. In fact, adolescence has been conceptualized as the second stage of individuation culminating in stable, clearly defined self and object representation (Blos, 1967). The amount of any up-heaval that may occur is determined in part by how success-fully the child has resolved the developmental crises of his or her life so far (A. Freud, 1946). At the same time, the recurring, universal developmental crises now re-emerge in the context of the early adolescent stage of development. Besides the previously mentioned major cognitive task of conquering thought, at least four major groups of univeral tasks can be defined: (1) defining one's own self, (2) achieving separation and coming to terms with specific feelings about one's family, (3) developing love relationships, and (4) achieving mastery over one's impulses and body functions and capacities.

IDENTITY

One major task of adolescence, then, is the consolidation of identity (Erikson, 1956, 1963; see Note 31). Besides the obvious conscious sense of individual identity and self-conscious intro-spective feeling, there is also an unconscious striving for a continuity of personal character.

REACTIONS TO IDENTITY TASKS

One often sees a young adolescent trying on different roles as he struggles with the task of identity—as if to see what role fits him best. He may also keep his identity, particularly his sexual identity, fluid and ambiguous. Or, again, the choice may be delayed and a psychosocial moratorium declared. The vari-ous roles played may also serve to counterbalance feelings of inadequacy. For example, a boy who feels that he is weak may parade as a bully and a girl who is concerned about her femininity may try to play the role of a femme fatale (Galdston, 1967).

Occasionally, the role adopted is like a suit of armor. And if the role is too rigid and fixed, occasionally it falls apart under pressure.

Daniel, a 15-year-old boy, had been conscientious and shy in his earlier years. He had grown up in a family disturbed by marital discord. In the year-and-a-half before he came to our attention he had a spurt of growth. He forced himself to socialize more and to go out for school teams. He wanted to be the perfect all-around boy, and as far as his parents were concerned, he appeared to be doing well. However, his work at school began to slip, and he had repeated angry outbursts against his mother and older sister. He also began talking with his peers about the hopelessness of the world situation, how rotten people were, and how he might as well die. He would strive harder in an attempt to prove himself by engaging in strenuous physical and academic work, but these periods of strenuous work alternated with periods of sadness and desperation. Nevertheless, Daniel's work did improve, and he decided to run for an important school office although, it was noted in retrospect, he appeared harassed and filled with remorse and hopelessness about his shortcomings. One day, just before the election and after having attended an important social event at school he felt he could not go on, and took a large dose of rat poison. He was brought to the hospital several hours later, and survived.

The boy simply could not live up to the rigid ideals that he had set for himself and that his parents' attitude encouraged him to live up to.

SEPARATION FROM AND FEELINGS TOWARD PARENTS

Separation from the family and coming to terms with specific feelings toward one's family and others is another major task of early adolescence. Sometimes, although seeming to be tearing himself away from the family abruptly, the young adolescent simultaneously displaces his longings onto other people, who either represent the parents or represent their very opposite. At the moment of transfer, the adolescent temporarily feels "free." However, his or her attachment to a leader of a group or gang may soon undergo the same vicissitudes as did his or her relationships with his or her parents. (Parents feel quite keenly the sudden loss of the adolescent who attempts to separate so suddenly.)

OTHER REACTIONS TO THE TASK OF SEPARATING

Other adolescents may reverse the tender feelings they have for their family members, and instead feel contempt or hate for them. Such an adolescent presents the picture of an uncooperative and hostile person. Sometimes the adolescent becomes excessively suspicious of others, and at other times he feels a sense of depression, depending on whether his hostile feelings are turned outward (projected) or inward (against the self). Depression in adolescents is often manifested by repetitive or frantic activity to ward off boredom, drug taking (see p. 290), and acts of violence or promiscuous sexual behavior (Toolan, 1962). Sometimes the adolescent succeeds in detaching himself from his family but for one reason or another is unable to find a person to love or be loved by. Such an adolescent may then turn his love interests inward and become intensely narcissistic. He either may feel enormously important, or, if his interests focus on his body, may become inordinately concerned with his physical state.

LOVE RELATIONSHIPS

The love relationships of adolescents also seem to follow a developmental sequence (Pearson, 1958), and achieving love relationships can be regarded as a separate developmental task. At the onset of adolescence, a furtive sexual interest in the opposite sex begins to occur in both boys and girls. This interest is soon followed by an at first unconscious desire to attract a person of the opposite sex that is manifested in feats of prowess among boys and giggling among girls. Very shortly the desire becomes conscious, and concerns about appearances are manifested. Boys and girls subsequently fall in love with persons of the opposite sex who usually are older—and ineligible. Girls tend to be more romantic in their fantasies and boys more erotic. Parents may resent these new attachments, and in so doing may contribute to the adolescents' conflicts. Gradually both boys and girls become more comfortable with their peers of the opposite sex, and tentative sexual explorations occur. At first, these explorations are somewhat aggressive (e.g., teasing and hair pulling) and seem to be regressive. Eventually, the boy or girl becomes attached to one peer of the opposite sex and experiences a sense of physical excitement in the presence of the person. Often that person is overvalued and exalted as a feeling of love replaces the urge for sexual gratification. At the same time the adolescent may feel unworthy of the object of his love. At first the adolescent's love relationships seem to be of limited duration and to consist mostly of talking, with some petting. As the adolescent becomes older and gains experience, his narcissism becomes less overriding and a genuine concern for the feelings of the person of the opposite sex emerges, together with an urge for genital sexual experiences. Among 13- and 14-year-old girls, more than 10% were reported to have had sexual intercourse at least once, while approximately 50% of 19-year-old girls reported that they had had sexual intercourse (Guttmacher, 1976). In a 7-year follow-up study of 45 normal adolescent boys who represented a significant segment of the adolescent population, 10% were reported to have had sexual intercourse by the end of the third year in high school; that figure rose to 50% by the middle of the third post-high-school year (Offer et al., 1970).

UNRESOLVED LOVE-RELATIONSHIP BEHAVIOR

Displaced feelings, infatuations, and disappointments are common enough in normal adolescents (A. Freud, 1958). Sometimes an infatuation seems in some ways to evoke the feelings of an earlier love affair; namely, the oedipal attachment of the younger child to the parent of the opposite sex. If the oedipal struggle had been particularly difficult, the young adolescent experiences a great deal of turmoil. The case of Cathy, mentioned earlier (p. 252) is relevant here.

Cathy, aged 15, became involved with a 24-year-old man. He was given to violence, and he had a criminal record that involved a holdup. Cathy became pregnant and had a miscarriage at three months. One month later, after an argument with her mother in which Cathy and her boyfriend were told to get out of the home, Cathy attempted suicide by swallowing an overdose of aspirin.

In the course of Cathy's treatment it was discovered that her father was an alcoholic. He was violent at times, and he often threatened Cathy's mother. Moreover, he had committed incest with Cathy when she was 6 or 7 years old.

In her relationship with her 24-year-old boyfriend, this adolescent girl seemed to be unconsciously repeating her earlier incestuous relationship with her father.

MASTERY OF IMPULSES AND OF THE BODY

The adolescent's tasks of comprehending and controlling the upsurge of impulses and the new powers of his or her changing body and mind seem formidable to him or her. Early in development, the child struggles to control his or her impulses. In early childhood, there is the tendency to act on each wish more or less as it arises. This impulsivity can be seen in the alternating loving, hating, caressing, and kicking behavior of some young children. Later, as more skills (e.g., language skills) become available the child learns to think about his wishes rather than always to act on them. The child also develops the capacity for play, in which he can actively work by means of repetition and trial solutions at mastering a problem that is beyond his capacity in real life. And, of course, he or she is usually reassured by the continuing presence of his or her parents and by their understanding support and encouragement on the one hand and their avoidance of excessive stimulation on the other hand. The child identifies with the parents and takes over their thoughts and ideals. Their modes of behavior become models for the child. In all these ways (that is, by initial impulsive discharge, by thinking and fantasizing, by trial solutions through play, and by identification), the child learns to cope with his or her strong instinctual urges. If the child is successful, he or she is free to learn at school and is prepared more or less for the onset of adolescence.

DRIVE REGRESSION

Many of the child's ways of coping are used again by the adolescent although perhaps in a more complex manner. Some adolescents become almost overwhelmed by the upsurge of their impulses, and they allow themselves to be indiscriminately messy, sloppy, or careless. An adolescent who does so may still feel like a young child inside a changing and relatively unfamiliar body, threatened by urges whose strength is also unfamiliar. (Many adults retain an area where they can be messy—the garage, the attic, their study, or their desk drawers.) Occasionally, the adolescent will feel overwhelmed and will act in a sexually impulsive manner. In another adolescent, a regression in sexual drive development occurs, leading to behavior in which the adolescent gratifies earlier components of the sexual instinct, including the voyeuristic urge, the urge to explore with the mouth, and the exhibitionistic urge.

INTELLECTUALIZATION AS A DEFENSE

Occasionally, the upsurging impulses are dealt with by repression. A common mechanism of defense employed by the adolescent to maintain that repression is intellectualization. In intellectualization, the body and its needs are almost totally disregarded and the intellect is exalted in its place. The adolescent calls into service his newly acquired cognitive skills. Until recently, intellectualization was regarded as the characteristic defense of adolescence. Today the observation does not appear to be so true. On the contrary, a more common tendency is toward activity or to what Hartmann (1969) refers to as the fashion of acting out in groups. At the same time, much of the activity of the adolescent is adaptive and devoted to change (Keniston, 1970c).

ALIENATION

Sometimes the so-called syndrome of alienation occurs (Halleck, 1967). Halleck originally described several characteristics of the alienated adolescent, who

1. Has a tendency to live in the present and to avoid commitment to people, causes, or ideas
2. Shows an almost total lack of communication with parents or other adults
3. Has an ill-defined self-concept
4. Has a tendency toward sudden severe depression often accompanied by attempts at suicide
5. Has an inability to concentrate or study
6. Shows promiscuous but ungratifying sexual behavior
7. Uses marijuana or LSD

Halleck postulated that the internal mechanisms that lead to the syndrome of alienation include a passive-aggresive rebellion against authority, fears of success or failure, and a feeling of being unloved. Also, several external forces contribute to the picture. The parents often give ambivalent messages to the child, and the forces and characteristics of society have a specific impact. For example, the increasing rate of social change and social values, the rapid development of automation, and the isolation of the generations are considered by Halleck to be important factors. The alienated adolescent also appears to have a pervasive distrust of what is said, how power is used, and of the motivations of those in power.

It is important to note, however, that not all these characteristics are always present. Indeed, contradictory characteristics are sometimes seen (Noshpitz, 1970; Wise, 1970). For example, far from having a tendency to avoid commitment to people, causes, or ideas, some adolescents who manifest other features of alienation may also have a passionate commitment to causes and ideas. Sometimes the alienation takes specific forms, e.g., the Hippie movement of the 1960's (Williams, 1970), while serving the same function. Recently, new religious sects, such as the Jesus Movement, Hare Krishna, Children of God, and Sun Myung Moon's "Unification Church," have similarly attracted a number of disillusioned adolescents (Plowman, 1971). At the same time, many adolescents are aware of and concerned about the irrational aspects of the adult world. Keniston (1970c) has made a special plea that more attention be given to the positive, adaptive attempts of the adolescent who is trying "to make the world a more livable place, to create new life styles, to change others."

ADOLESCENT EMOTIONS

Despite the foregoing descriptions of adolescents, most adolescents do *not* have any great psychologic upheaval or disturbance (Rutter et al., 1976). *Some* adolescents have transitory feelings of misery and self-depreciation and ideas of being laughed at. *Most* adolescents, however, far from being rebellious, are conforming persons, much like most parents. Indeed, most adolescents share the values of their parents (Offer and Offer, 1975; Rutter et al., 1976). Masterson (1968), in a 5-year controlled study of 101 adolescents, attempted to distinguish between so-called adolescent turmoil and psychiatric disorder; he regarded the psychiatric effects of adolescent turmoil as the product of the interaction between the turmoil and the personality structure of the adolescent. In the healthy personality, adolescent turmoil, when it occurred at all, produced, at most, subclinical anxiety and depression. Adolescents with a character neurosis suffered psychoneurotic symptoms during the period of adolescent turmoil but retained a residue of pathological character parts after the turmoil and the accompanying psychoneurotic symptoms subsided. Adolescents with preexisting schizophrenia and personality disorder, however, suffered a worsening of their condition during adolescent turmoil that also persisted into adulthood. Masterson was concerned that a psychiatrist who saw an adolescent with a personality disorder might attribute the difficulties in diagnosis to the fact that the patient was an adolescent rather than that the patient had a personality disorder. Normal adolescence, as Graham and Rutter (1976) point out, is a period of many psychological changes but psychiatric disorder is not one of them.

Psychological tasks and conflicts in adolescents may sometimes seek expression through an intercurrent event, such as a physical illness. Children with chronic illnesses often unconsciously make use of their condition to express their anxiety over problems involving control of the body and its impulses, and over their need for independence from parental restraints.

Johnny first came to the attention of the pediatrician when, at the age of 10, he had symptoms of diabetes. Initially, the management of the diabetes was not a problem. Then, as Johnny entered adolescence the pediatrician noticed that the diabetes was becoming more difficult to control. Johnny began having attacks of severe acidosis with coma. He also seemed uncooperative and unhappy and showed considerable lassitude. Further, he consistently aroused the antagonism of the medical staff during each of his many hospital stays. Each time his mother went out, Johnny seemed to have an extreme fear that she would desert him.

It soon became evident that there was more to the problem of controlling the diabetes than managing a refractory pancreas, difficult as that was. Attention was therefore focused on other aspects of Johnny's life, and many significant findings came to light.

Johnny's father had died when Johnny was 13, just before the diabetes became difficult to control. His father had also been diabetic and he had died tragically from a staphylococcal infection. Johnny did not believe his father had died when he first heard about it, and for a short while afterward he was angry at almost everyone.

Johnny's mother was hypertensive and obese. She seemed to have conflicts about dependency, but she had remained married to her husband. (She knew when she married him that he had diabetes.) The marriage seemed in some ways to fulfill her need to grapple with a situation that was bristling with difficulties.

After the father's death, the mother seemed to take an immense interest in Johnny's diabetes, to the extent that she herself decided what medication Johnny should have. At times she confused the many doctors she involved in Johnny's care. It appeared that her anxiety about Johnny's life expectancy prevented her from being able to trust doctors. Also, the anxiety seemed related to her own fears and wishes about death, in which, one might say, brinkmanship was constantly involved.

As far as Johnny was concerned, it became clear that the whole matter of "control" of the diabetes was related in part to his ability to "control" his body and his impulses. The illness itself seemed to be experienced as a threat to the integrity toward which he had been striving. The attacks of coma also bore a close affinity to an attempt to test out a self-destructive fantasy; that is, they appeared to be suicidal equivalents. It was as though Johnny was seeking to join his dead father and to identify with him. In addition, Johnny was violently struggling to free himself from his mother's control at the same time that he was acting out what seemed to be an unconscious wish of his mother, namely, to have Johnny replace her husband. (It should be emphasized that these aspects of Johnny's illness were clarified through intensive psychotherapy and are not immediately obvious from the skeleton of the case presented here.)

REACTIONS OF PARENTS

The adolescent is, of course, not behaving in a void; he or she behaves in the context of his or her family and society, who in turn react to the adolescent. For at least three reasons, parents cannot help reacting to the adolescent.

1. The parent is in a sense faced from the other side with the very same problems that face the adolescent. For example, in regard to identity choice, the parent may want the adolescent to follow a certain career, while the adolescent may have quite different ideas, and sometimes several at a time, for himself or herself. Involved in this, too, is the narcissistic wound that the parent feels and that often is expressed in a competitive relationship with the daughter or son. For example, a mother may unconsciously try to attract her daughter's date, or a father may do likewise toward his son's date. Some parents may be particularly

sensitive to the impending separation of their adolescent
and, instead of helping the adolescent make the transition, may actually try to increase his tie to family by
making the home too comfortable (e.g., by making his bed
or getting his breakfast). Then again, some parents un-
knowingly may find themselves uncomfortably aroused
by the sight, smell, or touch of their adolescent son or
daughter.

A mother once expressed concern, even alarm, that her 15-
year-old son, with whom she lived alone, was having violent
temper tantrums. When an inquiry was made as to what the
temper tantrums were like, it turned out that when the son
watched television and saw his team lose at football, he would
throw a pencil down on the floor (gently) and say "damn!"
(quietly). Subsequently, it was found out that the mother was
concerned about her own sexual and aggressive fantasies, which
were related in part to her husband, who had abandoned her
many years earlier. These fantasies were now being displaced
and projected onto her 15-year-old son, who was in fact a very
subdued adolescent.

Thus parents may unwittingly use an adolescent daughter or son to act out unconscious wishes of their own.

2. Parents react to adolescents because the defensive pattern of behavior of the adolescent arouses discomfort and
   concern. For example, if an adolescent is careless, messy,
   unreasonable, sarcastic, unpredictable, alternately affectionate or hostile, sometimes erupting into violent anger
   in response to an innocuous question, it is not surprising
   that a parent might react to him with feelings of anger or
   guilt or both. Sometimes the parents so react because the
   behavior of the adolescent is an uncomfortable invitation
   to them to act likewise, stirring up in the parents a
   tendency to regress. Sometimes the parents so react
   because the parents' own adolescent struggles were not
   completely mastered and the behavior of the adolescent
   arouses in the parents memories of conflicts that the
   parents do not wish to relive. The adolescent often senses
   this and may turn to a more neutral, less-highly-charged
   person, such as an uncle or an aunt. (However, it should
   also be said that some parents may also find that the
   presence of an adolescent offers them an opportunity for
   further working through of some of their own earlier
   conflicts.)

3. Parents of an adolescent may be in their forties, a period
   of life which has its own developmental features and
   corresponding anxieties. For these parents, the trou-

blesome adolescent may be a further source of anxiety. This anxiety is perceived by the adolescent, who in turn feels more insecure, thus creating a vicious cycle.

Sometimes, a family in crisis may use the adolescent as a scapegoat, perhaps because the adolescent is, for a variety of reasons, a source of great discomfort for the parents. The adolescent himself may contribute to the scapegoating and may aggravate the situation by his provocative behavior. When this interaction occurs, the adolescent is prone to act impulsively (e.g., by committing a petty crime). He may do this in part because his defenses are impaired and implicit sanction is given for the breakthrough of previous forbidden impulses (Courts, 1967). Sometimes such behavior occurs during a divorce and represents an adolescent's attempt to hold the family together.

SOCIETY AND ADOLESCENTS

Society* in general is also part of the environment with which the adolescent interacts. Society may play a structuring role. Evolving as it does through generation after generation of adults, society has over the years erected structures to channel the problems of adolescence, with varying success. Such structures range from primitive rites and rituals to highly organized systems of apprenticeships and examinations.

But by the same token, when society itself is in a state of turmoil, unrest, and danger, the adolescent will feel less secure and more upset. He or she may then feel impelled toward acts of violence against others or against himself or herself. The adolescent has to learn how to live with the constant and rapid social change that prevails today, as well as with uncertainty, ambiguity, and relativity. Adequate models for identification are less available as civilization becomes more complex. Many middle-aged parents today are utterly baffled by the social changes they are witnessing. The current information explosion in the midst of social misery has led some adolescents to

---

*"The term *society* denotes a continuing group of people who have developed certain relatively fixed ways of doing things which express their particular ways of viewing reality, and which employ specific symbols embodying these views. The society creates a whole universe of rules, laws, customs, mores, and practices to perpetuate the commonly accepted values and to cope with the various issues (birth, death, marriage, puberty, etc.) experienced by all members. All of these socially patterned ways of behaving constitute the society's culture." (G.A.P., 1968, p. 763).

seek "relevance" in social action, while others have tried to create a simpler society of their own. Previously held notions of child rearing and education may not be appropriate for the special adaptation to change that is now required. At this point, the question goes beyond the interaction between the adolescent and society and becomes one of priorities in living for the future of mankind.

TROUBLED ADOLESCENTS

Adolescents, who constitute 15% of the U.S. population (the percentage is declining), are mostly normal, even though their behavior is sometimes troubling to adults. Nevertheless, disorders do occur during adolescence, and it may be useful to describe briefly some of the more common or important ones.

DEATH IN AUTO ACCIDENTS

Accidents, particularly auto accidents, are the leading cause of death among adolescents. Twenty-five percent of all auto deaths in the state of Connecticut involve people from 16 to 19 years of age.

SUICIDE AND ATTEMPTED SUICIDE

Suicide now ranks fourth (after trauma, malignancy, and homicide) as a leading cause of death in adolescence (Surgeon General's Report, 1979). Further, the number of adolescent suicides is increasing; there are now about 5000 deaths per year. The ratio of boys to girls who commit suicide is 3:1. At the same time, for every reported suicide (and suicides are often not reported), there are between 50 and 200 attempted suicides (Committee on Adolescence, 1980). The ratio of boys to girls who attempt suicide is 1:3.

The ratio of attempted suicide goes up by a factor of 10 between ages 15 and 19 compared with the rate between ages 10 and 14. Thus, attempted suicide as a solution to life's problems has its peak incidence during adolescence. Many of the common dynamic factors involved in an attempted suicide in adolescents are related to the developmental tasks of adolescents (Lewis and Solnit, 1963), as shown in the following discussion of motivation for suicide attempts.

1. The adolescent may find himself overwhelmed by the task of dealing with his sexual and aggressive feelings toward his parents, or the persons on whom these feelings have

been displaced, and act impulsively. Sometimes cata-
strophic social events (e.g., plane crashes, civil disturbances, war) intensify the adolescent's problems and lead
to attempted suicide.

2. Occasionally, the adolescent is motivated by an unconscious wish to joint a dead relative (e.g., a father who died
when the adolescent was a young child).

3. When faced with the identity struggle, the adolescent
may fear his identity dissolution, and paradoxically attempt suicide to avoid that fate.

4. Some adolescents are simply desperate and can think of
no other solution for dealing with their depression, guilt
and anxiety, or their intolerable home situation. Fortunately, in some of these cases there is also a strong wish to
be rescued.

5. Occasionally, the adolescent attempts suicide as an act of
revenge, or as an attempt to manipulate his family into
change.

6. Sometimes the adolescent concerned is schizophrenic; or
his reality testing may be impaired by brain injury or
acute toxic states, caused by infection or drugs.

In short, depression, despair, poor impulse control, and
psychosis are some of the major causes of suicide in adolescence. Attention has recently been drawn to parental divorce
as an immediate cause of suicide attempts in adolescents
(Crumley, 1979; Rabin and Swenson, 1981).

DEPRESSION

Depression in adolescents is often the result of the interaction between biological, psychological, and social factors at a
particular development stage (Lewis and Lewis, 1980).
Kashani et al. (1981) have reviewed the biochemical, genetic,
psychosocial stress, behavioral reinforcement, and cognitive
theories used to understand depression in childhood and
adolescence. The normal hormonal changes of puberty have
already been mentioned. The lifetime risk for depression in a
child of a bipolar parent is about 10%, and the risk for a child of
a unipolar parent is about 15% (Cytryn et al., 1980).

McKnew and Cytryn (1979), following a controlled study of
nine children of ages 6 to 12 with a diagnosis of chronic
depression, suggested that a physiological counterpart to emotional "detachment" in children may be a suppression of the
general arousal system, mediated through the noradrenergic
network and centered on the locus ceruleus, resulting in a

reduction of urinary 3-methoxy-4-hydroxyphenylethylene glycol (MHPG). Puig-Antich et al. (1979) have demonstrated a cortisol hypersecretion in children diagnosed as suffering from a depressive syndrome. The various feelings of loss that may occur when separation and independence are attempted during adolescence may play an important role in adolescent depression. Laufer (1976) has speculated that the depressed adolescent experiences a fear of being abandoned by the superego rather than by the mother, although this is concurrent with a feeling of actual psychological abandonment by the mother. In his study of adolescents who had attempted suicide, Laufer found that the adolescent seemed to feel an inability to change the relationship to the mother. This feeling was associated with the experience of being rejected by another person.

In addition, the parents may play a role in the adolescent's depression, especially if they harbor strong ambivalent feelings toward the adolescent. Some illnesses that are common during adolescence, such as infectious mononucleosis, may precipitate a depression in an adolescent predisposed to depression, as may certain drugs such as barbiturates and alcohol.

The DSM-III diagnostic criteria for depression in children and adolescents are the same as those for depression in adults. They include (A) dysphoric mood or pervasive loss of interest or pleasure and (B) four of the following eight symptoms:

1. Change in appetite or weight
2. Sleep difficulty
3. Loss of energy
4. Psychomotor agitation or retardation
5. Loss of interest or pleasure in activities
6. Feelings of self-reproach or guilt
7. Complaints or evidence of diminished ability to concentrate or think
8. Recurrent thoughts of death or suicide

None of these symptoms should be due to organic disorder or uncomplicated bereavement.

Weinberg and his colleagues (1973) described the following 10 major categories of symptoms found in childhood depression: (1) dysphoric mood, (2) self-deprecatory ideation, (3) aggressive behavior (agitation), (4) sleep disturbance, (5) changes in school performance, (6) diminished socialization, (7) changes in attitude toward school, (8) somatic complaints, (9) loss of usual energy, and (10) unusual change in appetite and/or weight.

Depression in children also occurs without the classic unhappy, withdrawn picture that makes the diagnosis easy. Toolan (1962), for example, used the term depressive equivalents to denote the condition of the adolescent who "may deliberately mask his own feelings by a pretense of happiness and exhibit the picture of a smiling depression" (p. 407). Other possible presenting symptoms of a depression include enuresis, headache, school failure, school phobia (Agras, 1958; Watts, 1966), hyperactivity, and antisocial behavior. Renshaw (1972) has recently drawn attention to promiscuity, academic failure, and drug abuse as further depressive equivalents. Dorothy Otnow Lewis and her colleagues (1973) reported underlying depression to exist in many of the pregnant teenagers referred to a psychiatrist. Delinquent acts are sometimes an expression of a depression and are often accompanied by hostile and self-punishing behaviors. Kaufman (1959) has described a depressive core in children with antisocial aggressive behaviors. Burks and Harrison (1962) also cite aggressive behavior as a symptom of masked depression, in which the aggressive behavior is used to ward off depression. However, the concept of masked expression as described by Glaser (1967) has recently fallen into disfavor in that masked depression in childhood is no longer considered a separate entity (Cytryn and Bunney, 1980).

Depressed adolescents may lose or gain weight, gorge themselves or starve themselves, boast of their achievements or speak deprecatingly of themselves, become members of groups or isolate themselves, overimmerse themselves in work or refuse to work at all. In fact, the degree of what looks like reaction formation in depressed children and adolescents is quite striking. As stated earlier, an early experience of loss or abandonment and ungratified longing are common antecedents of depression in children and adolescents. Whether certain kinds of cognitive, emotional, or sensory deprivation at particular times of development permanently change the biochemical functions of the human organism and result in a chronic or recurrent dysphoric state remains an unanswered question (Lewis and Lewis, 1980).

JUVENILE DELINQUENCY

Juvenile delinquency has existed since at least the Sumerian culture of 4000 to 3000 B.C., when the first case was recorded on clay tablets (Kramer, 1959). Currently, 43.3% of people arrested for serious crimes are under the age of 18. In the United States, the number of arrests of people under 18 rose 27.5%

between 1968 and 1977, and the number of arrests for violent crimes rose 59.4%. Among girls under 18, arrests for violent crimes rose 138.8%. Fifty percent of all rapes and murders are committed by adolescents. Clearly, delinquent behavior reaches a peak during adolescence.

The term juvenile delinquency really has two definitions—one legal, the other psychological. The legal definition is based purely on age; that is, a juvenile delinquent is any person under the statutory age limit who has committed a legal offense. In most states the age limit is 16 to 20 years. Juvenile delinquency is classified legally into two categories: (1) criminal offenses, which are acts forbidden by adult criminal law (e.g., robbery, burglary), and (2) status offenses, which are acts that only minors can commit (e.g., truancy, running away, and incorrigibility).

The psychological definition of juvenile delinquency is based on motivation. Thus Eissler (1955) observed that "behavior patterns which may not fall into the arbitrary delineations of juristic definition might show all the earmarks of delinquent behavior in respect to their origin, motivation, clinical appearance, and also very often their social effect."

The literature on delinquency is monumental (see Lewis and Balla, 1976a; Scott, 1965). The Uniform Crime Report of the F.B.I. (see The Status of Children, Youth and Families, 1979, p. 106) revealed that in 1976 more than 2,000,000 arrests were made of adolescents between ages 11 and 17, comprising about 7% of the 28.8 million youth in that age group. Eighty-two percent of juveniles arrested were males. Males were arrested for serious violent offenses more often than females were; females were more likely than males to be referred to the court as status offenders. As the juvenile increases in age, the likelihood of court involvement increases; a 17-year-old was four times more likely to be processed by the court than a 13-year-old was. Interestingly, the number of status offender cases declined by 21% (from 355,000 to 280,000) between 1975 and 1976.

Delinquency is mentioned here to emphasize (1) that it is a phenomenon that characteristically occurs during adolescence and (2) that in many instances the problems of adolescence are part of the roots of the delinquent behavior although the delinquent behavior may have many roots and may manifest itself in many forms.

Wardrop (1967), for example, has identified five broad groups in delinquent behavior, each of which has a characteristic etiology:

1. Adolescents may have poor impulse control due to some degree of organic brain damage, including psychomotor epilepsy. In this group, family disturbance may be the factor that tips the balance in the direction of delinquency. Serious psychopathology may also be present (Lewis and Balla, 1976b).
2. Severe deprivation due, say, to illegitimacy or to frequent foster home changes leads to a tendency toward immediate impulse gratification. Sexual promiscuity and drug use may be a symptom.
3. Neurotic conflict, due to unresolved earlier problems, may result in inadequate sexual identification or strong feelings of guilt. Aggressive behavior that represents bravado or promiscuity that represents an attempt to bolster self-esteem and a feeling of inadequacy, as well as self-punishing behavior, may be seen.
4. The adolescent may be responding to a family upset or family encouragement.
5. The cultural environment may encourage the adolescent to identify with a gang in which violent behavior is the norm.

Many other classifications have been proposed (Scott, 1965). The virtue of the classification just given is that it tries to group in a broad way some of the biological and psychological causes of delinquency in the context of the social setting. Each classification usually implies a theory (Lewis and Balla, 1976a). For example, one theory suggests that delinquency is an attempt to deal actively with the misery, frustration, rage, and envy brought about by deprivation. Thus Cohen (1955) has suggested that "the hallmark of the delinquent subculture is the explicit and wholesale repudiation of middle class standards and the adoption of their very antithesis." Other theories stem from other points of view. For example, the observation that early deprivation and separation, particularly during the second year, is associated with delinquency during adolescence (Bennett, 1960) has given rise to a psychodynamic theory of delinquency involving the concepts of deformed ego and superego formation.

More recently, the importance of neuropsychiatric disorders in the etiology of violent delinquency has received careful and appropriate attention (Lewis et al., 1979). For example, Lewis and her colleagues suggest "that a single factor (e.g., brain damage, social deprivation, vulnerability to psychosis) is insufficient to engender violent delinquency. Unfortunately, often the combination of familial vulnerability (e.g., as indexed by the presence of a schizophrenic parent), trauma to the central nervous system (e.g., perinatal trauma, head injury), physical and psychological abuse from a parent, and social deprivation (e.g., failure of a physician to diagnose and treat correctly, or failure of society to provide adequate support systems in the form of community programs or residential treatment) is sufficient to create the violent young offender, and this combination of factors occurs frequently" (p. 13 ff.)

UNWED MOTHERHOOD IN ADOLESCENCE

Adolescent girls who become unwed mothers are not rare in our society and come from every social class. In an early study, 18% of 2000 single females who had premarital intercourse became pregnant (Kinsey, 1953). In 1971, 46% of unmarried 19-year-old women reported having had intercourse (Zelnik and Kantner, 1978), and in 1975, 69% of adolescent males were reported to be sexually experienced (Finkel and Finkel, 1975). Of approximately 1,000,000 adolescents who became pregnant, 570,622 gave birth and 370,000 had abortions (McAnarney and Greydanus, 1979). Of the 1,000,000 or more adolescents who become pregnant each year in the United States, about 300,000 are girls under 15 years (Lipsitz, 1979). Out-of-wedlock births among 14- to 17-year-olds increased by 75% between 1961 and 1974. Recently, in the District of Columbia, the number of out-of-wedlock births exceeded those in wedlock. More pregnant girls aged 14 have abortions than give birth. Of the babies born to 15-year-olds, 13% weighed less than 2500 gm, compared to 6% born to mothers aged 25 to 29.

However, it is important to note that these statistics are changing. Sexual activity among teenage girls in cities is increasing; e.g., for adolescents 15 to 18 years old (9th to 12th grade), from 14.4% in 1971 to 22.5% in 1979 (Zelnik and Kantner, 1980). However, in 1976, two thirds of all 16-year-old women and half of all 18-year-olds were still virgins (Zelnik et al., 1979). Further, although there was an increase in the number of births to young adolescents in the early 1970s, there is now a decline because of the reduced birth rate and smaller numbers in this age group (NCHS, 1978). In 1978, 10.9% of all births were to women 18 years and under, and only 2% of all births to teenagers occurred in women 15 years of age or younger (Dreisbach and Kasun, 1981). In 1977 there were 570,609 births and about 400,000 abortions in women under the age of 20, whereas for women under age 15, a pregnancy is more likely to be terminated by an abortion than a live birth

(Forrest et al., 1979). [The birth rate for girls at age 14 has risen recently (Hollingsworth and Kreutner, 1981).]

A recent report (Alan Guttmacher Institute, 1981) predicts that if current trends continue, 4 in 10 of today's 14-year-old girls will have at least 1 pregnancy, 2 in 10 will have at least 1 birth, and more than 1 in 7 will have at least 1 abortion while still in their teens.

For the adolescent, the event of pregnancy may be related to an attempt to cope with any of the developmental tasks described earlier. In many instances there is an unconscious or even a conscious wish to become pregnant. The wish may be derived from a number of sources. Some girls believe that by producing a baby they will be able to rid themselves of the feeling that they are defective (Bonan, 1963). In others, there are a depression and a fear of loss of the tie to the mother, which are dealt with in part by an attempt to identify strongly with the mother and to produce a child whom the adolescent can mother as she herself wished to be mothered. Occasionally, the wish to have a baby is an attempt to satisfy the adolescent's urge to give a baby to someone, often her mother. Indeed, the adolescent may be acting out the unconscious wish of her mother to have another baby. Often, pregnancy is the accidental result of a wish for closeness with a boy. Rarely is the unwed pregnant teenager promiscuous in the common sense of the word.

The wish of the adolescent's mother for a baby may arise because she is menopausal and feels particularly in need. Her wish may be conveyed to the adolescent for example, in the mother's turning a blind eye to the adolescent's late nights, by engaging in stimulating sexual conversation with the adolescent, by misplaced "permissiveness," or by providing the young adolescent with contraceptives. Sometimes a pregnancy results through a prophecy-fulfillment mechanism: the parents "expect the worst" of their child, and the child obligingly lives up to this expectation (Bowman, 1958). This phenomenon is sometimes seen in adopted girls who have assumed, as have their parents, that they were born out of wedlock.

Rarely, an adolescent will impulsively become pregnant in an attempt to rid herself of what she feels to be an intolerably bad wish, somewhat along the lines of Oscar Wilde's dictum that "the only way to get rid of a temptation is to yield to it." The conflict is then externalized as the parents and social agencies struggle to help the adolescent decide what to do about her pregnancy: whether the outcome will be abortion, adoption, marriage, or keeping the baby. For some deprived adolescent unwed mothers, the baby is a source of gratification (Khlentzos and Pagliaro, 1965).

During an out-of-wedlock pregnancy, the adolescent girl may experience feelings of shame, guilt, or helplessness and may not take adequate care of herself (perhaps in the hope of inducing an abortion). She usually has considerable fears about her parents' reactions. Parents in most cases find it hard to accept the pregnancy, no matter what their social class (Malinowski, 1966). There may also be much conflict about making suitable plans. Rarely does the unwed pregnant minor see her pregnancy as a symptom of emotional conflict.

Again, a striking aspect of such a pregnancy is its relationship to the adolescent's struggles with impulse control, concerns about the body, striving for a sense of integrity and identity, and regressive pull in the face of the demands of reality—all of which are part of the "normal disturbance" of adolescence.

ALCOHOL USE

Alcohol use (O'Connor, 1977), smoking, and drug taking are increasing among adolescents. In one study, 63% of boys and 53% of girls between ages 11 and 13 were reported to have tried alcohol and 1 in 7 17-year-olds to get drunk once a week. Nearly all (93%) high-school seniors in 1977 were reported to have tried alcohol, and 6% drank daily (The Status of Children, Youth and Families, 1979). Fifty percent of the people who die in car accidents in which drinking is involved are adolescents.

SMOKING

While there has been a 25% decline in smoking in adults, there was a 43% rise in smoking in adolescents between 1965 and 1975. However, the rate of smokers among adolescents dropped from 15.6% in 1974 to 11.7% in 1979, especially among males (The Status of Children, Youth and Families, 1979). The adolescent may start smoking because smoking makes him feel more adult, less anxious, and, in some instances, more accepted by peers. Other motivations are curiosity and rebellion.

DRUG USE

Drug use among adolescents changes with each generation. Nevertheless, some of the studies done when drug use was on the increase are relevant to the present-day habits of adolescents. In one study, it was reported that approximately 50% of the students enrolled in large universities or colleges near urban centers had tried marijuana and that many high school students had also tried it (Cohen, 1969). Blum and his colleagues (1969), in a survey of four high schools in the San Francisco Bay area, emphasized how rapidly the use of drugs seemed to have spread, especially marijuana but also LSD and the amphetamines; and they predicted that the use of opiates would also spread rapidly, a prediction that was subsequently confirmed (Kleber, 1970).

In another survey of 26,000 college students, 26% were reported to have used marijuana, 14% to have used amphetamines, and 5% to have used LSD (Mizner et al., 1970). Almost all LSD users had also tried marijuana, and most had used amphetamines. There is no evidence at present that all or most users of marijuana progress to heroin, and nothing to suggest that dependence on marijuana creates any kind of physiological need for heroin (Stafford-Clark, 1969).

Drug use in 1980, with the exception of stimulants and methaqualone (Quaaludes), declined, as did general cigarette smoking. The decline has been attributed to peer disapproval and heightened health consciousness (Institute for Social Research, 1981).

GLUE SNIFFING

A curious form of inhalation drug taking is seen in young adolescents, particularly 11- to 15-year-old boys—and usually boys of normal intelligence. The striking feature here is that almost any substance that can be vaporized is used (e.g., model-airplane glue, lighter fluid, paint, and gasoline), and the substance is inhaled in all kinds of ingenious methods (Glaser, 1966). The inhaled substance is used with tobacco and alcohol but not usually with other narcotics. The homes of some of these young adolescents have been broken by death, abandonment, or divorce. In some adolescents, the inhalation facilitates wish-fulfilling fantasies (Fawcett and Jensen, 1952), while in others it appears to be related to an erotic sensation derived during the act of sniffing, which itself may be a compulsive symptom. This symptom is often part of a regressive tendency during early adolescence.

NARCOTICS USE

The use of narcotics among adolescents is partly the result of the ready availability in high schools of such drugs as heroin at a time when the adolescents are curious and wish to experiment (Kleber, 1970). Chein and his colleagues (1964) found that 16 seemed to be the age at which most experimentation starts. Many observers now find that 14-year-olds are experimenting with narcotics. Ordinarily, if narcotics were not so readily available, drug use might end with experimenting. But with the ready availability of narcotics, the experimenter may go on to occasional use, then to regular or habitual use, and then he or she may try to break the habit. A user may go through all these stages, but he or she may also stop at any stage (Chein et al., 1964). Heroin is usually started by inhaling ("snorting") a mixture of heroin and quinine water. Subcutaneous injection ("skin popping") is then tried. Later, the adolescent may give himself or herself intravenous injections ("main line"). The adolescent reaches a "high" very quickly, perhaps in less than a minute, and then experiences a reversible drowsiness and sensual itching that may last from two to four hours. During the next four to 12 hours he or she may experience no particular sensations, but neither does he or she yet feel a need to take another dose. From 12 to 15 hours after taking a dose, the adolescent begins to show withdrawal signs. He begins to feel anxious, his eyes and nose start running, he gets gooseflesh, and his muscles twitch. During the next day or two, the withdrawal symptoms get worse, with abdominal cramps and chills. The adolescent will then often huddle in a blanket to keep warm. Usually the withdrawal symptoms subside after four or five days, leaving the adolescent feeling exhausted and achy.

Cocaine ("coke," "snow") is now widely used among young adolescents, having increased dramatically in use between 1975 and 1979. Some observers estimate that 10 to 15% of high school students in some communities use cocaine (Woolston, 1981). The drug, in the form of a white powder, is usually "snorted" through the nostrils, although it may also be smoked in a water pipe, or a solution of cocaine may be injected intravenously. The drug gives rise to a feeling of confidence, euphoria, and hyperarousal, often followed by a letdown that leads to the urge for another "hit." Chronic use may give rise to insomnia, depression, paranoid thinking, and physical debilitation. Repeated use may destroy the nasal mucous membrane. Overdose may cause headaches, nausea, convulsions, and cardiovascular collapse. Juveniles who need money to buy cocaine may become involved in delinquent acts.

Amphetamine ("speed") is popular although it is usually taken for a short period of time. If an overdose is taken, the adolescent will have hallucinations and become suspicious of others, and he or she may become wildly violent. After an amphetamine high, there is often a prolonged period of fatigue and depression that sometimes lasts for a week or two. Adolescents soon discover that heroin counteracts this aftereffect, and it is often that discovery that is the first step in heroin addiction.

Psychedelic drugs, such as LSD, mescaline, and STP, may also be taken by the adolescent. The complex etiology of adverse reactions ("bad trips") to LSD have been described elsewhere (Ungerleider et al., 1968). Phencyclidine (PCP, "angel dust") is rapidly becoming more popular. Unfortunately, PCP is a dangerous drug because it is unpredictable, associated with violence (Fauman and Fauman, 1979), and may result in death if an overdose is taken.

MOTIVATION FOR DRUG USE

The motivations of adolescents for taking drugs are multiple; some motivations seem to be relatively superficial ones, others to have complex roots. Mizner and his colleagues (in the study mentioned earlier) found that (1) 38% of those who used marijuana for the first time said they did so out of curiosity, (2) 60% of those who used amphetamines said they took the drug to help study or get through exams, and (3) 45% of first-time users of LSD felt it would be a worthwhile experience. At the same time, psychiatric problems are often associated with drug use. However, these psychiatric problems are comparable to the kinds of problems that beset students who avoid drugs. Paulsen (1969) has distinguished three prevailing elements in these problems: (1) disturbances of intellectual functioning (thinking), (2) anxiety, phobic, panic, or depressive episodes (feelings), and (3) behavioral disturbances (action). Other investigators have observed social factors in the motivation for drug use. Thus adolescents in the lower social classes tend to take drugs to suppress their awareness of the squalor in which they live, whereas adolescents from the upper social classes tend to take drugs for the sensual experience they afford them.

Findings from studies of adolescents who had taken drugs during psychoanalytic treatment revealed a wide range of psychopathology, none of which could be called pathognomonic for drug users or drug addicts (Hartmann, 1969). However, Hartmann did note that the young adolescents she studied had little tolerance of frustration and tension. Some of the adolescents who had a healthy earlier development had used drugs in defiance of their parents or out of "experimental curiosity."

Others had allowed themselves to be seduced into using drugs simply to avoid discomfort. "They remain in a group of other drug users in a pseudoclose relationship, without much emotional commitment; their sexual gratifications are on the level of masturbation; therefore they are as often homosexual as they are heterosexual; the more passive they were to begin with, the greater is the danger of their being seduced by this kind of gratification."

Attempts have been made to relate the adolescent's choice of drug to his specific psychological needs, even to the extent of hypothesizing that "different drugs induce different regressive states that resemble specific phases of early childhood development." The user is said to harbor wishes or tendencies for a particular regressive conflict situation, which the pharmacology of a particular drug is thought to facilitate; the repeated experience of "satisfaction" is then said to establish a preference for the specific drug (Wieder and Kaplan, 1969). For example, Wieder and Kaplan assert that (1) LSD states are comparable to the autistic phase, (2) opiate effects have similarities to the narcissistic regressive phenomena of the symbiotic state, and (3) amphetamine effects are reminiscent of the separation-individuation phase. Alcohol is said to be experienced by the younger adolescent as releasing too much drive, leading to fears of loss of control—and marijuana to be preferred because it is shorter acting, less diffuse, and more comfortable: the healthier adolescent will "use alcohol or marijuana only casually and intermittently, in the manner of the healthier adult." What can be said with a little more certainty is that the adolescent's personality determines in large measure how he experiences the pharmacological effects of the drug he uses. For example, an adolescent with an emotionally unstable personality may experience feelings of profound depersonalization, depression, and ideas of reference that may recur spontaneously for several weeks, all following a single marijuana cigarette (Klein and Davis, 1969).

In many instances, drugs are taken to ward off depression or feelings of inadequacy. For some, drug taking is a form of rebellion. For example, in the 1960s the Hippies in part expressed their antiestablishment feelings through drug taking. Other adolescents say that they take drugs because they like them and because they reject what they think are the hypocrisies of society, such as keeping marijuana illegal but allowing the use of tobacco and alcohol. Others are convinced that the drugs they take are helpful to them. Blum and his colleagues (1969) are careful to point out that there is no simple, universal motivation for the use of drugs in the young. Furthermore, they note that drug use among students is prevalent enough that it must be considered within the "normal range of behavior, at least on some campuses." Chein and his colleagues (1964) go farther and note that motivational factors change over a period of time, so that analyses of causes reported at one time at another time may be "hardly more than an historical curiosity rather than germane to pressing contemporary problems."

Since most of the drugs taken are obtained illegally, the meaning that breaking the law has for some adolescents is often intrinsic to the motivation. Some adolescents take drugs as part of a wish to be caught and punished. Others take drugs as a relatively safe and private means of defiance and ridicule.

In general, over a period of time, adolescents seem to prefer sedative drugs to stimulants. Class factors figure in the choice of certain drugs, but they are less clearly defined. Until recently, for example, heroin was rarely taken among the middle class, but that is no longer true. It is rare that an adolescent believes that he takes drugs because of an emotional disorder, and he rarely comes for treatment with the purpose of being weaned off a drug. Yet it seems so often that the drug taking, pleasurable as it may be, is still part of the adolescent's attempts to deal with the turmoil he feels at this stage in his development.

RUNNING AWAY

In 1976, about 733,000 youths (ages 10 to 17) left home without their parents' consent for at least overnight (The Status of Children, Youth and Families, 1979). Running away, like attempting suicide, is often an expression of despair, anger, and the wish to be loved (Lewis and Lewis, 1973). The runaway child often is a child who is running away from a hostile environment (Balser, 1939; Foster, 1962; Lowrey, 1941; Reimer, 1940; Robey et al., 1964; Staub, 1943; Wylie and Weinreb, 1958). The hostile environment may be in the home, the school, or the community—or in all three places (Shellow et al., 1967). The parents, as well as the child, may be psychologically disturbed or mentally retarded (Armstrong, 1937; Leventhal, 1964). A child who has not been enabled to work through the death of a parent earlier in his life may run away in an unconscious search for the lost love object. An adopted child who has not been enabled to work through his fantasies about his biological parents may run away in an unconscious search for his fantasized "true" parents. Children may run away from a family environment that aggravates the conflict surrounding a particular developmental task, such as the struggle for independence, which is accompanied by the child's feelings of helplessness and neediness. Sometimes the child is fleeing from the fantasized or real sexual or aggressive behavior of a parent. Many parents consciously or unconsciously wish that a child would leave home. In such cases, the runaway child is responding to the parents' message.

HOMOSEXUALITY

Mention has been made of the fact that the achievement of an appropriate sexual identity and a heterosexual relationship is a primary concern of the adolescent. Sometimes a shift toward homosexuality receives a particular impetus during adolescence. However, it is important to realize that a wide variety of homosexual experiences is normal during childhood and adolescence (Fraiberg, 1961) (see also p. 250). The following activities are normal during adolescence:

1. Visual comparison of the size of one another's penises
2. Group exhibitionism and grabbing of one another's penises
3. Mutual masturbation
4. Occasional fellatio
5. In girls, comparison of the size of breasts, hand holding, kissing, fondling of one another's breasts, and petting one another's genitals

These kinds of behaviors are almost age appropriate among adolescents, provided they are sporadic, not persistent, and not pervasive. Usually the behavior represents a temporary defense against the anxieties associated with heterosexual relationships.

On the other hand, a homosexual identity may become entrenched under certain conditions. For example, persistent homosexual behavior, particularly in late adolescence, with the beginnings of an exclusive preference in that direction, is an indication of such an entrenchment. Prolonged halting of heterosexual explorations because of anxiety may help turn the adolescent toward homosexuality. When less common homosexual activities are engaged in (e.g., anal intercourse), heterosexual relationships are less likely to occur. If the adolescent forms a love relationship with an adult of the same sex, it is difficult for the adolescent to relinquish that relationship.

ANOREXIA NERVOSA

Occasionally, the challenges of adolescence uncover the immaturity of the adolescent who is still dealing with conflicts from a much earlier period of development. The conflicts may represent, for example, fixation at earlier points in the sexual development of the child. Further, the child's level of object relations may be such that he still leans heavily on the need to be cared for, and unresolved earlier separation difficulties may persist. Sometimes these conflicts express themselves directly as a somatic illness. For example, among many girls who exhibit some form of the anorexia nervosa syndrome, there seems to be a regression as puberty approaches, with a recrudescence of oedipal and preoedipal conflicts.

Descriptively, the anorexia nervosa syndrome consists essentially of disturbances in the body image and the perception of the bodily state, along with a paralyzing sense of ineffectiveness (Bruch, 1962). An eating disturbance is prominent; it may include such symptoms as aversion to all food, strange diets, or eating at times to relieve anxiety. The girl (anorexia nervosa usually affects girls) may deny she is thin, and she seems unaware of fatigue. She may have feelings of shame and guilt, and she avoids the sexual function of the mouth (i.e., kissing). Most adolescents who have anorexia nervosa are perfectionistic, even obsessive-compulsive, with the thought of food as an obsession and the avoidance of food as a compulsion. At the same time, these adolescents are usually somewhat infantile, dependent, and tense, and they easily feel unwanted. In their object relations they are usually shallow, lacking in warmth, and have an ambivalent relationship with their mothers. Their self-concept is often unrealistic in that although they wish to be independent, they are, in fact, quite incapable of taking care of themselves. Last, in their sexual adjustment there are marked conflicts, with disgust of sex as a prominent reaction formation.

The symptoms seem to represent in part the adolescent's attempt to escape adult sexual roles. They may also serve to regain control of the body, the self, and the parents (Sours, 1969). More common than the girl with anorexia nervosa is the pubescent girl who attempts to reject her sexual role through milder food fads and diets that alter her body.

CONVERSION REACTION

Another example of how earlier unresolved difficulties and the onset of adolescence can join to produce a clinical syndrome is a conversion reaction, another disorder that occurs predominantly in girls. Descriptively, the syndrome in child-hood consists essentially of usually quite massive loss of functions without organic cause (Proctor, 1958; Rock, 1971). The commonest symptoms are blindness, deafness, inability to walk (astasia), inability to stand (abasia), great pain or no pain, and inhibition of movement or grossly excessive movements, often resembling seizures. Prazar and Friedman (1978) and Friedman (1973) have suggested the following diagnostic fea-tures of a conversion reaction: (1) a dramatic description of the symptom, (2) a symbolic meaning to the symptom, (3) the presence of so-called *la belle indifference*, (4) a family whose communication centers on health issues, (5) an adult model who has similar symptoms, and (6) a physical examination whose results are inconsistent with the presenting symptoms.

The symptoms of a conversion reaction may be part of a general hysterical personality, which usually consists of marked immaturity and labile emotions. The adolescent's emotional ties usually seem to be shallow, and the adolescent is often seductive and loves to be the center of attention. Often the adolescent imitates others. She may show an apparent lack of concern for the conversion symptom itself. Most adolescents who have a conversion reaction have a need to maintain a fiction of excellence and to control others, often in a demand-ing, dependent way. It should be emphasized that these needs or wishes are unconscious and that the adolescent does indeed feel pain or does believe she cannot walk.

What is again of interest here is that the conversion reaction commonly occurs at puberty. Problems and anxieties in these adolescents often arise from what the adolescent experienced in his childhood as seductions and repressed sexual conflicts. Excessive sexual stimulation of the child by immature par-ents, who at the same time imposed excessive taboos, may have contributed to the conflicts. All remains more or less quiescent until adolescence. At that point, a rekindling of the earlier conflicts occurs, with resultant florid symptom forma-tion. The conversion reaction persists until the anxiety can be successfully resolved or repressed again. Perhaps the similar-ity of the developmental problems of adolescence to the de-velopmental problems of earlier childhood arouses the earlier conflicts and leads to anxiety and symptom formation.

After this discussion of some of the troubling behavior that may occur in adolescents, it is important to emphasize once again that most adolescents are essentially normal. Ninety-eight percent of unmarried girls ages 15 to 17 do not get pregnant; arrests of persons under 18 for violent crimes are less than 1% of arrests for all ages (Lipsitz, 1979). The facts are that most adolescents cope with this time in their lives remarkably well and they are not at all homogeneous.

Psychiatric disorders do occur in adolescence, but when they do they have much in common with either conduct disorders and emotional disturbances of younger children or the psychoses and depressions of adults (Rutter and Hersov, 1976). Further, when psychiatric disorders in adolescence are discussed, it is important to keep in mind the order of magnitude. In a survey of the general population of adolescents on the Isle of Wight, Rutter and his colleagues (1976) found that the prevalence of psychiatric disorders, both those continuing from childhood into adolescence and those starting for the first time in adolescence, was from about 10% to 21%, depending on the criteria used. Of the adolescents with psychiatric disorders, about 40% were diagnosed as having anxiety, depression, or some kind of affective disorder, and 40% as having a conduct disorder. Twenty percent had a mixture of antisocial behavior and emotional disturbance. Obsessive-compulsive disorder, conversion reaction, phobias, and tics, although they affected a few of the adolescents with emotional disorders, were much less common, and psychoses were rare (less than 1 per 1000). Depression, either alone or associated with anxiety, is more common during adolescence than in childhood. School refusal also increases in prevalence again although when it occurs during adolescence it is more often part of a psychiatric disorder and carries a worse prognosis (Rodriquez et al., 1959). Other conditions that are rare before puberty (e.g., schizophrenia, manic-depressive psychosis, anorexia nervosa, and drug dependence) are more common during later adolescence. Last, during adolescence some preexisting disorders show important changes. Thus autistic children may develop seizures (Rutter, 1970), and hyperactive children may develop severe social problems.

In short, there are few, if any, disorders specific to adolescence; rather, psychiatric disorders during adolescence resemble those that occur either more commonly in childhood (e.g., conduct disorders and emotional disturbances) or more commonly in adulthood (e.g., depression and psychoses), with particular features associated with the developmental changes seen in adolescence (Graham and Rutter, 1976).

SUMMARY

Adolescence is a time of physical, cognitive, and emotional changes. Most adolescents seem to have little trouble coming to a satisfactory resolution of the problems they face. For them, reality and good judgment rule the day. Psychiatric disorders do occur during adolescence, and they should be diagnosed as such; they should not be confused with normal adolescent behavior and given the misleading label of adolescent turmoil.

Normal adolescents clearly can be sources of great pleasure. A good example was described by Calandra (see Guttman, 1965):

> ... a physics student who was fed up with college instructors trying to teach him how to think instead of "showing him the structure of the subject matter"... had been given a zero for his answer to a question on a physics examination. The question was: "Show how it is possible to determine the height of a tall building with the aid of a barometer." The student's answer: "Take the barometer to the top of the building, attach a long rope to it, lower the barometer to the street, and then bring it up, measuring the length of the rope. The length of the rope is the height of the building." Dissatisfied with this solution but conceding that it was not strictly incorrect, the physics teacher gave the student another chance to answer, this time in a way that would show some knowledge of physics. Having selected what he said was the best of many answers he had in his head, the student dashed off the following: "Take the barometer to the top of the building and lean over the edge of the roof. Drop the barometer, timing its fall with a stopwatch. Then, using the formula $S = \frac{1}{2} gt^2$, calculate the height of the building." (S = distance fallen, g = gravitational acceleration of the barometer, and t = time). This apparently satisfied the letter, if not the spirit, of the examination question, and the student received almost full credit for the answer. He was then asked what other answers he had had in mind and responded, in part, with the following: "You could take the barometer out on a sunny day and measure the height of the barometer, the length of its shadow, and the length of the shadow of the building, and, by the use of a simple proportion, determine the height of the building. Or, if not limited to physics, you could take the barometer to the basement and knock on the superintendent's door. When he answers you say: "Here, I have a very fine barometer. If you will tell me the height of this building, I will give you this barometer."

Note 30

J. Piaget (1969), The intellectual development of the adolescent. In: *Adolescence: Psychosocial Perspectives*, ed. G. Caplan and S. Lebovici. New York: Basic Books, pp. 22–26.

Now, the great novelty that characterises adolescent thought and that starts around the age of 11 to 12, but does not reach its point of equilibrium until the age of 14 or 15—this novelty consists in detaching the concrete logic from the objects themselves, so that it can function on verbal or symbolic statements without other support. Above all the novelty consists in generalising this logic and supplementing it with a set of combinations....

The great novelty that results consists in the possibility of manipulating ideas in themselves and no longer in merely manipulating objects. In a word, the adolescent is an individual who is capable (and this is where he reaches the level of the adult) of building or understanding ideal or abstract theories and concepts. . . . the adolescent is capable of projects for the future. . . . of nonpresent interests, and of a passion for ideas, ideals, or ideologies.

. . . it is apparent how these intellectual transformations typical of the adolescent's thinking enable him not only to achieve his integration into the social relationships of adults, which is, in fact, the most general characteristic of this period of development, but also to conquer a certain number of fundamental intellectual operations which constitute the basis for a scientific education at high school level. The problem that remains unresolved, however, is the generality of these intellectual transformations. . . . It is probable that in underdeveloped societies which still have a tribal organisation the individual remains throughout his entire life at the level of concrete operations, without ever reaching the level of formal or propositional operations that are characteristic of adolescents in our cultural environment. But in these societies the younger generations remain under the authority of the "elders" of the tribe, and the elders in turn remain subject to the conservative traditions of their ancestors. . . .

Note 31

E.H. Erikson (1962), *Childhood and Society*, 2nd Ed. New York: Norton, pp. 261–263.

. . . 5. IDENTITY VS. ROLE CONFUSION. With the establishment of a good initial relationship to the world of skills and tools, and with the advent of puberty, childhood proper comes to an end. Youth begins. But in puberty and adolescence all samenesses and continuities relied on earlier are more or less questioned again, because of a rapidity of body growth which equals that of early childhood and because of the new addition of genital maturity. The growing and developing youths, faced with this physiological revolution within them, and with tangible adult tasks ahead of them are now primarily concerned with what they appear to be in the eyes of others as compared with what they feel they are, and with the question of how to connect the roles and skills cultivated earlier with the occupational prototypes of the day. In their search for a new sense of continuity and sameness, adolescents have to refight many of the battles of earlier years, even though to do so they must artificially appoint perfectly well-meaning people to play the role of adversaries; and they are ever ready to install lasting idols and ideals as guardians of a final identity.

The integration now taking place in the form of ego identity is, as pointed out, more than the sum of the childhood identifications. It is the accrued experience of the ego's ability to integrate all identifications with the vicissitudes of the libido, with the aptitudes developed out of endowment, and with the opportunities offered in social roles. The sense of ego identity, then, is the accrued confidence that the inner sameness and continuity prepared in the past are matched by the sameness and continuity of one's meaning for others, as evidenced in the tangible promise of a "career."

The danger of this stage is role confusion.* Where this is based on a strong previous doubt as to one's sexual identity, delinquent and outright psychotic episodes are not uncommon. If diagnosed and treated correctly, these incidents do not have the same significance which they have at other ages. In most instances, however, it is the inability to settle on an occupational identity which disturbs individual young people. To keep themselves together they temporarily overidentify, to the point of apparent complete loss of identity, with the heroes of cliques and crowds. This initiates the stage of "falling in love," which is by no means entirely, or even primarily, a sexual matter—except where the mores demand it. To a considerable extent adolescent love is an attempt to arrive at a definition of one's identity by projecting one's diffused ego image on another and by seeing it thus reflected and gradually clarified. This is why so much of young love is conversation.

Young people can also be remarkably clannish, and cruel in their exclusion of all those who are "different," in skin color or cultural background in tastes and gifts, and often in such petty aspects of dress and gesture as have been temporarily selected as *the* signs of an in-grouper or out-grouper. It is important to understand (which does not mean condone or participate in) such intolerance as a defense against a sense of identity confusion. For adolescents not only help one another temporarily through much discomfort by forming cliques and by stereotyping themselves, their ideals, and their enemies; they also perversely test each others' capacity to pledge fidelity. The readiness for such testing also explains the appeal which simple and cruel totalitarian doctrines have on the minds of the youth of such countries and classes as have lost or are losing their group identities (feudal, agrarian, tribal, national) and face world-wide industrialization, emancipation, and wider communication.

The adolescent mind is essentially a mind of the *moratorium*, a psychosocial stage between childhood and adulthood, and between the morality learned by the child, and the ethics to be developed by the adult. It is an ideological mind—and, indeed, it is the ideological outlook of a society that speaks most clearly to the adolescent who is eager to be affirmed by his peers, and is ready to be confirmed by rituals, creeds, and programs which at the same time define what is evil, uncanny, and inimical. In searching for the social values which guide identity, one therefore confronts the problems of *ideology* and aristocracy, both in their widest possible sense which connotes that within a defined world image and a predestined course of history, the best people will come to rule and rule develops the best in people. In order not to become cynically or apathetically lost, young people must somehow be able to convince themselves that those who succeed in their anticipated adult world thereby shoulder the obligation of being the best. We will discuss later the dangers which emanate from human ideals harnessed to the management of super-machines, be they guided by nationalistic or international, communist or capitalist ideologies. In the last part of this book we shall discuss the way in

---

*See "The Problem of Ego-Identity," *J. Amer. Psa. Assoc.*, 4:56–121.

which the revolutions of our day attempt to solve and also to exploit the deep need of youth to redefine its identity in an industrialized world.

REFERENCES

Agras, S. (1958), The relationship of school phobia to childhood depression. *Am. J. Psychiatry*, 116:533–536.

Alan Guttmacher Institute (1981), *Teenage Pregnancy: The Problem That Hasn't Gone Away*. The Alan Guttmacher Institute, 360 Park Ave. So., New York, NY, 10010.

American Psychiatric Association (1980), DSM-III (*Diagnostic and Statistical Manual of Mental Disorders*, 3rd Ed.). Washington, D.C.

Armstrong, C.P. (1937), A psychoneurotic reaction of delinquent boys and girls. *J. Abnorm. Soc. Psychol.*, 32:329.

Balser, B.H. (1939), A behavior problem: Runaways. *Psychiatr. Q.*, 13:539.

Bennet, I. (1960), *Delinquent and Neurotic Children: A Comparative Study*. London: Tavistock.

Berger, B.M. (1969), The new stage of American man—Almost endless adolescence. *The New York Times Magazine*, Nov. 2, 1969, p. 32.

Blos, P. (1962), Phases of adolescence. In: *On Adolescence: A Psychoanalytic Interpretation*. New York: Free Press, pp. 52–157.

Blos, P. (1967), The second individuation process of adolescence. *Psychoanal. Study Child*, 22:162–187.

Blum, R.H. (1969), *Students and Drugs*. San Francisco: Jossey-Bass, p. 399.

Bonan, A.F. (1963), Psychoanalytic implications in treating unmarried mothers with narcissistic character structures. *Soc. Casework*, 44:323–339.

Bowman, L.A. (1958), The unmarried mother who is a minor. *Child Welfare*, 37:13–19.

Bruch, H. (1962), Perceptual and conceptual disturbances in anorexia nervosa. *Psychosom. Med.*, 24:187–194.

Burks, H., and Harrison, S. (1962), Aggressive behavior as a means of avoiding depression. *Am. J. Orthopsychiatry*, 32:416–422.

Chein, I., Gerard, D.I., Lee, R.S., and Rosenfeld, E. (1964), *The Road to H.: Narcotics, Delinquency and Social Policy*. New York: Basic Books.

Cohen, A.K. (1955), *Gang*. New York: Free Press, p. 129.

Cohen, S. (1969), Drug abuse. In: *Psychiatry Medical World News*. New York: McGraw-Hill.

Committee on Adolescence, American Academy of Pediatrics (1980), Teenage suicide. *Pediatrics*, 66:144–146.

Courts, R.M. (1967), Family crises and the impulsive adolescent. *Arch. Gen. Psychiat.*, 17:64–71.

Crumley, F.E. (1979), Adolescent suicide attempts. *JAMA*, 241:2404–2407.

Cytryn, L., McKnew, D.H., and Bunney, W.E. (1980), Diagnosis of depression in children: A reassessment. *Am. J. Psychiatry*, 137:22–25.

Daniel, W.A., Jr. (1970), *The Adolescent Patient*. St. Louis: Mosby.

Douglas, J.W.B., Ross, J.M., and Simpson, H.R. (1968), *All Our Future: A Longitudinal Study of Secondary Education*. London: Peter Davies.

Dreisbach, P.B., and Kasun, J.R. (1981), Teen-age pregnancy (letter). *N. Engl. J. Med.*, 304:121.

Eissler, K.R. (1955), Some problems of delinquency. In: *Searchlights on Delinquency*, 2nd Ed., ed. K.R. Eissler. New York: International Universities Press.

Elkind, D. (1967), Egocentrism in adolescence. *Child Dev.* 38:1025–1034.

Erikson, E.H. (1956), The problem of ego identity. *J. Am. Psychoanal. Assoc.*, 4:56.

Erikson, E.H. (1963), *Childhood and Society*, 2nd Ed., New York: Norton, pp. 261–263.

Fauman, M.A., and Fauman, B.J. (1979), Violence associated with phency-clidine abuse. *Am. J. Psychiatry*, 136:1584–1586.

Fawcett, R.L., and Jensen, R.A. (1952), Addiction to the inhalation of gasoline fumes in a child. *J. Pediatr.*, 41:364–368.

Finkel, M., and Finkel, D. (1975), Sexual and contraceptive knowledge, attitudes and behavior of male adolescents. *Farm. Plann. Perspect.*, 7:256.

Forrest, J.D., Sullivan, E., and Tietze, C. (1979), Abortion in the United States, 1977–1978. *Fam. Plann. Perspect.*, 11:329–341.

Foster, R. (1962), Intrapsychic and environmental factors in running away from home. *Am. J. Orthopsychiatry*, 32:486.

Fountain, G. (1961), Adolescent into adult: An inquiry. J. Am. Psychoanal. Assoc., 9:417–433.

Frailberg, S.H. (1961), Homosexual conflicts. In: *Adolescents*, ed. S. Lorand and H.I. Schneer. New York: Paul Hoeber, pp. 78–112.

Freud, A. (1946), *The Ego and the Mechanisms of Defense*. New York: International Universities Press, pp. 154–165.

Freud, A. (1958), Adolescence. *Psychoanal. Study Child*, 13:255–278.

Freud, A. (1969), Adolescence as a developmental disturbance. In: *Adolescence*, ed. G. Caplan and S. Lebovici. New York: Basic Books, pp. 5–10.

Friedman, S.B. (1973), Conversion symptoms in adolescents. *Pediatr. Clin. North Am.*, 20:873–882.

Galdston, R. (1967), Adolescence and the function of self-consciousness. *Ment. Hygiene*, 51:164–168.

G.A.P. Report No. 68, Vol. 6 (1968), Normal adolescence. New York: Group for the Advancement of Psychiatry, pp. 756–758; 841–846.

Glaser, K. (1967), Masked depression in children and adolescents. *Am. J. Psychother.*, 21:565–574.

Glasser, F.B. (1966), Inhalation psychosis and related states. *Arch. Gen. Psychiatry*, 14:315–322.

Graham, P., and Rutter, M. (1976), Adolescent disorders. In: *Child Psychiatry*, ed. M. Rutter and L. Hersov. Oxford: Blackwell, pp. 407–427.

Guttmacher, A. (1976), *11 Million Teenagers: What Can Be Done about the Epidemic of Adolescent Pregnancy in the United States?* New York: Planned Parenthood Federation of America. The Alan Guttmacher Institute. 1976.

Guttman, S.A. (1965), (Quoting A. Callandra) Some aspects of scientific theory construction and psycho-analysis. *Int. J. Psychoanal.*, 46:129–137.

Halleck, S. (1967), Psychosomatic treatment of the alienated college student. *Am. J. Psychiatry*, 124:642–650.

Hartmann, D. (1969), A study of drug-taking adolescents. *Psychoanal. Study Child*, 24:384–398.

Hauser, A. (1977), Drinking patterns of young people. In: *Alcoholism and Drug Dependence: A Multidisciplinary Approach*. Proc. Third Conf. Alcoholism and Drug Dependence. New York: Plenum.

Hauser, S.T. (1976), Self-image complexity and identity formation in adolescence. *J. Youth Adol.*, 5:161–178.

Hollingsworth, D.R., and Kreutner, A.K. (1981), Teen-aged pregnancy (letter). *N. Engl. J. Med.*, 304:321.

Inhelder, B., and Piaget, J. (1958), *The Growth of Logical Thinking from Childhood to Adolescence*. New York: Basic Books.

Institute for Social Research, University of Michigan (1981), Highlights from student drug use in America 1975–1980. DHHS Pub. No. (ADM) 81-1066.

Jones, M.C. (1957), The later careers of boys who were early- or late-maturing. *Child Dev.*, 28:113–128.

Kashani, J.H., Husain, A., Shekim, W.O., Hodges, K.K., Cytryn, L., and McKnew, D.H. (1981), Current perspectives on childhood depression: An overview. *Am. J. Psychiatry*, 138:143–153.

Kaufman, I., MacKay, E., and Zilbach, J. (1959), The impact of adolescence on girls with delinquent character formation. *Am. J. Orthopsychiatry*, 29:130–143.

Keniston, K. (1970a), Youth: A "new" stage of life. *Am. Scholar*, 39:631–653.
Keniston, K. (1970b), Student activism, moral development, and morality. *Am. J. Orthopsychiatry*, 40(4):577–592.
Kestenberg, H.S. (1961), Menarche. In: *Adolescents*. ed. S. Lorand and H. Schneer. New York: Paul B. Hoeber, pp. 19–50.
Khlentzos, M.T., and Pagliaro, M.A. (1965), Observations from psychotherapy with unwed mothers. *Am. J. Orthopsychiatry*, 35:779.
Kinsey, A.C. (1953), *Sexual Behavior in the Human Female*. Philadelphia: Saunders, p. 842.
Kleber, H. (1970), Personal communication.
Klein, D.F., and Davis, J.M. (1969), *Diagnosis and Drug Treatment of Psychiatric Disorders*. Baltimore: Williams & Wilkins, p. 417.
Kramer, S.N. (1959), *History Begins at Sumer*. New York: Garden City.
Laufer, M. (1976), Personal communication.
Leventhal, T. (1964), Inner control deficiencies in runaway children. *Arch. Gen. Psychiatry*, 11:169.
Lewis, D.O., and Balla, D.A. (1976a), Psychiatric and sociological viewpoints: Changing perspectives and emphases. In: *Delinquency and Psychopathology*, ed. D.O. Lewis and D.A. Balla. New York: Grune & Stratton, pp. 7–18.
Lewis, D.O., and Balla, D.A. (1976b), *Delinquency and Psychopathology*. New York: Grune & Stratton.
Lewis, D.O., Klerman, L., Jekel, J., and Curry, J. (1973), Experiences with psychiatric services in a program for pregnant teenage girls. *Soc. Psychiatry*, 8:16–25.
Lewis, D.O., Shanok, S.S., and Balla, D.A. (1979), Perinatal difficulties, head and face trauma, and child abuse in the medical histories of seriously delinquent children. *Am. J. Psychiatry*, 136:419–423.
Lewis, M., and Lewis, D.O. (1973), *Pediatric Management of Psychologic Crises*. Chicago: Year Book, p. 43.
Lewis, M., and Lewis, D.O. (1980), A psycho-biological view of childhood depression. In: *Clinical Approaches to Childhood Depression*, ed. A.L. French. New York: Human Sciences Press.
Lewis, M., and Solnit, A.J. (1963), The adolescent in a suicidal crisis. In: *Modern Perspectives in Child Development*. (In Honor of Milton J.E. Senn), ed. A.J. Solnit and S.A. Provence. New York: International Universities Press, pp. 229–245.
Lipsitz, J.S. (1979), Adolescent development. *Child. Today*, 8:2–7.
Lowrey, L.G. (1941), Runaways and nomads. *Am. J. Orthopsychiatry*, 11:775.
McAnarney, E.R., and Greydanus, D.E. (1979), Adolescent pregnancy: A multifaceted problem. *Pediatr. Rev.*, 1:123–126.
McKnew, D.H., and Cytryn, L. (1979), Urinary metabolites in chronically depressed children. *J. Am. Acad. Child Psychiatry*, 18:608–615.
Malinowski, B. (1966), Parenthood—The basis of social structure. In: *The Unwed Mother*, ed. R.W. Roberts. New York: Harper & Row, pp. 25–41.
Marshall, W.A., and Tanner, J.M. (1970), Variations in the pattern of pubertal changes in boys. *Arch. Dis. Child.*, 45:13.
Masterson, J.F., Jr. (1968), The psychiatric significance of adolescent turmoil. *Am. J. Psychiatry*, 124:1549–1553.
Mizner, G.L., Barter, J.T., and Werme, P.H. (1970), Patterns of drug use among college students: A preliminary report. *Am. J. Psychiatry*, 127:15–24.
Mussen, P.H., and Jones, M.C. (1957), Self-conceptions, motivations, and interpersonal attitude of late- and early-maturing boys. *Child Dev.*, 28:243–256.
NCHS (1978), National Center for Health Statistics. Advance report: Final natality statistics, 1978. Monthly Vital Statistics Report (Suppl.), April 28, 1980.
Noshpitz, J.D. (1970), Certain cultural and familial factors contributing to adolescent alienation. *J. Am. Acad. Child Psychiatry*, 9:216–223.
O'Connor, J. (1977), Normal and problem drinking among children. *J. Child Psychol. Psychiatry*, 18:229–284.

Offer, D., Marcus, D., and Offer, J.L. (1970), A longitudinal study of normal adolescent boys. *Am. J. Psychiatry*, 126:917–924.

Offer, D., and Offer, J. (1975), *From Teenage to Young Manhood: A Psychological Study*. New York: Basic Books.

Paulsen, J. (1969), Psychiatric problems. In: *Student and Drugs*, ed. Richard H. Blum and Associates. San Francisco: Jossey-Bass, pp. 291–304.

Paulson, M.J. and Lin, T.T. (1972), Family harmony: An etiologic factor in alienation. *Child Dev.*, 43:591–604.

Pearson, G.H.J. (1958), *Adolescence and the Conflict of Generations*. New York: Norton, pp. 101–126.

Phillips, E.L., Phillips, E.A., Fixsen, D.C., and Wolf, M.M. (1973), Achievement Place: Behavior shaping works for delinquents. *Psychology Today*, 7:75–79.

Piaget, J. (1962), Comments on Vygotsky's critical remarks concerning "The language and thought of the child" and "Judgment and reasoning in the child." Cambridge, Mass.: MIT Press, 71:473–490.

Piaget, J. (1969), The intellectual development of the adolescent. In: *Adolescence: Psychosocial Perspectives*, ed. G. Caplan and S. Lebovici. New York: Basic Books, pp. 22–26.

Plowman, E.E. (1971), *The Jesus Movement in America*. New York: Pyramid Books.

Prazar, G., and Friedman, S.B. (1978), Conversion reaction. In: *Principles of Pediatrics: Health Care of the Young*, ed. R.A. Hoekelman. New York: McGraw-Hill, pp. 687–693.

Proctor, J.T. (1958), Hysteria in childhood. *Am. J. Orthopsychiatry*, 28:394–407.

Puig-Antich, J., Chambers, W., Halpern, F., Hanlon, C., and Sachar, E.J. (1979), Cortisol hypersecretion in pre-pubertal depressive illness. *Psychoendocrinology*. 4:191–197.

Rabin, P.L. and Swenson, B.R. (1981), Teen-age suicide and parental divorce. *N. Engl. J. Med.*, 304:1048.

Renshaw, D.C. (1972), Depression of the 70's. *Dis. Nerv. Syst.*, 35:241–245.

Riemer, M.D. (1940), Runaway children. *Am. J. Orthopsychiatry*, 10:522.

Robey, A., Rosenwald, R.I., Snell, J.E., and Lee, R.E. (1964), The runaway girl: A reaction to family stress. *Am. J. Orthopsychiatry*, 34:762.

Rock, N.L. (1971), Conversion reactions in childhood: A clinical study of childhood neuroses. *J. Am. Acad. Child Psychiatry*, 10:65–93.

Rodriguez, A., Rodriguez, M., and Eisenberg, L. (1959), The outcome of school phobia: A follow-up study based on 41 cases. *Am. J. Psychiatry*, 116:1563–1577.

Rutter, M. (1970), Autistic children: Infancy to adulthood. *Semin. Psychiatry*, 2:435–450.

Rutter, M., Graham, P., Chadwick, O., and Yule, W. (1976), Adolescent turmoil: Fact or fiction? *J. Child Psychol. Psychiatry*, 17:35–56.

Rutter, M., and Hersov, L. (Eds.) (1976), *Child Psychiatry*. Oxford: Blackwell.

Scott, P.D. (1965), Delinquency. In: *Modern Perspectives in Child Psychiatry*, ed. J.G. Howells. Springfield, Ill.: Charles C Thomas, pp. 370–402.

Shellow, R., Schamp, J.R., Liebow, E., and Unger, E. (1967), *Suburban Runaways of the 1960's*. Society for Research in Child Development. Chicago: University of Chicago Press.

Sours, J.A. (1969), Anorexia nervosa: Nosology, diagnosis, developmental patterns, and power control dynamics. In: *Adolescence*, ed. G. Caplan and S. Lebovici. New York: Basic Books, pp. 185–212.

Stafford-Clark, D. (1969), Drug dependence. *Guy's Hospital Gazette*, 83:298–305.

The Status of Children, Youth and Families 1979 (1980), Washington, D.C.: DHHS Pub. No. (OHDS) 80-30274.

Staub, H. (1943), A runaway from home. *Psychoanal. Q.*, 12:1.

Surgeon General's Report on Health Promotion and Disease Control (1979),

Healthy People. Washington, D.C.: Dept. of Health, Education, and Welfare, Pub. No. 79-55071, pp. 5:1–5:15.

Tanner, J.M. (1962), *Growth at Adolescence,* 2nd Ed. Oxford: Blackwell.

Tanner, J.M. (1971), Sequence, tempo, and individual variations in growth and development of boys and girls aged twelve to sixteen. *Daedalus,* 100:907–930.

Toolan, J.M. (1962), Depression in children and adolescents. *Am. J. Orthopsychiatry,* 32:404–415.

Ungerleider, J.T., Fisher, D.D., Fuller, M., and Caldwell, S. (1968), The "bad trip"—The etiology of the adverse LSD reaction. *Am. J. Psychiatry,* 124:1483–1490.

Wardrop, K.R.H. (1967), Delinquent teenage types. *Br. J. Criminol.,* 7:371–380.

Watts, C.A.H. (1966), *Depressive Disorders in the Community.* Bristol: John Wright.

Weinberg, W., Rutman, J., Sullivan, L., Renick, E., and Dietz, S. (1973), The ten symptoms of childhood depression and the characteristic behavior for each symptom. *J. Pediatr.,* 83:1072.

Wieder, H., and Kaplan, E.H. (1969), Drug use in adolescents. *Psychoanal. Study Child,* 24:399–431.

Williams, F.S. (1970), Alienation of youth as reflected in the hippie movement. *J. Am. Acad. Child Psychiatry,* 9:251–263.

Wise, L.J. (1970), Alienation of present-day adolescents. *J. Am. Acad. Child Psychiatry,* 9:264–277.

Woolston, J.L. (1981), Personal communication.

Wylie, D.C., and Weinreb, J. (1958), The treatment of a runaway adolescent girl through treatment of the mother. *Am. J. Orthopsychiatry,* 28:188.

Young, H.B. (1971), The physiology of adolescence. In: *Modern Perspectives in Adolescent Psychiatry,* ed. H.G. Howells. Edinburgh: Oliver & Boyd.

Zelnik, M., and Kantner, J.S. (1978), First pregnancies to women aged 15–19: 1976 and 1971. *Fam. Plann. Perspect.,* 10:11.

Zelnik, M., and Kantner, J.S. (1980), Sexual activity, contraceptive use and pregnancy among metropolitan area teenagers, 1971–1979. *Fam. Plann. Perspect.,* 12:230.

Zelnik, M., Kim, Y.J., and Kantner, J.F. (1979), Probabilities of intercourse among U.S. teenage women, 1971–1976. *Fam. Plann. Perspect.,* 11:177.

Part Three

The Stress of Illness During Childhood

Chapter 17

PSYCHOLOGICAL REACTIONS TO ILLNESS AND HOSPITALIZATION

Illness is perhaps the most common and widespread stress that can befall the developing child. Every child who is ill has a psychological reaction to his illness. Some reactions are general; others are specific to the illness. The general reactions depend on several factors, including (1) the child's developmental stages (his or her emotional and cognitive levels of development and previous adaptive capacity), (2) the degree of pain or mutilation and the meaning the illness has for the child and parents, (3) the parent-child relationship and the child's response to the reaction of the parents, (4) the child's psychological reaction to medical and surgical procedures, separation, and hospitalization, and (5) the resultant interference with physical, psychological, and social functions. The specific reactions depend, in part, on the nature and severity of the illness.

BIRTH DEFECTS

Reaction of Parents

The antecedents of the psychological reactions of parents to a birth defect in their child are found in the pregnant woman's concerns and fantasies about possible fetal abnormalities. The actual presence of a live baby with a congenital defect mobilizes these latent fears and stimulates further reactions. The general reactions to a birth defect include feelings of revulsion, anger, and anxiety, as well as a precipitous drop in the self-esteem and sense of integrity of the mother. The parents of a defective infant feel guilty and resentful. The more visible the defect, the greater the reaction. Equally significant is the sense of loss that both parents experience as they painfully and slowly relinquish their ideal fantasies of the child during the process of adjusting to the sharply different realities and establishing new goals (Solnit and Stark, 1961). Because of the continuing presence of the defective child, the process of working through of loss is a continuing, changing process in that at each stage in the child's development the parents' other expectations for him or her may have to be modified or given up. And at each stage, new, often unanticipated, problems confront the parents. Some defects may not become known until a later stage of development. For example, certain congenital heart defects may be missed initially but may subsequently be discovered either routinely or as a result of a study for the cause of certain symptoms. Other defects may become apparent only at a later period of development. The process of giving up long-held expectations in such cases is often more difficult because of the tenacity with which those expectations are held.

The specific reactions of parents to a birth defect depend, in part, on the type of defect as well as on the personality of the parents. Ambiguity of the external genitalia, for example, or hypospadias may affect the parents' "gender attitude" toward their child, who in turn may have a heightened difficulty in accepting a clear sexual identification. In the specific instance of cryptorchism, the parents' attitudes seem to induce in the child a preoccupation with his testes, with associated disorders of behavior, including hyperactivity, accident proneness, lying, and learning difficulties (Blos, 1960). Mothers of children with cleft palate, on the other hand, seem to make especial use of the mechanism of denial and later avoid talking with their child about the deformity but may instead point out to others how "bright" the child is (Tisza et al., 1968). At the same time, since cleft palate is a more or less correctable defect, the drive toward restitution is strongly reinforced in these parents.

Reaction of the Child

The psychological reaction of the child to a birth defect is in large part related to the parental attitudes just mentioned. At the same time, the child also has his own characteristic reaction to his defect. Sometimes the physical defect is the starting point for a widespread interference with development to which the child then reacts. In children born with a cleft palate, for example, the interference with pleasurable sucking and feeding experiences, as well as the imbalance between gratifying and painful experiences, may lead later to speech difficulties and to a view of life as being essentially painful. Further, the frequent separations and surgical procedures required to correct this defect, especially during the child's first few years, may interrupt the continuity of affection he needs to develop the capacity for good relationships. Even when surgical correction has been achieved, previously established self-concepts, including low self-esteem, may persist and may make the child more vulnerable at each succeeding developmental period to adolescence and beyond (Schwartz and Landwirth, 1968).

BLIND CHILDREN

How complexly the combination of birth defect and the parents' reaction to the birth defect affects the development of the child is well illustrated in the case of children born totally blind. In a series of longitudinal studies of infants born totally blind, Fraiberg and her colleagues found that approximately 25% showed motor stereotypes, such as (1) rocking, lateral rotation of the head and trunk, and empty fingering, (2) no definition of body boundaries, and (3) delayed speech (Fraiberg, 1968; Fraiberg and Freedman, 1964; Fraiberg et al., 1966). Adaptive hand behavior (which ordinarily depends on the coordination of eye and hand schemas), gross motor achievements, and the constitution of a body- and self-image were all delayed. Most significant was the absence of or failure to achieve stable human object relations. For most of their 24-hour day, these infants lived in a "sensory desert."

The parents of these infants were markedly upset, often revealing their unconscious revulsion toward the baby by not touching the baby except when it was necessary. Some fathers had developed potency problems soon after the birth of the baby. There was also a conspiracy of silence on the part of other family members, who rarely said anything to indicate that the baby was at all attractive.

However, if the parents were able to perceive and interpret the infant's nonvisual signals and respond appropriately to its needs, the disastrous consequences just described could be avoided. For example, blind infants do, in fact, show a smile response to the mother's or father's *voice* at around the same time that sighted babies smile at the sight of the human face. When told that, and with the support and encouragement of a skilled person, the parents were able to avoid feeling rebuffed by the blind infant's failure to respond with a smile to the presentation of the parents' faces. Indeed, the parents felt elated at the infant's smile response to the presentation of the parent's voice, and they then related in a more affectionate way to their now "responsive" infant. Both parents and infant were then mutually responsive instead of mutually repelling.

One particular nonvisual mode of communication in the infant that was especially informative was the infant's expressive hand movements. Interventions designed to bring the hands together in the midline prevented empty fingering and promoted useful hand movement. Later, introduction of objects that had a sound as well as texture led to the infant's being able (at 10 months of age) to conceptualize an object with a sound (e.g., a bell). The infant could then search for a bell "out there" on hearing the sound alone. Once the infant was able to reach out on a sound cue, he was motivated to propel himself forward. At that point, creeping, which had been delayed, could proceed.

ACUTE ILLNESS

General Reactions

The general reactions of the child to acute illness again depend to a large extent on the child's developmental level and the reaction of the parents, and those reactions may be adaptive or maladaptive. Under the general impact of acute illness, most young children regress. They may return temporarily to bedwetting, thumb sucking, crying, and clinging behavior. Further, the young child, particularly, tends to interpret his illness as a punishment for something he has done wrong, and since he sometimes has difficulty in distinguishing between fantasy and reality, the wrongdoing could have been imaginary or actual. The young child who is hospitalized, especially the child under age 4, feels abandoned and fears what harm may come to him without the love and protection of his parents. He may also feel confused and anxious about the more or less sudden confrontations with people who are strange to him and about the strange routines (e.g., for eating, dressing, sleeping, and toileting), and special procedures (e.g., immobilizations and injections). These observations have been repeatedly documented. In a well-controlled study by Prugh and his colleagues, for example, children under 4 years of age screamed, had outbursts of anger when the parents visited, withdrew, and had difficulty eating and sleeping (Prugh et al., 1953; see Note 32). "In general, children with previously limited capacities for adaptation showed the greatest difficulty in adjusting comfortably to the ward milieu and showed as well the most severe reactions to the total experience of hospitalization." Furthermore, problems of adaptation occurred often about three months after the hospitalization, again with persistent signs of emotional disturbance tending to occur in children under age 4 and in children who had relatively unsatisfactory relationships with their parents, who had undergone severe stress in the hospital, and who had shown the greatest difficulty in adapting to the ward environment.

Anxiety is heightened when the special vulnerabilities of a particular developmental struggle are touched on. For example, an infant, who needs a sense of security and trust, may express through fretting and fussing his state of tension and insecurity when held by a mother who is anxious because of his illness. The fear of loss of love and loss of autonomy may be reinforced by separation and illness in the young infant. Castration anxiety may be heightened in the young child who is undergoing surgical procedures. Separation from peers may temporarily rob the school-age child of the comfort and sublimation activities he had previously enjoyed. And the adolescent may find increasing difficulty in dealing with the upset that may accompany such developmental tasks as body mastery, impulse control, and independence.

Adolescents may regard their illness with shame or as a sign of physical weakness, or as a punishment (for, say, masturbation). They may use illness or its management as an instrument for the expression of rebellion or as a convenient excuse for avoiding close relationships. At the same time, adolescents may fear loss of control. They may withdraw in the face of illness, either to conserve their strength or because they feel hopeless. Anxiety may be heightened if motor activity in particular is prevented by forced immobilization. A lowering of self-esteem may occur, accompanied by psychiatric illness and academic problems (Rutter et al., 1970). Illness may also be used to enlist help (Peterson, 1972). Last, adolescents may be surprisingly ignorant about their bodies and illnesses, and have unusual ideas about their illnesses (Kaufman, 1972).

The anxiety aroused in children and adolescents may be dealt with in different ways, depending in part on their level of development. The most common reaction—regression—has already been mentioned. On the other hand, some children fight hard to retain their recently acquired skills. They may, for example, resist bed rest when they have only just learned to walk (Freud, 1952). Other children deny their illness and their anxiety. Some children identify with the doctor or the nurse, who seems to them so aggressive. Aggression is particularly mobilized in the face of motor restraint (Wolff, 1969). Still others may withdraw or may become astonishingly compliant. The particular pattern of response depends on the many factors mentioned earlier (e.g., the state of the child's previous personality development, the degree of stress caused by the illness, and the reaction of the parents to the ill child).

Sometimes the anxiety becomes manifest after the acute episode has passed (Levy, 1945; Langford, 1948; Neill, 1967). Night terrors, dreams about being left alone in the dark, or fear of the dark may occur with increasing frequency. Negativistic behavior toward the parents often occurs on the child's return home.

Reactions to Specific Illnesses or Procedures

Certain illnesses and certain treatment procedures tend to produce characteristic reactions in the child.

Burns. Children who suffer burns often experience severe emotional reactions. Jackson said, "An extensive burn is an accident involving thirty seconds of terror, and it is often followed by years of suffering" (Jackson, 1968). Pain, fright, and body mutilation are, in fact, primary sources of psychological disturbance in the burned child and in a child traumatized in any other way. Further sources of disturbance in the burned child include (1) the child's guilt over disobeying a parent's admonition not to play with matches (for example), (2) the turmoil characteristic of the period of acute care, (3) the hospitalization and separation from parents, (4) the immobilization, exposure, and repeated immediate and long-term surgical procedures, (5) the metabolic changes induced by the burns, and (6) the reactions of the distressed and guilty parents and the frustrated and angry hospital staff.

Pain in itself is a significant factor in burns, and it often gives rise to anger, hostility, and depression in the child (Long and Cope, 1961). In an unusual study of the psychological reactions to a leg burn in a 5-year-old boy who had no pain sensation below the waist (because he had a myelomenin-gocele), Nover (1970) found that the child had a much less adverse reaction to the burn and was more cooperative in the extensive surgical treatments than are most burned children.

Preexisting emotional difficulties often seem to have predisposed the child to the burn "accident." In a study of 13 families of severely burned children, 10 families were found to have major psychological and social problems that were present prior to the burn (Holter and Friedman, 1969).

Fluid loss, medication, anorexia, and sleep interruption are important aggravating factors during the acute period. It has also been suggested that magnesium deficiency may aggravate the psychological symptoms associated with burns (Broughton et al., 1968).

Equally important are the long-term reactions. Grafting operations frequently extend over a period of 5 years, and in some cases as long as 15 years. Numerous concerns arise during this period. Jackson (1968) has observed that burned children ask such questions as, "Will my breasts develop normally?", "Will boys look at me with these scars?", and "Will I be able to have a baby?" The importance of these questions in the context of adolescent developmental concerns is obvious.

Tonsillectomy. Another type of specific reaction occurs in response to tonsillectomy. Here, the operation is performed on a well child who usually does not have a clear understanding of why he or she needs the operation or what is the nature of the operation. Curiously, the indications for tonsillectomy actually are not well defined, and there are no adequate controlled studies (Horstman, 1969). Indeed, in one study of 681 children in whom tonsillectomy was postponed because of a poliomyelitis outbreak, more than one-third were judged not to need the operation when they were reexamined 18 months later (Dey, 1952). Certainly scientific data do not support the need for so many tonsillectomies. Approximately 2,000,000 tonsillectomies are done each year, at a cost of about $150,000,000 and incurring 200 to 300 deaths. Interestingly, a study performed in 1938 reported that the operation was done twice as often when the family income was above $5000 a year (Collins, 1938).

In any event, the operation is most often performed at an age when fantasies of injury to body parts and fears of punishment and retribution are prominent. Moreover, for a number of reasons, the child is often inadequately prepared for the operation. Sometimes the sudden availability of a bed in the hospital forces a somewhat precipitous admission to hospital on short notice, perhaps following a telegram. Few explanations are given to the child as he or she is separated from his or her parents, turned over to strangers, and made to submit to routines that seem remote from the sore throat he or she once had and now has almost forgotten.

Lipton (1962) has further postulated that at least three powerful psychological factors help perpetuate this "attack" by the adult on the child. First is the adult's dread of passivity and of doing nothing. Second is the mobilization of aggression by both parents and doctors against the child as he is, in an effort to convert him into a projected ideal. Third, the ready availability of the tonsils lets them serve as a concrete representation of the undesirable impulses or attributes the adult has projected onto the child—removing the tonsils then symbolically removes those undesirable impulses.

The impact a tonsillectomy has on the child when these factors are operative is enormous and the risks are great (Jessner et al., 1952; Robertson, 1956). The child distorts the whole procedure and uses the distortion as an active, external representation of his current internal fears and fantasies. Anesthesia may be seen by the child as an oral attack. Separation anxiety and castration fears are heightened. The hospital staff members are perceived unconsciously or consciously as attackers and punishers, and fears of death arise.

Demandingness, irritability, aggressive behavior, temper tantrums, fears, and nightmares often are rampant. Defenses mobilized to contain this anxiety may include the mechanisms of denial and psychosomatic symptom formation. According to Lipton (1962), lasting character traits may be formed during such a psychic trauma. Fortunately, much of this harm can be attenuated and even turned into a constructive experience when the child is adequately prepared for, supported through, and helped after the operation (Robertson, 1956).

CHRONIC ILLNESS

General Reactions

In general, chronic illnesses impose psychological as well as physical strains on the developing child. The strains arise from a number of sources. For example, a particular treatment regimen (e.g., motor restriction, diet, medication, and surgical procedures) may foster passivity and dependence, against which the normal child struggles. The child's feeling of being different from other children arouses feelings of resentment and then guilt. Young children in particular find the illness and the treatment virtually incomprehensible, and they develop distorted ideas and frightening fantasies about the illness.

A 5-year-old boy with nephrosis was observed by the nurse to be unusually quiet and immobile. He would sit still in his wheel chair and would contrive to not even turn his head. In the course of an interview, the boy revealed his ideas and fantasies about his illness. He knew that there was something wrong with his kidneys, and that this caused "blood pressure." He was aware of everyone's efforts to keep down his blood pressure. He felt sure that if his blood pressure went up, it would blow off the top of his head. Not surprisingly, he avoided any movement that might increase the blood pressure and lead to such a feared disaster.

Children with chronic illness also react to the parents' attitudes and concerns or to their distorted perception of the parents' attitudes (Wolff, 1969). On the other hand, the actual attitudes of the parents are often a real source of anxiety for the child. In a study of family adaptation to cystic fibrosis in children, for example, McCollum and Gibson (1970) found that, first of all, incorrect or incomplete diagnoses generated in parents a mounting mistrust of the medical profession and hostility toward it. Further, since the infant patients were often unsatisfied by their feeds and had periods of fussiness, the mothers initially had feelings of self-doubt and self-reproach at their inability to nurture their infants. These feelings in the mothers led to feelings of despair and moments of frank hostility toward the infants, often accompanied by guilt. When the diagnosis of cystic fibrosis was confirmed, the threat posed by the child's having a fatal illness stimulated an acute, anticipatory mourning reaction in the parents. Feelings of helplessness aroused anxiety in the parents and stimulated thoughts about their own death. In an effort to avoid these thoughts, parents invoked such defenses as an apparent absence of affect, denial, avoidance, and forgetting. Parents suffered sleep and appetite disturbances. They often displaced their anger at the child onto others. Many other problems connected with the child's illness (e.g., the knowledge that there is a genetic factor, the impact of the illness on other family members, especially siblings, the need for separate accommodations to house a mist tent, the odor of the stool, the high medical expenses; and the parents' efforts to master the technique of postural drainage) contributed to the parents' anxiety. Long-term adaptation by the parent invariably involved some denial of the prognosis, a denial that was constantly challenged by certain intrusive characteristics of the disease, notably the odor and the persistent cough. The child, in turn, reacted to all these attitudes with anxiety.

Last, children may learn to use their chronic illness in the service of achieving other aims, as seen in the case of Johnny, who used his diabetes to satisfy certain psychological needs (see p. 275).

Specific Reactions

Specific chronic illnesses often evoke characteristic reactions in the child and his parents. The reactions of parents to the child with cystic fibrosis have already been mentioned. Another chronic illness that evokes specific reactions is hemophilia. In a study of 28 hemophiliac children and their families, Browne and his colleagues (1960) observed that the children tended to feel isolated and different. They often tried to conceal their illness, and they felt constantly watched. The enforced passivity prevented the discharge of tension through activity and led to anxiety about movement and action. Sometimes the children were outwardly docile and passive although they often showed evidence of subtle rebellion. For example, a child might revenge himself or his parents by deliberately bumping himself, by threatening to bleed, or by telling the doctor that his parents spanked him. Curiously, however, trauma was not the overriding factor in bleeding. Bleeding was often spontaneous, and it sometimes seemed to be related more to anxiety, especially anxiety about increased activity and independence, than to trauma. The bleeding would then serve to prevent the child from participating in these activities. Many of the children experienced anxiety around feelings of loss of masculinity. They felt unable to be active the way boys usually are, and they experienced their fathers' withdrawal from them as a denial of the boys' masculinity. Further, the episodes of uncontrolled bleeding were sometimes linked in their fantasies with the bleeding that occurs in females. Also, most of the boys knew that hemophilia is handed down through the female.

These specific reactions to hemophilia often lead to psychiatric disorders, the most frequent one being the development of passive-dependent characters, a tendency toward risk-taking (accident-prone) behavior, psychophysiological responses, such as bleeding in relation to anxiety, and sexual identity problems (Agle, 1964).

These reactions are related in part to the interaction with parents, who themselves showed characteristic responses to the illness. For example, Browne and his colleagues (1960) found that the mothers frequently felt guilt and anger at being the carrier. They tended to be ambivalent toward their sick child and overprotective of him. On the one hand, they saw themselves as the only effective protector of the child; on the other hand, they saw the child as a cross to bear. The child was restricted in his activities, since activity was equated with injury. The mothers often selected the child's playmates, and they usually selected younger, smaller, and passive children. Indeed, quiet little girls seemed the most desirable playmates. Markova and his colleagues (1980) found that mothers of hemophiliac boys were particularly anxious about their son's absence from school, although differences in childrearing seemed to vary with the degree of severity of the hemophilia.

Many of the fathers of hemophiliac boys seemed to lose interest in the child and were relieved that they were not involved genetically as carriers. They were afraid to play with their sons, saw school as dangerous, and sought desk jobs for their sons. The child resented the father who denied him any physical activity. In another study, the son tended to regard his father as a traitor to his sex because he felt his father prevented him from expressing his masculinity (Goldy and Katz, 1963).

Many other illnesses produce characteristic behavior traits. Sometimes the behavior traits seem to be secondary to the complex relationships and reactions to illness just described; at other times the behavior traits appear to be a primary factor in the production of the illness. Usually there is an inextricable interaction between primary and secondary factors.

One phenomenon that is seen more and more today is the reaction of pediatric cancer patients to survival. Koocher and his colleagues (1980), in a study of the psychological adjustment of 115 pediatric cancer survivors, found that in general the younger the child is at the time of diagnosis and treatment and the greater the number of years since the onset of the illness, the less likely the child is to have later adjustment problems or to have anxiety about recurrence, respectively. Children who have poorer socialization and self-help skills and poorer intellectual functioning are more likely than others to have difficulties in psychosocial adjustment (e.g., residual depression, anxiety, and poor self-esteem). Developmental disruptions caused by the cancer treatment experience are apparently more marked and persistent when they occur during middle childhood or adolescence than when they occur during infancy.

Note 32

Prugh, Dane G., Staub, E.M., Sands, H.H., Kurschbaum, R.M., and Lenihan, E.A., 1953. A study of the emotional reactions of children and families to hospitalization and illness. *Am. J. Orthopsychiatry*, 23(1):70–106.

... Two groups of 100 children each were selected for study, one designated as the *control* and the other, the *experimental* group.

... A base-line study of the control group was carried out initially, covering a period of approximately four months. The circumstances under which hospitalization was encountered by children during this period were those involving traditional practices of ward management, existing prior to the experimental nursing program.

... Following an interval sufficient to allow complete turnover of patients who had been in the control study, an experimental program of ward management was put into effect. This involved many of the practices employed in other hospitals and included daily visiting periods for parents, early ambulation of patients where medically feasible, a special play program employing a nursery-school teacher, psychological preparation for and support during potentially emotionally traumatic diagnostic or therapeutic procedures, an attempt at clearer definition and integration of the parent's role in the care of the child, and other techniques. Attention was paid to the handling of admission procedures, with parents accompanying the child to the ward to meet the staff and to assist in the child's initial adjustment. As a part of admission routine, parents were given a pamphlet prepared especially to enhance their understanding of their child's needs and their own role in his care.

In order to coordinate the activities of the professional staff in the management of patients, a weekly Ward Management Conference was held, directed by a pediatrician with psychiatric training. In attendance were the ward physician, head nurse, play supervisor, occupational therapist, dietitian, social worker, psychologist, and frequently a public health nurse. An attempt was made to discuss the adjustment of each child on the ward, although children presenting particular difficulties in adaptation received the most attention. Among other measures discussed and implemented in this interdisciplinary conference were: the assignment of one nurse to the principal care of a particularly anxious child; the scheduling of injections or other medical procedures at times other than feeding, nap, or play times; the use of appropriate psychological preparation for forthcoming procedures by physician, nurse, or play supervisor; the selection of particular play activities designed to meet the emotional needs of particular children; the special handling of feeding or other activities; the flexible arrangement of visiting periods or the encouragement of parental participation in ward care; and the provision of special psychological support for particular parents. Psychiatric consultation and psychological appraisal were provided where indicated, but the essential approach was in the direction of the coordination and potentiation of the efforts of all professional personnel involved in the care of the ill child. . . .

Results

Immediate reactions

. . . 92 per cent of the children in the control or unsupported group exhibited reactions of a degree indicating significant difficulties in adaptation. . . . In the experimental group, this figure totaled 68 per cent. . . .

. . . Immediate reactions to hospitalization were noted to be most marked in children from two through five years of age in both groups. . . .

. . . In general, children with previously limited capacities for adaptation showed the greatest difficulty in adjusting comfortably to the ward milieu and showed as well the most severe reactions to the total experience of hospitalization. . . .

Long-range reactions

. . . Children under four years of age and children who had relatively unsatisfying relationships with their parents, who had undergone very severe stress in the hospital, and who had shown the greatest difficulty in adapting to the ward milieu were those who tended to show persistent signs of emotional disturbance at three months following hospitalization. . . .

Types of individual reactions of children in the hospital

. . . The most common manifestation of disturbance in adaptation at any age level or in either group was that of overt anxiety. . . .

. . . (In) children from two to four years of age (in the) control group. . . anxiety over separation from parents was the most common manifestation and the most intense of any age level, occurring equally in both sexes and to some degree in all children. Anxiety was often associated with fear or anger at the time of departure of the parents. Constant crying, apprehensive behavior, outbursts of screaming, and acute panic when approached by an adult were frequent, together with occasional somatic concomitants of anxiety such as urinary frequency, diarrhea, vomiting, etc. Depression, at times resembling the anaclitic type described by Spitz . . . homesickness and withdrawal were observed in this group more than in older children, particularly at the outset of hospitalization. The need for tangible evidence of home and family, such as dolls, items of clothing, etc., was particularly manifest in this group, as demonstrated by the anxiety of many children over giving them up. At times, shoes and socks, for example, seemed to be incorporated into the body image, with marked anxiety shown whenever they were removed.

Reactions to the experiencing of overwhelming fear or anxiety showed some specificity for the children in this age group. . . Disturbances in feeding behavior, including anorexia, overeating, and refusal to chew food, often combined with regressive smearing of food or the demand for a return to bottle feeding, were more frequent and severe than in any other group. Changes in toilet behavior were next in incidence, involving regressive loss of control of bladder or bowel functions, most marked in the early phases of hospitalization. Fears of the toilet or of the loss of the stool, fear of loss of control of bowel or bladder functions, as well as guilt and fear of punishment over wishes to soil or wet, were handled by mechanisms of denial, projection, and other modes of adaptation available to the child of this age. Fears of the dark or of physical attack were common and were associated with sleep disturbances—insomnia, nightmares and restlessness. Increase of bedtime rituals and other compulsive acts during hospitalization was often seen.

... Open acting-out of infantile wishes and aggressive impulses appeared most frequently in this age group, with wild outbursts of frantic aggression and attendant guilt and anxiety. Marked inhibition of aggressive drives was observed in some children, together with turning inward of hostility. Restlessness, hyperactivity and irritability, with associated rocking, thumb-sucking or aggressive behavior, appeared in many children, particularly if they were confined to bed with the use of a "restrainer," as had been the practice for small or acute disoriented children in order to prevent their falling from bed. With ambulation, this behavior often disappeared or diminished markedly.

A variety of primitive gratifications of pregenital character... were employed to greater degree than prior to hospitalization. Thumb-sucking and rocking were common, associated with withdrawal and with masturbation in one third of the children. Headbanging was relatively infrequent. In many instances, as children established parent-surrogate relationships, often with the play supervisor or one particular nurse, gratifications of this type diminished, no longer interfering with adjustment to the group.

Among the defense mechanisms available to this younger group, regression was the most widespread. Libidinal regression was often uneven, associated with feeding, bowel and bladder symptomatology. Oral components were manifest through enhanced sucking, overeating, and demanding behavior, with occasional biting and other manifestations. Cruelty, sadistic enjoyment of the pain of others, pleasure in handling or smearing feces, and other regressive anal components of behavior were transparently or openly evident, particularly in children isolated for medical reasons.

In some instances, a nearly total regression of the ego to a relatively narcissistic level of psychosexual development, associated with disturbances in reality testing, was manifest....

Denial of illness or of the loss of the loved object, the mother, was observed in a number of children of this age. For example, one child, a boy of three and a half, insisted for three days that his mother was "downstairs" and that he was "all well now," in spite of the persistence of his dyspnea from a bronchopneumonia.

(In the) experimental group... the same types of disturbances in adaptation were noted as among the control or unsupported group. In general, however, manifestations were less severe and lighter in incidence....

Reactions to specific types of treatment or diagnostic procedures
... The impression was gained that any or all... procedures seemed to be interpreted by a child at a particular level of libidinal development in terms of the specific anxieties and fears characteristic of that level, and to be dealt with by means of his own previously developed

defenses, rather than in terms of the exact nature of the procedure itself. . . .

In the main, the younger children tended to react to such threatening procedures as to hostile attacks, often interpreted as punishment. . . . The impression was gained, however, that a great deal of the small child's fear of unknown procedures, of separation from the parents, of punishment, and of overwhelming attack was displaced much of the time onto such objectively less threatening but directly visible things as needles, tourniquets, etc. In the experimental group, aggressive responses in particular to various procedures were only half as frequent and were less intense than those in the control group. . . .

Post hospitalization reactions

. . . Following discharge, most of the regressive manifestations in the younger age group appeared to subside rather promptly. Behavior of an infantile or demanding nature, together with greater dependence on parents, persisted for several months in a number of children under five years of age. Wetting, soiling, and intensified pregenital gratifications, however, were ordinarily given up within three months' time.

The most common manifestations among children showing continuing disturbances were related to anxiety over separation from parents, apppearing most intensely in younger children but arising also in latency children. . . . All of these manifestations appeared to be milder in children in the experimental group (e.g., sleep disturbances were five times as common in the control as the experimental group). . . .

In general, symptoms which persisted were fewer in number and milder for each child at home than in the hospital. Such symptoms appeared to be related more directly to the personality structure and characteristic patterns of adaptation of the child prior to hospitalization. . . .

Reactions of parents and families

. . . Realistic fear in proportion to the severity of the child's illness, overt anxiety, guilt over possible involvement in the causation of illness or over previously hostile feelings toward the child, and other feelings were handled in various ways, dependent upon the character structure of the parent, the nature of the relationship with the child, experiences immediately preceding hospitalization, and other factors. . . .

. . . Marked ambivalence, even on the part of well-adjusted parents, was frequent in the face of behavioral regression on the part of the child, either during or following hospitalization.

. . . In general, the well adjusted parents whose children were hospitalized under the experimental program seemed more satisfied with visiting regulations than those in the control group, where visiting was strongly curtailed. . . .

Problems in ward management

. . . The common conception that crying occurs more frequently among children whose parents visit frequently was found to be erroneous in the experimental phase of the study. . . .

... (Moreover) the hazard of cross-infection is not appreciably increased under circumstances involving more frequent contact with parents.

REFERENCES

Agle, D.P. (1964), Psychiatric studies of patients with hemophilia and related states. *Arch. Int. Med.*, 114:76–82.

Blos, P. (1960), Comments on the psychological consequences of cryptorchism: A clinical study. *Psychoanal. Study Child*, 15:395–429.

Broughton, A., Anderson, M.B., and Bowden, C.H. (1968), Magnesium deficiency in burns. *Lancet*, 2:1156–1158.

Browne, W.J., Mally, M.A., and Kane, R.P. (1960), Psychosocial aspects of hemophilia. *Am. J. Orthopsychiatry*, 30:730–740.

Collins, S.D. (1938), Frequency of surgical procedures among 9,000 families, based on nation-wide periodic canvasses 1928–31. *Public Health Rep.*, 53:587–628.

Dey, D.L. (1952), A survey of 681 children awaiting tonsillectomy and the indications for operation in childhood. *Med. J. Aust.*, 1:510–514.

Fraiberg, S. (1968), Parallel and divergent patterns in blind and sighted infants. *Psychoanal. Study Child*, 23:264–300.

Fraiberg, S., and Freedman, D.A. (1964), Studies in the ego development of the congenitally blind child. *Psychoanal. Study Child*, 19:113–169.

Fraiberg, S., Siegel, B.L., and Gibson, R. (1966), The role of sound in the search behavior of a blind infant. *Psychoanal. Study Child*, 21:327–357.

Freud, A. (1952), The role of bodily illness in the mental life of children. *Psychoanal. Study Child*, 8:69.

Goldy, F.B., and Katz, A.H. (1963), Social adaptation in hemophilia. *Children*, 10:189–193.

Holter, J.C., and Friedman, S.B. (1969), Etiology and management of severely burned children. *Am. J. Dis. Child.*, 118:680–686.

Horstman, D. (1969), Personal communication.

Jackson, D.MacG. (1968), What the burnt child goes through. *Proc. Royal Soc. Med.*, 61:1085–1087.

Jessner, L., Blom, G.E., and Waldfogel, S. (1952), Emotional implications of tonsillectomy and adenoidectomy on children. *Psychoanal. Study Child*, 7:126–169.

Kaufman, R.V. (1972), Body image changes in physically ill teenagers. *J. Am. Acad. Child Psychiatry*, 11:157–170.

Koocher, G.P., O'Malley, J.E., Gogan, J.L., and Foster, D.J. (1980), Psychological adjustment among pediatric cancer survivors. *J. Child Psychol. Psychiatry*, 21:163–173.

Langford, W.S. (1948), Physical illness and convalescence: their meaning to the child. *J. Pediatr.*, 33:242.

Levy, D.M. (1945), Psychic trauma of operations in children and a note on combat neurosis. *Am. J. Dis. Child.*, 69:7.

Lipton, S.D. (1962), On the psychology of childhood tonsillectomy. *Psychoanal. Study Child*, 17:363–417.

Long, R., and Cope, O. (1961), Emotional problems of burned children. *N. Engl. J. Med.*, 264:1121.

McCollum, A.T., and Gibson, L.E. (1970), Family adaptation to the child with cystic fibrosis. *J. Pediatr.*, 77:571–578.

Markova, I., MacDonald, K., and Forbes, C. (1980), Impact of hemophilia on child-rearing practices and parent cooperation. *J. Child Psychol. Psychiatry*, 21:153–162.

Neill, C.A. (1967), The child and his family at home after hospitalization. In: *The Hospitalized Child and His Family*, ed. J.A. Haller, Jr. Baltimore: Johns Hopkins Press, pp. 67–77.

Nover, R. (1970), Personal communication.

Peterson, E.G. (1972), The impact of adolescent illness on parental relationships. *J. Health Soc. Behav.*, 13:429–437.

Prugh, D.G., Staub, E.M., Sands, H.H., Kirschbaum, R.M., and Lenihan, E.A. (1953), A study of the emotional reactions of children and families to hospitalization and illness. *Am. J. Orthopsychiatry*, 23:70.

Robertson, J. (1956), A mother's observation on the tonsillectomy of her four-year-old daughter, with comments by Anna Freud. *Psychoanal. Study Child*, 11:410–436.

Rutter, M., Tizard, J., and Whitmore, K. (1970), *Education, Health and Behavior*. London: Longmans, Green.

Schwartz, A.H., and Landwirth, J. (1968), Birth defects and the psychological development of the child: Some implications for management. *Conn. Med.*, 32:457–464.

Solnit, A.J., and Stark, M. (1961), Mourning and the birth of a defective child. *Psychoanal. Study Child*, 16:523–537.

Tisza, V., Selverstone, B., Rosenblum, G., and Hanlon, N. (1968), Psychiatric observations of children with cleft palate. *Am. J. Orthopsychiatry*, 28:416–423.

Wolff, S. (1969), *Children Under Stress*. London: Penguin, pp. 53–93.

Chapter 18*

DYING AND DEATH IN CHILDHOOD AND ADOLESCENCE: CONCEPTS AND CARE

Dying is a transitional state in which the child and the family may look to the physician for understanding, support, and direction. However, a physician may experience anxiety in the presence of a dying child because of (1) the feelings of impotence, failure, and anxiety that are aroused in the physician when confronted with his or her own limitations and mortality, (2) the regressive pull the child's loneliness, abandonment, neediness, and insecurity evoke in the physician, and (3) the difficulty of dealing with the parents' anxiety, depression, anger, resentment, and denial.

Yet there is probably almost nothing that the child or parent fears, imagines, feels, or experiences that cannot be discussed with the child in an honest way. The basis for the discussion is a trusting relationship. Children in particular soon learn whom they can trust and hence whom they can open up to. Indeed, the child often senses more accurately what the adult

---

*This chapter is modified from M. Lewis and D.O. Lewis (1973), *Pediatric Management of Psychological Crises*. Chicago: Year Book Medical Publishers, and from M. Lewis and D.O. Lewis (1980), Death and dying in children and their families. In: *The Physician and the Mental Health of the Child*, Vol. 2, Chicago: American Medical Association.

can tolerate than the adult senses how much the child can assimilate, and the child acts accordingly.

CHILDREN'S CONCEPTS OF DEATH

The child's reaction to his own dying or to the death of others is related in part to his or her concept of death (Anthony, 1940; Gartley and Bernasconi, 1967; Schilder and Wechsler, 1934; Wolff, 1969), which in turn is related to his or her developmental stage (see Table 18–1).

During the first few years, the child ordinarily has virtually no concept of death other than of death as a disappearance. However, when faced with traumatic events, such as the death of a parent, children under the age of 5 may develop what seems to be a precocious understanding of death.

Children between 5 and 10 years of age (approximately) are beginning to clarify their concepts of death but are still at times confused. For example, a child may say, "When I die, my heart stops, I can't see, and I can't hear. But if I'm buried, how will I breathe?" Some of the child's difficulty in thinking clearly about death is developmental, but some of the difficulty is emotional. If the child of this age has a heightened concern about a part of his body and its functioning, he or she may tend to think of death in terms of the harm to that part of his or her body and its functioning, especially since the child also tends to think in concrete terms at this stage.

Somewhere between 10 and 15 years of age, the child acquires a grasp of the meaning of mortality (Kastenbaum, 1959). His or her reaction to death at this time is influenced more by his emotional struggles than by his intellectual capacities. Thus a young adolescent who is concerned with, among other things, sexual performance, control of impulses, physical intactness, and separation from parents may react with anxiety if any one of these sensitive conflict areas is involved in the fatal illness.

THE CHILD'S REACTION TO HIS OR HER OWN DYING

The very young child is mostly preoccupied with the discomfort of the illness, whether acute or chronic, and the separation and withdrawal that occur when hospitalization is necessary. A somewhat older child, although also troubled by pain and separation, interprets his or her illness according to his or her level of cognitive development and emotional conflicts. Thus, he or she may interpret the illness as an act of "immanent

Table 18–1. DEATH AND CHILDHOOD

	BEFORE		Sudden	DURING Acute	Chronic	AFTER
Child	Ideas on Death	Death & Stage Anxieties				
0–5	Abandonment Punishment	Fear of loss of love		Avoidance of pain Need for love	Withdrawal Separation anxiety	
5–10	Concepts of inevitability Confusion	Castration anxiety		Guilt (bad) Regression Denial	Guilt (religious), regression, denial	
10–15	Reality	Control of body and other developmental tasks		Depression Despair for future	Depression Despair, anxiety, anger	

	Sudden	Acute	Chronic	Sudden	Acute	Chronic
Parents	Anxiety, Concern, Hopefulness	Premature mourning, anticipatory grief, guilt, reaction formation and displacements, need for information	Disbelief, Displaced rage, Accelerated grief, Prolonged numbness	Desperate concern, Denial, Guilt; Guilt, Mourning	Denial, Remorse, Resurgence of love; Anger at M.D., need for follow-up, over-idealizing, fantasy loss	Remorse, Relief and guilt
Siblings 0–5	Reactions to changes in parents (sense of loss of love and withdrawal)			1. Respond to reaction of parents	2. Survivor guilt	
5–10	Concern re their implication; Fearful for themselves					
10–15	Generally supportive					
Staff	Anxiety; Conspiracy of silence	Reaction: Withdraw. Tasks: 1. correct distortions, e.g., "am I safe?", "will someone be with me?", "will I be helped to feel better?"; 2. comfort parents; 3. allow hope and promote feeling of actively coping; 4. protect dignity of patient		Need for after care of survivors; Autopsy request tact; Accurate information regarding disposal of body; Delay billing		

justice" for the guilt he or she feels about some real or imagined misdeed. Usually he shows regressive behavior in the face of the illness, hospitalization, treatment techniques, and fear of mutilation. Occasionally he or she shows a denial of discomfort or dread (Solnit and Green, 1959; Solnit, 1963). An older child who is aware of the finality of death may deny his or her own anxiety but may exhibit a depression, occasionally mixed with outbursts of anger and anxiety. This reaction is especially common in adolescents. On the other hand, some children are astoundingly courageous and steadfast in the face of death.

The range of reactions is great. In a sense, all that has gone before contributes to the child's understanding of death and his or her reaction to it. Each child is an individual, and a myriad of variables influences the behavior of the child, his family, and the helping persons around him.

REACTION OF OTHERS TO THE DEATH OF A CHILD

An important determinant of the child's reaction to death is the reaction of those around him to death. Those others may be parents, siblings, or hospital staff members.

Reactions of Parents

General Reactions. The general reactions of parents have a chronological sequence, starting before and continuing during and after the moment of death. Initial shock and denial of the diagnosis may last from a few seconds to a few months. This stage may be followed by anger ("Why my child?") or guilt ("If only I had...). Sooner or later, the parent starts to bargain ("If he could only live to..."). This stage is followed by normal grieving and mourning over the impending loss and by the beginning of separation. Finally, a stage of resignation or acceptance can be reached.

Specific Reactions. Reactions to a Rapid Death. When the death has occurred relatively rapidly (e.g., perhaps as a consequence of a brief illness), the period prior to death is filled with anxiety and concern. The parents may be desperately hopeful, but they may also have feelings of guilt and have a need to deny the possibility of death as an eventual outcome. After a rapid death of their child, the parents may again feel some diffuse anger, which may be displaced onto the physician. This reaction may occur whether or not the physician has been diligent, but it is more likely to fester and be prolonged if the physician fails (out of his or her own discomfort) to show consideration at the time and to provide the opportunity for a follow-up interview. Over a period of time the parents will then go through their own characteristic mourning process. Their mourning may include some identification with the lost person and, occasionally, an overidealizing of the lost person (particularly in cases in which the parent also experiences the loss of what they had expected for the lost child). Further possible reactions may include (1) a displacement of attitudes toward the dead child onto one or more of the surviving children, (2) attempts to fill the loss by another pregnancy, or (3) withdrawal for a time. These and other normal reactions should be respected and left alone.

Reactions to Prolonged Dying. Occasionally, premature mourning may occur, with anticipatory grief and withdrawal of interest in the dying child, perhaps accompanied by the displacement of warm feelings onto an infant child in the family. Often, unacceptable thoughts arise. For example, a parent may find himself or herself wishing that the child would finally die and relieve everyone of the emotional and financial burden and suffering. Such a wish may horrify a parent and lead to the immediate mobilization of certain defense mechanisms. A common defense mechanism is that of reaction formation: the parent becomes extra protective in caring for the dying child. The parent may also feel guilty and may express his or her guilt (and anxiety) by asking repetitive questions that require tactful answers.

As a chronically ill child nears death, the parents may be filled with remorse and may experience a resurgence of love. Rarely, a denial that death is imminent may remain in force. After the death of a chronically ill child, parents may feel a mixture of relief and guilt, perhaps with feelings of remorse uppermost.

Reactions of Siblings

Siblings who are very young, especially those under the age of 5, feel the withdrawal of the parent intensely and consequently feel a loss of love. Young siblings may view the death as an abandonment, as punishment, as the realization of unacceptable wishes—or as all three. Children between about 5 and 10 years of age generally are somewhat more concerned for the dying child and may also be fearful for themselves. Although it is expected that older children usually can muster a supportive attitude and temporarily assume parental roles for the younger siblings at home, even teenagers feel and react to parental withdrawal and may "act up" during such a trying time. They too require special attention. Children as well as adults may experience survivor guilt after the death of a child (Lifton, 1967). Some surviving children suffer serious symptoms and subsequent distortions of character structure (Cain et al., 1964).

Reactions of the Hospital Staff

Hospital staff members also experience anxiety in the presence of a dying child or a grieving parent (Solnit and Green, 1959), and they tend sometimes to deal with that anxiety by withdrawal and a conspiracy of silence. These reactions may hamper them from giving the dying child and his family the best care possible and may prevent the staff members from carrying out certain essential psychological tasks. Besides comforting the parents, such tasks are helping the child feel as active as possible in his or her attempts to cope with anxiety and allowing the child some hope. Furthermore, the privacy and dignity of the child require protection. Last, certain distortions require correction. The child, for example, may show his or her concern by asking such questions as "Am I safe?"; "Will someone be with me when I need them?"; "Will I be helped to feel better?" The continuing need for tact carries through into the period of care for the survivors.

CLINICAL CARE OF THE DYING CHILD

Talking with the Parents about Fatal Illness

The hardest task for the physician is to tell the parents that their child is fatally ill. The physician should take the parents into a private office and allow at the very least half an hour, uninterrupted by telephone calls or other tasks. He or she can begin by telling the parents the diagnosis and the nature of the illness. He might then go on to describe the treatment that is available to offer some relief for the child's symptoms. At some point, he will have to tell the parents that there is no treatment that can cure the child of the illness. Throughout this interview he should pause and give the parents every opportunity to express their feelings and ask questions. He must resist his understandable impulse to "shut off" their grief. If they ask whether the child will die from the illness, the physician will have to say that he will. If they do not ask, he should at some point attempt to clarify that the illness is progressive and that the child will die. At the same time, the physician must remember that the parents will not necessarily understand or accept what they have been told.

The physician should not end the interview then but should stay with the parents as they experience their shock (and perhaps anger) and grief. He might then tell the parents how he plans to treat the child and help the parents feel some measure of participation in and control of the treatment.

The physician is obliged to tell the parents what to expect as the illness progresses. This information need not be given in full in the first interview; rather, it should be given in stages over an extended period. The goal is to give the parents information that will enable them to anticipate the child's needs at each stage. The parents usually will indicate by their questions what they need to know.

Regular contact with the parents then should be planned. The contact should take the form not of comments made in passing but of time set aside to talk, review, and listen in the privacy of an office. The physician should resist the natural impulse to avoid the parents or avoid the subject. In order to do this, he must recognize the impotence and anger he feels in the face of death. The parents will come to trust the physician and feel safe expressing, if they so wish, some of their less acceptable feelings if they are sure that he is available and ready to listen. During these planned interviews, the physician can discuss with the parents their child's behavior, their management of the child, what to tell his siblings, and whether and in what way they would like their minister, priest, or rabbi involved. The parents should be reassured about their own handling of the situation, and the physician should feel free to share his admiration for how well they are meeting the child's needs.

The physician may be asked for advice about religious rites for the sick. The practice of offering prayer with the child or administering the Sacrament of the Sick, although intended to comfort, may be anxiety arousing. Although it sometimes happens that the Sacrament of the Sick is given without the parents' consent, or even knowledge, most priests prefer to involve the parents and family first, and to have the family present in the room. However, administering the Sacrament of the Sick may cause as much upset in the family as in the child.

The 1972 modification* of the Sacrament of the Sick does not alter very much the way in which the child might experience the ritual. Indeed, there are no specific modifications for children other than those based on the judgment of the particular priest. The physician should discuss with the parents and the priest the child's needs and how the child might experience the praying or the Sacrament before any step is undertaken.

Talking with the Child

In regard to talking about death with the sick child, especially the young sick child, the parents' feelings and wishes must be respected. Some parents, for example, do not wish the child to be told that he is going to die, whereas others do. Some families need to use denial as a protective device.

There is no simple answer to the question of whether or not the particular child should be told. One useful approach is to discuss with the parents how they think they would respond if their dying child asked them whether he was going to die. There are several stages of response to such a question that might be suggested.

1. The child's reason for asking the question must be clarified. The child may be responding to the parents' or the hospital staff's anxious behavior, or the child may be concerned about such things as pain, mutilation, loneliness, and the needs of others. The child then can be given repeated opportunities to talk about what he is worried about.

2. If the parents decide that they want the child to know that his illness is fatal, the process of telling the child about the illness and impending death should have the characteristics of a dialogue rather than of an announcement. Some children simply cannot understand and do not want to hear the truth; they should not be told. Others have to arrive slowly at the realization of the significance of their illness; it is too much for them to understand and grasp at one time.

3. The child must be given hope. Even when he is told that the illness is one that causes death, he can and should be told that the physicians will do everything they can to fight the illness.

---

*Ordo Unctionis Infirmorum Eorumque Pastoralis Curae. In: *Rituale Romanum* Rome: Typis Polyglottis Vaticanis, 1972, pp. 10 and 15.

The adults must agree not only on *how* the child should be told but also on *who* should be the first to tell him. Sometimes the physician is not the right person to disclose this information. A parent or a clergyman who is close to the child may have a more sensitive understanding of the child's needs.

A discussion of this kind with parents often helps them to express some of their own concerns. It also promotes in them a feeling of trust and of being understood, as well as a feeling that they have some control over the care of their child. Nothing is so painful to the parents as their feeling of helplessness as their child's life ebbs.

Most important, the physician who has had a dialogue with the parents is prepared to have a dialogue with the child, always keeping in close touch with the parents. The physician, for example, can convey assuredness as he imparts to the child as much of the truth as the parents want and the child seems ready to know. There is no blueprint answer.

The ward staff members should be clear about who has the primary responsibility for talking with the parents and child about the seriousness of the illness. If it has been agreed on by the parents that the physician should tell the child, the physician should first establish a relationship of trust with the child. Before he talks with the child, he should make sure that someone is available to be with the child after he himself has left the room if the child so desires. The involved staff members should know how much the child knows about the illness so that the child does not receive conflicting and therefore puzzling information. Ward staff members also experience anxiety when in the presence of a dying child or his family. Their natural inclination to avoid these feelings may cause them to stay away from both the child and the grieving family. Such inclinations may be better controlled if the ward staff members have the opportunity to explore and share their feelings in meetings (Lewis, 1962).

Specific Management of the Child Who Is Dying

Kübler-Ross (1972) gives a beautiful description of a dying boy's expression of his thoughts and feelings:

> [The dying] boy tried to paint what he felt like. He drew a huge tank and in front of the barrel was a tiny little figure with a stop sign in his hand. This to me represents the fear of death, the fear of the catastrophic, destructive force that comes upon you and you cannot do anything about it. If you can respond to him by saying it must be terrible to feel so tiny and this thing is so big, he may be able to

verbally express a sense of smallness or impotence or rage. The next picture he drew was a beautiful bird flying up in the sky. A little bit of its upper wing was painted gold. When he was asked what this was, the boy said it was the peace bird flying up into the sky with a little bit of sunshine on its wing. It was the last picture he painted before he died. I think these are picture expressions of a stage of anger and the final stage of acceptance.

This description underscores the importance of one aspect of the care of the dying child: with the parents' permission and in the privacy of his own room, the young child should be given the opportunity on different occasions to express his concerns through drawings or through play with toys and dolls. If necessary, and if the parents agree, the collaboration of a child psychiatrist should be sought. The opportunity for expressive play enables the child to exercise some control over his anxiety. If the child expresses concern about such problems as pain, loneliness, and fear through this play, this fact should be noted mentally by the physician. At another time, the child could be reassured, without reference to the play session, that the physicians will make sure that he does not have pain, that there will always be someone available to help him, and that everything will be done to help him feel better. (Such a reassurance during the play itself may cause a child to feel tricked and exposed and so may inhibit future play.)

Patients—adults and children alike—feel threatened by the passivity imposed on them by illness. Every effort must be made to give the child a feeling of active participation in his treatment. He should be informed at each stage what is being done, why it is being done, and what he can expect. Some feeling of hope needs to be provided. Last, the dignity of the child requires protection, and his privacy should be ensured.

Denial of death in a child, as in an adult, is a defense against anxiety, and it should be respected. Each person must be allowed his own way of dealing with the dread of death. At the same time, certain distortions should be corrected. For example, the child may require reassurance that the illness was not brought about by anything the child did (or thinks he did). Reactions that generate further anxiety, such as regression, should be gently but firmly controlled by the parents as well as by the hospital staff; excessive regressive behavior is uncomfortable for a child as well as for those caring for him.

Children vary in their capacity to deal with the inevitability of their impending death or with the diagnosis that implies impending death. Some children, particularly older children, want to know, whereas others do not want to know or cannot comprehend.

The Moribund Child

In a situation in which a child has no brain activity and is being kept alive by artificial methods, and there is no hope of spontaneous respiration or recovery of brain function, the physician must proceed with tact. First, before any decision is made to stop artificial life supports, the parents must be fully informed and prepared. The physician first might tell them that the child is being kept alive by machines but that there is no possibility that he will breathe on his own or will recover brain function. He should explain why this is so. In some instances, the parents have already considered the issue and will have decided to discontinue artificial life supports. Such parents may also have decided whether they want to be in the room at the time of death. Other parents may experience great anguish at the burden of deciding to discontinue artificial respiration and may also prefer not to know exactly when it will be stopped. In a tactful way, the physician can say to such parents that there is nothing more that can be done. Then when the parents do decide to discontinue artificial respiration the physician should ask the parents where they want to be when it is discontinued.

The parents' wishes must be respected at all times; the child is theirs. The parents should not be rushed. It is always their decision to make, and they need all the help they can get.

It is essential also that the parents feel a sense of unanimity with and security in the entire ward staff. Therefore, before the plan is carried out, the staff physician should discuss with all the ward staff members the steps just outlined and encourage them to express their thoughts and feelings. Patients tend to seek different answers from different staff members, and it is essential that all the staff members are aware of the way in which an individual case is being handled so that their responses do not conflict.

If the child dies suddenly without the parents' being present, the parents should be informed of the death immediately, no matter what the time of day. The parents' sense of guilt at not being present when their child dies is an enormous one.

Management of Parents During Prolonged Illness in the Child

The many different reactions that parents may have when the period of dying is one of prolonged suffering necessitate sensitive management. Some parents may request other opinions regarding prognosis or treatment. Often they should be given this opportunity. Sometimes, however, a futile search for a magical cure may devastate a family emotionally and financially. The physician then should gently attempt to steer the parents toward a more realistic and helpful way of coping with their feeling of impotence. The physician can help parents by giving them opportunities to talk about their feelings in an accepting, nonjudgmental way. For example, parents often feel relieved when the physician reassures them that they are doing everything they can and that he knows how hard it is for them. He can also say, "Many parents have told me how at times they had wished it would all finally end, and then felt bad about thinking that. But it's a natural thought to occur. We all have all kinds of thoughts. What is important is that you have done everything that could possibly be done."

Questions may arise about childrearing during the long period of time during which remissions occur and treatment is administered. While his condition is far from normal, there is often a wish on the part of the child to feel normal. Perhaps this represents in part the child's wish that he or she no longer had the disease, that there was no longer a need for painful treatments, and that he or she could talk freely with others about feelings of frustration, anger, and resentment.

At the same time, parents may be in a quandary about how to rear the child, siblings about how to relate to the child and deal with their guilt, and teachers about how to educate and deal with the child and the other children in the classroom. Once again, there is no blueprint answer; indeed, blanket recommendations, (e.g., "Treat the child normally") may only burden the parents with more conflicts and guilt. Each situation must be thought out and managed individually, taking into account the many needs of the child, the parents, and the siblings.

Management of Siblings

Good medical management takes into account how the child's dying and death affect his siblings. Siblings of all ages need support and explanations, and the physician can help the parents provide them. He may suggest that the parents gather the family together and then give a simple explanation to all the children. The explanation should include the facts that Johnny is very ill, that everyone is doing his best to make him as comfortable as possible, that the illness Johnny has could not be prevented, that it is no one's fault, and that it is necessary to figure out together how everyone can help. Later, individual children in the family may be given more information as they give evidence that they require it. If the siblings are told that death is near, they will also need help on how to conduct themselves in the presence of the dying child. The dying child needs their support, and they can give it by doing such things as making drawings for the child, bringing messages from others, and getting things he or she may need. If the dying child asks them whether he or she is going to die, they can say, "I don't know. I know it's a serious illness. Would you like me to ask Mommy and Daddy, or do you want to ask them yourself?"

When the child dies, in order to avoid hurt feelings, all the siblings should be told of the death at the same time if possible. A simple account of the death can be given if the children ask about it. It is better to avoid such statements as, "He died in his sleep," especially when young children are present, because of the danger of engendering in them a fear of sleep.

A visit to the home by the physician is nearly always deeply appreciated by the parents and siblings of the dead child. If the physician has had a longstanding relationship with the family, he should ask about the funeral or memorial service, and he should attend the service. A physician who has provided extended care for a dying child may be remembered only for his failure to attend the funeral service or to convey his condolences.

Sometimes a parent will ask whether a young sibling should attend the funeral. The physician first should decide whether the parent will probably be in control of himself and who else will be present at the funeral who could support the child. For children under the age of about 5, the funeral can be a puzzling experience unless it is explained and unless a great deal of support is given by a familiar and caring adult. Attendance also depends on cultural practices. Children above the age of 5 often can utilize the funeral rite in the same way as adults do, especially if they have adults in attendance who can also explain to them their feelings and describe what is taking place. A child who does not wish to attend the funeral should not be made to feel guilty. Rather, arrangements should be made for him to be in the company of an understanding adult during the time of the funeral. Older children should be encouraged to attend the rites and observe the rituals the adults are attending and observing, since, again, these practices usually help one to deal with the reality of death. If the older child chooses not to attend the funeral, the reason for his choice should be explored with him, but if he continues to feel that he does not want to attend, his wishes should be respected. Each person mourns in his own way. In no circumstance should the subject of the dead person be closed off. A wall of silence hampers the child as he struggles with the reality of the death and his feelings about death. Some of the specific ways of helping children understand the many facets of death have been described by Wolf (1958).

Other questions involving siblings may arise later. A younger sibling may ask to have some of the dead child's toys. The transfer can be done in a helpful way by suggesting that the dead child would have wanted his or her younger brother or sister to have his or her toys. Other decisions, such as rearranging the dead child's room or giving a sibling the dead child's room, might be deferred until most of the work of mourning has been done. Such decisions can probably be made on a rational basis then, when the mourners are less affected by their emotions.

Requesting Autopsy Permission or Organ Donation

A difficult task for the physician is requesting autopsy permission or organ donation. Because of the difficulties, the request is frequently made in a hasty, tactless manner. The physician must be aware that many families have strong feelings against such procedures. For example, Orthodox Judaism prohibits the permanent removal of organs. Despite the physician's medical curiosity and zeal to learn, he must resist pressuring a family into agreeing to a procedure to which it objects. On the other hand, the physician may legitimately describe an autopsy to the parents as a postmortem internal examination that determines the cause of death and the effects of the treatment given. He can honestly present to them the possible potential benefits of an autopsy or organ donation to others. If the physician is asked whether the child will be cut open, he must answer honestly, even if he knows that the autopsy or donation request may then be refused. Families who refuse to agree to such procedures should not be made to feel guilty about their refusal.

WHEN A PARENT DIES

The Children

When a parent dies, the physician should help the surviving parent anticipate the reactions to be expected from the children. Children, particularly young children, are unable to tolerate—and therefore complete—the painful task of mourning the death of a parent. Sad feelings often are curtailed, and often the child quickly returns to everyday activities as if nothing had changed. Although mourning in extremely young children is brief, it is difficult to assess the impact of a parent's death on the child's future personality development. Occasionally, a child may express hostile feelings toward the surviving parent. The child may actually be angry at—and feel abandoned by—the parent who died. Since such feelings usually are experienced as unacceptable, the child displaces them onto the surviving parent. The expression of hostile feelings toward the surviving parent unfortunately invites punishment when it is misunderstood. Frequently, a child, by virtue of his still somewhat primitive way of viewing the world, is convinced that he caused his parent's death, either by not being a good child or by having at one time or another wished the parent dead. When the child provokes the surviving parent, he may in part be seeking punishment to assuage his feelings of guilt. Therefore, it is necessary to prepare a parent for these reactions as well as to attempt to correct the child's fantasies.

The child who has lost a parent is a child at psychiatric risk. This is particularly true of the child who loses a mother. Impairments in the child's capacity to form new, lasting relationships may show up later. Shame at being different may be experienced. Impaired sexual identity and conscience formation also may occur (Neubauer, 1960; Bonnard, 1962). In addition, the loss of a parent during childhood may predispose a child to attempted suicide during adolescence.

The family disruption and the reactions of the surviving parent may lead to a depression in the child. The presenting symptom may be a school learning problem or a behavior difficulty. Another hazard that sometimes occurs is a morbid attachment of the surviving parent to a child of either sex, particularly an adolescent. The adolescent in question may have great difficulty in separating from the parent or may develop along homosexual lines.

On the other hand, as development proceeds, the child may be able to continue the work of the mourning on a piecemeal basis. As his cognitive capacity matures and his reality testing is strengthened, the child may at some later date be able to express some of the feelings that he had repressed. These feelings may include yearning and sadness as well as anger and resentment.

The physician can help most if he can enable the parent, who is also in a state of mourning and withdrawal, to recognize the needs of the child. The child needs to know that there is someone he can depend on to meet his needs and to whom he can express his feelings. In some instances, the physician may appropriately support the parent in this role by making himself available to the child if the parent agrees. The pediatrician should not hesitate to suggest a consultation with a child psychiatrist if he is especially concerned about the child's behavior.

The Surviving Parent

The death of a parent almost always disrupts a family. As far as possible, the physician should help the family to maintain its stability and to avoid making hasty decisions while the family is in a state of acute grief. The services of a relative or a homemaker may be helpful during this acute period. Some tact is required as the physician tries to steer a course that will not be experienced by the parent either as intrusive or as an abandonment.

The disruption in the family caused by the death of a parent is not confined to the period of mourning. Loss of income, reduction in the amount of time that can be spent with the children, changed roles for the surviving spouse, caretaking responsibilities for the older children in the family, and altered social relationships are some of the repercussions that continue to affect the family. The physician should remain accessible to the members of the family. Sleep difficulties, psychosomatic disturbances, or school learning difficulties are some of the common signs of continuing distress. Psychiatric evaluation of these difficulties may be indicated (see Chap. 19).

REFERENCES

Anthony, S. (1940), *The Child's Discovery of Death*. New York: Harcourt, Brace & World.
Bonnard, A. (1962), Truancy and pilfering associated with bereavement. In: *Adolescents*, ed. S. Lorand and H.L. Schneer. New York: Paul Hoeber Medical Division, Harper & Row.
Cain, A.C., Fast, I., and Erickson, M.E. (1964), Children's disturbed reactions to the death of a sibling. *Am. J. Orthopsychiatry*, 34:741.
Gartley, W., and Bernasconi, M. (1967), The concept of death in children. *J. Genet. Psychol.*, 110:71–85.
Kastenbaum, R. (1959), Time and death in adolescence. In: *The Meaning of Death*, ed. H. Feifel. New York: McGraw-Hill.
Kübler-Ross, E. (1972), On death and dying. *J. Am. Med. Assoc.*, 221:174.

Lewis, M. (1962), The management of parents of acutely ill children in the hospital. *Am. J. Orthopsychiatry*, 30:60.

Lifton, R.J. (1967), *Death in Life*. New York: Random House.

Neubauer, P.B. (1960), The one-parent child and his oedipal development. *Psychoanal. Study Child*, 15:286.

Schilder, P., and Wechsler, D. (1934), The attitudes of children toward death. *J. Genet. Psychol.*, 45:405–451.

Solnit, A.J. (1963), The dying child. *Dev. Med. Child Neurol.*, 7:693.

Solnit, A.J., and Green, M. (1959), Psychologic considerations in the management of deaths on pediatric hospital services. I. The doctor and the child's family. *Pediatrics*, 24:106.

Wolf, A.W.M. (1958), *Helping Your Child to Understand Death*. New York: Child Study Association of America, Inc., pp. 7–44.

Wolff, S. (1969), *Children Under Stress*. London: Penguin.

Part Four

Introduction to Clinical Psychiatric
Diagnosis

Chapter 19

THE PSYCHIATRIC EVALUATION OF THE CHILD

The immediate aims of the psychiatric evaluation of the child are to define the child's behavior as accurately as possible, including the context in which it occurs, and to seek its causes. The ultimate aims are to assess normality, strengths, and psychopathology in order to recommend treatment, to predict the future course, to communicate to others, and to devise preventive interventions.

In a screening intake procedure, which may be done by telephone, the clinician obtains the patient's full name and telephone number and the name of the referring person. He or she then attempts to clarify the problem and the appropriateness of the referral (e.g., by asking, "Can you tell me something about the problem?"). The clinician also initiates the evaluation process by outlining briefly the steps and procedures (e.g., the number and kinds of interviews, and the administrative practices for such matters as permission forms and fees).

There are some built-in biases that affect how the clinician approaches the child and his family. For example, the source of the referral may be reflected in the diagnostic label. Children referred by school officials are often labeled as having "learning difficulties," and the request is to "rule out organic disorder," almost as a ticket of admission. Children referred by juvenile court officials are readily viewed as "delinquent" or "sociopathic," with the bias that they are somehow therefore untreatable. Parents' concerns about a child often reflect their concerns about themselves or some prevailing family attitudes or worries. The clinician also has to assess the reliability of the witness or the history giver. Finally, there may be a hidden agenda, such as a custody suit that is pending.

In addition, clinicians, like other people, all have certain bêtes noirs: deformed children may repel the clinician at first; aggression in children often mobilizes strong defenses in the clinician; and mentally retarded children are often overlooked or given inadequate attention.

In approaching a diagnostic evaluation, the clinician should have in the back of his or her mind some idea of the important possibilities, along the lines of a psychiatric sieve. For the sake of simplicity, it can be said clinically that there are eight major basic categories of psychopathology to be screened for and assessed. The italic type in the following questions indicates what those categories are.

1. What is the level of *development* of the child? Is there a *developmental delay*?
2. What degree of *organic dysfunction* is present, and to what degree does it affect perception, coordination, attention, learning, emotions, and impulse control?
3. Is there any evidence of a *thought disorder*?
4. What evidence is there of *anxiety, conflict, or neurotic symptoms* (e.g., phobic behavior, obsessive-compulsive behavior, hysterical behavior, or depression)?
5. Is there a *temperament* difficulty or *personality* disorder?
6. Is there a *psychophysiological* disorder?
7. Is the child *mentally retarded*?
8. Is the child *reacting to an unfavorable environment* (family, school, community, society)?

The categories are not mutually exclusive. In fact, problem behaviors from all categories may be present in some degree. Sometimes the behaviors are a cause of other behaviors; sometimes they are a consequence of a particular behavior. (The particular functions will be discussed in greater detail later in the chapter.)

Also to be kept in mind are possible significant predisposing or causative factors, which can be put into five major groups:

1. *Genetic factors*, as expressed, say, in developmental dyslexia, attention disorders, mental retardation, autism, and schizophrenia
2. *Organic causes*, including prenatal factors (e.g., malnutrition, exposure to radiation, the use of drugs during pregnancy, prematurity), traumatic factors (e.g., head injury),

infective factors (e.g., encephalitis), neoplastic factors (e.g., brain tumors), degenerative factors (e.g., cerebromacular degenerations), metabolic factors (e.g., thyrotoxicosis), and toxic factors (e.g., ingestion of amphetamines, steroids, bromides, and lead)

3. *Developmental immaturity*, whether due to intrinsic factors or external environmental factors (e.g., stimulus deprivation) or both

4. *Inadequate parenting*, e.g., parental deprivation, separation, loss, abuse by parents (including sexual and physical abuse), ambivalence in parents, and psychiatric disorders in parents

5. *Stress factors*, including illness, injury, surgery, and hospitalization, school failure, poverty, and racial discrimination

Again, all five groups of factors may interact.

THE PARENTS

With these "sets" in mind, the clinician starts usually by interviewing both parents together. Adolescents may prefer that they be seen alone first, and they might be given the choice. In some instances, seeing the whole family together may be useful, especially for diagnostic purposes. Each spouse should also be seen individually in addition to being seen together with the other spouse.

There are six parts to the evaluative process as far as the parents are concerned:

1. The clinician strives to get a detailed history of the child, which includes (a) a careful description of the problem and the parents' view of the problem, (b) the personal history, (c) the developmental history, (d) the history of previous illnesses, (e) the social history, (f) the family history, (g) the school history, (h) the history of such biological functions as appetite, sleep, bladder and bowel control, and menstruation, (i) a description of the child's relationships within the family and with peers, (j) a description of significant events, such as separations and losses, and (k) information about previous psychiatric, psychological, and neurological evaluations.

2. The clinician strives also to assess the psychiatric state of each parent, the marriage and the family relationships, both nuclear and extended.

3. The parents should be given an opportunity to ask questions.

4. The clinician should again outline for the parents both the subsequent procedure and how the parents might prepare the child for it.
5. Various administrative matters (e.g., those regarding the fee, consent forms, and requests for outside information) should be discussed and settled.
6. The clinician must make a final review and recommendation.

THE CHILD

Before the child is seen, space and time for the appointment should be set aside. The child should have enough space and the proper equipment to play with such things as a ball, crayons and paper, Play-Doh, a dollhouse, rubber dolls, puppets, toy guns, a doctor's bag, and a few games, such as checkers and cards. The list of toys can, of course, be expanded (e.g., to include toy telephones). The space and furniture in the room should be scaled to the child. Some small (one-inch) cubes are needed for the preschool-age child.

The developmental assessment of the preschool-age child requires a special approach. Developmental scales and assessment techniques commonly used in the United States include the original Gesell and Amatruda scales as updated by Knobloch and Pasamanick (1974), the Bayley Scale (1969), the Denver Developmental Screening Test (Frankenburg and Dodds, 1967), and the Yale Revised Developmental Schedules. However, for screening purposes, the items listed in Table 19–1 are useful.

Two, three, or more interviews of approximately 30 to 60 minutes each are needed to allow for the child's anxiety over the unfamiliar and to get a better sample of his behavior.

The areas that will require closest examination are usually suggested in the interview with the child's parents. Thus the clinician might want to pay special attention to, say, organicity, a thought disorder, a developmental delay, mental retardation, or a specific syndrome, such as Gilles de la Tourette syndrome.

In the organization of the interview with the child, a frame of reference is useful. The interview consists of four parts: (1) the introductory statements, (2) free play, (3) the mental status examination, and (4) the conclusion. In practice, these parts are not distinct; there is considerable overlapping, depending on the behavior of the particular child. (For example, some children want to play right away; others will not play or

Table 19–1. CHECKLIST FOR ASSESSMENT BY OBSERVATION
OF DEVELOPMENTAL LEVEL OF PRESCHOOL-AGE CHILD

Age	Historical (or Observed) Items	Items to be Tested
2 years	Runs well Walks up and down stairs—one step at a time Opens doors Climbs on furniture Puts 3 words together Handles spoon well Helps to undress Listens to stories with pictures	Builds tower of 6 cubes Circular scribbling Copies horizontal stroke with pencil Folds paper once
2½ years	Jumps Knows full name Refers to self by pronoun "I" Helps put things away	Builds tower of 8 cubes Copies horizontal and vertical strokes (not a cross)
3 years	Goes upstairs, alternating feet Rides tricycle Stands momentarily on one foot Knows age and sex Plays simple games Helps in dressing Washes hands	Builds tower of 9 cubes Imitates construction of bridge with 3 cubes Imitates a cross and circle

4 years	Hops on one foot
	Throws ball overhand
	Climbs well
	Uses scissors to cut out pictures
	
	Counts 4 pennies accurately
	Tells a story
	
	Plays with several children
	Goes to toilet alone
		Copies bridges from a model
		Imitates construction of a gate with
		  5 cubes
		Copies a cross and circle
		Draws a man with 2 to 4
		  parts—other than head
		Names longer of two lines

5 years	Skips Names 4 colors Counts 10 pennies correctly Dresses and undresses Asks questions about meaning of words	Copies a square and triangle Names 4 colors Names heavier of 2 weights

R.S. Paine, and T.E. Oppé (1966), *Neurological Examination of Children*. New
York: Heinemann, p. 40.

say a word.) The four parts of the interview are discussed
separately in the paragraphs that follow.

The Introductory Statements

The clinician should keep a reasonable physical distance
from the child in the waiting room in order not to loom too
large and forbidding. He should introduce himself to the child,
and invite the child to accompany him to the office, reassuring

the child that his parents will be in the waiting room when he returns. Once inside the office, the clinician should ask the child what he prefers to be called, and he should make sure the child knows the clinician's name. The clinician should clarify what is the child's understanding of why he has come and then give his own understanding of why the child has come. Next he should tell the child what will take place: "It's a time set aside to see if I can help you understand what may be bothering you. We will have 45 minutes together, at the end of which you will return to your parents." The clinician should clarify the extent of the confidentiality: "I *will* be meeting with your parents, but I will *first* discuss with you what I will or will not say to your parents." In some circumstances, e.g., a court-ordered evaluation, there is no confidentiality, and a report must be rendered to the court. The clinician should inform the child of this fact.

It is probably best not to take notes during the interview. Note taking might inhibit the child, and it will inhibit the clinician in observing. The clinician should avoid asking leading questions or any kind of demanding interrogation since that too is unproductive and may inhibit the play and communication. Open-ended questions (e.g., "What happened then?") are better than leading questions or questions that require only a single answer. (A short bibliography covering the various practical techniques used in psychiatric interviews with children is given in the references for this chapter.)

Free Play

The clinician should invite the child to play (e.g., by saying, "Is there anything you would like to play with?") and should observe the play, perhaps encouraging the child with a word or two if he appears interested in playing with a particular toy. If appropriate, the clinician should engage in the play in an accepting, nondirective, noncompetitive manner.

One need not be rigid about this. One may also begin by asking the child "Who is in your family?" and may use the child's response as an opportunity to begin exploring the child's relationships with various family members.

The Mental Status Examination

What and how the child plays, says, and does constitute the raw data for the mental status examination of the child. To bring some order to the understanding of what seems like random play, it is useful to have an outline of things one particularly wants to observe and of why one wants to observe them. When completed, such an outline constitutes the report of the child's mental status.

Some of the data emerge spontaneously, some only after questioning. The categories in the outline that follows are for convenience only; they are made up of behavior items that are not isolated, and the behaviors listed usually do not occur in any special sequence. The child acts as a whole and in the context of a given environment, and the child's present behavior is always continuous with his past behavior. It is not necessary to elicit the information in the precise order presented here, and all these categories need not be covered in equal detail or in one sitting. The clinician should use his clinical judgment as to how fast and in what detail he should proceed and as to what he wants to look for. He should also consider the age of the child when assessing a given response.

1. Physical Appearance
   a. Small stature is often associated with a more infantile self image; the child who is short may also be depressed because of his size. The cause of the shortness will have to be determined (e.g., the child may have a pituitary disorder).
   b. Head size may indicate microcephaly and mental retardation, or hydrocephaly.
   c. Physical signs of a chromosomal disorder may be present (e.g., Down's syndrome or Turner's syndrome).
   d. Neurological signs, such as strabismus, may suggest organicity (see the discussion of soft neurological signs, p. 353).
   e. Bruising may indicate child abuse.
   f. Nutritional state may indicate an eating disorder, ranging from anorexia nervosa to obesity.
   g. Level of anxiety may be manifested by hyperalertness, tics, biting of lips or nails, and hair pulling. The activity may have a "driven" quality: the child cannot sit still, has motor overflow as he moves from one thing to another, is easily distracted, and has a "short attention span," a low frustration tolerance, and labile emotions. All these may suggest an attention deficit disorder as well as anxiety.
   h. Momentary lapses of attention (staring, head nodding, eye blinking) may indicate epilepsy or hallucinatory phenomena. The clinician will subsequently inquire

about such seizure phenomena as auras (nausea, vomiting, epigastric sensations), micropsia ("Do things seem to get smaller as you look at them?") or macropsia ("Do things seem to get bigger as you look at them?"), or about hallucinations (see 9d).

i. Gait may indicate a particular disorder (e.g., walking on tiptoe may indicate childhood autism; a stiff gait may indicate cerebral palsy).

j. Dress gives some idea of the care the child has received and how much the child cares for himself or herself. Sexual preferences and conflicts may be expressed in attitudes, behavior, and dress.

k. Mannerisms may provide a clue to a disorder (e.g., smelling everything may be a sign of childhood autism, tics a sign of anxiety, thumb sucking or repetitive play a sign of regression).

2. Separation
Some caution is usually appropriate. Too much ease in separating may indicate superficial relationships associated with maternal deprivation. Difficulty in separating may indicate an ambivalent parent-child relationship.

3. Manner of Relating
The child usually relates to the clinician cautiously at first. However, some children are indiscriminately friendly and are shallow. Autistic children appear to "look through" one.

4. Orientation to Time and Place
This may be impaired by organic factors, intelligence, anxiety, or a thought disorder.

5. Central Nervous System Functioning
Child psychiatrists are often particularly interested in the presence of so-called soft neurological signs as a possible indication of organicity. The concept of soft neurological signs was introduced by Paul Schilder, and the term was first used by Lauretta Bender (1956). Soft neurological signs are those signs that do not in themselves signify a definitive, manifest, specific neurological lesion but taken together may indicate organicity. They constitute a statistical association rather than a pathognomonic finding. They are often neurodevelopmental immaturities which have persisted.
There is no completely satisfactory classification of soft neurological signs. One classification is as follows:

a. Group A signs. A developmental delay in relation to chronological and mental age is reliably present. The delay may be in such functions as speech, motor coordination, right/left discrimination, and perception; and it may be associated with (1) mental retardation, (2) specific, genetically determined maturational disorders, and/or (3) brain damage.

b. Group B signs. A reliable single sign, such as nystagmus or strabismus, that may or may not have a determinable neurological cause.

c. Group C signs. Slight, unreliably present signs, such as asymmetry of tone or asymmetry of reflexes, which may be associated with various deprivational states or any of the conditions just mentioned.

Soft neurological signs include deficiencies in:

a. Gross motor coordination. Awkwardness, clumsiness, motor overflow with extraneous movements, and contralateral "minor" movements of the opposite limb seen in posture, gait, balance, skill in climbing stairs, and ball throwing and catching.

b. Fine motor coordination (perceptuo-motor capacities). The child is asked to copy the following designs:

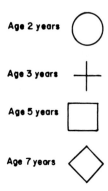

Age 2 years

Age 3 years

Age 5 years

Age 7 years

c. Performance of the Bender gestalt test. Clinically, it is useful to ask the child to copy various Bender designs (see Fig. 19–1). Formal testing is required if the child has difficulty copying the designs.

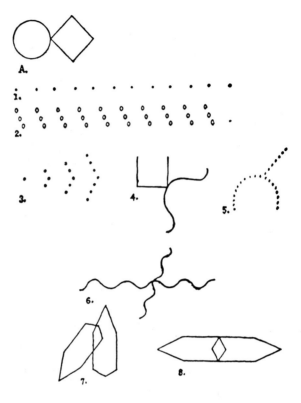

Fig. 19–1. The visual motor Gestalt test figures.
L. Bender, *The Bender Visual Motor Gestalt Test,* published by The American Orthopsychiatric Association, Inc.

The difficulties may include:
a. Trouble with angulation and juxtaposition

b. A tendency to verticalize a diagonal

c. Substitution of loops for dots

It is important to take into account the child's developmental level (see Fig. 19–2).

d. Laterality (Laterality is sometimes achieved by age 3 and usually achieved by age 7)

  (1) Eye (The child might be asked to look through a telescope.)

  (2) Hand (while the child is writing)

  (3) Foot (while the child is kicking a ball)

Laterality, preference, and dominance are not identical. Clinically, one may merely be testing preference, which in

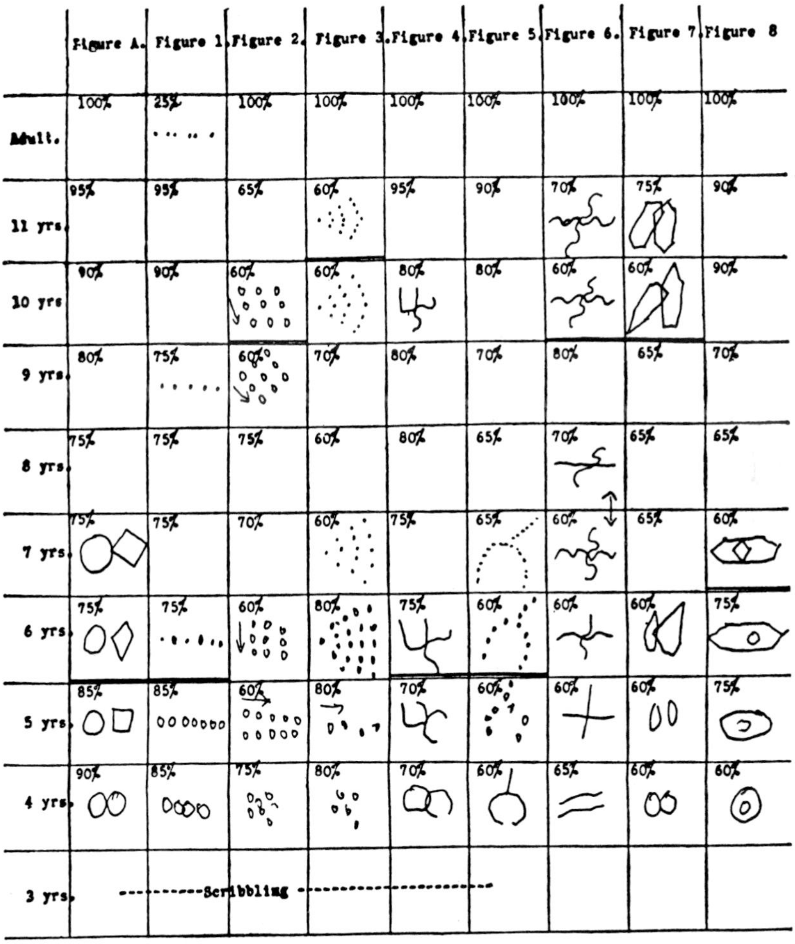

	Figure A.	Figure 1	Figure 2	Figure 3	Figure 4	Figure 5	Figure 6.	Figure 7	Figure 8
Adult	100%	25%	100%	100%	100%	100%	100%	100%	100%
11 yrs	95%	95%	65%	60%	95%	90%	70%	75%	90%
10 yrs	90%	90%	60%	60%	80%	80%	60%	60%	90%
9 yrs	80%	75%	60%	70%	80%	70%	80%	65%	70%
8 yrs	75%	75%	75%	60%	80%	65%	70%	65%	65%
7 yrs	75%	75%	70%	60%	75%	65%	60%	65%	60%
6 yrs	75%	75%	60%	80%	75%	60%	60%	60%	75%
5 yrs	85%	85%	60%	80%	70%	60%	60%	60%	75%
4 yrs	90%	85%	75%	80%	70%	60%	65%	60%	60%
3 yrs	-----------Scribbling -----------------------								

Fig. 19–2. Norms for the visual motor Gestalt test.

L. Bender, *The Bender Visual Motor Gestalt Test,* published by The American Orthopsychiatric Association, Inc.

turn may depend more on the peripheral organ than on any central mechanism (see pp. 235–236).

e. Right/left discrimination (The child should be asked to put his right hand to his left ear, his left hand to his right knee, etc.)

f. Muscle tone. The clinician should observe how the child handles toys, or crayons.

g. Tremors

h. Eye tracking. The child should be asked to look right or left at a picture on the wall, with just his eye. The clinician should observe whether the child turns his entire body.

i. Extension test. The child extends his arms. If the arms have greater tone when they are elevated, the test is positive.

j. Rapid alternating movements
   (1) Wrist rotation (pronation and supination)
   (2) Patting back of one hand with middle finger of the other hand (finger tapping)

k. Heel-to-toe walking and hopping on one foot (usually by age 7).

l. Reflex symmetry

m. Short attention span, which may be due to:
   (1) Distractibility or poor discrimination of foreground from background
   (2) Task too difficult
   (3) Fatigue
   (4) Anxiety

n. Hyperactivity. More often than not hyperactivity is disorganized activity that appears to be hyperactive. The "hyperactivity" seems to be more noticeable in the classroom than in one-to-one situations.

o. Motor overflow, especially when excited (e.g., when throwing a ball)

p. Strabismus

q. Nystagmus

r. Convergence difficulties

s. Delayed or absent light reflexes

t. Speech defects (poor modulation of voice)

u. Reading and writing difficulties, e.g., (1) reversals; (2) struggle to write or read; (3) reckless speed; (4) poor spelling

Rutter, Graham, and Yule describe a useful, brief (20-minute) neurological examination for screening purposes only. If the screening procedures reveal that the child has soft neurological signs, a comprehensive neurological examination is required.

6. Language and Speech

Children who do not use words by 18 months or phrases by 2½ to 3 years, but who have a history of normal babbling, who understand commands, and who use as well as respond to nonverbal cues are probably developing normally. Delays beyond these ages or disturbances in these other forms of communication are indications for further diagnostic evaluation.

The general signs of a language dysfunction include:

a. Reduced vocabulary, especially for abstract concepts, such as feelings
b. Delay in the acquisition of two sentences, usually acquired by age 2
c. Overuse of concrete nouns and verbs
d. Underuse or omission of abstract word classes (e.g., adjectives, adverbs, prepositions, articles, and conjunctions), giving rise to telegraphic or unintelligible speech. Some children may avoid speaking or may have "interpreters," who speak for them.

Language delay may be due to sensory impairment (e.g., blindness or deafness), neurologic damage (e.g., cerebral palsy), mental retardation, or developmental delay. Developmental dysplasia may be *receptive* (there is often an associated high-tone deafness), or *expressive* (there is often a family history of delay in language development).

The clinician therefore looks for the child's

a. Receptive abilities

	Deafness	Mental retardation	Infantile autism	Elective mutism
Sound discrimination	↓	Normal	Normal	Normal
Attentiveness	↓ Watches face	↓	↓ ↓	Normal
Understanding complex orders	↓	↓	↓ ↓ ↓	Normal

b. Expressive language abilities
  (1) Quality of babbling (by history)
  (2) Use of gestures to communicate
  (3) Developmental level of spoken language

          (a) Syntax. At age 18 months the normal child can make one-word utterances, at age 30 months the child can make 2- to 3-word phrases, and at age 40 months the child can speak in 4-word sentences.

          (b) Semantics. The child is able to use words correctly (in regard to meaning).

          (c) Abnormalities: persistent echolalia or persistent use of neologisms

  c. Speech difficulties

     (1) Defective speech due to deafness; normal facial expressions

     (2) Dysarthria due to anatomical defect

     (3) Developmental delay, as in mental retardation

     (4) Disturbance of rhythm (stuttering beyond age 4), rate, and pitch

  d. Cognitive and psychosocial factors

     (1) Intelligence

     (2) Stimulation

     (3) Socialization

     (4) Attachments

Language and/or speech impairments may be present in the following conditions:

          (a) Childhood autism: echolalia, delayed echolalia, misuse of pronouns and gender; lack of nonverbal communication behavior, including lack of eye contact and lack of facial expression

          (b) Mental retardation: delayed language and speech

          (c) Organic brain damage: scanning speech

          (d) Deprivation: too many concrete words; too few abstract words

          (e) Anxiety: high-pitched, "tight" voice

          (f) Drug intoxication: dysarthria

          (g) Regression: infantile speech

(The reader who wishes a more comprehensive assessment of language and its disorders is referred to Rutter [1972].)

7. Intelligence

A rough idea of the child's intelligence may be assessed by an evaluation of the child's

  a. General vocabulary, responsiveness, and level of comprehension and curiosity

  b. Ability to identify the parts of his body. For example, at age 5, the normal child can identify his jaw, temples, forearms, and shins.

   c. Drawing ability (see pp. 43, 44, and 45)

   d. Performance on the Wechsler Intelligence Scale for Children (revised version)

   e. Ability to subtract serial 7s or serial 3s

8. Memory

   a. At age 8, the normal child can count five digits forward and two or three digits backward; at age 10 he can count six digits forward and four digits backward. Very poor performance on the digit span test may indicate brain damage (particularly left-hemisphere damage) or mental retardation. Minor difficulties may simply reflect anxiety.

   b. The child can repeat three items five minutes after having been told them.

9. Thinking Processes

   a. Disorder of speed (e.g., retardation and push of thinking and speaking)

   b. Disorder of flow (e.g., blocking and excessive repetition of words and sentences)

   c. Disorder of content including:

      (1) Neologisms

      (2) Idiosyncratic logic or reasoning (e.g., transductive reasoning, in which things that are related in time and space are believed to be related causally)

      (3) Excessive concreteness

      (4) Difficulty in discerning similarities and differences and in discerning what is relevant and what is irrelevant

   d. Disorder of perception (for example, the clinician should ask about auditory and visual hallucinations as though he were taking a medical history of the eyes and ears [Lewis, 1981]). He might ask, "Do you have any trouble with your ears?" "Do your ears ever hurt you?" "Do your ears ever play tricks on you?" "Do you ever think you hear something, but nothing is there?" A similar sequence can be designed for inquiring about visual hallucinations.

   e. Paranoid ideation

10. Fantasies and Inferred Conflicts

The clinician might evaluate:

   a. The child's response to the following: "Do you have good dreams or bad dreams?" "Tell me one of your dreams."

   b. The child's response to the question, "If you could have three wishes, what would you wish for?"

    c. The child's drawings of (1) a person, or (2) whatever the child wants to draw.

    d. The child's squiggles (Winnicott, 1971; Berger, 1980).

    e. The child's spontaneous play

    f. A story the child makes up in response, say, to a question about his drawing of a person; e.g., "Suppose that the person has just finished doing something, is doing something now, and is going to do something soon; what do you think he or she is doing?"

    g. The child's response to the request, "Tell me about a TV program you watch."

11. Affects

Observe affects such as anxiety, depression, apathy, guilt, and anger, which may be caused by such factors as withdrawal, mental retardation, the deprivational syndromes, substance intoxication, depression, and neurotic conflicts. If depression is present (or conspicuously absent), one should inquire about suicidal ideation; e.g., "Have you ever had thoughts of hurting (or killing) yourself?"

12. Object Relations

    a. With the family. The clinician might ask the child (1) who is in his family and (2) what family members the child gets along with best and least.

    b. With peers. The clinician might ask the child (1) who his friends are and (2) whom he likes best and least.

    c. With teachers. The clinician might ask the child what teachers he likes and dislikes.

13. Drive Behavior

    a. Sexual: Is the child seductive? Autoerotic?

    b. Aggressive: Is the child violent? Destructive?

14. Defense Organization

    a. Is the child phobic (e.g., is he afraid of something in the room, such as a radiator?)?

    b. Is the child obsessive (e.g., are his drawings too neat?)?

    c. Does the child show denial (e.g., does he say that he has no problems?)?

    d. Does the child show a reaction formation (e.g., could he be described as too good to be true?)?

15. Judgment and Insight

To evaluate the child's judgment and his insight, the clinician should try to assess:

    a. what the child thinks caused his problem

    b. how upset the child appears to be about the problem

    c. what the child thinks might help solve his problem

    d. how the child thinks the clinician can help him

16. Self-Esteem
    The child who has low self-esteem often makes such remarks as "I can't do that" and "I'm no good at all."
17. Adaptive Capacities
    The child is adept at many different kinds of problem-solving activities.
18. Positive Attributes
    The following description of a child who has many positive attributes might help the clinician decide what positive attributes the child he is examining has:
    The child is attractive looking, is of normal height, and has normal vision, and hearing. He is a likeable person and seems to be happy. He relates to peers and adults easily, and he has formed a number of suitable and lasting friendships. He plays well (e.g., he is imaginative, has themes, and is sustained in his play). He is active and has sustained attention. He draws well and he is good at ball play (he is well coordinated). He enjoys playing on teams. He has healthy concepts (e.g., of a person or his body), and he is of normal intelligence. His emotional responses are appropriate, and he does not have extreme mood swings. He is in touch with his feelings and fantasies, he has a good command of language, and he can verbalize his thoughts and feelings. He is not easily made anxious, nor is he rigid (i.e., he is not obsessional, phobic, or denying). He does not shirk problems. He feels good about himself. He does well at school, both academically and socially.

Conclusion

In the course of the evaluation of the child, the clinician establishes a trusting relationship with the child and the parents. Consequently, the clinician considers the feelings of the child and the parents during the conclusion phase of the evaluation. For example, the clinician informs the child ahead of time when the last session will take place. Then, during the final interview, the clinician ensures that the child knows what will take place next. This can be done by asking the child: "Are there any things you would particularly like me to tell your parents?" "Are there any things you don't want me to say to your parents?" "This is what I plan to say to your parents" (see below) "How does that sound to you?" "Do you have any questions?" Sometimes a child will express feelings about the ending. These feelings should be recognized, acknowledged, and dealt with sympathetically and realistically.

At the final review meeting with the parents, the clinician may start by asking how the child reacted to coming for his or her interviews. Sometimes information comes to light that may help the clinician in assessing the child's capacity to make a relationship and engage in psychotherapy. The clinician can then give the parents an account of the child's strengths. Every child has some strengths (the child may be attractive, intelligent, delightful to be with, well-coordinated, able to think clearly), and it is important that the parents be told about such qualities by the clinician.

Next, the clinician talks with the parents about his or her assessment of the child's difficulties. The assessment should be discussed in clear language and documented with vignettes from the clinical interviews and/or any of the special tests that help to illustrate and make clear the nature of the difficulty. If psychological tests have been performed, the psychologist may wish to participate in the review meeting with the parents.

The parents should be given every opportunity to ask questions. Reactions on the part of the parents should be recognized and understood; the parents need the support of the clinician. The parents will need an explanation of the possible causes for the child's condition. They should also be reassured about all the good things they have done to help the child. Finally, treatment options and recommendations should be discussed with the parents. The parents should not be rushed, and they may be invited to telephone or return if they so wish.

Documentation of the basis for the findings is particularly important when a written report has to be submitted, say, to a court for evidence in a custody conflict (Lewis, 1974). When appropriate and with the parents' permission, the clinician should also send a report to the referring person. The limits of the confidentiality must be clearly understood by the child, the parents, and the clinician, and the clinician must exercise special care to safeguard this confidentiality.

Taking the history, performing the mental status examination, and observing during the clinical interviews are problem-solving exercises for the diagnostician. He or she observes, asks questions, and elicits responses for the purpose of confirming or refuting the presence of a symptom or sign that may be pathognomonic, cardinal, or important for a particular condition. Obviously he or she must be selective, since it is not practical to ask every imaginable question (Cox, Rutter, and Holbrook, 1981). Each observation, question, or special test should have a purpose and should have been selected carefully—on the bases of priority and probability.

Table 19-2. SELECTED DEVELOPMENTAL AND PSYCHOLOGICAL TESTS

Test Category	Age Range	Test Description
Developmental Assessments		
Gesell Infant Scale	8 wks–3½ yrs	mostly motor development in
Catell Infant Scale		the first year, with some social and language assessment
Bayley Infant Scale of Development	8 wks–2½ yrs	motor and social
Denver Developmental Screening Test	2 mos–6 yrs	screening
Yale Revised Developmental Schedule	4 wks–6 yrs	gross motor, fine motor, adaptive, personal/social, language
Individual Intelligence Tests		
Stanford-Binet Test	2 yrs–Adult	heavily verbal
Wechsler Intelligence Scale for Children—Revised (WISC-R)	6 yrs–17 yrs	verbal, performance and full-scale IQ
McCarthy Scales of Children's Abilities	2½ yrs–8 yrs	general cognitive index (IQ equivalent) scores for: verbal perceptual performance quantitative memory motor laterality
Motor Skills		
Bruininks-Oseretsky Test of Motor Proficiency	4½ yrs–14½ yrs	8 subtests gross and fine motor balance
Perceptual and Perceptuomotor		
Bender Visual-Motor Gestalt Test	4 yrs–12 yrs	
Draw-A-Person	All ages	
Benton Visual Retention Test (BVRT)	8 yrs–Adult	
Porteus Mazes	3 yrs–Adult	
Beery Test of Visual Motor Integration (VMI)	2:11 yrs–16 yrs	
Purdue Perceptual Motor Survey		
Speech and Language		
Peabody Picture Vocabulary Test-Revised	2½ yrs–Adult	screening
Illinois Test of Psycholinguistic Ability (ITPA)	2 yrs–11 yrs	reception, expression and processing of language
Personality		
Rorschach Test	3 yrs–Adult	
Thematic Apperception Test (TAT)	6 yrs–Adult	
Children's Apperception Test (CAT)	2½ yrs–Adult	
Social Maturity—Adaptive Behavior		interview with parent
Vineland Social Maturity Scale	0—Adult	or caregiver on
Vineland Social Maturity Scale-Revised	0—Adult	communication, motor skills, daily living, socialization, and leisure time.
School Grade Level Skills		
Wide Range Achievement Test (WRAT)	5 yrs–Adult	reading, spelling, math
Peabody Individual Achievement Test	5:4 yrs–18:3 yrs	word identification spelling math reading comprehension general information
Gray Oral Reading Test	Grades 1–12	oral reading and comprehension

I am grateful to Sara Sparrow, PhD for her assistance in the preparation of this table.

Since troubled children and their families are often anxious or even distraught, the diagnostician asks his questions tactfully and thoughtfully.

The many practical techniques for history taking and interviewing have been described elsewhere (see the references for this chapter). Experience is an important ingredient. Psychological tests have been reviewed elsewhere (Gittelman, 1980) (see Table 19–2), as have neurological examinations (Paine and Oppé, 1966) and EEG examinations (Solomon, 1975).

Finally, it is important to remember that the psychiatric evaluation of the child and his or her family goes beyond the diagnosis. Each child and family member has his or her own private experience of life. In a good psychiatric evaluation, the clinician is privileged to enter that private experience momentarily, and to empathize with that person's feelings, hopes, and fears. We try to capture this aspect of an individual's life in the descriptive diagnostic formulation that follows the formal diagnosis.

REFERENCES

Bayley, N. (1969), *Bayley Scales of Infant Development Manual*. New York: The Psychological Corporation.

Bender, L. (1956), *Psychopathology of Children with Organic Brain Damage*. Springfield, Ill.: Charles C Thomas.

Cox, A., Rutter, M., and Holbrook, D. (1981), Psychiatric interviewing techniques. V. Experimental study. Eliciting factual information. *Br. J. Psychiatry*, 139:29–37.

Frankenburg, W.K., and Dodds, J.B. (1967), The Denver Developmental Screening Test. *J. Pediatr.*, 71:181–191.

Gittelman, R. (1980), The role of psychological tests for differential diagnosis in child psychiatry. *J. Am. Acad. Child Psychiatry*, 19:413–438.

Knobloch, H., and Pasamanick, B. (Eds.) (1974), *Gesell and Amatruda's Developmental Diagnosis*, 3rd Ed. New York: Harper & Row.

Lewis, D.O. (1981), Personal communication.

Lewis, M. (1974), The latency child in a custody conflict. *J. Am. Acad. Child Psychiatry*, 13:635–647.

Paine, R.S., and Oppé, T.E. (1966), *Neurological Examination of Children*. Clinics in Developmental Medicine, Vols. 20, 21. London: Heinemann, p. 40.

Rutter, M. (1972), Clinical assessment of language disorders in the young child. In: *The Child with Delayed Speech*, ed. M. Rutter and J.A.M. Martin. Clinics in Developmental Medicine, No. 43. London: SIMP/Heinemann.

Solomon, S. (1975), Neurological evaluation. In: *Comprehensive Textbook of Psychiatry*, Vol. 2, ed. A.M. Freedman, H.I. Kaplan, and B.J. Sadock. Baltimore: Williams & Wilkins, pp. 188–212.

Winnicott, D.W. (1971), *Therapeutic Consultation in Child Psychiatry*. New York: Basic Books.

Child Psychiatric Interviewing Techniques

Anthony, E.J., and Bene, E. (1957), A technique for the objective assessment of the child's family relationships. *J. Ment. Sci.*, 103:541–555.

Beiser, H.R. (1979), Formal games in diagnosis and therapy. J. Am. Acad. Child Psychiatry, 18:480–491.

Beiser, H.R. (1962), Psychiatric diagnostic interviews with children. *J. Am. Acad. Child Psychiatry*, 1:652–670.

Bender, L. (1952), *Child Psychiatric Techniques*. Springfield, Ill.: Charles C Thomas, p. 335.

Berger, L.R. (1980), Winnicott squiggle game. *Pediatrics*, 66:921–924.

Conn, J.H. (1939), The play interview: A method of studying children's attitudes. *Am. J. Dis. Child.*, 58:1199–1214.

Cox, A., and Rutter, M. (1976), Diagnostic appraisal and interviewing. In: *Child Psychiatry*, ed. M. Rutter and L. Hersov. Oxford: Blackwell.

Despert, J.L. (1937), Technical approaches used in the study and treatment of emotional problems in children. 5. The playroom. *Psychiatr. Q.*, 11:677–693.

DiLeo, J.H. (1970), *Young Children and Their Drawings*. New York: Brunner/Mazel, p. 386.

DiLeo, J.H. (1973), *Children's Drawings as Diagnostic Aids*. New York: Brunner/Mazel, p. 227.

Felice, M., and Friedman, S.B. (1978), The adolescent as a patient. *J.C.E. Pediatr.*, October, 15–28.

G.A.P. Report No. 38 (1957), The diagnostic process in child psychiatry. New York: Group for the Advancement of Psychiatry, p. 44.

G.A.P. Report No. 87 (1973), From diagnosis to treament: An approach to treatment planning for the emotionally disturbed child. New York: Group for the Advancement of Psychiatry, p. 139.

Goodman, J., and Sours, J. (1967), *The Child Mental Status Examination*. New York: Basic Books, p. 134.

Gubbay, S.S., Ellis, E., Walton, J.N., and Court, S.D.M. (1965), Clumsy children: A study of apraxic and agnosic defects in 21 children. *Brain*, 88:295–312.

Levy, D.M. (1933), Use of play technic as experimental procedure. *Am. J. Orthopsychiatry*, 3:266–277.

Lowe, M. (1975), Trends in the development of representational play in infants from one to three years: An observational study. *J. Child Psychol. Psychiatry*, 16:33–47.

MacCarthy, D. (1974), Communication between children and doctors. *Dev. Med. Child Neurol.*, 16:279–285.

McDonald, P.F. (1965), The psychiatric evaluation of children. *J. Am. Acad. Child Psychiatry*, 4:569–612.

Paine, R.S. and Oppé, T.E. (1966), *Neurological Examination of Children*. Clinics in Developmental Medicine, Vols. 20, 21. London: Heinemann, p. 40.

Reisman, J.M. (1973), *Principles of Psychotherapy with Children*. New York: Wiley.

Rutter, M. (1972), Clinical assessment of language disorders in the young child. In: *The Child with Delayed Speech*, ed. M. Rutter and J.A.M. Martin. Clinics in Developmental Medicine. No. 43. London: SIMP/Heinemann.

Rutter, M., Graham, P., and Yule, W. (1970). *A Neurological Examination: Description*. London: SIMP/Heinemann, pp. 27–39.

Rutter, M., Graham, P., and Yule, W. (1970), *A Neuropsychiatric Study in Childhood*. Clinics in Developmental Medicine, Nos. 35, 36. London: SIMP/Heinemann.

Simmons, J.E. (1974), *Psychiatric Examination of Children*, 2nd Ed. Philadelphia: Lea & Febiger, p. 239.

Werkman, S.C. (1965), The psychiatric diagnostic interview with children. *Am. J. Orthopsychiatry*, 35:764–771.

Winnicott, D.W. (1971), *Therapeutic Consultations in Child Psychiatry*. New York: Basic Books.

Yarrow, L.J. (1960), Interviewing children. In: *Handbook of Research Methods in Child Development*, ed. P.H. Mussen. New York: Wiley, pp. 561–602.

Chapter 20

*DIFFERENTIAL DIAGNOSIS**

From all the information that has been gathered, it should be possible to narrow the possibilities down for a differential diagnosis. The differential diagnosis aims at distinguishing among the various conditions which may have similar symptoms in order to arrive at an accurate diagnosis as a basis for specific treatment and preventive measures, communication, and research.

Difficulties arise in child psychiatry because symptoms, the conditions from which they arise, and the causes of these conditions are not well defined (Zigler and Phillips, 1961). In practice, the term symptom in child psychiatry may mean almost any behavioral manifestation that comes to the attention of the observer. When certain traits, signs, or behaviors are particularly prominent and occur together frequently, conventional labels are commonly applied to define a condition or syndrome; for example, the symptom cluster short attention span, hyperactivity, labile emotions, and clumsiness is conventionally represented by the label attention deficit disorder. These labels, in turn, may imply an etiology, a treatment, or a prognosis. However, in many cases the causes are many, the treatment is untested, and the prognosis is unknown. In the example given, genetic, congenital, traumatic, infective, neo-

*Material for this chapter was drawn largely from my chapter "Differential Diagnosis" in *Basic Handbook of Child Psychiatry*, edited by J.D. Noshpitz, and I gratefully acknowledge the permission of Basic Books, Inc., to use this material.

plastic, metabolic, psychodynamic, and environmental factors may give rise to the same behavioral manifestations. The treatment is also nonspecific, and the prognosis is wide ranging. In many instances, each factor in such a symptom cluster is in itself complex and it interacts with the other factors in the cluster in a complex manner. Finally, the validity of any such grouping will depend ultimately on the accuracy with which each symptom was defined initially.

A second class of difficulties arises because there is no satisfactory or universally accepted classification of diagnostic entities. Many attempts have been made to improve the definition and classification of diagnoses (Feighner et al., 1972; G.A.P., 1966; Rutter et al., 1975; Spitzer and Cantwell, 1980). However, the problem remains unsolved. The classification currently used in the United States is that given in the *Diagnostic and Statistical Manual of the American Psychiatric Association* (DSM-III). The relevant DSM-III categories of disorders that arise during childhood and adolescence are given in Appendix A. (Rutter and Schaffer [1980] have made an excellent critique of DSM-III.)

Yet a third class of difficulties arises because methods of eliciting data are either inadequate or not standardized (Rutter and Schaffer, 1980). This defect leads to a loss of reliability and, consequently, of validity (Rutter and Graham, 1968). Reliability is measured by the degree of agreement between independent, trained observers, and the use of the term reliability here refers to the consistency with which disorders are classified, however unsatisfactory the classification system. Attempts have been made to improve reliability through meticulous and standardized interview structures and rating scales (Chambers, Puig-Antich, and Tabrizi, 1978; Carlson and Cantwell, 1980; Goodman and Sours, 1961; Kovacs and Beck, 1977; McKnew and Cytryn, 1979; Orvashel, Sholomskas, and Weissman, 1980; Petti, 1978; Simmons, 1974; Spitzer et al., 1970; Rutter and Schaffer, 1980). The skill of the observer and the setting in which the observations are made must also be taken into account. Observer bias is particularly troublesome (see Chapter 19). At present there is no universally agreed on method of data collection.

Perhaps a fourth class of difficulties arises from the fact that the same maladaptive behavior may have arisen out of different factors (Rubin et al., 1972), including (1) intrinsic defects or immaturities in the child that render him or her vulnerable to normal demands in the family, school, and society; and/or (2) such factors as deprivation, rejection, hostility, inconsistencies, and bizarre parental behavior acting upon a child at specific stages in development.

The immediate tasks in differential diagnosis are to define as carefully as possible the behavior in question and to assess its significance. This raises the question of normality. Normal behavior is behavior that conforms to the expectations of the majority in a given society at a given time. Normality is not an absolute; it is a function of the prevailing historical, cultural, and social factors. By the same token, disordered behavior in a child is behavior that the majority of adults consider inappropriate either in form, frequency, or intensity in the particular circumstances in which the behavior occurs. In effect, the child psychiatrist is sanctioned by society to make a judgment about normality, much as the judge and the jury are sanctioned by society to make a judgment about guilt and innocence.

Unfortunately, the criteria for such judgments are often nebulous. The reliability of the witnesses, the tolerance of the child, family, school, and community, and the context of the psychiatrist's observations, as well as the psychiatrist's biases and thresholds, must all be taken into account by the psychiatrist in reaching a judgment. Further, as Ross (1974) has pointed out, "behavior that is observed at any point in time represents the end point of the interaction of four variables: genetic constitutional endowment, past learning, the individual's current physiological state, and his current environmental conditions." The practical question then is, Under what conditions does the so-called abnormal behavior appear? For example, even when a definite organic condition, such as psychomotor epilepsy, is present, a seizure may occur only under certain conditions, such as stress, anxiety, fatigue, rage, and excitement.

Assessments of the nature, sources, and conditions under which a problem arises need to be made systematically. As described in Chapter 19, the work-up should include information about the pediatric and psychiatric history, the child's mental status, the parents' and the family's relationships, the school and community environments, and the confirmatory studies, such as the neurological examinations, EEGs, psychological tests, and educational tests. Data from such an exploration should enable a diagnosis to be made.

However, there remain a considerable number of cases in which the data do not fit neatly into the diagnostic categories suggested by the classifications. Indeed, most of the descriptions of syndromes depict a more or less typical or prototypical clinical picture. In practice, most cases either lack all the diagnostic features of a given syndrome or include diagnostic features that are not ordinarily considered part of that syndrome. Further, there appears to be a gradient of exactitude in syndromes, extending from certain clear-cut conditions, such as the Gilles de la Tourette syndrome (Tourette's disorder, 307.23), to increasingly amorphous categories, such as "atypical child" or "borderline child." The more amorphous a category is, of course, the less useful it is. Nonetheless, it may have some limited communication value for clinicians, particularly those in a specific setting. For example, the label borderline might be a useful one for clinicians in a residential treatment center. Those clinicians are working with children whose egos are unstable and whose behaviors are characterized by unpredictability and marked fluctuations. Such children, for example, have immature object relations and poor social relationships. They have temper tantrums during which they are out of contact with reality and act as if they are warding off an attacker; at moments they may even become quite paranoid and regressed. Their behavior is like that of a younger child: when they feel unloved, they will either withdraw or become hostile or aggressive. They need the presence of the love object to maintain their hold on reality; that is, they have a limited "reality span." They are often obsessional and have difficulty in thinking abstractly. The particular usefulness of this clustering under the heading borderline is that it can lead to specific interventions within the residential setting. Sooner or later, however, a resolution of the diagnosis should occur—in this case, perhaps to childhood onset pervasive developmental disorder (299.94) or to atypical pervasive developmental disorder (299.84).

Thus diagnosis is a means, not an end, and differential diagnosis begins with a differentiation of symptoms. In childhood, the range of behavior is wide but not infinite. Most behavior items can be covered in such lists as that given in Appendix B.

When clusters of these behavior items occur with some regularity, they give rise to the so-called syndromes. Besides the small, subtype clusters that constitute the syndromes, larger correlations of symptoms may also occur. For example, in a factor-analysis study by Achenbach (1966), phobias, stomachaches, fearfulness, and pains had a high correlation with one another, constituting a group of so-called internalizing symptoms. Other symptoms found in this group include shyness, worrying, seclusiveness, withdrawal and apathy, headaches, nausea and vomiting, obsessions, and compulsions, crying, and preoccupation with fantasy. In this internalizing group, the number of girls was twice that of boys.

At the other end of the pole, symptoms such as disobedience, stealing, lying, fighting, cruelty, destructiveness, vandalism, firesetting, inadequate guilt feelings, swearing, temper tantrums, showing off, hyperactivity, truancy, and running away constituted a group of so-called externalizing symptoms. Externalizers tended to move often, have poor school performance and a history of psychiatric, school, and police problems. Aggression, in fact, was more poorly controlled in this group. In this externalizing group, the number of boys was twice that of girls. Interestingly, the parents of children in this externalizing group tended to more often have psychiatric and criminal records. The family histories spoke of alcoholism, divorce, neglect, desertion, and illegitimacy.

This categorization, of course, is too global for clinical purposes. Many of the symptoms subsumed under either category may have multiple causes. Such symptoms as daydreaming, impulsiveness, nervous movements, including twitching, frequent dizziness, staring blankly, sudden changes in mood or feelings, sleepwalking, and talking while asleep may have a variety of causes.

Nevertheless, it should be possible to construct an index of differential diagnosis of symptoms in child psychiatry. To illustrate, an introductory partial index follows of just a few of the symptoms or symptom disorders that commonly require a differential diagnosis. A more comprehensive index is in preparation (Lewis, 1982).

SYMPTOMS THAT COMMONLY REQUIRE DIFFERENTIATION

Attention Difficulties: Short Attention Span; Hyperactivity

These terms are usually descriptive rather than truly quantitative. In any case, there is little agreement on what is meant by attention (Taylor, 1980). Short attention span is frequently a result of fatigability, which in turn is a function of the amount of effort the child has to expend to overcome any difficulty he has in discriminating background from foreground or in trying to hold onto more units of data than he can manage. Similarly, so-called hyperactivity is often a form of disorganized motor activity that becomes worse in a 1:30 classroom situation rather than an excess of normal, organized behavior. Anxiety may account for this behavior. However, in addition the child may have signs of clumsiness, extraneous movements, confusions of right and left, front and back, before and after, together with so-called soft neurological signs, particularly asymmetries of reflexes or of fine finger and hand movements. In such instances, attention deficit disorder may be present.

Psychiatric interviews, classroom observations, psychological tests including the Bender gestalt test, neurological examination, and, if necessary, an EEG, will help in deciding among these possibilities.

Bed Wetting

Bed wetting may be maturational, organic, or psychological. When bed wetting is due to a maturational lag, the child characteristically is in Stage 4 NREM sleep when a burst of delta waves occurs; the sleep pattern then changes to Stage 2 or Stage 1, during which micturition occurs (Gastaut and Broughton, 1964). Dreaming during REM sleep may occur subsequently, in which case the bed wetting may be incorporated into the dream. In these cases of maturational lag, there is often a strong family history of bed wetting, with a specific age at which the symptom ceased in the family members. Maturational delay may also occur when the child's parents have had little expectation that the child will achieve bladder control.

Diurnal as well as nocturnal enuresis, and dysuria, may indicate the presence of an organic disorder, such as posterior urethral valve obstruction, a double ureter, or cystitis.

Psychological causes are likely when the child had been successfully toilet trained. After a dry interval, enuresis begins, following psychological stress associated with, say, the birth of a sibling, the loss of a parent, or illness.

Hallucinations

Hallucinations in childhood are almost always pathological, although the literature is confusing (see Rothstein, 1981). The following clinical categories should be considered.

Drug Intoxication. Many drugs are potentially hallucinogenic; they include marijuana, mescaline, psilocybin, LSD, STP, amphetamines, barbiturates, bromides, MAO inhibitors, antihistamines, and atropine-like drugs. At the same time, children and adolescents who take drugs may have an antecedent psychiatric disturbance (Paulsen, 1969). Sometimes the timing and form of the hallucinations suggest the possibility of drug ingestion. Other symptoms of drug ingestion may be present, including drowsiness, paranoid behavior, confusion, restlessness, excitement, violence, dilated pupils, ataxia, dysmetria, tremor, dysarthria, dyskinesia, akathisia, and hypotensive signs. The clinician must ask about drug ingestion.

Urine and blood samples must be tested when drug ingestion is suspected.

Seizure Disorder. Hallucinations, particularly hypnagogic hallucinations, may occur in narcolepsy and other seizure disorders. Hallucinations may be the first symptoms of degeneration following previous encephalitic illness. A neurological examination and an EEG are required.

Metabolic Disorders. The metabolic disorders that may give rise to hallucinations include adrenal cortical hypofunction, thyroid and parathyroid disease, hepatolenticular degeneration, porphyria, beriberi, hypomagnesemia (secondary to prolonged parenteral fluid replacement therapy, diuretic therapy, excess vitamin D intake, or diabetic acidosis). Signs of the primary metabolic disorder are usually present.

Infection. Encephalitis, meningitis, and acute febrile illnesses (especially in young children) may give rise to hallucinations.

Immaturity and Stress. Acute grief reactions following the death of a parent may give rise to hallucinations. Usually these hallucinations are auditory and consist of admonitions and prohibitions attributed to the dead parent.

Hallucinations following severe anxiety may occur when the anxiety overwhelms the child. Young children who are under severe stress and resort to the defense mechanisms of repression, projection, and displacement may also have hallucinations. The hallucinations appear to be part of a regressive phenomenon, in which the distinction between fantasy and reality is temporarily lost. Often the stress is sexual, and the child may have been exposed to too much stimulation. The content of the hallucination may suggest the underlying psychological conflict.

In older children, external conflicts rarely, if ever, give rise to hallucinations. However, if the stress is massive and overwhelms the child, it can lead to profound regression. The circumstances in which this occurs include severe and sudden illness. For example, a previously healthy 15-year-old girl suddenly developed hemolytic uremic syndrome, with acute renal shutdown that necessitated immediate hemodialysis.

While undergoing hemodialysis, the girl began to hallucinate. For another example, an active child who is suddenly immobilized to treat a fractured limb may hallucinate during moments of acute anxiety.

In some instances, severe cultural deprivation, *together* with a disturbed parent-child relationship, may determine the prevalence and the form of the hallucinations. The hallucinations in this setting are said to be localized, orderly, and related to reality, consisting of forbidding voices and overt wish fulfillments (Wilking and Paoli, 1966). Often the hallucinations in this setting are consistent with the superstitions of the parents. The child may appear to be well organized in other ways. However, there is usually evidence of a personality disturbance in the child and psychosis in the parent, suggesting at least the possibility of a genetic or organic component as well as powerful sociocultural influences (Esman, 1962). In fundamentalist sects, a high value is placed on being possessed by the spirit. Hysterically inclined children and youths may lend themselves to this experience and may "hear voices."

Schizophrenia. When hallucinations are more fragmented, incoherent, and bizarre in content, there is a greater likelihood that schizophrenia is present (Bender, 1954). Bodily complaints and paranoid delusions may be associated with the psychosis. The child is often frightened and secretive about the hallucinations. There are usually other signs of a thought disorder, including disordered, illogical thought processes and inappropriate affect. A history of psychiatric disturbance in the family and maternal deprivation during infancy are often present. Sometimes the child presents with delinquent behavior (Lewis, 1975). Psychological tests, particularly projective tests, are indicated.

Language and Speech Dysfunction

The general signs of a language dysfunction include (1) a reduced vocabulary, especially for abstractions, such as feelings, (2) a delay in the acquisition of two-word sentences (usually acquired by 24 months of age), (3) an overuse of concrete nouns and verbs, and (4) an underuse or lack of use of abstract word classes (e.g., adjectives, adverbs, prepositions, articles, and conjunctions), which gives rise to telegraphic or unintelligible speech. Subsequently, some children may also avoid speaking and tend to have "interpreters," who speak for them.

Language dysfunction may arise as a result of a hearing loss, understimulation, mental retardation, a psychosis, a central nervous system impairment, a developmental language disorder (developmental aphasia), or an anatomical defect in any of the apparatuses serving speech. These are the major categories the psychiatrist must consider. In screening for specific conditions within these categories, the minimal requirements are a detailed history, a physical examination, a psychiatric evaluation, and psychological tests. Depending on what condition seems most probable, more specific studies are then required.

Children with a developmental language disorder may have receptive or expressive language disorders. Receptive language disorders are usually characterized by a difficulty in (1) understanding language at one or more of the various stages of decoding (including auditory or visual perception of particular sounds or pictures), (2) integration, (3) storage, and (4) sequence recall.

Children with an expressive language disorder have a normal and appropriate level of understanding language and concepts but have difficulties in articulation and in "getting the words out." Their vocabulary and grammar are usually below age level.

Certain associated speech patterns may reflect the level of integration at which the central nervous system is affected. For example, (1) aphonia may occur when the neuromuscular level is involved, including involvement of such apparatuses as the lips, tongue, larynx, and medulla oblongata, (2) dysarthria may occur when the corticobulbar level is involved, (3) scanning, explosive, and monotonous speech may occur when the cerebellar level is affected, and agnosia (failure to understand symbols) and aphasia (failure to understand the spoken word and/or to speak) may occur when the cerebral level is affected. Dysrhythmias, such as cluttering, stuttering, and/or stammering, and rapid speech, may be exaggerations of normal errors of speech. Idioglossia occurs typically among twins.

Specific language dysfunctions, such as echolalia, idioglossia, and pronoun reversal, may occur in childhood autism and hyperlexia.

Reading Difficulty

Children who have difficulty in learning to read may be suffering from visual or auditory perceptual handicaps, mental retardation, psychological disturbances, maturational lags,

poor teaching, adverse family environments, linguistic problems, or specific reading disabilities. The etiology of a specific
reading disability may include those factors associated with
attention deficit disorders. It is obvious that each of these
factors must be considered and investigated. The work-up
must therefore include tests for hearing and vision, a careful
neurological examination, the Wechsler Intelligence Scale for
Children, the Rorschach and TAT tests, the Bender visual-
motor test, an evaluation of the child, the family, and the
school, and specific reading tests, such as the Wide Range
Achievement Test. Psychiatric interviews alone are rarely
sufficient.

Pure (but by no means simple) developmental dyslexia usually becomes apparent after the first grade. Many of the
children with this problem have to repeat first grade. Clinically, reading is an effort for the child, and he makes many
omissions and guesses. His comprehension is poor. His handwriting is poor, with many rotations, confusions, and transpositions. All-around frustration, anxiety, and anger are almost
inevitable. There are usually no convincing neurological
findings.

The rare syndrome of hyperlexia is occasionally encountered, predominantly in boys (Silberberg and Silberberg, 1967).
Children with hyperlexia are often clumsy, and have a marked
apraxia (an inability to copy simple figures). They also have
some difficulty in comprehension, with an impaired ability to
relate speech sounds to meaning, poor relationships, and such
language disorders as echolalia, idioglossia, and pronoun reversal. These symptoms are also found in childhood autism; in
fact, a common neuropathology, possibly one involving the
parietal lobe, has been postulated for both disorders (Huttenlocher and Huttenlocher, 1973).

Seizure Behavior

A frequent and important differential diagnosis is that
between a paroxysmal epileptic disorder and a conversion
reaction. In a conversion reaction there is rarely any aura, and
consciousness is impaired but not lost. Sequential movements
are uncommon. Loss of bladder or bowel control and tongue
biting do not usually occur. The attack may end suddenly, and
there is no postictal confusion. The EEG is normal.

Breath-holding spells may sometimes be confused with seizures. Children under the age of 6 may hold their breath
during a crying spell, become cyanotic, and then lose con-

sciousness. In epilepsy, the cyanosis follows the seizure. In hysterical adolescents, hyperventilation may given rise to fainting, presenting as a transient loss of consciousness. Actual loss of consciousness, especially if prolonged, suggests epilepsy. Syncope, of course, may precipitate a seizure in an epileptic child.

Sleep Disturbances

Sleep disturbances are primary or secondary. The major primary sleep disorders include somnambulism, nightmares and night terrors, delta wave disturbance with enuresis, narcolepsy, and hypersomnia (Kales and Kales, 1974).

Secondary sleep disturbances are associated with pain, physical discomfort, anxiety, excitement, depression, neurosis (particularly obsessive-compulsive neurosis), and psychosis (including borderline disturbances and schizophrenia).

Sleepwalking, found more often in boys than in girls, usually occurs in Stage 3 or Stage 4 sleep and lasts for a few minutes. There is often some awareness during the episode but usually no memory of the event once the child is awakened.

Children who are sleepwalkers also commonly have night terrors, which consist of intense anxiety, outbursts of screaming and thrashing, rapid heart rate, and deep, rapid breathing. All these phenomena last for a few minutes, but again, the child has little or no memory of the event after he has awakened. Night terrors, like sleepwalking, occur early in Stage 4 sleep. Both conditions have been considered to be arousal disorders, consisting of delayed or impaired arousal out of Stage 3 or Stage 4 sleep, perhaps as a result of delay in maturation (Broughton, 1968).

Spontaneous remission usually occurs as the child grows older. It is comparatively unusual to find any pathognomonic psychopathology in these children. However, of those who remain sleepwalkers during young adulthood, approximately one-third are schizophrenic (Sours et al., 1963).

Unlike children who sleepwalk and who have night terrors, children who have anxiety dreams ("bad dreams") may have psychological problems. Essentially, these easily remembered frightening dreams occur during REM sleep from which the child is easily aroused.

Some adolescents are prone to sudden, irresistible, brief attacks of shallow sleep (narcolepsy), often accompanied by sudden, fleeting attacks of loss of muscle tone (cataplexy). Narcolepsy and cataplexy are especially likely to occur during strong emotional states, such as anger. The child is easily aroused from his sleep and has no postictal confusion. Consciousness is not lost in cataplexy.

Spelling Difficulties

Spelling difficulties are often accompanied by reading difficulties, and when they are there often is a common basic language deficit (Nelson and Warrington, 1974). The work-up then is identical to that for the differential diagnosis of a reading or language difficulty. However, sometimes there is a specific problem unrelated to reading. The causes are virtually unknown in these cases (Frith, 1980).

Stealing

The symptom of stealing may have many causes. Sometimes the symptom is due to a failure in distinguishing between "what's mine" and "what's not mine." That failure in turn may be due to immaturity. If there is also an organic component, the compulsive defenses that are usually prominent in such children will lead to an exaggeration of the "hoarding" tendency of young children. This may prepare the ground for the child, who subsequently feels unloved and ungratified, to then steal to obtain love. If the child is also frustrated and enraged at the ungiving adult, he will steal specifically from that person, representing in part the mixed dependency and hostility he feels toward that person. (Such ambivalence is not uncommon.) When the child's personality development has been considerably distorted, the child may steal because there have been no parental sanctions against stealing. In such cases the child rarely feels guilty.

Indiscriminate, repeated stealing is often a sign of poor impulse control, particularly true in children who have poor parental models, who are deprived, or who live in a subculture in which stealing has other meanings. Sometimes the stealing is an attempt to find a place in and identify oneself with a peer group of equally deprived children who roam and steal.

The child who feels guilty about stealing may steal in such a way that he is very likely to be caught and punished. In such a child, the punishment assuages his feelings of guilt, and his basic (unconscious) motivation for stealing may escape detection.

Stealing may first appear or become aggravated when the

child is under stress; in this sense, it is a regressive phenomenon, much as enuresis is sometimes a regressive phenomenon.

Temper Tantrums

The differentiation of the symptom temper tantrum requires attention to the following clinical points. Temper tantrums that represent motor discharge occur typically in young children and are accompanied by screaming and hand flailing. This motor behavior usually occurs before the child is able to speak.

Children with infantile autism may also have temper tantrums. However, the child with infantile autism will almost certainly be markedly deviant in other ways, whereas the normal infant will not.

Anger and frustration are frequent causes of temper tantrums. When the tantrums give rise to violent and aggressive behavior with destructive components, they become clinical issues. The frustrations may be the normal frustrations encountered in growing up, but they may also be chronic frustrations arising out of a feeling of being unloved or deprived or out of too much stimulation. A search for these sources of frustration is the first step toward solving the problem.

Panic or anxiety may be manifested as temper tantrums (or, in a sense, "terror tantrums"). Usually other signs associated with the cause are present (e.g., decompensating phobic or obsessional symptoms, signs of an attention deficit disorder, or signs of a pervasive developmental disorder).

In some cases, the parents' tolerance level may be too low, leading them to describe an item of their child's behavior as maladaptive when, in fact, the behavior is normal—or at any rate, characteristic of the particular child.

Further, even when the behavior is so severe that it suggests a problem, the behavior may still be adaptive. For example, a child may be appropriately enraged at a frustrating social situation although not mature enough to change the situation. In such a circumstance, the behavior (the rage) is adaptive.

Thought Disorder

The process of thinking has three major clinical dimensions: actual thought content, speed of thinking, and ease of flow. A variation in any of these dimensions may be of such a degree and duration as to constitute a thought disorder (see Chap. 19).

Disordered thought content may take the form of neologisms and idiosyncratic logic, including transductive reasoning (things that are related in time or space are believed to be related causally), difficulty in discerning differences and similarities, difficulty in distinguishing the relevant from the irrelevant, and excessive concreteness.

Disordered speed of thinking may take the form of retardation or a push of thinking and speaking. Disorders of flow may take the form of blocking, muteness, and excessive repetitions of words and sentences.

A child may experience any of these manifestations subjectively as being alien, out of his control, and, sometimes, frightening.

There may be an associated disorder (1) of mood (depression, elation, inappropriateness, or paranoid rage), (2) of behavior (disorganized, regressive, aggressive, withdrawn, or bizarre behavior) or (3) of perception (delusions or hallucinations).

Thought disorder is another example of a cluster of symptoms which is not in itself a diagnosis. The possible causes of the thought disorder cluster may be classified clinically as follows:

1. Psychological (e.g., acute and massive psychological stress reaction)
2. Genetic (e.g., inborn errors of metabolism, such as Hartnup's disease and Kufs' disease, and schizophrenia)
3. Traumatic (e.g., postconcussion syndrome)
4. Infective (e.g., viral encephalitis and brain abscesses)
5. Neoplastic (e.g., brain tumor)
6. Toxic (e.g., amphetamines, steroids, bromism)
7. Deficiencies (e.g., pellagra)
8. Endocrine (e.g., thyrotoxicosis)
9. Multiple (e.g., pervasive developmental disorder, schizophrenia)

The examples just given are illustrative rather than comprehensive. The important point here is to think of the classes of possible causes.

The symptoms, or rather the cluster of symptoms, that constitute a thought disorder should lead to a systematic review of these possible causes. Obviously, some causes will be easily ruled out, while others will immediately appear to be more likely possibilities. Once the field has been narrowed in this way, a more detailed study can lead to a further narrowing. For example, the associated presence of hallucinations (see p. 371) may give a cross-differential diagnosis of specific syndromes.

Violent Behavior

Important psychiatric and neurological factors may give rise to delinquent behavior (Lewis, 1975). The severity of the offense is not a reliable guide. An inability to remember violent acts should raise the possibility of some form of seizure disorder, including psychomotor epilepsy or episodic dyscontrol. A history of birth difficulty, cerebral infection, or head injury may be an important forerunner of an organic condition resulting in poor impulse control or a seizure disorder. Early child abuse, interpersonal difficulties, and behavior problems at school may be important harbingers of later psychotic symptoms, including hallucinations and paranoid thinking associated with violent acts (Lewis et al., 1973). A history of psychiatric disturbance in the family is significant. Living with a psychiatrically impaired relative may be a contributing factor. Antisocial behavior is sometimes the child's way of calling attention to the parent's disturbance. Poor socioeconomic conditions (Cloward and Ohln, 1960; Cohen, 1965; Merton, 1938; Matza, 1964; Shaw and McKay, 1969), as well as psychodynamic factors (Aichorn, 1935; Glueck and Glueck, 1970; Jenkins and Hewitt, 1944; Johnson, 1949; Schmideberg, 1953), must also be evaluated as possible causes of violent delinquent behavior. Depression may be an important component of the child's antisocial behavior. The label sociopathic should be avoided (Lewis and Balla, 1975). Rather, a specific psychiatric and/or neurological diagnosis is required.

THE DIAGNOSTIC FORMULATION

It can be seen that even a differential diagnosis of symptoms or symptom clusters does not lead directly to a diagnosis. Such an approach merely opens up possibilities to be considered. In the final analysis, the actual diagnosis depends on a careful and meticulous assessment of all the available data. The data must be judged in the context of the child's equipment, vulnerabilities, and developmental level, his or her family and his or her other environmental factors, and the circumstances of the evaluation process itself. Actually, an accurate description of an individual child goes beyond the assigned stereotyped diagnostic category. Each child requires an individual diagnostic formulation. It is here that the various metapsychological profiles have their best use (see Appendix C).

REFERENCES

Achenbach, T. (1966), The classification of children's psychiatric symptoms: A factor-analytic study. Psychol. Monog., 80(615).

Aichorn, A. (1935), *Wayward Youth*. New York: Viking.

Bender, L (1954), Imaginary companion: Hallucinations in children. In *A Dynamic Psychopathology of Childhood*. Springfield, Ill.: Charles C Thomas.

Broughton, R.J. (1968), Sleep disorders: Disorders of arousal. *Science*, 159:1070–1078

Carlson, G.A., and Cantwell, D.P. (1980), A survey of depressive symptoms, syndromes and disorders in a child psychiatric population. *J. Child Psychol. Psychiatry*, 21:19–25.

Chambers, W., Puig-Antich, J., and Tabrizi, M.A. (1978), The ongoing development of the Kiddie-SADS (Schedule for Affective Disorders and Schizophrenia for School-Age Children). Paper read at Annual Meeting of American Academy of Child Psychiatry, San Diego, CA.

Cloward, R.A., and Ohln, L.E. (1960), *Delinquency and Opportunity: A Theory of Delinquent Gangs*. New York: Free Press.

Cohen, A.K. (1965), The sociology of the deviant act: Anomie theory and beyond. *Am. Soc. Rev.*, 30:5–14.

Esman, A.H. (1962), Visual hallucinosis in young children. *Psychoanal. Study Child*, 17:334–343.

Feighner, J.P., et al. (1972), Diagnostic criteria for use in psychiatric research. *Arch. Gen. Psychiatry*, 26:57–63.

Frith, U. (1980), Reading and spelling skills. In: *Scientific Foundations of Developmental Psychiatry*, ed. M. Rutter. London: Heinemann, pp. 220–229.

G.A.P. Report No. 62 (1966), Psychopathological disorders in childhood: Theoretical considerations and a proposed classification. New York: Group for the Advancement of Psychiatry.

Gastaut, H., and Broughton, R. (1964), A clinical and polygraphic study of episodic phenomena during sleep. In: *Recent Advances in Biological Psychiatry*, ed. J. Wortis. New York, Plenum, pp. 197–221.

Glueck, S., and Glueck, E. (1970), *Toward a Typology of Juvenile Offenders: Implications for Therapy and Prevention*. New York: Grune & Stratton.

Goodman, J.E., and Sours, J.A. (1967), *The Child Mental Status Examination*. New York: Basic Books.

Huttenlocher, P.R., and Huttenlocher, J. (1973), A study of children with hyperlexia. *Neurology*, 23:1107–1116.

Jenkins, R.L., and Hewitt, L. (1944), Types of personality structure encountered in child guidance clinics. *Am. J. Orthopsychiatry*, 14:84–94.

Johnson, A.A. (1949), Sanctions for superego lacunae of adolescents. In: *Searchlights on Delinquency*, ed. K.R. Eissler. New York: International Universities Press.

Kales, A., and Kales, J. (1974), Sleep disorders. *N. Engl. J. Med.*, 290:487–499.

Kovacs, M., and Beck, A.T. (1977), An empirical approach toward a definition of childhood depression. In: *Depression in Childhood*. ed. J.G. Schulterbrandt and A. Raskin. New York: Raven Press, pp. 21–25.

Lewis, D.O. (1975), Diagnostic evaluation of the juvenile offender. *Child Psychiatry Hum. Dev.*, 6:198–213.

Lewis, D.O., and Balla, D. (1975), "Sociopathy" and its synonyms: Inappropriate diagnoses in child psychiatry. *Am. J. Psychiatry*, 132:720–722.

Lewis, D.O., et al. (1973), Psychotic symptomatology in a juvenile court clinic population. *J. Am. Acad. Child Psychiatry*, 124:660–675.

Lewis, M. (1982), *An Index of Differential Diagnosis in Child Psychiatry* (in preparation).

McKnew, D.H., and Cytryn, L. (1979), Urinary metabolites in chronically depressed children. *J. Am. Acad. Child Psychiatry*, 18:608–615.

Matza, D. (1964), *Delinquency and Drift*. New York: Wiley.

Merton, R.K. (1938), Social structure and anomie. *Am. Soc. Rev.*, 3:672–682.

Nelson, H.E., and Warrington, E.K. (1974), Developmental spelling retardation and its relation to other cognitive abilities. *Br. J. Psychol.*, 65:265–274.

Orvaschel, H., Sholomskas, D., and Weissman, M.M. (1980), The Assessment of Psychopathology and Behavioral Problems in Children: A Review of Scales Suitable for Epidemiological and Clinical Research (1967–1979). Mental Health Service System Reports. Series AN, No. 1., U.S. Department of Health and Human Services, Rockville, MD.

Paulsen, J. (1969), Psychiatric problems. In: *Students and Drugs*, ed. R.H. Blum and Associates. San Francisco: Jossey-Bass.

Petti, T.A. (1978), Depression in hospitalized child psychiatry patients. *J. Am. Acad. Child Psychiatry*, 17:49–59.

Ross, A.O. (1974), *Psychological Disorders of Children*. New York: McGraw-Hill.

Rothstein, A. (1981), Hallucinatory phenomena in childhood. *J. Am. Acad. Child Psychiatry*, 20:623–635.

Rubin, E.Z., et al. (1972), *Cognitive Perceptual Motor Dysfunction*. Detroit: Wayne State University Press.

Rutter, M.L., and Graham, P.J. (1968), The reliability and validity of the psychiatric assessment of the child. I. Interview with the child. *Br. J. Psychiatry*, 114:563–579.

Rutter, M.L., and Schaffer, D. (1980), DSM-III: A step forward or back in terms of the classification of child psychiatric disorders? *J. Am. Acad. Child Psychiatry*, 19:371–394.

Rutter, M.L., Schaffer, D., and Shepherd, M. (1975), *A Multi-Axial Classification of Child Psychiatric Disorders*. Geneva: World Health Organization.

Schmideberg, M. (1953), The psychoanalysis of delinquents. *Am. J. Orthopsychiatry*, 23:13–19.

Shaw, C.R., and McKay, H.D. (1969), *Juvenile Delinquency and Urban Areas*. Chicago: University of Chicago Press.

Silberberg, N.E., and Silberberg, M.D. (1967), Hyperlexia: Specific word recognition skills in young children. *Except. Child.*, 34:41–42.

Simmons, J.E. (1974), *Psychiatric Examination of Children*. Philadelphia, Lea & Febiger.

Sours, J.A., Frumken, P., and Inderwell, R.R. (1963), Somnambulism. *Arch. Gen. Psychiatry*, 9:400–413.

Spitzer, R.L., and Cantwell, D.P. (1980), The DSM-III classification of the psychiatric disorders of infancy, childhood, and adolescence. *J. Am. Acad. Child Psychiatry*, 19:356–370.

Spitzer, R.L., Fleiss, J.C., and Cohen, J. (1970), Psychiatric status schedule: A technique for evaluating psychopathology and impairment in role functioning. *Arch Psychiatry*, 23:41–55.

Taylor, E. (1980), Development of attention. In: *Scientific Foundation of Developmental Psychiatry*, ed. M. Rutter. London: Heinemann, pp. 185–197.

Wilking, V.N., and Paoli, C. (1966), The hallucinatory experience. *J. Am. Acad. Child Psychiatry*, 5:431–440.

Zigler, E., and Phillips, L. (1961), Psychiatric diagnosis: A critique. *J. Abnorm. Soc. Psychol.*, 63:607–618.

Appendix A
DSM-III* Classification of Disorders Usually First Evident in Infancy, Childhood or Adolescence

The disorders described in Appendix A are classified by DSM-III into the following five major groups, based on the predominant area of disturbance: intellectual, behavioral, emotional, physical, and developmental.

I. INTELLECTUAL DISORDERS

Mental Retardation

The essential features are: (1) significantly subaverage general intellectual functioning, (2) resulting in, or associated with, deficits or impairments in adaptive behavior, (3) with onset before the age of 18. The diagnosis is made regardless of whether or not there is a coexisting mental or physical disorder.

317.0 ↓	Mild	IQ 50–70
318.0 ↓	Moderate	IQ 35–49
318.1 ↓	Severe	IQ 20–34
318.2 ↓	Profound	IQ below 20
319.0 ↓	Unspecified	

*More specific information on the differential diagnosis and diagnostic criteria is given in the *Diagnostic and Statistical Manual of Mental Disorders* (Third Edition) (DSM-III), American Psychiatric Association, 1980, from which the material in this appendix was obtained, with permission.

II. BEHAVIORAL DISORDERS (OVERT)

Attention Deficit Disorder

The essential features are signs of developmentally inappropriate inattention and impulsivity.
  314.01 Attention deficit disorder with hyperactivity
  314.00 Attention deficit disorder without hyperactivity
  314.80 Attention deficit disorder, residual type

Conduct Disorder

The essential feature is a repetitive and persistent pattern of conduct in which either the basic rights of others or major age-appropriate societal norms or rules are violated. The conduct is more serious than the ordinary mischief and pranks of children and adolescents.

  312.00 Conduct disorder, undersocialized, aggressive
  312.10 Conduct disorder, undersocialized, nonaggressive
  312.23 Conduct disorder, socialized, aggressive
  312.21 Conduct disorder, socialized, nonaggressive
  312.90 Atypical conduct disorder

III. EMOTIONAL DISORDERS

309.21 Separation Anxiety Disorder

The essential feature is a clinical picture in which the predominant disturbance is excessive anxiety on separation from major attachment figures or from home or other familiar surroundings. When separation occurs, the child may experience anxiety to the point of panic. The reaction is beyond that expected at the child's developmental level.

313.21 Avoidant Disorder of Childhood or Adolescence

The essential feature is a clinical picture in which the predominant disturbance is a persistent and excessive shrinking from contact with strangers of sufficient severity so as to interfere with social functioning in peer relationships, coupled with a clear desire for affection and acceptance, and relationships with family members and other familiar figures that are warm and satisfying.

313.00 Overanxious Disorder

The essential feature is a clinical picture in which the predominant disturbance is excessive worrying and fearful behavior that is not focused on a specific situation or object (such as separation from a parent or entering new social interaction) and that is not due to a recent psychosocial stressor.

313.89 Reactive Attachment Disorder of Infancy

The essential features of this disorder are signs of poor emotional development (lack of age-appropriate signs of social responsiveness, apathetic mood) and physical development (failure to thrive), with onset before 8 months of age, because of lack of adequate caretaking. The disturbance is not due to a physical disorder, mental retardation, or infantile autism. Some severe cases of this disorder have also been called "failure to thrive" or "hospitalism."

313.22 Schizoid Disorder of Childhood or Adolescence

The essential feature is a defect in the capacity to form social relationships that is not due to any other mental disorder, such as pervasive developmental disorder, conduct disorder, undersocialized, nonaggressive, or any psychotic disorder, such as schizophrenia.

313.23 Elective Mutism

The essential feature is continuous refusal to speak in almost all social situations, including at school, despite ability to comprehend spoken language and to speak. These children may communicate via gestures, by nodding or shaking the head, or, in some cases, by monosyllabic or short, monotone utterances.

313.81 Oppositional Disorder

The essential feature is a pattern of disobedient, negativistic, and provocative opposition to authority figures. The diagnosis is not made if there is a pattern in which the basic rights of others or major age-appropriate societal norms or rules are violated, in which case the diagnosis of conduct disorder is made, or if the disturbance is due to another mental disorder, such as schizophrenia or pervasive developmental disorder. If the individual is 18 years or older, the disturbance does not meet the criteria for passive-aggressive personality disorder.

313.82 Identity Disorder

The essential feature is severe subjective distress regarding inability to reconcile aspects of the self into a relatively coherent and acceptable sense of self. There is uncertainty about a variety of issues relating to identity, including long-term goals, career choice, friendship patterns, sexual orientation and behavior, religious identification, moral values, and group loyalties. These symptoms last at least three months and result in impairment in social or occupational (including academic) functioning. The disturbance is not due to another mental disorder, such as affective disorder, schizophrenia, or schizophreniform disorder; and if the individual is 18 years or older, the disturbance does not meet the criteria for borderline personality disorder.

IV. PHYSICAL DISORDERS

307.10 Anorexia Nervosa

The essential features are intense fear of becoming obese, distortion of body image, significant weight loss, refusal to maintain a minimal body weight, and amenorrhea (in females). The disturbance cannot be accounted for by a known physical disorder. (The term anorexia is a misnomer, since loss of appetite is usually rare until late in the illness.)

307.51 Bulimia

The essential features are episodic binge eating accompanied by an awareness that the eating pattern is abnormal, fear of not being able to stop eating voluntarily, and depressed mood and self-deprecating thoughts following the eating binges. The bulimic episodes are not due to anorexia nervosa or any known physical disorder.

307.52 Pica

The essential feature is the persistent eating of a nonnutritive substance. Infants with the disorder typically eat paint, plaster, string, hair, or cloth. Older children may eat animal droppings, sand, bugs, leaves, or pebbles. There is no aversion to food.

307.53 Rumination Disorder of Infancy

The essential feature is repeated regurgitation of food, with weight loss or failure to gain expected weight, developing after a period of normal functioning. Partially digested food is brought up into the mouth without nausea, retching, disgust, or associated gastrointestinal disorder. The food is then ejected from the mouth or chewed and reswallowed. A characteristic position of straining and arching the back with the head held back is observed. Sucking movements of the tongue occur, and the infant gives the impression of gaining considerable satisfaction from the activity.

307.50 Atypical Eating Disorder

This category is a residual category for eating disorders that cannot be adequately classified in any of the previous categories.

307.21 Transient Tic Disorder

The essential features are recurrent, involuntary, repetitive, rapid movements (tics). The movements can be voluntarily suppressed for minutes to hours. The intensity of the symptoms varies over weeks or months. The onset is during childhood or adolescence. The duration is at least one month, but not more than one year.

307.22 Chronic Motor Tic Disorder

The essential features are recurrent, involuntary, repetitive, rapid movements (tics), usually involving no more than three muscle groups at any one time. The movements can be voluntarily suppressed for minutes to hours. The intensity of the symptoms is constant over weeks or months, and the duration is at least one year. Vocal tics occur infrequently. When present, they are not loud, intense or noticeable; frequently they are grunts or other noises caused by thoracic, abdominal, or diaphragmatic contractions.

307.23 Tourette's Disorder

The essential features are recurrent, involuntary, repetitive, rapid movements (tics), including multiple vocal tics. The movements can be voluntarily suppressed for minutes to hours; and the intensity, frequency, and location of the symptoms vary over weeks or months.

307.20 Atypical Tic Disorder

307.30 Atypical Stereotyped Movement Disorders

This category is for conditions such as head banging, rocking, repetitive hand movements consisting of quick, rhythmic, small hand rotations, or repetitive voluntary movements that typically involve the fingers or arms. These disorders are distinguishable from tics in that they consist of voluntary movements and are not spasmodic. Moreover, unlike individuals with a tic disorder, those with these conditions are not distressed by the symptoms and may even appear to derive enjoyment from the repetitive activities. Though bizarre posturing or movements may occur in adults, these conditions are found almost exclusively in children. They are especially prevalent among individuals with mental retardation or pervasive developmental disorders and among children suffering from grossly inadequate social stimulation, but they also occur in the absence of a concurrent mental disorder.

307.00 Stuttering

The essential features are frequent repetitions or prolongations of sounds, syllables, or words or frequent, unusual hesitations and pauses that disrupt the rhythmic flow of speech. The extent of the disturbance varies from situation to situation, and is most severe when there is special pressure to communicate, as during a job interview.

307.60 Functional Enuresis

The essential feature is repeated involuntary voiding of urine during the day or at night, after an age at which continence is expected, that is not due to any physical disorder. The disorder is somewhat arbitrarily defined as involuntary voiding of urine at least twice a month for children between the age of 5 and 6 and once a month for older children.

307.70 Functional Encopresis

The essential feature is repeated voluntary or involuntary passage of feces of normal or near-normal consistency into places not appropriate for that purpose in the individual's own sociocultural setting, not due to any physical disorder. Encopresis is generally referred to as *primary* if it occurs after the child has reached the age of 4 and has not been preceded by fecal incontinence for at least one year and *secondary* if it has been preceded by a period of fecal continence for at least one year. There is no provision for recording the primary-secondary distinction. When the passage of feces in functional encopresis is involuntary rather than deliberate, it is often related to constipation, impaction, or retention with subsequent overflow. In such cases there often is soiling of clothes shortly after bathing because of reflex stimulation.

307.46 Sleepwalking Disorder

The essential features are repeated episodes of a sequence of complex behaviors that frequently, though not always, progress—without full consciousness or later memory of the episode—to leaving bed and walking about. The episode usually occurs between 30 and 200 minutes after onset of sleep (the interval of nonrapid eye movement [NREM] sleep that typically contains EEG delta activity, sleep Stages 3 and 4) and lasts from a few minutes to about a half hour.

307.46 Sleep Terror Disorder

The essential features are repeated episodes of abrupt awakening from sleep, usually beginning with a panicky scream. The episode usually occurs between 30 and 200 minutes (the interval of nonrapid eye movement [NREM] sleep that typically contains EEG delta activity, sleep Stages 3 and 4), and lasts 1 to 10 minutes. This condition has also been called pavor nocturnus.

V. DEVELOPMENTAL DISORDERS

299.0 Infantile Autism

The essential features are a lack of responsiveness to other people (autism), gross impairment in communicative skills, and bizarre responses to various aspects of the environment, all developing within the first 30 months of age. Infantile autism may be associated with known organic conditions, such as maternal rubella or phenylketonuria. In such cases the behavioral syndrome infantile autism should be recorded on Axis I, and the physical disorder on Axis III.

299.00 Infantile autism, full syndrome present
299.01 Infantile autism, residual state

Pervasive Developmental Disorder

The essential features are a profound disturbance in social relations and multiple oddities of behavior, all developing after 30 months of age and before 12 years.

299.90 Childhood onset pervasive developmental disorder, full syndrome present
299.91 Childhood onset pervasive developmental disorder, residual state

299.80 Atypical Pervasive Developmental Disorder

This category should be used for distortions in the development of multiple basic psychological functions that are involved in the development of social skills and language and that cannot be classified under either infantile autism or childhood onset pervasive developmental disorder.

315.00 Developmental Reading Disorder

The essential feature is significant impairment in the development of reading skills not accounted for by chronological age, mental age, or inadequate schooling. "Significant" impairment differs somewhat with age: a 1-to-2 year discrepancy in reading skill for ages 8 to 13 is significant, but it is difficult to specify how great a discrepancy is significant below age 8.

315.10 Developmental Arithmetic Disorder

The essential feature is significant impairment in the development of arithmetic skills not accountable for by chronological age, mental age, or inadequate schooling. The diagnosis can be made only by individually administered IQ tests that yield a level of full-scale IQ, plus a variety of academic achievement tests that include arithmetic subtests.

315.31 Developmental Language Disorder

There are three major types of language disorder: (1) failure to acquire any language, (2) acquired language disability, and (3) delayed language acquisition (developmental language disorder). Failure to acquire any language is rare and is virtually always a result of profound mental retardation. Acquired language disabilities are usually the result of trauma or neurological disorder. Developmental language disorder, the most common type of language disorder, involves difficulty in comprehending oral language (receptive type) or in expressing verbal language (expressive type). (Although these two subtypes are described separately, no digit is available for indicating them separately.) These conditions have each been referred to as developmental aphasia, but the term is technically not correct, since aphasia means loss of language that has already been acquired.

315.39 Developmental Articulation Disorder

The essential feature is failure to develop consistent articulations of the later-acquired speech sounds, such as r, sh, th, f, z, l, or ch. Omissions occur or substitutions are made for these sounds, giving the impression of baby talk. Vocabulary and grammatical structures are within age norms. This disorder encompasses a range from the misarticulation of one sound (e.g., l or n, as in lalling) to mispronouncing several sounds (e.g., s, z, sh, ch, as in lisping).

315.50 Mixed Specific Developmental Disorder

The category should be used when there is more than one specific developmental disorder but none is predominant. It is common for a delay in the development of one skill (e.g., reading, arithmetic, or language) to be associated with delays in other skills. The mixed specific developmental disorder category should be used when the mixture of delayed skills is such that all skills are impaired to relatively the same degree. When the skills are impaired to varying degrees, multiple diagnoses should be recorded, the skill most seriously impaired being recorded first.

315.90 Atypical Specific Developmental Disorder

This is a residual category for use when there is a specific developmental disorder not covered by any of the previous specific categories.

COMMENTS

1. Gender identity disorders are classified with the other psychosexual disorders.
2. Disorders classified elsewhere in DSM-III may also be appropriate for children and adolescents.
3. A diagnosis of unspecified mental disorder may be used for those problems that are not subsumed within a specific DSM-III category (e.g., precocious sexual activity and aggressive behavior).
4. There is no separate category for child abuse in DSM-III.
5. A multiaxial classification should be used (see Table 1).
6. The decision tree shown in Table 2 may be helpful.

Table 1.   MULTIAXIAL EVALUATION

Axis I	Clinical Syndromes, Conditions Not Attributable to a Mental Disorder That Are a Focus of Attention or Treatment, and Additional Codes
Axis II	Personality Disorders and Specific Developmental Disorders
Axis III	Physical Disorders and Conditions

Axes IV and V are available for use in special clinical and research settings and provide information supplementing the official DSM-III diagnoses (Axes I, II, and III) that may be useful for planning treatment and predicting outcome:

Axis IV	Severity of Psychosocial Stressors
Axis V	Highest Level of Adaptive Functioning Past Year

Table 2. DISORDERS USUALLY FIRST EVIDENT IN INFANCY, CHILDHOOD, OR ADOLESCENCE*

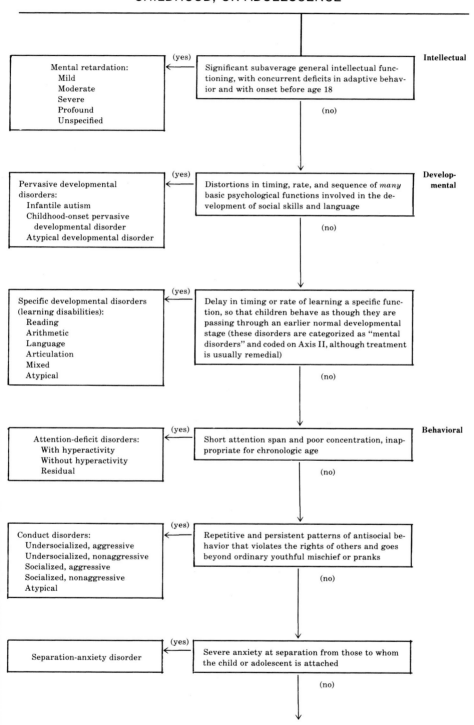

Intellectual

(yes) Mental retardation:
Mild
Moderate
Severe
Profound
Unspecified

← Significant subaverage general intellectual functioning, with concurrent deficits in adaptive behavior and with onset before age 18

(no)

Developmental

(yes) Pervasive developmental disorders:
Infantile autism
Childhood-onset pervasive developmental disorder
Atypical developmental disorder

← Distortions in timing, rate, and sequence of *many* basic psychological functions involved in the development of social skills and language

(no)

(yes) Specific developmental disorders (learning disabilities):
Reading
Arithmetic
Language
Articulation
Mixed
Atypical

← Delay in timing or rate of learning a specific function, so that children behave as though they are passing through an earlier normal developmental stage (these disorders are categorized as "mental disorders" and coded on Axis II, although treatment is usually remedial)

(no)

Behavioral

(yes) Attention-deficit disorders:
With hyperactivity
Without hyperactivity
Residual

← Short attention span and poor concentration, inappropriate for chronologic age

(no)

(yes) Conduct disorders:
Undersocialized, aggressive
Undersocialized, nonaggressive
Socialized, aggressive
Socialized, nonaggressive
Atypical

← Repetitive and persistent patterns of antisocial behavior that violates the rights of others and goes beyond ordinary youthful mischief or pranks

(no)

(yes) Separation-anxiety disorder

← Severe anxiety at separation from those to whom the child or adolescent is attached

(no)

393

Table 2.   DISORDERS USUALLY FIRST EVIDENT IN INFANCY, CHILDHOOD, OR ADOLESCENCE* (Continued)

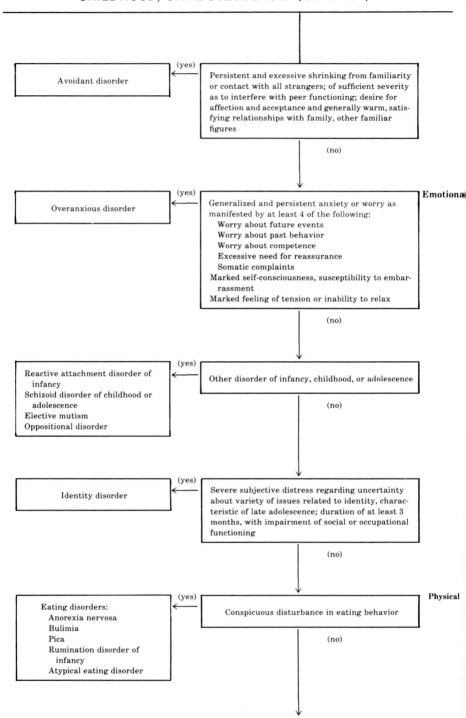

Table 2. DISORDERS USUALLY FIRST EVIDENT IN INFANCY, CHILDHOOD, OR ADOLESCENCE* (Continued)

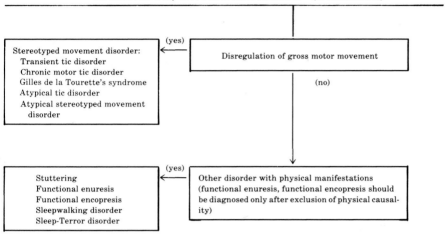

Stereotyped movement disorder: (yes) ← Disregulation of gross motor movement
  Transient tic disorder
  Chronic motor tic disorder
  Gilles de la Tourette's syndrome   (no)
  Atypical tic disorder
  Atypical stereotyped movement
    disorder

Stuttering (yes) ← Other disorder with physical manifestations
Functional enuresis   (functional enuresis, functional encopresis should
Functional encopresis   be diagnosed only after exclusion of physical causal-
Sleepwalking disorder   ity)
Sleep-Terror disorder

N.B. Any appropriate adult diagnosis can be used for diagnosing a child.

* Reprinted with permission from Janicak, P.G., and Andriukaitis, S.M. (1980), DSM-III: Seeing the Forest Through the Trees. *Psychiatric Annals*, 10:284–297.

Appendix B
Child Behavior Checklist for Ages 4–16

CHILD'S NAME

PARENT'S TYPE OF WORK (Please be specific—for example: auto mechanic, high school teacher, homemaker, laborer, lathe operator, shoe salesman, army sergeant, even if parent does not live with child.)

SEX	AGE	RACE
☐ Boy		
☐ Girl		

FATHER'S TYPE OF WORK: _____

MOTHER'S TYPE OF WORK: _____

TODAY'S DATE

Mo. _____ Day _____ Yr. _____

CHILD'S BIRTHDATE

Mo. _____ Day _____ Yr. _____

THIS FORM FILLED OUT BY:

☐ Mother
☐ Father
☐ Other (Specify)

I. Please list the sports your child most likes to take part in. For example: swimming, baseball, skating, skate boarding, bike riding, fishing, etc.

☐ None

Compared to other children of the same age, about how much time does he/she spend in each?

Compared to other children of the same age, how well does he/she do each one?

	Don't Know	Less Than Average	Average	More Than Average	Don't Know	Below Average	Average	Above Average
a. _____	☐	☐	☐	☐	☐	☐	☐	☐
b. _____	☐	☐	☐	☐	☐	☐	☐	☐
c. _____	☐	☐	☐	☐	☐	☐	☐	☐

II. Please list your child's favorite hobbies, activities, and games, other than sports. For example: stamps, dolls, books, piano, crafts, singing, etc. (Do not include T.V.)

☐ None

Compared to other children of the same age, about how much time does he/she spend in each?

Compared to other children of the same age, how well does he/she do each one?

	Don't Know	Less Than Average	Average	More Than Average	Don't Know	Below Average	Average	Above Average
a. _____	☐	☐	☐	☐	☐	☐	☐	☐
b. _____	☐	☐	☐	☐	☐	☐	☐	☐
c. _____	☐	☐	☐	☐	☐	☐	☐	☐

III. Please list any organizations, clubs, teams, or groups your child belongs to.

☐ None

Compared to other children of the same age, how active is he/she in each?

	Don't Know	Less Active	Average	More Active
a. _____	☐	☐	☐	☐
b. _____	☐	☐	☐	☐
c. _____	☐	☐	☐	☐

IV. Please list any jobs or chores your child has. For example: paper route, babysitting, making bed, etc.

☐ None

Compared to other children of the same age, how well does he/she carry them out?

	Don't Know	Below Average	Average	Above Average
a. _____	☐	☐	☐	☐
b. _____	☐	☐	☐	☐
c. _____	☐	☐	☐	☐

Reprinted with permission of T. Achenbach, University of Vermont, Burlington, VT 05405

V. **1. About how many close friends does your child have?** ☐ None ☐ 1 ☐ 2 or 3 ☐ 4 or more

2. About how many times a week does your child do things with them? ☐ less than 1 ☐ 1 or 2 ☐ 3 or more

VI. Compared to other children of his/her age, how well does your child:

		Worse	About the same	Better
a.	Get along with his/her brothers & sisters?	☐	☐	☐
b.	Get along with other children?	☐	☐	☐
c.	Behave with his/her parents?	☐	☐	☐
d.	Play and work by himself/herself?	☐	☐	☐

VII. **1. Current school performance—for children aged 6 and older:**

☐ Does not go to school

	Failing	Below average	Average	Above average
a. Reading or English	☐	☐	☐	☐
b. Writing	☐	☐	☐	☐
c. Arithmetic or Math	☐	☐	☐	☐
d. Spelling	☐	☐	☐	☐
Other academic subjects: for example: history, science, foreign language, geography. e. _____	☐	☐	☐	☐
f. _____	☐	☐	☐	☐
g. _____	☐	☐	☐	☐

2. Is your child in a special class?

☐ No ☐ Yes—what kind?

3. Has your child ever repeated a grade?

☐ No ☐ Yes—grade and reason

4. Has your child had any academic or other problems in school?

☐ No ☐ Yes—please describe

When did these problems start and end?

VIII. Below is a list of items that describe children. For each item that describes your child *now* or *within the past 6 months*, please circle the *2* if the item is *very true* or *often true* of your child. Circle the *1* if the item is *somewhat* or *sometimes true* of your child. If the item is *not true* of your child, circle the *0*.

0 1 2	1.	Acts too young for his/her age	16	0 1 2	31.	Fears he/she might think or do something bad	
0 1 2	2.	Allergy (describe): _____					
		_____		n 1 2	32.	Feels he/she has to be perfect	
				0 1 2	33.	Feels or complains that no one loves him/her	
0 1 2	3.	Argues a lot					
0 1 2	4.	Asthma		0 1 2	34.	Feels others are out to get him/her	
				0 1 2	35.	Feels worthless or inferior	50
0 1 2	5.	Behaves like opposite sex	20				
0 1 2	6.	Bowel movements outside toilet		0 1 2	36.	Gets hurt a lot, accident-prone	
				0 1 2	37.	Gets in many fights	
0 1 2	7.	Bragging, boasting					
0 1 2	8.	Can't concentrate, can't pay attention for long		0 1 2	38.	Gets teased a lot	
				0 1 2	39.	Hangs around with children who get in trouble	
0 1 2	9.	Can't get his/her mind off certain thoughts; obsessions (describe): _____		0 1 2	40.	Hears things that aren't there (describe):	
						_____	55
0 1 2	10.	Can't sit still, restless, or hyperactive	25	0 1 2	41.	Impulsive or acts without thinking	
0 1 2	11.	Clings to adults or too dependent					
0 1 2	12.	Complains of loneliness		0 1 2	42.	Likes to be alone	
				0 1 2	43.	Lying or cheating	
0 1 2	13.	Confused or seems to be in a fog					
0 1 2	14.	Cries a lot		0 1 2	44.	Bites fingernails	
				0 1 2	45.	Nervous, highstrung, or tense	60
0 1 2	15.	Cruel to animals	30				
0 1 2	16.	Cruelty, bullying, or meanness to others		0 1 2	46.	Nervous movements or twitching (describe):	
						_____	
0 1 2	17.	Day-dreams or gets lost in his/her thoughts					
0 1 2	18.	Deliberately harms self or attempts suicide		0 1 2	47.	Nightmares	
0 1 2	19.	Demands a lot of attention		0 1 2	48.	Not liked by other children	
0 1 2	20.	Destroys his/her own things	35	0 1 2	49.	Constipated, doesn't move bowels	
0 1 2	21.	Destroys things belonging to his/her family or other children		0 1 2	50.	Too fearful or anxious	65
				0 1 2	51.	Feels dizzy	
0 1 2	22.	Disobedient at home					
				0 1 2	52.	Feels too guilty	
0 1 2	23.	Disobedient at school		0 1 2	53.	Overeating	
0 1 2	24.	Doesn't eat well					
				0 1 2	54.	Overtired	
0 1 2	25.	Doesn't get along with other children	40	0 1 2	55.	Overweight	70
0 1 2	26.	Doesn't seem to feel guilty after misbehaving					
				0 1 2	56.	Physical problems without known medical cause:	
0 1 2	27.	Easily jealous		0 1 2	a.	Aches or pains	
0 1 2	28.	Eats or drinks things that are not food (describe): _____		0 1 2	b.	Headaches	
				0 1 2	c.	Nausea, feels sick	
		_____		0 1 2	d.	Problems with eyes (describe):	
0 1 2	29.	Fears certain animals, situations, or places, other than school (describe): _____		0 1 2	e.	Rashes or other skin problems	75
				0 1 2	f.	Stomachaches or cramps	
		_____		0 1 2	g.	Vomiting, throwing up	
0 1 2	30.	Fears going to school	45	0 1 2	h.	Other (describe): _____	
						_____	

Please see other side

0 1 2	57.	Physically attacks people	0 1 2	84.	Strange behavior (describe): _____
0 1 2	58.	Picks nose, skin, or other parts of body (describe): _____			
		_____ 80	0 1 2	85.	Strange ideas (describe):
0 1 2	59.	Plays with own sex parts in public 16			_____
0 1 2	60.	Plays with own sex parts too much	0 1 2	86.	Stubborn, sullen, or irritable
0 1 2	61.	Poor school work	0 1 2	87.	Sudden changes in mood or feelings
0 1 2	62.	Poorly coordinated or clumsy	0 1 2	88.	Sulks a lot 45
0 1 2	63.	Prefers playing with older children 20	0 1 2	89.	Suspicious
0 1 2	64.	Prefers playing with younger children	0 1 2	90.	Swearing or obscene language
0 1 2	65.	Refuses to talk	0 1 2	91.	Talks about killing self
0 1 2	66.	Repeats certain acts over and over; compulsions (describe): _____	0 1 2	92.	Talks or walks in sleep (describe):
					_____
			0 1 2	93.	Talks too much 50
0 1 2	67.	Runs away from home	0 1 2	94.	Teases a lot
0 1 2	68.	Screams a lot 25			
			0 1 2	95.	Temper tantrums or hot temper
0 1 2	69.	Secretive, keeps things to self	0 1 2	96.	Thinks about sex too much
0 1 2	70.	Sees things that aren't there (describe):			
			0 1 2	97.	Threatens people
		_____	0 1 2	98.	Thumb-sucking 55
		_____	0 1 2	99.	Too concerned with neatness or cleanliness
0 1 2	71.	Self-conscious or easily embarrassed	0 1 2	100.	Trouble sleeping (describe):
0 1 2	72.	Sets fires			_____
0 1 2	73.	Sexual problems (describe):	0 1 2	101.	Truancy, skips school
			0 1 2	102.	Underactive, slow moving, or lacks energy
			0 1 2	103.	Unhappy, sad, or depressed 60
		_____ 30	0 1 2	104.	Unusually loud
0 1 2	74.	Showing off or clowning			
			0 1 2	105.	Uses alcohol or drugs (describe):
0 1 2	75.	Shy or timid			
0 1 2	76.	Sleeps less than most children	0 1 2	106.	Vandalism
0 1 2	77.	Sleeps more than most children during day and/or night (describe): _____	0 1 2	107.	Wets self during the day
			0 1 2	108.	Wets the bed 65
0 1 2	78.	Smears or plays with bowel movements 35	0 1 2	109.	Whining
			0 1 2	110.	Wishes to be of opposite sex
0 1 2	79.	Speech problem (describe): _____	0 1 2	111.	Withdrawn, doesn't get involved with others
			0 1 2	112.	Worrying
0 1 2	80.	Stares blankly	0 1 2	113.	Please write in any problems your child has that were not listed above:
0 1 2	81.	Steals at home			
0 1 2	82.	Steals outside the home	0 1 2		_____ 70
0 1 2	83.	Stores up things he/she doesn't need (describe): 40	0 1 2		_____
			0 1 2		_____

PLEASE BE SURE YOU HAVE ANSWERED ALL ITEMS.　　　　UNDERLINE ANY YOU ARE CONCERNED ABOUT.

Appendix C
The Developmental Profile

In 1945, Anna Freud pointed out the hazard of making assumptions on the basis of manifest childhood symptomatology. She directed attention instead to the child's development and the need to assess those factors that might threaten that development (A. Freud, 1945). In 1962, she began to formulate a psychoanalytic "profile of development" (A. Freud, 1962). Part of this profile was subsequently elaborated in her "Concept of Developmental Lines" (A. Freud, 1963). Two years later, her *Outline of the Developmental Profile* was published (A. Freud, 1965).

The purposes of the profile are to assess the development of the child as a basis for deciding on the indication for child psychoanalysis and to assess the child's readiness for certain experiences, such as entering nursery school. In practice, both kinds of assessments are usually made on much simpler information.

In its general form, the profile consists of a number of headings under which data can be organized (see *General Child Metapsychological Profile*, p. 402). It attempts to combine clinical observations with metapsychological considerations. Over the years, this general profile has been elaborated and modified into profiles for different developmental periods: a baby profile (W.E. Freud, 1967), a latency profile (Meers, 1966), the Adolescent Profile (Laufer, 1965), and a profile for adulthood (A. Freud et al., 1965). Within these categories, the profile has been applied to the study of borderline and psychotic children, blind children, and children with impulse character disorders (see *References* pp. 402–403).

The major differences between the general profile and the baby profile, besides the obvious detailed description of the pregnancy, labor and perinatal period, are that the baby profile provides opportunities to describe the mother and father, and aspects of the infant's behavior under various conditions. The aims of the baby profile are to (1) permit thinking metapsychologically about the infant, (2) to convey a global, overall picture of the infant's personality, (3) to point to phenomena that might otherwise be overlooked, and (4) to provide a systematic schema for monitoring normal development and early recognition of pathology.

The major differences in the Adolescent Profile are in its elaboration of ego development, particularly in regard to defenses, affects, and identifications. Special attention is also given to superego development and the development of the total personality.

Although the literature on the profile has grown (see *References*, p. 402), most of the work on the profile has been confined to the Hampstead Child Therapy Clinic in London. Few other centers use the profile in a systematic way. Indeed, the profile is now used almost exclusively by only a small number of the relatively few child psychoanalysts, each of whom sees only a few children in psychoanalysis.

Perhaps part of the reason for this limited application is that the profile is only as good as the experience of the investigator and is sometimes time-consuming to use. Further, the profile is not standardized within a given setting, much less from institution to institution. There are no criteria or units for measurement, and categories within the profile are at different levels of abstraction and inference. Nevertheless, it is reproduced here since it is one of the few attempts to provide an in-depth picture of an individual child, a picture that goes beyond the diagnostic level.

GENERAL CHILD METAPSYCHOLOGICAL PROFILE

   I. Reason for referral
  II. Description of child
 III. Pediatric history, including family, personal, developmental, social, and history of previous illnesses
 IV. Environmental influences
  V. Assessments of development
     A. Drives
        1. Libido
           a. Level and dominance of phase development
           b. Distribution to self, object
           c. Level, quality, and dominance of object libido

2. Aggression
   a. Quantity
   b. Quality; i.e., correspondence with libido development
   c. Direction (self; object world)
B. Ego and superego
   a. Ego functions—perception, memory, motility, reality testing, synthesis, speech, secondary process
   b. Defense organization—against which drive? age adequate? balance? effectiveness? dependence on object world?
   c. Secondary interference of defense activity with ego achievements
   d. Consider developmental lines here (see Chap. 7)
VI. Genetic assessments (regression and fixation points)
   a. By manifest behavior
   b. By fantasy activity
   c. By symptomatology
VII. Dynamic and structural assessments
   a. External (fear)
   b. Internalized (guilt)
   c. Internal conflicts (unsolved ambivalence, activity vs. passivity, masculinity vs. passivity, etc.)
   Assess:
   i. Level of maturity (relative independence)
   ii. Severity of disturbance
   iii. Intensity of therapy needed for alleviation or removal of the disturbance
VIII. Assessment of some general characteristics
   a. Frustration tolerance
   b. Sublimation potential
   c. Overall attitude to anxiety (retreat or mastery)
   d. Progressive vs. developmental forces
IX. Diagnosis
   a. Variations of normality
   b. Transitory symptoms as by-products of developmental strain
   c. Permanent drive regression and fixation → neurotic conflicts → infantile neuroses and character disorders
   d. Drive regression and ego and superego regression → infantilisms, borderline, delinquent, or psychotic disturbances

e. Primary deficiencies of an organic nature, or early deprivations that distort development and structuralization → retarded, defective, and nontypical personalities

f. Destructive processes at work (organic, toxic, psychic—known or unknown)

REFERENCES

Normality

Diagnostic Profile

Freud, A. (1962), Assessment of childhood disturbances. *Psychoanal. Study Child*, 17:149–158.

Freud, A. (1963), The concept of developmental lines. *Psychoanal. Study Child*, 18:245–265.

Freud, A. (1965), *Normality and Pathology in Childhood*. New York: International Universities Press.

Nagera,* H. (1963), The developmental profile: Notes on some practical considerations regarding its use. *Psychoanal. Study Child*, 18:511–540.

Babies

Freud, W.E. (1967), Assessment of early infancy. *Psychoanal. Study Child*, 22:216–238.

Latency

Meers, D.R., (1966), A diagnostic profile of psychopathology in a latency child. *Psychoanal. Study Child*, 21:483–526.

Adolescents

Laufer, M. (1965), Assessment of adolescent disturbances. *Psychoanal. Study Child*, 20:99–123.

Adults

Freud, A., Nagera, H., and Freud, W.E. (1965), Metapsychological assessment of the adult personality. *Psychoanal. Study Child*, 20:9–41.

Pathology

Blind Children

Burlington, D. (1975), Special problems of blind infants. Blind Baby Profile. *Psychoanal. Study Child*, 30:3–14.

Colonna, A. (1968), Discussion (The re-education of a retarded blind child.) *Psychoanal. Study Child*, 23:386–390.

Nagera, H., and Colonna, A. (1965), Aspects of the contribution of sight to ego and drive development: A comparison of the development of some blind and sighted children. *Psychoanal. Study Child*, 20:267–287.

---

* First published case.

Impulsive Psychopathological Character

Michaels, J.J., and Stiver, I.P. (1965), The impulsive psychopathic character according to the Diagnostic Profile. *Psychoanal. Study Child*, 20:124–141.

Psychotic Children (4), aged 7 to 10

Thomas, R., et al. (1966), Comments on some aspects of self and object representation in a group of psychotic children: An application of Anna Freud's Diagnostic Profile. *Psychoanal. Study Child*, 21:527–580.

Borderline Twin, aged 14

Maenchen, A. (1968), Object cathexis in a borderline twin. *Psychoanal. Study Child*, 23:438–456.

Borderline States

Frijling-Schreuder, E.C.M. (1969), Borderline states in children. *Psychoanal. Study Child*, 24:307–327.

Epilog

RESEARCH, DEVELOPMENT, AND PSYCHOPATHOLOGY: RECENT TRENDS

In this epilog we will attempt to highlight briefly a few of the questions that today challenge investigators in the growing fields of developmental psychiatry and developmental psychopathology.

CONTINUITY

Developmentalists have held on with great tenacity to the idea that there is an inherent continuity of development from the conceptus through to old age and death, and that this continuity is all-encompassing. The concept of continuity is implied, for example, when psychoanalysts talk about transference and the compulsion to repeat in psychoanalysis (S. Freud, 1920).

Recent observations, however, have suggested that perhaps continuity is not as all-encompassing as was once believed, and that there may be certain discontinuities. Kagan (1979), for example, has noted that the enhancement of memory between 8 and 12 months of age and the shift from a perceptual mode to a symbolic-linguistic mode at about 17 months may be related more to maturation of special areas in the central nervous system than to the mother-child bond. The significance of this, according to Kagan, is that the experiences of the average infant with his or her parents might not, after all, have any long-lasting, cumulative effects. The argument is an important one, since it suggests, among other things, that the present is as important as the past. It also suggests an almost serendipitous, discontinuous emergence of new functions unrelated, as it were, to past events, that adds to the generous plasticity of the neonate and young infant. This plasticity allows for great leeway in early child-rearing and, in the end, provides further opportunity for later development to supersede previous experiences. Kagan (1978; Kagan, et al., 1978) once went so far as to make the startling statement that "there is little support for the view that the behavior of the 1- or 2-year-old provides a clear picture of the adult behavior profile. Differences among infants in activity, irritability and affectivity do not predict profiles during later childhood;" and more specifically, "Neither maternal behavior nor the child's psychological profile during the first three years of life seems to be related in any serious way to future intellectual talent, after the effects of the child's social class are taken into account." This is an extreme view, however, and extrapolations beyond intellectual capacity, in any case, are not justified.

INFANTILE AMNESIA

Few of us remember much, if anything, from our first or second year of life. Psychoanalysis has suggested the concept of infantile amnesia to account for this phenomenon, with the expectation that repressed memories will be recovered during analysis. An alternative hypothesis has now been suggested, however, by studies in cognitive development. The observed behavior may now be understood in part as the result of new cognitive schemata superseding, and therefore obliterating, previous schemata. One further extension of this newer concept is the idea that what we have previously thought of as transferences from early periods instead may be merely reconstructions of that earlier time. Piaget, for example, has commented that we reconstruct the past as a function of the present and that there may be no such thing as pure memories, i.e., all memories of early childhood, to a greater or lesser extent, may be "created" (reconstructed) from later material, with inferences and fantasies interwoven. Piaget once gave a fascinating example from his own memories of early childhood (Bringuier, 1980):

"... I have a childhood memory of my own that would be absolutely splendid if it were authentic, because it goes back to an age when one doesn't usually have memories of childhood. I was still in a baby carriage, taken out by a nurse, and she took me down the Champs-Élysées, near the Rond-Point. I was the object of an attempted kidnapping. Someone tried to grab me out of the buggy. The straps held me in, and the nurse scuffled with the man, who scratched her forehead; something worse might have happened if a policeman hadn't come by just then. I can see him now as if it were yesterday— that was when they wore the little cape that comes down to here (he motions with his hand) and carried a little white stick, and all that, and the man fled. That's the story. As a child I had the glorious memory of having been the object of an attempted kidnapping. Then—I must have been about fifteen—my parents received a letter from the nurse, saying that she had just converted and wanted to confess all her sins, and that she had invented the kidnapping story herself, that she had scratched her own forehead, and that she now offered to return the watch she'd been given in recognition of her courage. In other words, there wasn't an iota of truth in the memory. And I have a very vivid memory of the experience, even today. I can tell you just where it happened on Champs-Élysées, and I can still see the whole thing."

This focus on the present, of course, is not to be construed as a discounting of the past; it merely serves to remind us, first, that there is a present during which development continues, and second, that although developmental processes may begin with genetic coding, the phenotypic expression is continuously modulated by interactions with the environment at each stage of development (Eisenberg, 1977). For example, environmental variables may determine which identical twin develops schizophrenia (Kety, 1976), which children with neurologic deficits at 1 year of age subsequently will show signs of an attention deficit disorder (Rutter, et al., 1970), or which child who experiences a separation from parents subsequently will show a disturbance (Rutter, 1972a). Even the temperament of the child does not remain fixed, but varies with the successive environments in which he or she develops (Chess, 1978; Graham, et al., 1973). In short, nowadays we attempt to see the child in his or her biologic and social context as well as intrapsychically, and to see this whole within a developmental frame of reference.

TRANSITIONAL OBJECT

What is the clinical significance of the so-called transitional object? Recently, Sherman and her co-workers at Cornell University performed a study using data collected from parents of 171 normal children between 9 and 13 years of age from the middle to upper socioeconomic class. (Sherman, et al., 1981). Briefly, their study did not substantiate earlier theoretic formulations on the use of treasured objects in relation to psychologic health or illness. In fact, they documented no significant differences between those children who were attached to a treasured object and those who were not, or between those children who continue to use a soft object after age 9 and those who never had a treasured object. This finding is interesting for two reasons: It underscores the necessity of testing a clinical hypothesis with scientific method (in this case an epidemiologic study) and highlights again "the diversity and richness of individual experience that falls within that larger category called 'normal'" (p. 383). We need studies that establish what is normal behavior in a child; at the same time we also need reliable methods. A recent study by Nye (1982) of 199 first-year psychology students first found that 62% said that they had been attached to a special, soft object during childhood. When 80 mothers of the students were asked the same question, however, nearly a quarter of the mothers' answers did not agree with those of their sons or daughters. Moreover, nearly one fifth of the students disagreed with their own answers 1 year later. The study clearly showed that retrospective evidence about attachment to objects is unreliable.

FIXATION

Is there such a thing as pure fixation? Findings from cognitive-developmental research now suggest that each later stage of development supersedes all earlier stages and that constructs developed at a given stage appear to become an integral part of the qualitatively new constructs that follow in an invariant sequence.

Further, we must look at the biologic component of such phenomena as phobias, as well as their intrapsychic and social components. For example, Donald Klein recently postulated that some agoraphobic adult patients suffered from a disruption of biologic processes that regulate separation anxiety. During childhood, these patients experienced panic and severe clinging, dependent behavior associated with separation. Both propranolol and imipramine appear to block the unpredictable and spontaneous attacks, apparently associated with an outpouring of catecholamines, in such adults. Consequently, imipramine was used in children with severe separation anxiety, e.g., "school phobia," with some startling, if transient, success

(Gittleman-Klein and Klein, 1971, 1973). This biologic component is now an important part of our new understanding of severe phobias in children, which are beginning to be viewed now from the multidisciplinary perspectives of developmental psychopathology.

DREAMS, MIND, AND BODY

The neurobiology of dreaming, particularly the work of Hobson and McCarley at Harvard, similarly seems to throw new light or, at any rate, raises new questions on the nature of dreams. Essentially, Hobson and McCarley (1977) postulate that the giant neurons of the pontine reticular formation, the so-called frontal gigantocellular field (FTG) neurons, fire off during the desynchronized sleep state (D sleep) and bombard the forebrain, which then must make sense of the messages received, resulting in the "dreamy" quality of dreams. This FTG cell activity increases just before a REM period and peaks during REM sleep. The FTG cell activity also activates cells in other parts of the brain, including the visual centers and the vestibular system.

One important aspect of these findings and theory is that a new dimension is added to our understanding of dreaming, if not to our understanding of the role of the forebrain in a particular dream. What this may mean is that an important set of developmental and physiologic variables may have to be taken into account in any comprehensive account of the meaning of a dream. Although this does not invalidate the psychoanalytic theory of manifest and latent dream content and intermediate dream work, it does considerably broaden the basis for our understanding and opens up new possibilities for dream exploration.

FETAL PERIOD

A great deal of evidence now confirms the importance of environmental variables on the outcome of pregnancy. For example, a weight gain of at least 25 pounds during pregnancy is now considered important for fetal growth (Winick, 1981). Prenatal sex hormones have a powerful effect on the developing brain and psychosexual differentiation (Ehrhardt and Meyer-Bahlburg, 1979), and differences in the frequency of aggressive behavior between males and females may be related to prenatal variations in hormone levels (Reinisch, 1981). These few items are mentioned only to underline again the importance of a thorough knowledge of the contribution of biologic factors to the behavior of the newborn. Once more, our psychologic theories, although necessary, are not sufficient if we want to aim for a complete understanding of behavior that includes the developmental origins of behavior.

INFANT STUDIES

What is striking now is the wealth of new data on the earliest dyadic relationship and the astonishing capacities of the newborn. Feature perception and visual organization can be demonstrated at birth (Kessen and Bornstein, 1978). At 1 week of age, the infant can be seen to be attracted to strongly patterned stimuli, e.g., horizontal shapes, concentric circles, and face-like mosaics. Pattern is also preferred over color or brightness or size, again indicating some degree of form perception in the neonate. Infants also appear to be attracted by complex patterns rather than simple ones and by objects that are in motion rather than those that are stationary. It soon becomes clear that the infant prefers to look at an object that: (1) is in almost constant motion, (2) emits a great deal of highly varied stimuli, (3) appeals to several different sensory modalities, (4) is complex, (5) possesses a distinctive pattern, and (6) is responsive to the infant's own behavior (Fagan, 1979; Fantz, 1975).

If we look at these characteristics, we see at once that they are all contained in the mother's face—not her breast, but her face—suggesting that perhaps we should talk about the good face and the bad face! At any rate, there is a strong developmental biologic guarantee that, given a responsive adult, attachment will occur within the context of that dyadic relationship. Klaus and Kennell (1976) have suggested that the infant utilizes all these capacities in its earliest bonding behavior. At one time they went as far as to suggest that the neonate must have close contact with the mother and father as early as during the first minutes and hours of life, so that the adult can make a species-specific response to the infant that will set in motion the process of bonding. Certainly the general idea of early bonding has been reiterated by Hales and associates (1977) and others.

Much of this research is consonant with the current trend in which the dyadic relationship is included in all studies of infant development, a point emphasized by Schaffer (1977) and others. Nevertheless, what is being suggested here again is that even within the dyadic relationship there is a complex biologic component for the earliest adaptive behavior of the neonate and infant, and that this biologic component probably plays an important part in the subsequent formation of object relationships (or attachments) of the individual. It may even be that, in many instances, the major thrust of the infant's genetic programming again outweighs minor variations in parental behavior.

Emde (1981) recently reviewed a large corpus of child development research (Bell and Harper, 1977; Clarke and Clarke, 1976; Clark-Stewart, 1977; Kagan, Kearsley, and Zelazo, 1978; Osofsky, 1979; Sameroff, 1978) and noted a number of challenges to clinical theory in psychoanalysis:

1. The infant constructs his or her own reality, and what analysts "reconstruct" for the patient in fact may never have happened. Analysts therefore perhaps should renew their emphasis on recent and current experience and not be so concerned to understand or modify early experiences. Analysts have identified, as it were, too much with the "helpless infant" who, it turns out, is not so helpless.

2. Discontinuities are prominent in development, suggesting too that we modify the theory of so-called reorganization of experience that is said to take place, for example, at puberty. Discontinuities may occur not only during infancy, but also during so-called "latency" (see the following) and, indeed, at puberty, when new myelination arcs occur (Yakovlev and Lecours, 1967).

3. Since there is a strong self-righting tendency after deflection from a developmental pathway, a single traumatic episode is unlikely to be pathogenic.

4. The concept of irreversibility of adverse effects, such as major maternal deprivation, should be modified, since it has been shown that environmental changes can offer major compensation for early environmental deficits.

5. The term "object relations" is unfortunate in the light of recent findings of social reciprocity and mutual interaction and change between infant and caregiver; the "object" is not simply the "target" of drives.

6. Psychoanalysts have not given sufficient attention to transactions within the family that determine which opportunities prevail and what early experience endures. Psychoanalysts now should look to the environment as well as to the individual, to the interface as well as to the intrapsychic.

7. Developmental phases other than infancy are equally
   important, and subsequent experiences continue to modify early experiences.

ATTACHMENT BEHAVIOR AND REGRESSION

Studies on attachment (Bowlby, 1969; Ainsworth, 1973) now
raise interesting questions about so-called regression.

The observation of interest here is that attachment behaviors, such as crying and clinging, become more prominent at
times of stress, including separation, sickness, and death,
particularly when there is no alternative solution. Clinically,
one might ordinarily regard this behavior as regression. However, it is important to emphasize, as Bowlby does, that such
behaviors may represent instead an intensification of attachment behavior, and not regression. The significance of this
difference is twofold. First, intensification of attachment behavior must be recognized as a normal phenomenon and
should be distinguished from pathologic or pathogenic regression. Second, even when regression does occur, it may at times
similarly represent a return to an earlier, more stable level
of organization and may therefore represent, in essence, a
normal activity.

STRANGER ANXIETY

The idea of intensified attachment behavior immediately
raises the question of the meaning of stranger anxiety in 6- to
8-month-old infants. Psychoanalysts emphasize the frailty of
object constancy in its early stages of development, when
object constancy is threatened by overriding drive needs and
the anxiety precipitated by the danger of loss of the object
when the familiar mother is replaced by the stranger.

Here too, however, we now have an alternative hypothesis
derived from cognitive developmental theory. One could say,
using cognitive developmental terms, that the infant's behavior in reaction to the stranger is actually a reaction to a
discrepancy that is beyond the infant's capacity to assimilate
or otherwise respond to constructively (Kagan, 1976). More
formally, the hypothesis would state that an event (such as the
presentation of a stranger) that activates existing structures
(the schema of a known person), but that cannot be assimilated
into these structures, creates arousal. If the discrepancy and
arousal are too great because of a failure of assimilation and

accommodation, disequilibrium occurs and negative affect is experienced.

Again, this suggests a biologic maturational phenomenon as much as it does anxiety and regression in the face of the threat of loss and as such raises the question of the meaning of the experience for the future development of the infant. What may be important here is the infant's experience of being able or not being able actively to do something about the experience of discrepancy, and it may be just that experience that is the precursor of a behavioral pattern that will persist as an established trait.

INFANTILE SEXUALITY

Recently, questions have been raised about Freud's theory of infantile sexuality. For example, some scholars now believe there is evidence to suggest that Freud was wrong in assuming that his patients' accounts of their being sexually abused by a parent (often the father) in early childhood were only fantasy (Klein and Tribich, 1980; Masson, 1981). The evidence in Freud's own reports, including the Dora case (S. Freud, 1905), reveals abundant information about sexually destructive behavior by the parents toward the child, and overwhelming data gathered since the 1960s attest to the great numbers of children who are in fact abused by their parents.

The importance of this new challenge is that it draws attention back to the real world in which the child lives as an important element in the development of the child, an hitherto neglected area in psychoanalysis.

LATENCY

The concept of latency in particular requires revision. The term is problematic at two levels: First, at the level of the reliability of the observations and clinical data, and second, at the conceptual level. At the observational level, several empiric studies have shown, if anything, an *increase* in sexual activities during this age period (Reese, 1966; Broderick, 1966; Janus and Bess, 1976). Rutter (1980) reviewed this evidence and concluded that sexual development clearly continues to proceed during these years.

At the conceptual level, we can turn to the work of Shapiro and Perry, who in 1976 carefully and systematically reviewed three major areas of information about biopsychologic events during this developmental period. Specifically, they reviewed the data on perceptual-postural maturation, temporospatial orientation, and cognitive changes. On the basis of this thoughtful survey, they concluded that the psychoanalytic idea of a biphasic growth of sexual drives is *not* the significant substratum on which the biologic timetable for this period of development is based. Rather, they noted (correctly) that processes within the central nervous system, together with cognitive strategies derived from *maturation*, probably provide the biologic clock basis for this developmental period. Furthermore, they view this maturation as a significant *discontinuity* in behavioral development. Shapiro and Perry then attempted to incorporate all this new multilevel information on the 7-year-old child under the old term of latency. It was a procrustean effort, rather like fitting all the knowledge in modern chemistry under the heading of alchemy. Obviously, psychoanalysts are loath to discard a term. The assumptions made when the concept first derived 75 years ago, however, are no longer sufficient, particularly in the light of new epidemiologic and biologic knowledge. We must insist now on a careful definition of what exactly a particular term means. Perhaps it would be better in this case to refer to the specific function being discussed, e.g., neurologic maturation, Gestalt perception, temporospatial orientation, and no longer use the somewhat misleading, global term, "latency." What is important here is that new data are enabling us to take a fresh look at an old concept, and that the fresh look encompasses a biopsychosocial perspective within the context of a comprehensive developmental approach.

ADOLESCENT TURMOIL

Is adolescent turmoil a common, or even normative, phenomenon, as some eminent authors have espoused (Erikson, 1955; A. Freud, 1958; and Blos, 1970)? One analyst went so far as to state that she "would feel great concern for the adolescent who causes no trouble and feels no disturbance" (Geleerd, 1961, p. 267). Unfortunately, as Rutter (1976) pointed out, these vivid descriptions of turmoil in adolescents are based for the most part only on "anecdote and opinion." What are the facts?

If we turn to the Isle of Wight Study (Rutter, Tizard, and Whitmore, 1970), the data show that "alienation from parents is *not* common in 14-year-olds" (p. 40) and that most young teenagers in a general population in fact get on well with their parents, who in turn continue to have a "substantial influence on their children right through adolescence" (p. 54).

Moreover, interviews with 96 boys and 88 girls revealed that at least half the group did not experience anything that could be called inner turmoil, and only a small minority appeared to be clinically depressed. Further, the data provided no support for the idea that psychiatric disorder is much more common during the middle teens; rather, most adolescents do *not* show psychiatric disorders (although the pattern of disorders shows a shift in terms of an increased prevalence of both depression and school refusal).

In short, Rutter convincingly demonstrated that the psychiatric importance of adolescent turmoil has probably been overestimated in the past, a conclusion based on sound epidemiologic data rather than clinical anecdote.

Let us turn now to just a few of the relatively recent ideas on certain disorders that hitherto have been explained largely on the basis of psychodynamic explanations.

INFANTILE AUTISM

Recent studies on infantile autism now reveal strong evidence for a group in which there is a genetic factor (Folstein and Rutter, 1978; Ritvo, 1979, August 1981). Infantile autism is now considered by many scientists to be the result, in many instances, of a "central disorder of cognition" involving language (Rutter, 1972a). Thus, the genetic influence "concerns some broader linguistic or cognitive impairment, of which autism is one result" (Folstein and Rutter, 1978, p. 220). This is a remarkable change in our thinking, rendering obsolete some of the earlier ideas put forward by a number of prominent psychoanalytic conceptualisers.

BEDWETTING

Bedwetting hardly seems to be considered a psychiatric disorder anymore. Many of the beautiful anecdotal case descriptions by Gerard (1939), Katan (1946), and others, in which bedwetting was attributed to intricate psychodynamic conflicts, today might be considered instances of a general developmental disorder (Shaffer and Gardner, 1981). In any event, controlled studies (e.g., Achenbach and Lewis, 1971), have not found evidence to support many of these psychodynamic hypotheses as being of primary etiologic importance.

OBSESSIONAL NEUROSIS

Entrenched notions about the psychodynamic causes of obsessive-compulsive disorders are also now being reappraised. For example, some evidence now supports a neurobiologic hypothesis (Elkins, Rapoport, and Lipsky, 1980). The evidence, which includes twin studies, association with Tourette's syndrome, neuropsychologic test data, psychosurgery reports, association with brain damage, and psychopharmacologic effects, although only suggestive at this stage, is nevertheless of great interest.

More specifically, a serotonin hypothesis has been suggested by the finding that clomipramine has been shown to be more efficacious than a placebo in the treatment of obsessive-compulsive disorders (Marks, et al., 1980; Thoren, et al., 1980). In fact, correlations have been found between clinical response to clomipramine and changes in the cerebrospinal fluid levels of 5-hydroxyindoleacetic acid (a serotonin metabolite) and L-tryptophan (a serotonin precursor) (Insel and Murphy, 1982).

All of these findings, although tantalizing, are still inconclusive. What they again suggest, however, is the importance of remaining open to a biopsychosocial developmental viewpoint of human behavior and its disorders.

DEPRESSION

Some of the earlier psychoanalytic views on depression in childhood (e.g., Sandler and Joffe, 1965) are still of interest, but again remain to be confirmed by controlled studies. What is now of equal interest is the biologic developmental understanding of the disorder based on controlled studies. For example, McKnew and Cytryn (1979), in a controlled study of nine children 6- to 12-years-old with diagnosed cases of depression, suggested that a physiologic counterpart to emotional "detachment" in children may be a suppression of the general arousal system, mediated through the nonadrenergic network and centered on the locus ceruleus, resulting in a reduction in the level of 3-methoxy-4-hydroxyphenylethylene glycol (MHPG). Puig-Antich and associates (1979) have demonstrated hypersecretion of cortisol in children suffering from a depressive syndrome. Puig-Antich essentially demonstrated that prepubertal children who fit the Research Diagnostic Criteria (RDC) for major depressive illness have a disturbance of the circadian rhythm of cortisol excretion similar to that of depressed adults: In the evening and early morning, secretion ceases in control subjects but continues in depressed patients.

Also of interest from a biopsychosocial-developmental perspective is the hypothesis (Brumback and Staton, 1981) that dysfunctional aminergic neurotransmission associated with depression may unmask previously subclinical neurologic signs. Signs of left hemiparesis (including pronation drift of the outstretched left arm, hyperactive left-sided tendon reflexes, and left extensor plantar responses), found during a major depressive disorder suffered by the two children studied, disappeared when the depression was temporarily relieved by treatment with tricyclic antidepressant medication (Staton, Wilson, and Brumback, 1981). They also observed, in 21 children with major depressive illness, that treatment with amitriptyline was associated with improvement in the results of right-hemisphere and frontal-lobe tests, including improvement in IQ on the WISC(R) Performance Scale (Brumback, Staton, and Wilson, 1980).

Recently, evidence has been found for a specific genetic marker for depressive disorders. Weitkamp et al. (1981) have found that depressive disorders segregate along with HLA (human leukocyte antigen) in families, which suggests that a locus on the sixth chromosome contributes to the risk factors for depression. This is important because "linkage of depressive disorders to a specific genetic marker raises the possibility of early detection of persons at risk and even the possibility of discovering the gene product through techniques of molecular biology" (Matthysse and Kidd, 1981, p. 1341).

None of these findings explains depression in children, but together they broaden the basis for our understanding of the condition far beyond the simple notion of anger turned inwards. Mandell (1976), for example, has hypothesized a psychobiologic developmental theory of altered biochemical state to explain the persistence of depressive affect even after the neurotic conflicts related to depression have been resolved. He suggested that this could conceivably arise because the developing nervous system of the young infant is particularly vulnerable to impingement in its biochemical balance. Thus, if a depletion of monoamine transmitters occurs in response, say, to an early and persistent psychologic loss, that altered biochemical state may then become the "normal," permanent biochemical state for that individual throughout his or her life. Any subsequent return to a more gratifying environment, either temporarily during an interpretation, or for more prolonged periods as a result of psychotherapy or a changed social environment, still eventually would be perceived as though that were, so to speak, the "deviant" state of mind, in the sense that the prevailing tendency of the biochemical response would always remain in the direction of returning to the previously acquired, permanent "depressive" baseline state.

Here, then, is another attempt to derive a superordinate developmental theory to account for both psychologic and biochemical mechanisms of disorder, in this case, major depressive disorder (296.0).

NEW TECHNOLOGY

Finally, some exciting technologic breakthroughs can be seen on the horizon. Bax (1980) recently reviewed some of the new possibilities for research that are becoming available. For example, using a sophisticated combination of radioactive labelling of oxygen, carbon dioxide, and glucose with a computerized scanning technique called proton emission tomography (PET), Lassen (1977) has reported fascinating studies of cerebral blood flow during a whole range of normal cerebral activities. Phelps et al. (1981) have shown how "positron computed tomography can map the distribution of local cerebral metabolic functions in humans in a safe and noninvasive manner that is not possible by any other technique" (p. 1447).

Computerized axial tomography (CAT) also has revealed such abnormalities as cerebral atrophy, and asymmetry in 32% of children aged 4 to 15 years who had a diagnosis of minimal brain damage (Bergstrom and Bille, 1978). Evoked potentials combined with computer technology have similarly given rise to a new technique of "neurometrics" (John, et al., 1977) for the study of children with learning disorders.

These techniques offer the opportunities for potential advances in the understanding of conditions such as learning disorders, for which we are still groping in the dark.

An astonishing new technique is Nuclear Magnetic Resonance (NMR), which in the future may yield information on tissue chemistry and may provide images of brain anatomy. The measure used is the "relaxation" time required for atomic nuclei to lose the energy gained after being placed in a strong magnetic field. A tentative finding is that relaxation times in the brains of manic-depressive patients are longer than normal and return to normal with lithium treatment.

In summary, scientific research in child psychiatry using sophisticated methods is on the threshold of giving us new windows through which to study and understand human behavior. In the light of these studies, some of our ideas have held up remarkably well; many, however, have crumbled.

Psychoanalysts doing research in psychoanalysis have formidable problems in establishing reliability and validity. Kaplan (1981), in his Presidential Address to the American Psychoanalytic Association, noted that the fundamental challenge to psychoanalysis was still "a much needed validation of . . . basic theoretical and clinical concepts." (p. 23). More specifically, he told analysts that "any progress in psychoanalysis must include an evaluation of the psychoanalytic process which involves making all of the data public by notes, tape recording, etc., . . ." (p. 19). It remains to be seen how many analysts will accept this challenge. Sophisticated work is being done, for instance, on object relations by Blatt and others (Blatt and Lerner, 1982), but such work is rare. One consequence of this relative sterility in child psychoanalytic research is that many of the concepts in psychoanalysis are now considered by many analysts as metaphor rather than true theory. Yet we should not throw out the baby with the bathwater. Although relatively little in psychoanalysis has been proven, much remains to be tested. The wealth of accumulated clinical experience still awaits scientific validation through suitable technologic methods still to be devised: This is the first challenge for child analysis.

The second challenge for psychoanalysis is to locate itself within and relate itself to the spectrum of biologic sciences that form part of the foundation for human behavior. Neither psychoanalysis nor the neurochemistry of the synapse alone, nor perhaps even both together, are sufficient to explain all of human behavior. Behavior that may appear to have (and that may indeed have) strong psychodynamic determinants may also be associated with significant biologic origins. To give just one brief clinical example, a jocular repetitive pattern of speech in a child might be interpreted as a resistance or defense, but it might also be associated with the Fragile-X syndrome recently described in the pediatric and genetic literature (Gerald, 1981; Jacobs, et al., 1980).

At the very least, a rapprochement between the psychologic and biologic sciences is needed. Better still, we need a superordinate general developmental theory that will incorporate knowledge from many different fields. For that we may have to wait for the next genius of the order of magnitude of Copernicus, Darwin, Freud, Watson, or Crick to come along. In the meantime, isolation of any one field benefits no one.

REFERENCES

Achenbach, T., and Lewis, M. (1971), A proposed model for clinical research and its application to encopresis and enuresis. *J. Am. Acad. Child Psychiatry*, 10:535.

Ainsworth, M.D.S. (1973), The development of infant-mother attachment. In: *Review of Child Development Research*, Vol. 3, eds. B.M. Caldwell and H.N. Ricciuti. Chicago: University of Chicago Press, pp. 1–94.

August, G.J., Stewart, M.A., and Tsai, L. (1981), The incidence of cognitive disabilities in the siblings of autistic children. *Br. J. Psychiatry*. (in press).

Bax, M.C.O. (1980), Future trends and problems. In: *Scientific Foundations of Developmental Psychiatry*, ed. M. Rutter. London: Heinemann, pp. 371–373.

Bell, R.Q., and Harper, L.V. (1977), *Child Effects on Adults*. New York: Halsted.

Bergstrom, K., and Bille, B. (1978), Computed tomography of the brain in children with minimal brain damage: A preliminary study of 46 children. *Neuropediatrie*, 9:378–384.

Blatt, S.J., and Lerner, H. (1982), Investigations in the psychoanalytic theory of object relations and object representations. In: *Empirical Studies on Psychoanalytic Theories*, ed. J. Masling. New York: Halsted.

Blos, P. (1970), *The Young Adolescent: Clinical Studies*. London: Collier-Macmillan.

Bowlby, J. (1969), *Attachment and Loss*, Vol. 1. New York: Basic Books.

Bringuier, J.-C. (1980), *Conversations with Jean Piaget*. Chicago: University of Chicago Press, p. 120.

Broderick, C.B. (1966), Sexual behavior among preadolescents. *J. Soc. Issues*, 22:6–21.

Brumback, R.A., and Staton, R.D. (1981), Depression-induced neurological dysfunction. *N. Engl. J. Med.*, 355:642.

Brumback, R.A., Staton, R.D., and Wilson, H. (1980), Neuropsychological study of children during and after remission of endogenous depressive episodes. *Percept. Mot. Skills*, 50:1163–1167.

Chess, S. (1978), The plasticity of human development. *J. Am. Acad. Child Psychiatry*, 17:80–91.

Clark-Stewart, A. (1977), *Child Care in the Family: A Review of Research and Some Propositions for Policy*. New York: Academic Press.

Clarke, A.M., and Clarke, A.D.B. (1976), *Early Experience: Myth and Evidence*. London: Open Books.

Ehrhardt, A.A., and Meyer-Bahlburg, H.F.L. (1979), Prenatal sex hormones and the developing brain: Effects on psychosexual differentiations and cognitive functions. *Annu. Rev. Med.*, 30:417–430.

Eisenberg, L. (1977), Development as a unifying concept in psychiatry. *Am. J. Psychiatry*, 133:225–237.

Elkins, R., Rapoport, J.L., and Lipsky, A. (1980), Obsessive-compulsive disorder of childhood and adolescence: A neurobiological viewpoint. *J. Am. Acad. Child Psychiatry*, 19:511–525.

Emde, R.N. (1981), Changing models of infancy and the nature of early development: Remodeling the foundation. *J. Am. Psychoan. Assoc.*, 29:179–219.

Erikson, E.H. (1955), The problem of ego identity. *J. Am. Psychoanal. Assoc.*, 4:56–121.

Fagan, J.F. (1979), The origins of facial pattern recognition. In: *Psychological Development from Infancy: Image to Intention*, eds. M.H. Bornstein and W. Kessen. New York: Halsted.

Fantz, R.L. (1975), Early visual selectivity. In: *Infant Perception*, eds. L.B. Cohen and P. Salapatek. New York: Academic Press.

Fish, B., and Ritvo, E.R. (1979), Psychoses of childhood. In: *Basic Handbook of Child Psychiatry*, Vol. 2, ed. J.D. Noshpitz. New York: Basic Books.

Folstein, S., and Rutter, M. (1978), A twin study of individuals with infantile autism. In: *Autism: A Reappraisal of Concepts and Treatment*, eds. M. Rutter and E. Schopler. New York: Plenum Press, pp. 219–241.

Freud, A. (1958), Adolescence. *Psychoanal. Study Child*, 13:255–278.

Freud, S. (1920), Beyond the pleasure principle. *Standard Edition*, Vol. 18, ed. J. Strachey. London: Hogarth Press, 1955.

Freud, S. (1905), Fragment of an analysis of a case of hysteria. *Standard Edition*, Vol. 7, ed. J. Strachey. London: Hogarth Press, 1953.

Geleerd, E.R. (1961), Some aspects of psychoanalytic technique in adolescence. *Psychoanal. Study Child*, 12:263–283.

Gerald, P.S. (1981), X-linked mental retardation and the Fragile-X syndrome. *Pediatrics*, 68:594–595.

Gerard, M.W. (1939), Enuresis: A study in etiology. *Am. J. Orthopsychiatry*, 9:48–58.

Gittleman-Klein, R., and Klein, D. (1973), School phobia: Diagnostic considerations in the light of imipramine effects. *J. Nerv. Ment. Dis.*, 156:199–215.

Gittleman-Klein, R., and Klein, D. (1971), Controlled imipramine treatment of school phobia. *Arch. Gen. Psychiatry*, 25:204–207.

Graham, P., Rutter, M., and George, S. (1973), Temperamental characteristics as predictors of behavior disorders in children. *Am. J. Orthopsychiatry*, 43:328–339.

Hales, D., Lozoff, B., Sosa, R., and Kennell, J. (1977), Defining the limits of the sensitive period. *Dev. Med. Child Neurol.*, 19:454–461.

Hobson, J.A., and McCarley, R.W. (1977), The brain as a dream state generator: An activation-synthesis hypothesis of the dream process. *Am. J. Psychiatry*, 134:1335–1348.

Insel, T.R., and Murphy, D.L. (1982), The psychopharmacologic treatment of obsessive compulsive disorder: A review. *J. Clin. Psychopharmacol.*, (in press).

Jacobs, P.A., et al. (1980), X-linked mental retardation; A study of seven families. *Am. J. Med. Genet.*, 7:471.

Janus, S.S., and Bess, B.E. (1976), Latency: Fact or fiction. *Am. J. Psychoanal.*, 36:339–346.

John, E.R., et al., (1977), Neurometrics: Numerical taxonomy identifies different profiles of brain functions within groups of behaviorally similar people. *Science*, 196:1393–1410.

Kagan, J. (1979), The form of early development. *Arch. Gen. Psychiatry*, 36:1047–1054.

Kagan, J. (1978), *The Growth of the Child: Reflections on Human Development*. New York: Norton.

Kagan, J. (1976), Emergent themes in human development. *Am. Sci.*, 64:186–196.

Kagan, J., Kearsley, R.B., and Zelazo, P.R. (1978), *Infancy: Its Place in Human Development*. Cambridge: Harvard University Press.

Kaplan, A.H. (1981), From discovery to validation: A basic challenge to psychoanalysis. *J. Am. Psychoanal. Assoc.*, 29:3–26.

Katan, A. (1946), Experiences with enuretics. *Psychoanal. Study Child*, 2:244–255.

Kessen, W., and Bornstein, M.H. (1978), Discrimination of brightness change for infants. *J. Exp. Child Psychol.*, 25:526–530.

Kety, S.S. (1976), Studies designed to disentangle genetic and environmental variables in schizophrenia. *Am. J. Psychiatry*, 133:1134–1137.

Klaus, M.H., and Kennell, J.H. (1976), *Maternal-Infant Bonding*. St. Louis: Mosby.

Klein, M. and Tribich, D. (1980), On Freud's blindness. *Colloquium*, 3:52–59.

Lassen, N.A., et al., (1977), Cerebral function, metabolism and circulation. *Acta Neurol. Scand.*, Suppl. 64.

Mandell, A.J. (1976) Neurobiological mechanisms of adaptation in relation to models of psychobiological development. In: *Psychopathology and Child Development*, eds. E. Schopler and R.J. Reichler. New York: Plenum Press, pp. 21–22.

Marks, I.M., et al., (1980), Clomipramine and exposure for obsessive compulsive rituals: I. *Br. J. Psychiatry*, 136:1–25.

Masson, J.M. (1981), The seduction hypothesis in the light of new documents. Paper presented at the Western New England Psychoanalytic Society, New Haven, CT, June 6, 1981.

Matthysse, S. and Kidd, K.K. (1981), Evidence of HLA linkage in depressive disorders. *N. Engl. J. Med.*, 305:1340–1341.

McKnew, D.H., and Cytryn, L. (1979), Urinary metabolites in chronically depressed children. *J. Am. Acad. Child Psychiatry*, 18:608–615.

Nye, P.A. (1982), The reliability of memories for attachment to special, soft objects during childhood. *J. Am. Acad. Child Psychiatry*, (in press).

Osofsky, J. (1979) (ed.), *Handbook of Infant Development*. New York: Wiley.

Phelps, M.E., Kuhl, D.E., and Mazziotta, J.C. (1981), Metabolic mapping of the brain's response to visual stimulation: Studies in humans. *Science*, 221:1445:1448.

Puig-Antich, J., et al., (1979), Plasma levels of imipramine (IMI) and desmethylimipramine (DMI) and clinical response in prepubertal major depressive disorder. *J. Am. Acad. Child Psychiatry*, 18:616–627.

Reese, H.W. (1966), Attitudes toward the opposite sex in late childhood. *Merrill-Palmer Quart.*, 12:157–163.

Reinisch, J.M. (1981), Prenatal exposure to synthetic progesterins increases potential for aggression in humans. *Science*, 2:1171–1173.

Rutter, M. (1980), Psychosexual development. In: *Scientific Foundations of Developmental Psychiatry*, ed. M. Rutter. London: Heinemann, pp. 332–338.

Rutter, M. (1972a), *Maternal Deprivation Reassessed*. Harmondsworth: Penguin.

Rutter, M. (1972b), Clinical assessment of language disorders in the young child. In: *The Child with Delayed Speech*, eds. M. Rutter and J.A.M. Martin. Clinics in Developmental Medicine, No. 43. London: Heinemann/SIMP.

Rutter, M., Graham, P., Chadwick, O.F.D., and Yule, W. (1976), Adolescent turmoil: Fact or fiction? *J. Child Psychol. Psychiatry*, 17:35–56.

Rutter, M., and Schopler, E. (eds.) (1978), *Autism: A Reappraisal of Concepts and Treatment*. New York: Plenum Press.

Rutter, M., Tizard, J., and Whitmore, K. (1970), *Education, Health and Behavior*. London: Longmans, Green.

Sameroff, A. (ed.) (1978). Organization and stability of newborn behavior. *Monogr. Soc. Res. Child Dev.*, 43(5–6).

Sandler, J., and Joffe, W.S. (1965), Notes on childhood depression. *Int. J. Psychoanal.*, 46:88–96.

Schaffer, H.R. (1977), Introduction: Early interactive development. In: *Studies in Mother-Infant Interaction*, ed. H.R. Schaffer. London: Academic Press.

Shaffer, D., and Gardner, A. (1981), Classification of enuresis. Paper presented at the 28th Annual Meeting of the American Academy of Child Psychiatry, Dallas, TX, October 15, 1981.

Shapiro, T., and Perry, T. (1976), Latency revisited: The age of seven plus or minus one. *Psychoanal. Study Child*, 31:79–105.

Sherman, M., Hertzig, M., Austrian, R., and Shapiro, T. (1981), Treasured objects in school-aged children. *Pediatrics*, 68:379–386.

Staton, R.D., Wilson, H., and Brumback, R.A. (1981), Cognitive improvement associated with tricyclic antidepressant treatment of childhood major depressive illness. *Percept. Mot. Skills.*, (in press).

Thoren, P., et al., (1980), Clomipramine treatment of obsessive compulsive disorder: A controlled clinical trial. *Arch. Gen. Psychiatry*, 37:1281–1289.

Weitkamp, L.R., et al. (1981), Depressive disorders and HLA: A gene on chromosome 6 that can affect behavior. *N. Engl. J. Med.*, 305:1301–1306.

Winick, M. (1981), Food and the fetus. *Natural History*, 90:76–81.

Yakovlev, P.I., and Lecours, A.R. (1967), The myelogenetic cycles of regional maturation of the brain. In: *Regional Development of the Brain*, ed. A. Kinkonski. Oxford: Blackwell Scientific Publications.

Index